THE STATE OF
JEWISH
STUDIES

THE STATE OF
JEWISH
STUDIES

Edited by

Shaye J. D. Cohen and Edward L. Greenstein

A PUBLICATION OF

The Jewish Theological Seminary of America

WAYNE STATE UNIVERSITY PRESS   DETROIT
1990

Copyright © 1990 by the Jewish Theological Seminary of America.
Published by Wayne State University Press, Detroit, Michigan
48202. All rights are reserved.
No part of this book may be reproduced without formal permission.
94 93 92 91 90   5 4 3 2 1

Library of Congress Cataloging-in-Publication Data

The State of Jewish studies / edited by Shaye J. D. Cohen and Edward L.
Greenstein.
       p.   cm.
    "A Publication of the Jewish Theological Seminary of America."
    Includes bibliographical references.
    ISBN 0–8143–2194–1. — ISBN 0–8143–2195–X (pbk.)
    1. Jews—History—Research—Congresses.   2. Judaism—History—
Research—Congresses.   I. Cohen, Shaye J. D.   II. Greenstein,
Edward L.
DS115.95.S73   1990
909'.04924'0072—dc20   89–39860
                                                         CIP

CONTENTS

Contents

CONTRIBUTORS

BARUCH M. BOKSER: Professor of Talmud at the Jewish Theological Seminary (hereafter JTS). Author of *Samuel's Commentary on the Mishnah, The Passover Seder,* and numerous articles on rabbinic religion and literature. Currently completing a translation of tractate *Pesaḥim* of the Palestinian Talmud.

SHAYE J. D. COHEN: Professor of Jewish History at JTS. Author of *Josephus in Galilee and Rome* and *From the Maccabees to the Mishnah.* Currently working on a history of conversion to Judaism and a history of menstrual taboos in Judaism.

TODD M. ENDELMAN: Professor of History at the University of Michigan (Ann Arbor). Author of *The Jews of Georgian England* and other works in modern, particularly British, Jewish history. Currently writing a history of conversion from Judaism in the modern period.

NEIL GILLMAN: Associate Professor of Jewish Thought at JTS. Author of a study of Gabriel Marcel and several articles on contemporary Jewish theology.

EDWARD L. GREENSTEIN: Professor of Bible at JTS. Author of *Essays on Biblical Method and Translation* and numerous articles on the ancient Near East and literary interpretation of the Hebrew Bible.

JOSEPH GUTMANN: Professor of Art History at Wayne State University and author of numerous books and articles on the history of Jewish art.

7

Contributors

PAULA E. HYMAN: Professor of Modern Jewish History at Yale University. Author of *From Dreyfus to Vichy* and numerous articles on modern French Jewish history and Jewish family history. Completing a social history of Jews of Alsace in the early nineteenth century.

STEVEN T. KATZ: Professor of Near Eastern Studies at Cornell University. Author of *Post Holocaust Dialogues* and author and editor of numerous books and articles on modern Jewish thought. Currently completing a study of the philosophy of Martin Buber.

JON D. LEVENSON: Formerly Associate Professor of Hebrew Bible at the University of Chicago Divinity School, currently List Professor at the Harvard Divinity School. Author of *Theology of the Program of Restoration of Ezekiel 40–48* and *Sinai and Zion*.

JOSEPH LUKINSKY: Professor of Education at JTS. Author of numerous studies in curriculum development and educational theory.

IVAN G. MARCUS: Professor of Jewish History at JTS. Author of *Piety and Society: The Jewish Pietists of Medieval Germany*. Completing a one-volume history of the Jews and a translation of *Sefer Hasidim*, the major work of German-Jewish pietism.

JAROSLAV PELIKAN: Professor of History and the Humanities at Yale University. Author of *Jesus through the Centuries* and many other books on the history of Christian theology and dogma.

DAVID G. ROSKIES: Professor of Jewish Literature at JTS. Author of *Against the Apocalypse*, founding editor of *Prooftexts*, and author of numerous articles on modern Jewish, especially Yiddish, literature. Currently writing a study of Jewish storytelling.

RICHARD S. SARASON: Associate Professor of Rabbinic Literature at the Hebrew Union College. Author of *A History of the Mishnaic Law of Agriculture* and numerous articles on rabbinic religion and literature.

ISMAR SCHORSCH: Professor of Jewish History and Chancellor at JTS. Author of *Organized Jewish Reactions to German Anti-Semitism* and *The Structure of Jewish History and Other Essays of Heinrich Graetz*. Currently completing a study of the social setting of the *Wissenschaft des Judentums* movement in the nineteenth century.

GERSHON SHAKED: Professor of Hebrew Literature at the Hebrew University (Jerusalem). Author of *Hebrew Narrative Fiction* and numerous books and articles on modern Hebrew and Jewish literature.

MOSHE SOKOLOW: Associate Professor of Jewish Studies at Yeshiva University. Author of articles on Bible exegesis and on religious education. Currently consultant on curriculum and education to the World Zionist Organization.

HAVA TIROSH-ROTHSCHILD: Formerly Assistant Professor of History at Columbia University, currently Assistant Professor of Religion at Emory University. Author of numerous articles on medieval Jewish intellectual history and mysticism.

I
INTRODUCTION

1

EDITORS' INTRODUCTION

During the past twenty years the academic study of Judaism and Jewish culture has enjoyed remarkable growth. Numerous universities and colleges, large and small, now offer courses in Judaica; many even grant a Ph.D. in Jewish History, Jewish Studies, or Religion with a specialization in Judaism. Recent years have witnessed not only spectacular growth in the number of academic specialists in Judaica but also the emergence of large numbers of scholars in other disciplines who have turned their attention to some aspect of Jewish culture or history. In sum, in the past twenty years the study of Judaism has not only grown, it has matured.

To celebrate this phenomenon and to celebrate its own centennial, in May 1987 the Jewish Theological Seminary of America hosted a three-day conference on "The State of Jewish Studies." The conference featured two plenary addresses as well as seven papers and responses. The presenters were members and former members of the seminary faculty, and the respondents were scholars from other institutions. The presentations and responses, revised and annotated by their authors and supplemented by two specially commissioned papers, make up the essays of this volume.

Perhaps the major theme of the essays in the central part of the volume, whether explicit or implicit, is the *normality* of Jewish studies. The academic study of Judaism is becoming more and more just another humanistic discipline, attracting students from diverse backgrounds and for diverse reasons. The methods, assumptions, and questions that govern the specific fields within Jewish studies (for example, ancient Judaism or Jewish literature) are, and ought to be, the same as those that govern the study of the parallel fields within the humanities. Some of the essays strengthen this point with the plea that Jewish studies be integrated even more fully into the general humanistic disciplines. Some scholars see themselves not so much as practitioners of Judaica but as students of a field within the humanities (for example, late antiquity or contemporary literature) who happen to have a particular interest in the Jewish dimension of their subject.

The founders of the *Wissenschaft des Judentums* (the scientific study of Judaism) movement in nineteenth-century Germany yearned for the time when Jewish studies would be normalized and accorded a place in university curricula. They did not achieve their ambition. Jewish studies remained almost exclusively an internal Jewish phenomenon, intimately linked to the social and cultural issues of the day. Some scholars used their scholarship to legitimate reform, others to affirm orthodoxy. Some used scholarship to demonstrate Judaism's capacity to enrich and be enriched by enlightened host cultures, whereas others sought to show that "the essence of Judaism" remained inviolate through the centuries. Some used scholarship to affirm that Judaism was a creed or a religion; others used it to demonstrate that it was a nationality. Some maintained the viability of the diaspora, others the inevitability of Zionism. But all, despite their ideological diversity, regarded Jewish studies as an extension of Judaism, not as a discipline within the humanities.

The essays in this volume attest to how much we owe our nineteenth-century forebears—and how far we have progressed beyond them. Our scholarship, no less than theirs, is shaped by ideological and existential needs, but we are far more methodologically self-aware than they, and we are far more conscious of the limitations of our knowledge. We recognize our prejudices and admit the futility of pursuing "pure" or "value-free" scholarship. We study a much broader range of questions than did our predecessors, and have an incomparably greater amount of available data. But we no longer believe in the absoluteness of our "facts." Even religious classics such as the Tanakh and the Talmud often reveal their truth only in nonfactual (or counterfactual) ways. We know both more and less than our predecessors. It is no surprise that most of the essays in this volume focus on questions of method and hermeneutics.

Even as positivistic research continues to discover and create new "facts," our inherited "facts" continue to be questioned and tested. Yesterday's facts were produced by yesterday's methods; newer methods, or a different configuration of methods, often yield different facts. Yesterday's revisionism provides the targets for today's revisionism. This general trend in the humanities has become equally characteristic of Jewish studies. Indeed, Judaic scholarship, by working within the disciplines of the university, is able to inject fresh thinking into the humanities in general as well as continue to draw on the richness of other academic disciplines. More and more are scholars in other fields entertaining paradigms and procedures of classical and contemporary Jewish learning.

While Jewish scholarship has become a full partner in humanistic studies, it also remains part of Judaism. Scholarship is of this world. Historiography becomes history, literary criticism becomes literature, and the study of religion becomes part of religion. The Jewish Theological Seminary, like other modern religious institutions, is dedicated both to the critical, multidisciplined study of its religious heritage and to the normative observance of that heritage. This dual commitment is beset with tension. If our store of "facts" diminishes with every increase in knowledge, and if through dispassionate scholarship and the hermeneutics of suspicion we question everything and believe nothing, how do we maintain our allegiance to Judaism? What authority binds us to Judaism and how do we teach Judaism to the next generation? The essays of the third part of this volume explicitly address these questions, but in fact all the essays grapple with these issues in one way or another. Every contributor to this volume—with the exception, of course, of Jaroslav Pelikan, a committed Christian—in one way or another writes as both a Jew and a scholar.

We are indebted to many individuals for their assistance, encouragement, and support. The provost of the Jewish Theological Seminary, Raymond P. Scheindlin, with our colleagues Ivan G. Marcus and David G. Roskies, were our partners in bringing the conference from imagination to reality. Cindy Slavin supervised publicity, and John Ruskay advised on many matters of program and logistics. Throughout the planning and implementation we were ably assisted by Lorne Hanick. Jean Highland helped us place the book with its publisher, and Anne Adamus has seen the volume through the press. In preparing the manuscript we have enjoyed the invaluable aid of Jodie Futornick. We are grateful to all the scholars who attended the conference and participated in the discussions; we have learned from their wisdom. Above all, we thank our fellow contributors for their cooperation. We hope that at the seminary bicentennial in 2086/87 scholars will look back on our generation as a "golden age" in the development of Jewish studies.

2

THE PLACE OF JEWISH STUDIES IN CONTEMPORARY SCHOLARSHIP

Ismar Schorsch

Anyone acquainted with the contemporary academic scene must be impressed by the burgeoning of Jewish studies in colleges and universities across North America. In numerical terms alone the growth of Judaic studies as an academic discipline is astonishing. Well over a thousand courses in the field are presently offered in institutions of higher learning outside Israel. In addition to all this, we are witnessing the proliferation of new subfields and the appearance of new centers of scholarly productivity around the world. These numbers are indeed impressive, but a skeptic might still question how deeply the academic study of Judaism has filtered into the general scholarship of religious studies. A subtle but significant index of the secure place of Judaica in the comtemporary study of religion is the recently published fifteen-volume *Encyclopedia of Religion*, edited by the late Mircea Eliade (Macmillan, 1987).

This majestic collective work uniquely confirms the status attained in our day by the field of Jewish studies within the American university and may even offer a clue as to the source of that incredible success. It is a work inspired by a generosity of spirit quite alien to the Christian bias and categories that colored its pedantic English predecessor, the thirteen-volume

This essay originally appeared in slightly different form in *Moment* 12/7 (October 1987), pp. 53–55, and is reprinted here with permission.

Encyclopedia of Religion and Ethics, edited by James Hastings from 1908 to 1926.

In the midst of that earlier venture, in 1921, Harry Austryn Wolfson, still an insecure and underpaid instructor of Hebrew literature and philosophy at Harvard, appealed to the pride of American Jewry to fund the publication of the classics of medieval Jewish philosophy. His justification of the project poignantly betrayed the unaltered peripheral status of Jewish studies within the scholarly world after a century of awesome productivity.

> When I speak of the importance of this unpublished part of Jewish philosophic literature, I do not mean to imply that I consider medieval Jewish philosophy to be the most important field of Jewish study. Hardly that. For I believe, just as our pious ancestors believed, though for different reasons, that the Talmud with its literature is the most promising field of study, the most fertile field of original research and investigation. But I believe that medieval Jewish philosophy is the only branch of Jewish literature, next to the Bible, which binds us to the rest of the literary world. In it we meet on common ground with civilized Europe and with part of civilized Asia and civilized Africa. (*Menorah Journal,*7 [1921], p. 32)

In other words, to get a hearing in the Western world, the study of Judaism had to start off center, on a body of literature—no matter how glorious—that was tangential to its essential character. Admission to the academy imposed subordination to external values and perspectives. It is worth noting that back in 1818, Leopold Zunz, the young visionary founder of the academic study of Judaism in Germany, had proposed a strikingly similar project, though in terms far less conciliatory to traditional rabbinics and more overtly apologetic.

This is not to say that the Hastings *Encyclopedia of Religion and Ethics* willfully overlooked the role of Judaism in the history of religion. On the contrary, its editors invited serious Anglo-Jewish scholars like Israel Abrahams, Elkan Adler, and Herbert Loewe and Christian authorities like Hermann Strack and Travers Herford to compose often substantial articles on Jewish subjects. Strack's lengthy treatment of anti-Semitism and Loewe's sympathetic survey of *kabbala* are but two of the more memorable contributions. It may well be that the dramatic publication of *The Jewish Encyclopedia* in New York from 1901 to 1906—the first encyclopedic distillation of modern Jewish scholarship—served to induce Hastings and his colleagues to accord greater attention to Judaism.

Yet the overall coverage of Judaism proved to be sparse and subordinate, a victim of the imperious Christian tone that marked Hasting's entire work. For all its historical erudition, the Hastings encyclopedia treated non-Christian religions from a developmental perspective that impeded empathy and encouraged invidious comparisons. Generally entries were authored by outsiders. Thus, Islam was actually portrayed under the rubric "Muhammadanism," an inaccurate Western appellation patterned after the formation of the name for Christianity. The 46-page entry on "Jesus Christ" opened with a volley of aggressive assertions about the inferiority of Buddhism and Islam to Christianity. And the long article on Israelite history and religion, written by the Regius Professor of Hebrew at Cambridge, ended on a decidedly Christian note. The Maccabean martyrs, it said, pointed to the emergence of the universal church, the true heir of ancient Israel. In short, the Hastings encyclopedia cast the religions of humanity in a hierarchical, theistic, and ethical mode forged by the Christian experience.

Not so the new *Encyclopedia of Religion*. Its scholarly ethos is militantly non-evolutionary and consequently non-judgmental. Its authors do not speak of higher and lower forms of religion and steadfastly shun the use of such loaded terms as "primitive." The working definition of religion throughout is consciously non-theistic. "Religion is the organization of life around the depth dimensions of experience—varied in form, completeness, and clarity in accordance with the environing culture" (vol. 12, p. 286). From that definition flows an expansive and holistic spirit of inquiry that lavishes caring attention on the non-Western experience of the sacred and on the full scope of each religious experience—its social, ritual, and theological expressions.

The tone is set by the very manner of dating. Gone from every article, except those of manifestly Christian content, are the Christian calendrical referents B.C. (before Christ) and A.D. (*anno domini*—in the year of the Lord), which characterized Hastings and even George Foot Moore's eminently fair study of rabbinic Judaism done in the 1920s. In deference to the religious sensibilities of non-Christians, the editors of the new encyclopedia chose to employ the more neutral referents B.C.E. (before the common era) and C.E. (of the common era). Their handiwork—a collective triumph of the contemporary study of religion—is firmly anchored in the seminal ecumenism of Mircea Eliade, its editor (who sadly did not live to see the child of his old age), as well as in the still vital legacy of Rudolf Otto, whose book *The Idea of the Holy* published seventy years ago first broke through to the non-rational core of the religious experience.

The coverage of Judaism is a direct beneficiary of that propitiously open-minded setting. Never before has a general encyclopedia devoted so much space to expounding the sundry deposits of Judaism's millennial religious dynamism. If this new work be compared to "a garden of nearly three thousand flowers, grown from seeds sown in scholarly fields around the globe" (vol 1, p. xvii), then the variety called "Judaism" represents well over ten percent of the vegetation, arranged in separate historical entries and in subdivisions of broadly thematic and synthetic entries. The presence of Judaism pervades the pages of the encyclopedia.

Even more important than quantity is the qualitative intent to survey Judaism from within, on its own terms. Criteria intrinsic to the nature and development of Judaism clearly determine the selection of topics. In consequence, a host of talmudic sages, medieval rabbis, and modern Orthodox leaders, who are not exactly household names even in the Jewish world, merit the honor of a biographical entry. Similarly, searching articles abound on religious institutions and bodies of literature that neither border on nor blend with Christian consciousness, but assuredly define the realm of the sacred in Judaism. How many general encyclopedias have devoted an article to the medieval Ashkenazic glossators of the Talmud, the *Tosafot*, or to the vital and multifaceted concept of Torah? A profound respect for the uniqueness of religious phenomena motivated Eliade and his circle to illuminate the central expressions of Judaism, as understood by the best of Jewish scholarship in our day.

No Jewish scholar contributed more to deepening the academic appreciation of Judaism as a religion than the late Gershom Scholem, and it is altogether apposite that Eliade singled him out for praise in his brief preface. But beyond the accolade, it was the readiness of the encyclopedia to involve Jewish scholars from start to finish that enabled it to do justice to Judaism. The appointment of Robert M. Seltzer, professor of Jewish history at Hunter College and the author of a splendid one-volume history of the Jews, as one of the eight senior editors ensured that Judaism would be accorded an integral part in the very conceptualization of the project. And the energetic recruitment of Jewish scholars to write the articles, even in the area of Biblical scholarship, long a contested turf, gave "insiders" a generous chance to be heard. The result is a plethora of well-informed expositions equally sensitive to inner meanings and outer settings.

The Encyclopedia of Religion is resounding evidence that the field of Jewish studies is at last not only in the university but of it. The subject is no longer a mere structural appendage, the product of enlightened Jewish donors in an age of affluence and the insatiable academic need for fresh funds. It has finally been woven into the very fabric of American scholarship because of the inherent human value of the Jewish experience. Admission into the university has gradually culminated in scholarly acceptance.

Many developments have contributed to this historic achievement. Neither American society nor the Jewish world nor the university are what they were when Wolfson tactfully stressed what connected Judaism to the mainstream. But publication of the new encyclopedia should also alert us to the formative role played by the discipline of religious studies. Its successful entry into the university in the decades after World War II heralded not only the importance of religion generically for the humanities but also the value specifically of non-Western religions for an institution that presumed to be universal. Along with other factors, the discipline of religious studies, often spearheaded by emigré scholars, helped to expand the parochial horizon of the university, and led eventually to a greater receptivity for the study of Judaism. Many of the early positions in Jewish studies were located within departments of religion.

This encyclopedia—a dazzling specimen of the humanity that currently informs the discipline of religious studies—also reminds us of the paradoxical link between value-free scholarship and the creation of new values. Broadening the intellectual horizon through non-partisan, comparative scholarship surely helps to foster a respect for individuality and diversity and a spirit of kinship and interdependence vital to an ethos of ethnic and religious pluralism.

Above all, the achievement of this encyclopedia is meant to enlarge religious commitment, not to erode it. In the words of Eliade, "Knowledge of the religious ideas and practices of other traditions better enables anyone to understand his or her own" (vol. 1, p. xi). A measure of distance yields a myriad of insights. Would that those tempted by the resurgent dogmatism abroad in the land permit themselves to savor of the wisdom so lovingly assembled in this encyclopedia. No gentler antidote has been devised.

II
THE STUDY OF JUDAISM

Biblical Studies

3

BIBLICAL STUDIES IN A STATE

Edward L. Greenstein

Biblical studies has grown into a multidisciplined field, seeming to expand in several directions at the same time. We are experiencing a somewhat dizzying development, similar to one that scholars in many other disciplines have recently undergone. Instead of building up the body of knowledge through the progressive accumulation of data and insights, practitioners have struck out centrifugally into uncharted terrain, extending the field laterally without necessarily enhancing its depth.[1] Whereas on the one hand the exposure to new and different disciplinary approaches bespeaks a maturation of Biblical studies as an academic field, on the other it reflects a more and more widely spreading "crisis" in our faith in the methods that have traditionally been cultivated within the confines of our own criticism.[2] In this essay I examine the background and nature of the "crisis" state in the Biblical field and explore the foundations underlying the sorts of historical and ahistorical approaches that various scholars take. Rather than bemoan an apparent lack of direction, in the end I celebrate the rich new possibilities that have opened up to us for the construction of meaning.

In 1964 the Anchor Bible published the first volume in its popular series, E. A. Speiser's *Genesis*. In one of his most original suggestions in that commentary, Speiser contended that the story in Genesis 14 of the battle between the four kings from the North and East and the five kings from the Dead Sea region represents a Hebrew transformation of an authentic non-Israelite chronicle, probably composed in Akkadian, from a time close to

23

the events themselves, the eighteenth century B.C.E.[3] "The narrative," Speiser concluded, " . . . has all the ingredients of historicity."[4] Among the foundations on which Speiser based his argument were certain linguistic features that struck him as Akkadian and the resemblance between the names of some of the protagonists in Genesis 14 and the names discovered on three cuneiform tablets, the so-called Spartoli texts, known by Bible scholars as the Chedorlaomer texts since the early twentieth century. What was at stake for Speiser in presenting this hypothesis he himself made clear: "If Abraham was cited in a historical or quasi-historical narrative that was written not by Israelites but by outsiders, it necessarily follows that Abraham was not a nebulous literary figure but a real person who was attested in contemporary sources."[5]

At about the same time M. Astour published a lengthy and highly detailed study of Genesis 14 in which he concluded that the Biblical narrative is a piece of late Deuteronomistic historiography.[6] He reached this finding through two general lines of investigation. On the one hand, he compared the narrative style of Genesis 14 with specimens of Deuteronomistic writing in 2 Kings. On the other, he examined the onomastics and typologies in Genesis 14 and found them to reflect a genre of late date in Mesopotamia. The Spartoli tablets, which Astour like Speiser connects with the Biblical text, come from the second century B.C.E. and represent originals that cannot be dated earlier than the seventh century. Genesis 14 in this view, is not a genuine historical document from 1700 B.C.E. but a symbolic fiction of no earlier than 700 B.C.E.[7]

Anyone acquainted with Biblical scholarship knows well that the antithesis between early and late dating of the patriarchal narratives is altogether typical of the state of the field. Some seek to establish the authenticity of the patriarchal period and accordingly look for parallels to the accounts in Genesis in ancient Near Eastern documents of the second millennium. Others, such as Van Seters, seek to establish the lateness of Genesis's composition and accordingly look for parallels to the accounts of Genesis and its literary style in the mid-first millennium.[8] Such a situation does not inspire confidence in the student who would like to know the history of Israel in the early Biblical period. Skepticism has earned a respectable place in the field.[9]

This skepticism is hardly new. Contemporary Biblical studies still hold largely to the assumptions of Wellhausen and other scholars of a century ago.[10] Virtually axiomatic in Wellhausen's approach was that narratives reflect events, or reflect events accurately, only when they are composed near the time in which the events are supposed to have transpired. Facts are recorded in writing. What is not recorded in writing is suspect and unreliable for historical reconstruction. As M. Noth put it in the middle of this

24

century, "History can only be described on the basis of literary traditions, which record events and specify persons and places."[11] More recently, Van Seters, who conceives of history somewhat differently from Noth, cannot conceive of it apart from the medium of writing.[12] The patriarchal stories bear no presumption of reliability because, among other things, no one believes they were written down in the period they are said to represent.

Now, one might think that the influence of Gunkel in the early part of this century had weakened scholars' attachment to Wellhausen's axiom. Gunkel argued eloquently for the existence of prior stages of oral transmission of traditions preceding the writing down of Biblical texts.[13] Gunkel has made a lasting impact on the way some historians of ancient Israel do their work. W. F. Albright and his students J. Bright, F. M. Cross, and others have attempted to posit years and sometimes centuries of oral transmission, more specifically epic narration, prior to the composition of Biblical prose narratives.[14] Like the Israeli scholar Cassuto,[15] many scholars of the so-called Albright school interpret units of parallelistic verse in the Torah and the Deuteronomistic history as evidence of an earlier Israelite historical epic. They will look to ancient Near Eastern models and typologies for explaining the historical and literary contexts of Biblical materials, arguing for their antiquity on the ground of these parallels. Yet in working this way even the Albright school displays the pervasive effects of Wellhausen's methodology.

Let us turn briefly to a recent historiographic effort by a former student of Cross. In *The Emergence of Israel in Canaan*, B. Halpern tries to reconstruct what he can of the "premonarchic" history of Israel.[16] He readily avers that the narratives of the Books of Joshua and Judges betray tendentious stories that read later monarchic institutions and ideology back into the earlier periods. "It is impossible to determine," he writes, "whether a character named Joshua ben-Nun led more than a few souls . . . into the Aijalon Pass."[17] Distrusting whatever orally transmitted traditions might lie behind that story (and I do not mean to imply that I put any stock in them either), Halpern establishes his conclusions on what he can glean from written documents. In this case they are the El Amarna letters from the fourteenth century, the Song of Deborah and the Song at the Sea—which, following Albright, Halpern dates to the so-called Period of the Judges—and large parts of the Deuteronomistic history that he ascribes to the early sources of that later historiographic composition. Tellingly, Halpern writes that the Song of Deborah "marks the beginning of the period for the recovery of which Israelite sources are of significant value (and basically historical character)."[18]

For similar reasons G. W. Ahlström locates the beginning of the national entity named Israel in the period of Saul, the first who attempted to unify the people that took upon itself the name Israel.[19] It is hardly a co-incidence that Ahlström regards the Biblical traditions about Saul to be the earliest that are historically reliable.

Virtually all modern Biblicists accept the overall historicity of the narratives from the monarchy on. In large measure this is because so many believe that the story of David and the succession to his throne was composed close to the time of David, perhaps during the "golden" era of Solomon.[20] The David story has been understood by many as an eyewitness version that served as a primary source for the Deuteronomist.[21] Its reliability is directly bound up with the theory that Israelite history writing began formally in the era of David and Solomon. Gottwald, who radically diverges from the Bible's account of the conquest and settlement of Canaan,[22] treats the Bible's account of the early monarchy with a high degree of credibility. Gottwald does recognize the genre of the David story as a novella of sorts,[23] yet in his synthesis of Israelite history he accepts the particulars of the Biblical sources. Unsurprisingly, Gottwald attributes the first great Israelite history writing to the period of David and Solomon: "A connected story of Israel's beginning from the creation of the world to at least the verge of Israel's entrance into Canaan was composed ca. 960–930 B.C.E., during the reign of Solomon, in the view of many scholars, although others date it later by as much as a century or more. . . . We do not know the name of the writer. Apparently it was someone in governmental favor—if not actual government service—who provided a kind of 'national epic' for the young kingdom of David and Solomon."[24] Gottwald, in line with conventional scholarship, is referring, of course, to J.[25]

A leading scholar who more than most exhibits the strong influence of Gunkel is R. Rendtorff. In his recent *The Old Testament: An Introduction*, Rendtorff's historical synthesis hews closely to the Bible's own historiography.[26] He endeavors to combine traditional source criticism with a history of traditions.[27] Following Noth and von Rad, Rendtorff identifies the earliest sources in the tradition as the earliest written embodiments of particular traditions. He posits the preliterary, oral transmission of traditions as "fact."[28] He does not account to the preliterary "sagas," however, the historical value that he ascribes to the narratives that might have originated in writing—the history from David onward. He believes the sagas' reports that Israel's ancestors led a "nomadic life-style,"[29] but the "various and sometimes independent traditions from the nomadic sphere" possess an inchoate form until they are "introduced into the later cult of all Israel."[30] This seems just another way of saying that whatever authentic traditions may be preserved in Biblical narrative, they have been made over in the period after Israel had become a nation-state, after the monarchy was established.

Rendtorff's historical reconstruction is founded almost entirely on the Biblical text: "The OT largely remains our only source for the history of Israel."[31] What the texts do not relate, we do not know: "The texts themselves do not make reference to the matter, so that in my view a tolerable historical reconstruction is impossible."[32] How do we know when the text is giving an authentic account of a tradition? Here Rendtorff trusts in the god of consistency. If two passages report the same thing, the truth of the thing is established. For this purpose extra-Biblical documents may also be adduced.[33] When Rendtorff asserts that "the periods into which [the Bible] divides [its] history have been confirmed in all essential points,"[34] what he is saying is that powerful traditions are historically valid. This is effectively no different from affirming one's credence in the historicity of Biblical traditions.[35]

For many Biblicists the early nineteenth century "Quest for the Historical Jesus" has turned into the Quest for the Historical Abraham, or, that having mainly failed, the Quest for the Historical David. It must be remembered that a historian who trusts all traditions that one cannot disprove is no more or less predisposed than a historian who distrusts all traditions that one cannot corroborate or deduce with conviction. In scholarship, cynicism is no worse than credulity. A scion of the Albright school, and a believer in the Bible's historical reliability, P. K. McCarter, Jr., begins from a position of trust. He writes, for example: "The stories of David's rise to power and the rebellion of Absalom *seem easiest to understand* [my emphasis] in the context of David's own lifetime. They were composed as attempts to sway public opinion in his favor and, more specifically, to defend him against charges or suspicions of wrongdoing—thus, to legitimate and solidify his claim to the throne."[36] Note in McCarter's statement that he merges his view of the story's essential historicity with his estimation of its dating to the period of David. One wonders whether McCarter and others would accept the historicity of the David narratives were they convinced that those narratives were set in writing at a much later date.

In characteristically maverick fashion, Van Seters has argued that the source-critical analysis of the Book of Samuel that segregates an early Davidic or Solomonic stratum in the David story is wrong.[37] Van Seters endeavors to demonstrate that the very passages that earlier scholars had assumed to be ancient show signs of having been produced *de novo* by the Deuteronomist historian. More precisely, Van Seters finds the story of David's early career to be of a piece with Deuteronomistic historiography. The so-called Court History of David is, in Van Seter's judgment, "a bitter attack upon the whole royal ideology of a 'sure house' for David."[38] Since the Deuteronomist is pro-Davidic, the Court History must have been added to the David narrative in the postexilic period. It should go without saying

27

that Van Seters puts little store in the reliability of the Davidic "history." Written late, it is not based on historical sources; it is contrived.

What is curious is that critical historians of opposing positions manifest trust in Biblical traditions only when they are found in near-contemporary written documents. With all the theorizing that has gone on since Gunkel concerning the oral transmission of Biblical narratives and other traditions, even scholars such as Rendtorff and McCarter will place confidence only in a written report. In this respect they are not far from Wellhausen. The believing historian, unlike the uncritical believer, does not accept the Bible as a historical witness. The believing historian by virtue of the academic discipline of history, begins from a position of distrust.[39]

Some will justify their skepticism by pointing to the literary genre of the Biblical narrative, its presumed intention. Zakovitch, for example, maintains that the extensive and multifaceted literary patterning of the Biblical "history" betrays its artificial, novelistic quality.[40] Although my own sympathies are with Zakovitch on this, the following represents a more widely shared perspective: "Although, admittedly, the Biblical authors made use of historical facts, they did so to convince the reader of the validity of the religious, moral and social concepts being urged, and they kneaded the raw material of historical facts into the message they were trying to convey. In short, when historical facts fit into the message, the Biblical authors used them; when the historical facts did not support the message, the facts were molded by rearranging them or elaborating them until they did support the message."[41] The author of these remarks, Y. T. Radday, goes on to delineate a large number of Biblical claims that cannot be factual, in particular matters of geography and chronology. Now, if these fundamentals of historiography are unreliable, in what can the historian trust? Indeed, on what basis does Radday assert that "the Biblical authors made use of historical facts"? To what extent is what the Bible says factual, and how can one tell? We have seen above that Rendtorff applies the standard of coherence: if the same fact is reported in different texts, it may be believed.

Others adduce the confirmation of archaeological exploration. Although historical geographers can often link up archaeological sites with Biblical toponyms,[42] the fact is that archaeology can readily be used to demonstrate the historical *un*reliability of what the Bible reports. The cases of Ha-ai and Jericho are well known.[43] Let me illustrate with a less familiar but hardly obscure instance. Textual and artifactual evidence had convinced scholars such as W. F. Albright that the camel had not been domesticated in the Levant until the twelfth century B.C.E. Accordingly, Albright viewed the references to camels in Genesis as "anachronistic."[44] Albright did not mean that the patriarchal narratives were late inventions. He thought that a later tradent replaced an earlier beast in the original narrative with a more fashionable, contemporary one. "Of course," Albright was quick to add, "such anachronisms in local color no more disprove the historicity of the underlying tradition than Tissot's painted scenes of Bible life falsify the biblical story by depicting its heroes as modern Palestinian Arabs."[45] In drawing the conclusion that the archaeological data do not indicate the time of the events being narrated in the Bible, Albright is in effect discounting the relevance of the archaeological evidence for dating or authenticating Biblical reports. Material evidence does not budge his trust in the historicity of the narratives. His initial presumption of historicity predetermined the way he handled the archaeological data.

The most recent data on the camel in the ancient land of Israel, from the excavation of numerous animal bones at Tel Jemmeh, an ancient crossroads near Gaza, indicate that camel caravans were not employed in what archaeologists call Syro-Palestine until around 600 B.C.E.[46] Thus, unless the trip of Abraham's servant in Genesis 24 and the visit of the Queen of Sheba to Solomon are but "singular events,"[47] the reference to camels in Biblical narrative are grossly anachronistic. One can argue that earlier stories were modernized by a later editor who inserted camels where there had been none in the source. But one will follow this strategy only under the presumption that the Biblical narratives are essentially historical. A historian who adds this particular anachronism to the many others that have been suggested may also conclude that the narratives were composed at a late date, and that they are historically unreliable.

The archaeologist William Dever has in a number of manifestos contended that recent studies and excavations in the near Middle East can best be explained if one does not accept the historical authenticity of the major episodes in the narrative from Genesis through Kings,[48] the so-called Primary History.[49] In his view there was no exodus of masses of Hebrews from Egypt in the thirteenth century, no sojourn in the Sinai wilderness, no military conquest of Canaan by the Israelites. Excavations by Israeli and American scholars in the Galilee and Negev in particular indicate that Israelites took up residence in places that had no preceding settlement.[50] To many, including Dever, the Israelites were Canaanites who moved to the hill country and Negev because those were sparsely populated areas that would offer them little resistance. Accordingly, Dever believes that recent archaeology conforms more closely to the settlement model proposed by Mendenhall and Gottwald[51] than the invasion model that had been favored by the Albright school, represented, for example, by Bright's *History of Israel*.[52] In the third edition of this widely used volume Bright attempts to assimilate some of the recent opposition but retains the historicity of the exodus and military conquest. He regards the events as complexes of various distinct

29

group movements that have been telescoped, and he lowers the numbers of people involved.

The editor of *Biblical Archaeology Review*, Hershel Shanks, has correctly defined the difference between the approach of scholars such as Dever and that of scholars such as Bright.[53] Dever begins without any commitment to the historical truth of the Biblical narrative, whereas Bright begins from a position of faith. Shanks maintains that "for Dever, any collision he can identify between the archaeological evidence and the Biblical evidence requires him to reject the Biblical evidence."[54] Shanks justifiably labels Dever's approach an "anti-biblical bias."[55] If one means by that a considered distrust of the Bible's historicity concerning the early stages of Israel's history, that characterization may be valid. But Shanks also condemns Dever's approach as "a fundamental methodological error."[56] Shanks is effectively saying that good methodology posits the authenticity of the Biblical record, or, more generously, that good methodology must exclude bias for or against both the Biblical record and one's interpretation of archaeological data. The exclusion of bias or presupposition, however, is no more than a comforting illusion, as we have seen. One always begins from a position of greater credence or of greater skepticism. One's methodology will be fundamentally affected by that opening stance.[57]

Aware of contrary possibilities for constructing a convincing model of what early Israel looked like, Cross has candidly admitted: "I doubt that Biblical archaeology can ever establish that the traditional events of Israel's early epic are historical, and certainly the archaeologist cannot prove these events were truly interpreted, even if established as historical."[58] Nevertheless, while Cross acknowledges the limitations of the historical disciplines in reaching decisive conclusions, he confesses his personal outlook, what Shanks would have to call a "bias": "Israel uniquely was plunged into history, into a perennial grappling with history as the realm of meaning, and it would not be surprising, I think, if this plunge were precipitated by Israel's own historical experience."[59] In other words, Cross admits to his predisposition to trust the contours of the Biblical tradition. At the same time, it is evident that historians and archaeologists with different predispositions will assemble their data into different models of historical reconstruction. Data do not by themselves congeal into theories. Scholars shape the data into configurations of their own imagination.[60]

The same may be said of philological analysis. In a recent publication two Israeli scholars, Y. Klein and Y. Zakovitch, assign the Book of Ruth to two different periods, one preexilic and one postexilic.[61] Zakovitch advocates the later dating on the basis of the text's affinities to postexilic Hebrew and its putative Aramaisms, its postclassical orthography, and its morphology (for example, no distinction between masculine and feminine in the plural possessive suffixes). Klein defends the earlier dating by pointing out that many of the text's peculiar expressions (lexical and morphological) occur in preexilic sources, too—and some of them only in early sources. To account for this he hypothesizes that what occurred late in written Hebrew may have developed early in spoken Hebrew.[62] The text's orthography may, in Klein's view, reflect the results of scribal transmission, not the stage of composition. Both Zakovitch and Klein acknowledge the archaic literary style of Ruth. But for Klein it is an authentically classical style, and for Zakovitch it is deliberately archaizing. Each scholar defines and adapts the evidence according to his own point of view.[63]

Nowhere is this situation more obvious in Biblical studies than in the state of affairs of the source-critical analysis of the Bible, and of the Torah in particular.[64] Source criticism of the Torah has loomed large in modern Biblical studies—so much so that Weinfeld has virtually equated source criticism with Biblical criticism in general in a recent encyclopedia article.[65] All questions concerning the early history of Israel and the development of Biblical religion—including the divine character of the Torah—presuppose certain conclusions about the Torah's literary origins. Both Wellhausen's and Kaufmann's almost antithetical visions of ancient Israelite religious history depend on closely kindred theories of the Torah's literary development.[66] Both Wellhausen and Kaufmann accept the division of the Torah into four documents, J, E, D, and P—except that for Kaufmann nothing is exilic or later, and P precedes D. In assaulting Wellhausen's reconstruction of Israelite history, Kaufmann does not challenge the assumptions and methods of source-critical analysis.

F. V. Winnett and his former student J. Van Seters have posed such a challenge, but only a partial one.[67] Van Seters objects not to source division but to the minute dissection of passages into small fragments; and more significant, he interprets the sources distinguished by documentary theorists not as parallel texts that have been redacted together but rather as literary supplements by what is often the same writer. The writer, in this view, fleshes out and revises earlier sources not by altering them but by adding to them. Alternatively, an ancient Israelite historian might compose a narrative of whole cloth, alluding to imaginary sources at times in order to give an aura of authenticity to his work.[68] Whereas in the Torah, the former model of composition prevails, in the Deuteronomistic history one finds a mix of both types.[69] The classical Documentary hypothesis and the Winnett–Van Seters theory apply different compositional models.[70] The Documentary theory regards the redactor of the Torah as an ancient Jewish predecessor of the author of a synoptic Gospel, redacting together two or more sources into a new version. Van Seters sees the Torah's author as a contemporary of Herodotus, composing history using similar methods.

The implications of the two opposing models for the reconstruction of Israelite history are profound. Within the first model, which posits earlier sources, it is possible to assume the antiquity and historicity of various Biblical traditions. The second model obstructs any attempt to posit early historical traditions.

The theory of the Torah's composition delineated by Rendtorff is both more revolutionary and more conservative than those just discussed.[71] Instead of beginning with written sources, Rendtorff follows Gunkel, Noth, and von Rad in tracing the written materials from units of tradition. These units take literary shape independently until they are later assembled into more extensive narrative works. These are then composed into the Torah through various processes resembling at times the model of documentary redaction and at times the model of literary supplementation. It is again unsurprising that in positing ancient oral traditions behind the earliest written stages of the Torah's development Rendtorff affirms the general historicity of the Biblical traditions, as we have seen. Just as historical reconstruction depends on a theory of literary composition, so does one's approach to literary composition reflect one's perspective on Israelite history, or the Bible's account of it.

Rendtorff considers himself to have made "a fundamental break with the traditional methods of analyzing pentateuchal texts."[72] He explains the nature of that break this way:

> Scholars usually begin their study of a pentateuchal text by dividing sources within the text. . . . But in my opinion this is wrong because it presupposes that there must be sources running through the whole Pentateuch. . . . According to the traditional method of literary critique it is not for the scholar to demonstrate that the respective text is not uniform and composed by different sources but it is for the text itself to prove this unity. This approach must be reversed. First of all we have to take the text as a unity and have to try and understand its structure and particular intention.[73]

Rendtorff would have us replace the dogmatism of source analysis with the dogmatism of synthesis. Viewing the text phenomenologically, from a presumption of unity, is no more or less theoretical than viewing the text as a composite. He is opposing a newer theory to the older one.[74]

Rendtorff's position is symptomatic of two important tendencies among many contemporary Biblicists. One is a disaffection from historical paradigms of Biblical study. The other, concomitant trend is attention to the text's unity, or, put differently, applying synchronic paradigms of study to the final form of the Biblical text. I shall take up these two points together because they are interdependent. The application of synchronic modes of analysis to the Bible, in step with other academic disciplines, seems often to flow from a reaction against or restlessness with the more entrenched historical methods of research.[75]

The frustration of many Biblicists with historical study is evinced in the recent introduction to the Hebrew Bible (or, in Christian terms, the "Old Testament") by Crenshaw. On account of the complicated and obscure literary development of the Biblical text, Crenshaw says: "A purely historical analysis of the literature cannot yield satisfactory results. Efforts to specify dates for biblical books and to examine them according to their historical sequence are doomed from the start. It has become increasingly clear that no satisfactory history of the literature can be written. . . . Thus far, no suitable criteria exist by which to separate later glosses from early writings, and every indication points to extremely active editorial work in updating ancient traditions."[76]

If we cannot with confidence distinguish historical strata in a Biblical text, we can only doubtfully engage in historical reconstruction. The Bible is, after all, our major source. We can, however, study and interpret the final form of the text, putting into practice strategies of analysis that deal with the form, style, and underlying ideas of the literature as we have it. Synchronic methods generally presuppose the integrity of the text.

The function of textual criticism has always been to restore an earlier, more original document. Versions of the Hebrew Bible, such as the Septuagint, have been compared in order to evaluate the Massoretic text and correct it where necessary with readings in the versions that for various reasons seemed better to the critic. There is now, however, a newer tendency to view the versions as independent traditions. The Septuagint, too, is a textual unity.[77] Only after being studied as a total structure should a text such as the Septuagint be compared with the Massoretic text, or with a Dead Sea fragment for that matter. M. Greenberg, in an examination of the Massoretic and Greek texts of Ezekiel, regards each as an independent entity: "We have two versions, each with its own quality and its own coherence."[78] Out of respect for the integrity of the Massoretic text (MT), the received text is regularly compared in order to trace the literary history of the versions. Compare the following conclusion from a recent study of the Exodus scroll from Qumran Cave 4: "[The Qumran text] represents a textual tradition that is very close to that known to us in the Massoretic text. Working from a base very much like what has come down to us as [the Massoretic text], one or several scribes expanded certain specific sections of the text, with the result that many columns of the scroll look quite similar to [the Massoretic text], while other columns—even in their present fragmentary state—have six or seven lines not found in [the Massoretic text].''[79] Implicit in these remarks are the following premises: MT is a distinct text; the Qumran scroll is a distinct text; material in the latter that is missing in the former is the result of expansion in the scroll rather than deletion in the source; and, most fundamentally, there is a historical connection between the Massoretic and Qumran texts. We may tend to forget that the connections we take for granted are the products of our prior hypotheses and conclusions. We do not simply see the connections; we first draw them. Our changing perspectives are not the naked fruits of new research. They are just that—"changing perspectives," a different way of looking at things.

This newer synchronic vision is most evident in our approaches to exegesis. Whatever disciplines scholars work in—whether anthropology, sociology, rhetoric, or theology—more and more analyze the Bible as a contained system of structurally related components. The models many Biblicists are increasingly adopting are structural, paradigmatic.[80] The difference in what the Bible means between the historical and synchronic methods of exegesis is analogous to the difference between the chronicle of a person's life and a psychoanalysis of that person.

Let me illustrate by referring to Biblical prophecy. Whereas scholars had typically attempted to segregate what the prophet said from what later interpolators and editors had added,[81] some recent work such as the Ezekiel commentary by Greenberg and the studies of First and Second Isaiah by Gitay start with the assumption of textual order.[82] They then apply diverse literary and rhetorical strategies to account for and make good sense of the present form of the text. We then read of the "consistent trend of thought" and "distinctive style" of Ezekiel,[83] or of the "order" and "art of persuasion" of Second Isaiah.[84] Applying synchronic analysis from a sociological perspective, Robert Wilson has endeavored to examine not so much the history of prophecy in ancient Israel as the relations of Biblical prophets to their society.[85] So, too, Michael Fishbane, rather than reconstruct the development of Israelite prophecy, has summarized a phenomenology of Biblical prophecy, placing it in the context of other elements in the Bible's conceptual framework (such as covenant and worship).[86] The significance of the prophet and the meaning of his message are determined in these models by their function within a given system, whether social or literary.

Various forms of literary criticism largely find the meaning of Biblical texts in the linguistic configurations and/or semantic and psychological deep structures that are manifest in them. Like a wave touched off by new and different disturbances in the field of literary theory, Biblical studies has of late reacted routinely to the latest literary vibrations. We have nothing like the widespread paradigm shifts in Biblical studies that would, in Thomas Kuhn's terminology, mark the equivalent of a "scientific revolution,"[87] but if there is any single new wave in Biblical criticism, it is the application of synchronic modes of literary interpretation. Even within historical approaches, synchronic analysis is often adduced to determine the meaning of a historical period or literary stratum, as in, for example, the studies of the Deuteronomist's work by Polzin[88] and Van Seters;[89] Harold Bloom's essays on "J," the Bible's, and perhaps the world's, most original writer;[90] and canonical criticism in general—the study of Biblical texts with regard to their position in the canon.[91]

Synchronic analysis, as the study of the text as a relatively closed system, is attractive for at least three reasons, apart from its trendiness. First, it interprets what we have—rather than a reconstructed version of it. Although interpreting what we have involves the same degree of theorizing as does interpreting what we must first reconstruct,[92] many feel more comfortable with the received text. Biblicists are only recently beginning to acknowledge the hypothetical nature of all the approaches they take. The matter has been put well by Barton:

> Biblical "methods" are *theories* rather than methods: theories which result from the formalizing of intelligent intuitions about meaning of biblical texts. Texts are perceived as having certain sorts of meaning—or, just as interestingly, as failing to convey meaning—by reading them with certain vague expectations about genre, coherence, and consistency, which are either confirmed and clarified, or disappointed and frustrated. Then reading begins again, this time with a sharper focus; and at the end of the process there emerges a distinct impression of what the text means, together with an explanatory theory as to how it comes to mean it. But the theory—which, when codified, will become source analysis or redaction criticism or whatever—is logically subsequent to the intuition about meaning.[93]

Accordingly, preference for the received text adumbrates an epistemological position. Many trust our means of making meaning more than our means of reconstructing a text.

A second reason for the popularity of synchronic analysis is also epistemological. We find the sense of a text, or anything else, to be more significant or fuller by studying it in terms of its shape and function than by studying its historical evolution. We have touched on this matter above.

A third, rather pragmatic reason for doing synchronic analysis is that its practice requires fewer accessory disciplines than historical investigation. That is, one does not have to be as well educated in languages, scripts, archaeology, history and historiography, textual criticism, and comparative Semitic philology to analyze the Biblical text within a synchronic paradigm. The synchronic approach either depends on the prior and fundamental work of historical scholarship, or it ignores it.[94] There is no question that synchronic methods produce rich and revealing meaning in the text, in particular with respect to the themes and typologies that have come to constitute the frameworks of the great religions that base themselves on the Hebrew Bible.[95] But in order to perform synchronic analysis on the Bible one need know only Hebrew, or even no Hebrew at all.[96]

Synchronic methods also serve us well in our teaching. We can train our students to apply literary, structural modes of analysis to the text in far less time than it would take to develop their skills in diachronic forms of analysis. Moreover, teaching historical method almost necessarily conveys a hierarchical or authoritarian view of the teacher-student relationship—that of learned master vis-à-vis ignorant disciple. Utilizing a synchronic approach, in little time the student can contribute and almost democratically participate in learning. The preference for synchronic paradigms of study by teachers and students may well reflect such an egalitarian political agenda.

If our object is to find meaning in the Bible in as many ways or on as many levels as possible, we should attempt to see the text within both historical and synchronic matrices. In his superb new introduction to the Hebrew Bible, Norman Gottwald assesses the values of the many paradigms of study—as religious testimony, historical witness, literary world, social world, to use his terms.[97] It is the merit of Gottwald's book to explain how different epistemological paradigms—what he calls "angles of vision"— yield different views of the Bible and the various parts of the world in which it was first produced. Before discussing the major Biblical themes or traditions, Gottwald does his best to place the literary sources in their historical, and if possible even their sociological, context.

That will work for Gottwald, who, as we saw above, appears relatively confident in the potential of historical reconstruction. It will not work for someone like literary critic Meir Sternberg, who would like to read the Bible against the enriching background of its historical world but does not because, as he says, "When all is said and done, the independent knowledge we possess of the 'real world' behind the Bible remains absurdly meager."[98]

Many contemporary Biblicists are experiencing a crisis in faith. I do not mean faith in the Bible's history, which, as we have seen, is hardly new; but faith in believing the results of our study. The objective truths of the past we increasingly understand as the creations of our own vision. The words of Christian Scriptures scholar John Dominic Crossan describe what we have found: "We found not a picture but a mirror, and the dust of ages was but the images of our ancestors. In a mirror, however, we see not just ourselves but ourselves *looking*. We see eyes before we see all else."[99] But rather than lament our loss of absolute knowledge, Crossan relishes the new hermeneutical possibilities that we have gained by this self-awareness of our ideas and sensibilities: "The fact that the mirror is overlaid with images, with multiple interpretations, is not our failure but our success."[100]

The effect of recognizing that all scholarship relies on theories and methods that come and go, and that modern critical approaches are no more or less than our own midrash, places us, if we are informed and responsible, on the same footing as our predecessors.[101] We should do our work as well as we can, using the paradigms and tools in which we can put our trust. Those paradigms and tools will play a role that serves our objectives and concerns. Feminist critics of the Bible, for example, have learned to appreciate the value of midrashic types of hermeneutics in order to make of the Bible a text with which and by which they can live.[102] Other feminist critics, using more conventional secular approaches, may decide that within their paradigms the Bible is hopelessly androcentric and demeaning to women.[103] Obviously, women who are committed to the centrality of the Bible will take the former approach, analogous to classical rabbinic midrash, because it will foster their personal or ideological needs. Women, or men for that matter, who lack that commitment, or who seek to dislodge the Bible from its historical position as a foundation of faith, will apply those analytical strategies that expose the Bible's antifemale bias.[104]

As a Jew, I welcome the greater freedom that issues from the crisis of faith in the older methods and conceptual constructs of Biblical studies. For several years now, Jewish Biblicists in Israel and in the United States have pointed to the fact that so many categories in the study of Biblical literature, and its religion in particular, derive from patently Christian doctrines.[105] We are only beginning—at least in widely circulating print—to produce a phenomenology of Biblical religion, or religions, that expresses a traditional Jewish framework.[106] It is significant, too, that Jewish scholars with historical training are attempting to reconstruct the development of classical Jewish hermeneutics from the Biblical world itself.[107] The Bible is no longer seen as a sphere apart from later Jewish tradition. For a time Jews engaging in the predominantly Christian field of Biblical studies seemed to feel constrained from reading their own religious outlook into the earlier Scriptures. Y. Kaufmann recognized that Biblical scholarship had in fact been presupposing certain Christian ideas, such as the priority of ethics and faith over ritual and community.[108] Kaufmann did not overly force the Bible into a traditional Jewish framework; but it is clear that his own dogmas concerning the distinctiveness of the People of Israel and their worldview went hand in glove with his strong Zionist ideology.[109]

Before concluding, it should be observed that not only Kaufmann's scholarship but historical modes of research are still prevalent in contemporary Israeli Biblical studies.[110] Although it is best to eschew the search for single, simple explanation for this phenomenon, one should not in pondering it overlook the effect of environment, as well as ideology, on scholarship. Israelis live with the world of the Bible; its history haunts their land. The Biblical encyclopedia produced in Israel, as Simon has noted, is distinguished from scholarship elsewhere not by its disciplinary approaches but by its extraordinary attention to the archaeology and realia of the Land of Israel.[111] We in the diaspora find the text, the literature, closer at hand. Our milieu is the library more than the countryside.

In Umberto Eco's mystery novel *The Name of the Rose,* the detective monk's amenuensis, Adso, asks his master, Brother William:

"Therefore you don't have a single answer to your questions?"

"Adso, if I did I would teach theology in Paris."

"In Paris do they always have the true answer?"

"Never," William said, "but they are very sure of their errors."

"And you," I said with childish impertinence, "never commit errors?"

"Often," he answered. "But instead of conceiving only one, I imagine many, so I may become the slave of none."[112]

The newer thinking in Biblical studies is open to new disciplines and conceptual models, as well as to newly discovered tells and texts.

Notes

1. Cf., e.g., William E. Cain, *The Crisis in Criticism: Theory, Literature, and Reform in English Studies* (Baltimore, 1984); Donald W. Fiske and Richard A. Shweder, eds., *Metatheory in Social Science* (Chicago, 1986).

2. Quite presciently R. M. Polzin some time ago put his finger on the problem: "If there is a crisis in biblical scholarship today, it does not consist in the present almost healthy tension between historical and literary criticism of the Bible, but rather in the destructive self image both may have concerning their status as scholarly disciplines modeled after the natural sciences"; see Robert M. Polzin, "Literary and Historical Criticism of the Bible: A Crisis in Scholarship," in Richard A. Spencer, ed., *Orientation by Disorientation: Studies in Literary Criticism and Biblical Literary Criticism* (Pittsburgh, 1980), pp. 99–114; here, p. 100. I must register my dissent from Polzin's assumption that synchronic (or any other) analysis can operate without any preconceived theories; see further my "Theory and Argument in Biblical Criticism," *Hebrew Annual Review* 10 (1987), pp. 77–92.

In the end Polzin attributes the "true crisis" to the fact that through historical criticism "so many . . . believe that they are actually understanding the Bible's claims on its own terms, when in fact they are not" (p. 108). Although I agree with this assessment, it must be acknowledged that synchronic or ahistorical critics are no more free of presupposition than the historians; see further below and cf. Alan Cooper, "On Reading the Bible Critically and Otherwise," in Richard E. Friedman and H. G. M. Williamson, eds., *The Future of Biblical Studies: The Hebrew Scriptures* (Atlanta, 1987), pp. 61–79.

3. E. A. Speiser, *Genesis,* Anchor Bible 1 (Garden City, N.Y., 1964), pp. 105–9.

4. Ibid., p. 109.

5. Ibid., p. 108.

6. Michael C. Astour, "Political and Cosmic Symbolism in Genesis 14 and in Its Babylonian Sources," in Alexander Altmann, ed., *Biblical Motifs* (Cambridge, Mass., 1966), pp. 65–112.

7. On Genesis 14, see further J. A. Emerton, "The Riddle of Genesis XIV," *Vetus Testamentum* 21 (1971), pp. 403–39, with bibliography; John Van Seters, *Abraham in History and Tradition* (New Haven, Conn., 1975), pp. 296ff.

8. Cf. Van Seters, *Abraham;* see also T. L. Thompson, *The Historicity of the Patriarchal Narratives* (Berlin, 1974).

9. Consider, e.g., both the contents and tone of the following remarks by a historian of the Biblical period: "It is time we stopped kidding ourselves; the patriarchal and conquest narratives represent at best the traditions of the end of the Late Bronze and the beginning of the Iron Age with thorough reworking in the late monarchy and beyond"; Anson F. Rainey, review of *The Tribes of Yahweh* by N. K. Gottwald, *Journal of the American Oriental Society* 107 (1987), pp. 541–43; here, p. 542b.

10. See esp. Julius Wellhausen, *Prolegomena to the History of Ancient Israel* (Cleveland, 1957; first published 1878).

11. Martin Noth, *The History of Israel,* rev. ed. (New York, 1960), p. 42.

12. Van Seters, *Abraham;* idem, *In Search of History: Historiography in the Ancient World and the Origins of Biblical History* (New Haven, Conn., 1983).

13. Esp. Hermann Gunkel, *Genesis* (Göttingen, 1966; first published 1901); idem, *The Legends of Genesis* (New York, 1966; first English ed., 1901).

14. E.g., William F. Albright, *From the Stone Age to Christianity,* 2d ed. (Garden City, N.Y., 1957); idem, *Archaeology and the Religion of Israel,* 5th ed. (Garden City, N.Y., 1969); John Bright, *A History of Israel,* 3rd rev. ed. (Philadelphia, 1981); Frank M. Cross, *Canaanite Myth and Hebrew Epic* (Cambridge, Mass., 1973). For Gunkel's influence on Albright, see Albright's introduction to the 1966 edition of Gunkel's *Legends.*

15. See esp. Umberto Cassuto, "The Israelite Epic," *Biblical and Oriental Studies,* trans. I. Abrahams (Jerusalem, 1975), vol. 2, pp. 69–109. Note the criticism of Van Seters, *In Search of History,* pp. 226–27; but see, too, my "Theory and Argument."

16. Baruch Halpern, *The Emergence of Israel in Canaan* (Chico, Calif., 1983).

17. Ibid., p. 8.

18. Ibid., p. 32; cf. p. 8.

19. Gösta W. Ahlström, *Who Were the Israelites?* (Winona Lake, Ind., 1986).

20. Cf., e.g., Gerhard von Rad, "The Beginnings of Historical Writing in Ancient Israel," in *The Problem of the Hexateuch and Other Essays,* trans. E. W. Trueman Dicken (Edinburgh, 1966), pp. 166–204, esp. p. 195.

21. For a literary critique of this position, see Yair Zakovitch, "Story Versus History," in *Proceedings of the Eighth World Congress of Jewish Studies,* Panel Sessions, Bible Studies and Hebrew Language (Jerusalem, 1983), pp. 47–60.

22. Norman K. Gottwald, *The Tribes of Yahweh: A Sociology of the Religion of Liberated Israel, 1250–1050* B.C.E. (Maryknoll, N.Y., 1979). See also his more synoptic presentation in "The Israelite Settlement as a Social Revolutionary Movement," in Janet Amitai, ed., *Biblical Archaeology Today: Proceedings of the International Congress on Biblical Archaeology, Jerusalem, April 1984* (Jerusalem, 1985), pp. 34–46.

23. Norman K. Gottwald, *The Hebrew Bible: A Socio-Literary Introduction* (Philadelphia, 1985), pp. 317–18.

24. Gottwald, *The Hebrew Bible,* p. 137.

25. Cf. this recent summary of contemporary thinking: "There seems to be plenty of reason to argue that J was created for and reflects the enthusiastic achievement of Davidic-Solomonic nationalism. To date it anytime during the period of the Divided Kingdom, and even after refugees from the North have been assimilated into the Hezekian community, seems less than satisfactory"; Simon J. De Vries, "A Review of Recent Research in the Tradition History of the Pentateuch," in Kent H. Richards, ed., *Society of Biblical Literature 1987 Seminar Papers* (Atlanta, 1987), pp. 459–502, at 500.

26. Rolf Rendtorff, *The Old Testament: An Introduction,* trans. John Bowden (Philadelphia, 1986).

27. For a comprehensive survey of tradition historical work, see De Vries, "A Review of Recent Research." De Vries is far more conventional than Rendtorff, however, and remains mystified at Rendtorff's departures from normative source theory.

28. Rendtorff, *The Old Testament,* p. 79.

29. Ibid., p. 86.

30. Ibid., p. 20.

31. Ibid., p. 5.

32. Ibid., p. 70.

33. Ibid., pp. 11, 19, and passim.

34. Ibid., p. 5.

35. For a recent positivistic assertion that the Bible's historical reliability should be presumed, see Tomoo Ishida, "Adonijah the Son of Hagith and His Supporters: An Inquiry into Problems about History and Historiography," in Friedman and Williamson, eds., *The Future of Biblical Studies,* pp. 165–87.

36. P. Kyle McCarter, Jr., "The Historical David," *Interpretation* 40 (1986), pp. 117–29; here, p. 118.

37. Van Seters, *In Search of History,* esp. chap. 8, pp. 249–91.

38. Ibid., p. 290.

39. For further discussion of this topic, see Ivan G. Marcus, "The Jewish Historian and the Believer," in Nina B. Cardin and David W. Silverman, eds., *The Seminary at 100: Reflections on the Jewish Theological Seminary and the Conservative Movement* (New York, 1987), pp. 215–22.

40. Zakovitch, "Story Versus History."

41. Yehuda T. Radday, "A Bible Scholar Looks at BAR's Coverage of the Exodus," *Biblical Archaeology Review* 8/6 (Nov./Dec. 1982), pp. 68–71; here, pp. 68–69. For the view that the Biblical history of the monarchy was less than tendentious, see Baruch Halpern, "Biblical or Israelite History?" in Friedman and Williamson, eds., *The Future of Biblical Studies,* pp. 103–39.

42. See esp. Yohanan Aharoni, *The Land of the Bible,* rev. and enl. Anson F. Rainey (Philadelphia, 1979).

43. Cf., e.g., Bright, *History,* pp. 130–31. For further discussion, see Roland De Vaux, *The Early History of Israel,* trans. David Smith (Philadelphia, 1978), esp. pp. 475–87.

44. William F. Albright, *The Archaeology of Palestine,* rev. ed. (London, 1954), pp. 206–7.

45. Ibid., p. 207.

46. Paula Wapnish, "Camel Caravans and Camel Pastoralists at Tell Jemmeh," *Journal of the Ancient Near Eastern Society* 13 (1981), pp. 101–21.

47. Ibid., p. 112. It should be noted that Wapnish appears conservative in her suggestion that the Queen of Sheba might have made an extraordinary journey to the Land of Israel in the tenth century B.C.E. by camel. Wapnish takes the narrative at its face value, in spite of its fairy-tale-like quality.

48. For a summary and bibliography, see William G. Dever, "Syro-Palestinian and Biblical Archaeology," in Douglas A. Knight and Gene M. Tucker, eds., *The Hebrew Bible and Its Modern Interpreters* (Chico, Calif., 1985), pp. 31–74. For a similar position, cf. Max Miller, "Old Testament History and Archaeology," *Biblical Archaeologist* 50/1 (Mar. 1987), pp. 55–63.

49. For the term "Primary History," see David N. Freedman, "The Earliest Bible," in Michael P. O'Connor and D. N. Freedman, eds., *Backgrounds for the Bible* (Winona Lake, Ind., 1987), pp. 29–37.

50. For summary discussion and bibliography, see Moshe Kochavi, "The Israelite Settlement in Canaan in the Light of Archaeological Surveys," in Amitai, ed., *Biblical Archaeology Today*, pp. 54–60. See also, in addition to the articles by Aharoni cited there, Aharon Kempinski, "Israelite Conquest or Settlement? New Light from Tell Masos," *Biblical Archaeology Review* 2/3 (Sept. 1976), pp. 25–30. Cf. Kempinski's conclusion: "The first appearance of the Israelites at Tell Masos in the northern Negev and the new cultural elements which they brought with them is in total harmony with the settlement theory of [Albrecht] Alt. . . . Tell Masos establishes that the Israelite settlers of the second half of the 13th century B.C.E. were not simply nomads who 'emerged from the desert' but were a people who already had a building tradition going back to the Bronze Age traditions of the mountainous areas" (p. 30b). Contrast the somewhat more traditional views of Amihai Mazar in *Biblical Archaeology Today*, pp. 61–71.

51. George E. Mendenhall, "The Hebrew Conquest of Palestine," *Biblical Archaeologist* 25/3 (Sept. 1962), pp. 66–87, reprinted in Edward F. Campbell, Jr., and David N. Freedman, eds., *The Biblical Archaeologist Reader* 3 (Garden City, N.Y., 1970), pp. 100–120; idem, *The Tenth Generation: The Origins of the Biblical Tradition* (Baltimore, 1973); Gottwald, *The Tribes of Yahweh*.

52. Bright, *A History of Israel*, esp. pp. 133–43.

53. Hershel Shanks, "Dever's 'Sermon on the Mound,' " *Biblical Archaeology Review* 13/1 (Mar./Apr. 1987), pp. 54–57.

54. Ibid., p. 57.

55. Ibid., p. 56.

56. Ibid., p. 57.

57. Cf. Frederic Brandton, "The Limits of Evidence: Archaeology and Objectivity," *Maarav* 4/1 (Spring 1987), pp. 5–43, who concludes: "As it turns out, the material evidence, although exceptionally valuable, is no more intrinsically accurate or objective than any other kind of evidence" (p. 43). Concerning the nonobjective use of archaeological evidence for ascertaining the historicity or date of any events reported in the Bible, one can hardly gainsay the characteristically thoughtful perspective of S. R. Driver, first published in 1904: "The monuments, again, . . . though they have thrown some light on the kings' names in Gen. 14:1, and have shown that it would be no impossibility for a Babylonian or Elamite king of the 23rd century B.C. to undertake an expedition to the far West, make no mention of the *particular* expedition recorded in Gen. 14: they consequently furnish no independent corroboration of it. . . . The case is similar in the later parts of Genesis. The argument which has been advanced, for instance, to show that the narrative of the purchase of the cave of Machpelah (ch. 23) is the work of a contemporary hand, breaks down completely: the expressions alleged in proof of the assertion are not *confined* to the age of Hammurabi; they one and all . . . occur, in some cases repeatedly, in the period of the kings, and even later: they consequently furnish no evidence that the narrative was written at any earlier date. There is no antecedent reason why Abraham should not have purchased a plot of ground near Hebron from the native inhabitants of the place: but to suppose that this is proven, or even made probable, by archaeology, is completely to misinterpret the evidence which it furnishes"; Driver, *The Book of Genesis*, 2d ed. (London, 1904), pp. xlix–l. See, too, my "Theory and Argument."

58. Frank M. Cross, "Biblical Archaeology Today: The Biblical Aspect," in Amitai, ed., *Biblical Archaeology Today*, pp. 9–15; here, p. 14.

59. Ibid.

60. Cf. Luis Alonso Schökel, "Of Methods and Models," *Supplements to Vetus Testamentum* 36 (Leiden, 1985), pp. 3–13; and my "Theory and Argument."

61. In *'Entsiqlopedya 'olam hattenakh*, vol. 16a, ed. Yaakov Klein (Tel Aviv, 1987), pp. 72–73.

62. Cf. Abba Bendavid, *Leshon miqra' uleshon hakhamin* (Tel Aviv, 1967), 2 vols.

63. Were I writing on the dating of Ruth based on the linguistic evidence, rather than take one or the other side I would explain that one could for very cogent reasons formulate the evidence in either direction. We are not in a position philologically to make a call either way.

64. Cf., e.g., John Van Seters, "Recent Studies on the Pentateuch: A Crisis in Method," *Journal of the American Oriental Society* 99 (1979), pp. 663–73; my "Sources of the Pentateuch," in Paul Achtemeier, ed., *Harper's Bible Dictionary* (San Francisco, 1985), pp. 983–86; and see further Douglas A. Knight, "The Pentateuch," in Knight and Tucker, eds., *The Hebrew Bible*, pp. 263–96.

65. Moshe Weinfeld, "Biblical Criticism," in Arthur A. Cohen and Paul Mendes-Flohr, eds., *Contemporary Jewish Religious Thought* (New York, 1987), pp. 35–40.

66. Wellhausen, *Prolegomena;* Yehezkel Kaufmann, *Toledot ha'emuna hayyisre'elit* (Tel Aviv, 1955–60), 8 vols.; see also his *Gola venekhar* (Tel Aviv, 1929–32), 2 vols. for the theoretical assumptions underlying much of his historiography.

67. Frederick V. Winnett, "Re-examining the Foundations," *Journal of Biblical Literature* 84 (1965), pp. 1–19; Van Seters, *Abraham* and *In Search of History.*

68. Van Seters, *In Search of History*, e.g., pp. 40–49 (see the index there for further references).

69. Ibid., pp. 267–69.

70. Cf. Alonso Schökel, "Of Methods and Models," esp. pp. 5–6.

71. Rolf Rendtorff, *Das überlieferungsgeschichtliche Problem des Pentateuch* (Berlin, 1977); idem, "The Future of Pentateuchal Criticism," *Henoch* 6 (1984), pp. 1–14; cf. Erhard Blum, *Die Komposition der Vätergeschichte* (Neukirchen-Vluyn, 1984). For a critique of Rendtorff's approach, see Van Seters, "Recent Studies on the Pentateuch."

72. Rendtorff, "The Future of Pentateuchal Criticism," p. 11.

73. Ibid.; cf., e.g., Bernhard W. Anderson, "From Analysis to Synthesis: The Interpretation of Genesis 1–11," *Journal of Biblical Literature* 97 (1978), pp. 23–39; Moshe Greenberg, *Ezekiel 1–20*, Anchor Bible 22 (Garden City, N.Y., 1983), pp. 18–27; idem, "What Are Valid Criteria for Determining Inauthentic Matter in Ezekiel?" in J. Lust, ed., *Ezekiel and His Book* (Leuven, 1986), pp. 123–35.

74. See further my "Theory and Argument."

75. Cf. my "The Torah as She Is Read," *Response* 47 (Winter 1985), pp. 17–40, with references.

76. James L. Crenshaw, *Story and Faith: A Guide to the Old Testament* (New York, 1986), p. 2.

77. See, e.g., Emanuel Tov, "Jewish Greek Scriptures," in Robert A. Kraft and George W. E. Nickelsburg, eds., *Early Judaism and Its Modern Interpreters* (Philadelphia, 1986), pp. 223–37, esp. p. 229.

78. Moshe Greenberg, "The Use of the Ancient Versions for Interpreting the Hebrew Text," *Supplements to Vetus Testamentum* 29 (Leiden, 1978), pp. 131–48; here, p. 140.

79. Judith E. Sanderson, *An Exodus Scroll from Qumran* (Atlanta, 1986), p. 308.

80. See, e.g., Roland Barthes et al., *Structural Analysis and Biblical Exegesis*, trans. Alfred M. Johnson, Jr. (Pittsburgh, 1974); Robert M. Polzin, *Biblical Structuralism* (Philadel-

phia, 1977); Robert Detweiler, *Story, Sign, and Self: Phenomenology and Structuralism as Literary-Critical Methods* (Philadelphia, 1978). The book *Structuralism and Biblical Hermeneutics* (Pittsburgh, 1979), ed. and trans. Alfred M. Johnson, Jr., deals directly very little with the Scriptures, and then mostly with the Christian ones. The fact, however, that the book is primarily addressed to Biblicists bespeaks the editor's presumption that structuralist methods are vital to Biblical studies.

81. For a recent approach to Jeremiah that attributes the book to layers of redactional work, see Robert P. Carroll, *From Chaos to Covenant: Prophecy in the Book of Jeremiah* (New York, 1981); *Jeremiah: A Commentary* (Philadelphia, 1986). Carroll clearly distinguishes modern approaches to Jeremiah in their theoretical oppositions in his "Introduction" to *Jeremiah*, esp. pp. 38–50. For an exemplary discussion of the ways that theory and method impinge on the literary historical analysis of Jeremiah, see W. McKane, "Relations between Prose and Poetry in the Book of Jeremiah . . . ," in Leo G. Perdue and Brian W. Kovacs, eds., *A Prophet to the Nations: Essays in Jeremiah Studies* (Winona Lake, Ind., 1984), pp. 269–84.

82. For Greenberg, see the references in n. 73 above; Yehoshua Gitay, "Reflections on the Study of Prophetic Discourse," *Vetus Testamentum* 33 (1983), pp. 207–21; "Isaiah and His Audience," *Prooftexts* 3 (1983), pp. 223–30; "The Effectiveness of Isaiah's Speech," *Jewish Quarterly Review* 75 (1984), pp. 162–72; *Prophecy and Persuasion: A Study of Isaiah 40–48* (Bonn, 1981). Although Greenberg maintains that his conclusion of the text's integrity "is no *a priori* stance" but his "critical assessment of the evidence" ("What Are Valid Criteria?" p. 135), by his applying the criteria that he himself sets forth in "What Are Valid Criteria?" p. 133, he could hardly have reached a different conclusion.

83. Greenberg, *Ezekiel 1–20*, p. 26.

84. Gitay, *Prophecy and Persuasion*, p. 232.

85. Robert R. Wilson, *Prophecy and Society in Ancient Israel* (Philadelphia, 1980); cf. idem, *Sociological Approaches to the Old Testament* (Philadelphia, 1984).

86. Michael Fishbane, "Biblical Prophecy as a Religious Phenomenon," in Arthur Green, ed., *Jewish Spirituality from the Bible through the Middle Ages* (New York, 1986), pp. 62–81.

87. Thomas S. Kuhn, *The Structure of Scientific Revolutions*, 2d ed. (Chicago, 1970). John Dominic Crossan exaggerates in seeing a current revolution in Kuhn's sense in the Biblical field; see his " 'Ruth Amid the Alien Corn': Perspectives and Methods in Contemporary Biblical Criticism," in Robert M. Polzin and Eugene Rothman, eds., *The Biblical Mosaic* (Philadelphia, 1982), pp. 199–210.

88. Robert Polzin, *Moses and the Deuteronomist* (New York, 1980).

89. Van Seters, *In Search of History*, pp. 249–353.

90. E.g., Harold Bloom, "Introduction" to Martin Buber, *On the Bible*, ed. Nahum N. Glatzer (New York, 1982), pp. ix–xxxii; "Criticism, Canon-Formation, and Prophecy," *Raritan* 3/3 (Winter 1984), pp. 1–20; and "Exodus: From J to K, or The Uncanniness of the Yahwist," in David Rosenberg, ed., *Congregation* (New York, 1987), pp. 9–26.

91. See esp. James A. Sanders, *Torah and Canon* (Philadelphia, 1972); Brevard S. Childs, *Introduction to the Old Testament as Scripture* (Philadelphia, 1979). In canonical criticism the text is read in its final form against the background of the faith community that created it. Child's approach differs somewhat from Sanders's in that Childs is more concerned with the meaning of the final form within the faith traditions that have preserved and transmitted it.

92. It is for this reason that I would not adopt the suggestion made to me by Professor Gershon Shaked that instead of contrasting, as I do, the historical/diachronic with the phenomenological/synchronic, I should contrast the positivist with the poeticist. In my view, positiv-

ism may characterize poetic analysis as well as historical reconstruction. An example might be Meir Sternberg's magnificent *The Poetics of Biblical Narrative* (Bloomington, Ind., 1985). To positivism I would oppose a perspective more akin to relativism, pluralism, or deconstruction—terms that many will regard as apt for classifying this essay.

93. John Barton, *Reading the Old Testament* (Philadelphia, 1984), p. 205.

94. Neglect of historical Biblical scholarship is manifest, for example, in the work of Robert Alter, *The Art of Biblical Narrative* (New York, 1981) and *The Art of Biblical Poetry* (New York, 1985). See, e.g., the criticisms in the following reviews: Jon D. Levenson, *Biblical Archaeologist* 46/2 (Spring 1983), pp. 124–25; Baruch Schwartz, *Shnaton: An Annual for Biblical and Ancient Near Eastern Studies* 5–6 (1982), esp. pp. 268–69 [in Hebrew]; Edward L. Greenstein, *Hebrew Studies* 27 (1986), pp. 82–91; James L. Kugel, *Journal of Religion* 67 (1987), pp. 66–79.

95. Cf., e.g., Michael Fishbane, "The Sacred Center: The Symbolic Structure of the Bible," in M. A. Fishbane and Paul Mendes-Flohr, eds., *Texts and Responses* (Leiden, 1975), pp. 6–27; Northrop Frye, *The Great Code: The Bible and Literature* (New York, 1982).

96. Distinguished examples are Roland Barthes, "The Struggle with the Angel," in Barthes et al., *Structural Analysis and Biblical Exegesis*, pp. 21–33 = Barthes, *Image/Music/Text* (New York, 1977), pp. 125–41; Mary Douglas, "The Abominations of Leviticus," in her *Purity and Danger* (New York, 1966), pp. 41–58.

97. Gottwald, *The Hebrew Bible*, esp. pp. 31–33.

98. Sternberg, *The Poetics of Biblical Narrative*, p. 16.

99. John Dominic Crossan, "The Hermeneutical Jesus," in O'Connor and Freedman, eds., *Backgrounds for the Bible*, pp. 15–27; here, p. 27.

100. Ibid.

101. This, for example, is the inevitable conclusion of James L. Kugel's review of the history of Biblical poetics in *The Idea of Biblical Poetry: Parallelism and Its History* (New Haven, Conn., 1981). Cf., e.g., Ismar Schorsch, "Message of the Chancellor," *[Jewish Theological] Seminary Progress* (March 1987), p. 16: "Critical scholarship is the *midrash* of the modern Jew, the application of Western modes of cognition to ancient texts that resonate with sense and meaning."

102. Cf., e.g., Phyllis Bird, "Images of Women in the Old Testament," in Rosemary Radford Reuther, ed., *Religion and Sexism* (New York, 1974), pp. 41–88; Phyllis Trible, "Feminist Hermeneutics and Biblical Studies," *Christian Century* 3/10 (Feb. 1982), pp. 116–18; idem, *God and the Rhetoric of Sexuality* (Philadelphia, 1978); idem, *Texts of Terror: Literary-Feminist Readings of Biblical Narratives* (Philadelphia, 1984).

103. Cf., e.g., Mieke Bal, *Lethal Love: Feminist Literary Readings of Biblical Love Stories* (Bloomington, Ind., 1987); J. Cheryl Exum, " 'Mother in Israel': A Familiar Figure Reconsidered," in Letty M. Russell, ed., *Feminist Interpretation of the Bible* (Philadelphia, 1985), pp. 73–85; Esther Fuchs, "The Literary Characterization of Mothers and Sexual Politics in the Hebrew Bible," in Adela Y. Collins, ed., *Feminist Perspectives on Biblical Scholarship* (Chico, Calif., 1985), pp. 117–36; idem, "Who Is Hiding the Truth? Deceptive Women and Biblical Androcentrism," in Collins, ed., *Feminist Perspectives*, pp. 137–44; idem, "Structure and Patriarchal Functions in the Biblical Betrothal Type-Scene," *Journal of Feminist Studies in Religion* 3 (1987), pp. 7–13.

104. Cf., e.g., Carol Meyers's review of *Feminist Interpretation of the Bible*, in *Journal of the American Academy of Religion* 54 (1986), pp. 608–9; Danna Nolan Fewell, "Feminist Reading of the Hebrew Bible: Affirmation, Resistance, and Transformation," *Journal for the Study of the Old Testament* 39 (Oct. 1987), pp. 77–87. Consider, for example, the contrast Fewell draws between Trible's and Fuchs's treatment of the character Ruth: "While Trible sees the character Ruth exemplifying radical commitment, Fuchs sees the character Ruth complying with patriarchal ethos" (p. 81).

105. See esp. Moshe Goshen-Gottstein, "Jewish Biblical Theology and the Study of Biblical Religion," *Tarbiz* 50 (1980–81), pp. 37–64 [in Hebrew]; idem, "Tanakh Theology: The Religion of the Old Testament and the Place of Jewish Biblical Theology," in Patrick D. Miller, Jr., and Paul D. Hanson, eds., *Ancient Israelite Religion: Essays in Honor of Frank Moore Cross* (Philadelphia, 1987), pp. 617–44; Jon D. Levenson, "The Hebrew Bible, the Old Testament, and Historical Criticism," in Friedman and Williamson, eds., *The Future of Biblical Studies*, pp. 19–59; idem, "Why Jews Are Not Interested in Biblical Theology," in Jacob Neusner, Baruch A. Levine, and Ernest S. Frerichs, eds., *Judaic Perspectives on Ancient Israel* (Philadelphia, 1987), pp. 281–307. Cf., too, Michael Fishbane, "The Role of Biblical Studies within Jewish Studies," *AJS Newsletter* 36 (Fall 1986), pp. 19–21; James L. Kugel, "Biblical Studies and Jewish Studies," in *AJS Newsletter* 36 (Fall 1986), pp. 22–24.

Recently a Christian scholar, Rolf Rendtorff, has discussed the Christian orientation of "Old Testament Theology" in "Must 'Biblical Theology' Be Christian Theology?" *Bible Review* 4/3 (June 1988), pp. 40–43. Although I appreciate Rendtorff's criticism of current "Biblical theology," I find him somewhat naive in thinking that anyone could compose a theology of the Hebrew Bible without some ideological slant. His own reading of Genesis and Exodus (p. 43), for example, omits any mention of the particularism that characterizes the covenant between YHWH and Abraham. That is—as I read it—after unsuccessful attempts to form covenants with the progenitors of all humankind, YHWH initiates and cultivates a relationship with a single tribe, the Hebrews. I suspect that Rendtorff's being a Christian and my being a Jew has something to do with our differences in interpreting the trajectory of the narrative.

106. See, more explicitly, Jon D. Levenson, *Sinai and Zion: An Entry into the Jewish Bible* (Minneapolis, 1985); and less explicitly, a study such as Jacob Milgrom's *Cult and Conscience: The* asham *and the Priestly Doctrine of Repentance* (Leiden, 1976). Note the assessment of the latter by Z. W. Falk in *Bibliotheca Orientalis* 39 (1982), cols. 377–79: "Thus while studying minutiae of *sancta* and ritual, the author presents us with a major insight on biblical theology. Repentance is seen as the central goal of piety and as an integral part of legal and cultic procedure. . . . In this sense the author has discovered in the Levitical code a central idea of rabbinical law" (col. 379).

Jewish in their orientation, too, are the articles on Biblical religion in Green, ed., *Jewish Spirituality* 1: David Sperling, "Israel's Religion in the Ancient Near East" (pp. 5–31); Jon D. Levenson, "The Jerusalem Temple in Devotional and Visionary Experience" (pp. 32–61); Fishbane, "Biblical Prophecy"; Joel Rosenberg, "Biblical Tradition: Literature and Spirit in Ancient Israel" (pp. 82–112); and James L. Kugel, "Topics in the History and Spirituality of the Psalms" (pp. 113–44). Cf. also many of the contributions to *Judaic Perspectives on Ancient Israel.*

I do not mean to imply that studies of Biblical religion by non-Jews are necessarily incompatible with Jewish views. I am sympathetic, to take merely one example, with aspects of John Barton, "The Old Testament," in Cheslyn Jones, Geoffrey Wainwright, and Edward Yarnold, eds., *The Study of Spirituality* (New York, 1986), pp. 47–57.

107. Cf. Nahum M. Sarna, "Psalm 89: A Study in Inner Biblical Exegesis," in Alexander Altmann, ed., *Biblical and Other Studies* (Cambridge, Mass., 1963), pp. 29–46; Michael Fishbane, *Biblical Interpretation in Ancient Israel* (Oxford, 1985); James L. Kugel, pt. 1 of Kugel and Rowan A. Greer, *Early Biblical Interpretation* (Philadelphia, 1986); Avigdor Shinan and Yair Zakovitch, "Midrash on Scripture and Midrash within Scripture" in Sara Japhet, ed., *Studies in Bible 1986* (Jerusalem, 1986), pp. 257–77; and cf. Jeffrey H. Tigay, "An Early Technique of Aggadic Exegesis," in H. Tadmor and M. Weinfeld, eds., *History, Historiography and Interpretation* (Jerusalem, 1982), pp. 169–89. Pertinent, too, are the anthologies of Jewish exegesis collected by Yair Zakovitch and Avigdor Shinan: *The Story about Reuben and Bilhah* (Jerusalem, 1983; in Hebrew); *And Jacob Came "Shalem"* (Jerusalem,

Now, if change is of the essence, the norm rather than the exception, then sequence is everything: put the chimpanzee before the cockroach and you have described both but accounted for neither. It is this eagerness to do justice to sequence that accounts for the preoccupation among Biblical scholars in the last century and into this one with source criticism. In a scholar such as Wellhausen, the dissection of the text into its constituent elements was in the service of the construction of a relative chronology: the presence of J and P in the same book was as profoundly misleading as the presence of dinosaur bones and human bones in the same pit would be to a paleontologist. To this sort of Biblicist, the manifest text is like a virgin tell to an archaeologist: it is something to be attacked and taken apart in order to understand the uneven process that brought it to its present deceptively placid condition. Or, to change the simile, the manifest text is like *Homo sapiens* to the evolutionist or like the conscious mind of the adult to a psychoanalyst—the beginning of investigation, but not its end, not its *telos.*

If I seem to be belaboring the point, it is largely because increasingly I hear synchronic critics of the literary sort (those who are in English departments or ought to be) expressing impatience with Biblicists for our concern for source criticism and chronology. "Why can't you just look at the text as it is?" they ask us impatiently. I have considerable sympathy with the question, but I must still point out that the unqualified acceptance of "the text as it is" requires some operations that the historian cannot responsibly perform and disallows others that historical analysis cannot forego. For example, it requires harmonization: the flat prohibition on a man's marrying his brother's wife in Lev. 20:21 must be seen, in good rabbinic fashion, as still allowing for the institution of levirate marriage in Deut. 25:5–10. Conversely, synchronic criticism forbids historians the solution that to them seems the most natural, the assignment of the two texts to different sources from different periods or social sectors (again, conflict rather than harmony). At issue here is what operations are most fruitfully performed on "the text as it is." This is not to deny that both diachronic and synchronic operations can be legitimate—I have danced at both weddings myself—but it is to say that they are different procedures with different goals, and I do not yet see on the horizon the unified field theory that can reconcile them.

Many of the inconcinnities upon which the source critics built their case were recognized by medieval commentators. Abraham ibn Ezra, for example, hinted that the statement that "the Canaanite was then in the land" in Gen. 12:6 undermines the old idea that Moses wrote the Pentateuch. Who did write it he does not tell us. The reason can, I think, be seen in the words of Joseph Bonfils (Hebraized as Tob Elem), the author of the fourteenth-century supercommentary on ibn Ezra, *Tsafenat Pa'aneah:* "What should I care whether it was Moses or another prophet who wrote it, since the words of all of them are true and inspired?"[1] I take this to mean that if the real author is God, then which human vessel he inspired at which time with any given verse is of no import. Divine authorship overrides human authorship, even to the point that Moses can be dispensed with painlessly. This theology does have affinities with some modern strategies to accept the historico-critical method without giving up the essential Jewish and Christian notions of revelation and inspiration. I am thinking of Franz Rosenzweig's moving remark that the deeper meaning of the siglum *R* is not "redactor" but *rabbenu,* "our teacher."[2]

Still, I think the claim of some nonfundamentalist Jewish traditionalists that modern Biblical criticism belongs on the same continuum with medieval exegesis is wrong.[3] To the medievals, authorship is a minor matter, if it figures at all; to the moderns, the determination of authorship is the *conditio sine qua non* of responsible interpretation, or at least it was until the recent emergence of the synchronic approaches.

The classical critical judgment on authorship can be seen in Benjamin Jowett's celebrated essay "On the Interpretation of Scripture," published in 1860, eighteen years before Wellhausen's *Prolegomena.* "Scripture has one meaning," wrote Jowett—"the meaning which it had to the mind of the Prophet or Evangelist who first uttered or wrote, to the hearers or readers who first received it."[4] This historico-critical notion that Scripture has only one meaning contrasts vividly with the pluralism of some earlier hermeneutical systems, for example, the Talmudic notion that the Torah has seventy "facets" *(panim),* the kabbalistic idea that the meanings of the Torah are infinite, and even the more sober medieval Jewish and Christian concepts of the fourfold sense of Scripture.[5] Equally striking is the exclusive identification of meaning with authorial intention. If this is valid, then only as we have ascertained authorship can we state meaning. Jowett's quote seems to suggest that in good Romantic fashion he thought of the author as a discrete individual, whereas Wellhausen, more realistically, treated the author as the mouthpiece for a whole spiritual-cultural situation. But with either understanding, the greatest sin the interpreter can commit is the sin of anachronism, the eisegetical ascription to authors of meanings unattested in their own time. The methodological implication is clear: since the text is not autonomous but rather the expression of an author, and since the author was a living person responding to his environment, then only as we reconstruct that environment can we understand the text.

To this, our synchronic literary critic might retort that it is surely possible and probably more fruitful to view the text as autonomous, as a closed system, a world to itself—and again I do not wish altogether to deny value to that exercise. In particular, I agree that a text is not simply the extension of an author's mind and experience; it has borders, even a measure of independence. Still, it must not be overlooked that this idea of a totally synchronic approach is an illusion. As soon as you interpret the discolorations on the page as the representation of a language, you have made a historical judgment. Barton's example is perfect: "Charles II, when he visited the new St. Paul's during its construction, complimented the architect on producing 'so awful and artificial' a building."[6] "So awful and artificial"—is this a compliment or an insult? "The text as it is," the text as a closed system, cannot tell us, but one familiar with Charles II and seventeenth-century English knows that it was a great compliment indeed. The issue is not whether we use extratextual evidence, but whether we do so responsibly.

It was about the turn of the century, at the end of Wellhausen's life, that the idea of recovering the "Biblical world," as it came to be called, first took hold of the minds of many scholars. The immediate cause is obvious: the dribble of ancient Near Eastern texts that had been coming in for half a century swelled into a flood, as one discovery after another inundated the tiny band of scholars able to process them in a torrent that has not ceased—Amarna, Ugarit, Qumran, Ebla, to name only a few outstanding sites. Involvement in this new material could be defended on the grounds that it is essential to the effort to reconstruct the author's meaning—"author" here understood in the broad cultural sense. In the English-speaking world, however, scholarship tended to take a different turn. Now the emphasis shifted from the meaning of the text to the historicity of the events it narrates. In Hans Frei's terms, the concern with text as narrative was subordinated to concern for the text as a source of historical information.[7]

It is this exercise in historical verification whose current difficulty Greenstein outlined in the first part of his essay. He is surely right that as practiced by such scholars as Albright, Speiser, and my own teacher, Frank Moore Cross, the Near Eastern method presupposed a powerful predisposition to believe. It also expressed a certain quintessentially American preference for facts, for the nuts and bolts of things, over the highfalutin theories of Continental Biblicists—especially the Germans with their endlessly complicated form-critical theories and their abstruse theological systems. This practical turn of mind helped forge a natural alliance with Israeli scholarship, which, for obvious reasons, often tends to excel in matters of topography, archaeology, and military history. This conservative tendency fits nicely with a certain rhetoric of reenactment that one finds in Zionism: how can we reenact a story that didn't happen that way at all? One does not have to be a sociological reductionist to suggest that the kind of Biblical scholarship a culture fosters will be partly a function of the role of the Bible in it. Not being a reductionist, I think such an explanation can never be exhaustive.

Brevard Childs points out that those who set about restoring the "original historical setting" of a Biblical text have "difficulty applying it to the modern religious context."[8] Historical study pushes the text further into the past, which, especially in the Near Eastern mode, means a vanished past. The appropriate rebuttal to Childs on the part of those who believe that we can talk about the meaning of the text in the present tense and not just the past is that the recovery of the "Biblical world" is not pursued to distance the text from us, but to reclaim it by bringing it alive again, making it, in the words of the midrash, *kifrozdigma hadasha shehakkol ratsim liqrotah,* "like a new decree that everyone is running to read."[9] So learned a scholar as Childs would not make this accusation, however, if the general practice of Biblical scholars in fact implemented a strategy of retrieval and reclamation. Instead, a large part of Biblical scholarship, especially in America, moves from the text to the underlying history or the cognate cultures and never returns. Many scholars whose deans think they are studying the Hebrew Bible are, instead, concentrating on Syro-Palestinian archaeology, the historical grammar of Biblical Hebrew, Northwest Semitic epigraphy, or the like—all of which are essential, but no combination of which produces a Biblical scholar. The context often supplants the text and, far worse, blinds the interpreters to features of the text that their method has not predisposed them to see.

I can illustrate this by returning, like Greenstein, to Speiser's *Genesis.* Chapter 38 of Genesis, the episode of Judah and Tamar, follows the sale of Joseph into slavery in Egypt and precedes the account of his ill-fated resistance to seduction by his owner's wife. In Speiser's view, "the narrative is a completely independent unit. It has no connection with the drama of Joseph," an observation that Speiser buttressed by noting the chronological oddity that while Joseph is being bought by Potiphar, Judah is able to beget and raise three sons to adulthood.[10] Had Speiser wished to carry on a conversation with midrash, however, he would have noticed, as did Rabbi Yohanan, a precise verbal connection with the preceding story of the sale of Joseph: the brothers say to their father, "Examine *(hakker-na')* this coat: is it your son's or not?" (Gen. 37:32), and Tamar now says to Judah, who suggested that sale, "Examine *(hakker-na')* these: whose seal, cord, and staff are these?" (38:25).[11] We can go further. In chapter 38 Judah finds himself bereaved of two sons and unwilling to surrender the third, precisely the state of Jacob four chapters later when, having lost Joseph and probably Simeon, he refuses to surrender Benjamin, though the survival of the family depends on it (42:36–38). What breaks this deadly impasse is Judah's own willingness to stand surety for the youngest son (43:9)—the same Judah who in chapter 37 sold Joseph into slavery and in chapter 38 withheld his own youngest from Tamar. What Speiser called "a completely indepen-

51

dent unit [with] no connection with the drama of Joseph'' is actually more like one of Shakespeare's subplots, reflecting, encapsulating, and commenting on the larger drama.

Why did so learned and careful a man as E. A. Speiser not see this? The reason, I think, has to do with his interest in the two main foci of historical or diachronic Biblical study—source-critical differentiation and connections with the larger ''Biblical world,'' in his case, Mesopotamian texts. Neither of these interests is likely to suggest the interpretation just offered. Instead, both of them draw the interpreter's attention away from the manifest text into the antecedent history. Speiser's opinion that *originally* the tale of Judah and Tamar was unrelated to the Joseph story is quite plausible, but the point is that the two narratives are *now* read together, and it is this point that the classical diachronic methods, with their focus on sequence, miss. It is to the credit of the synchronic approaches that they are restoring the Bible to Biblical studies.

What is, I believe, emerging nowadays is a scene of rich methodological pluralism. Diachronic investigation is by no means at an end, even though its past practice often seems unsophisticated. The question of sources continues to receive attention, as well it should, and new texts from the ancient Near East are still steadily being discovered and processed. Unless historical consciousness disappears, involvement in historical study will be mandatory for Biblicists. Perhaps I am more sanguine about the future of diachronic investigation than Greenstein because, unlike him, I consider sociological and anthropological studies to be historical, even when they are structural or paradigmatic in method. It would be unfortunate if historical study of the Bible were thought to be limited to the dating of sources and the ascertainment of the veracity of reports of events. Biblical archaeology (if we may still use the term) has been steadily shifting its interest from proving or falsifying these reports to larger issues at the interface of social anthropology, geography, and political science.

In light of this rich fare of methods and interests, Jowett's pronouncement that ''Scripture has one meaning'' (the author's) seems woefully simplistic. Perhaps we are being returned to something akin to the late antique and medieval concepts of the plural senses of Scripture. In that case, the question is: what are the limits to interpretation? Not even the rabbinic *dar-shanim* or the kabbalists held that *every* interpretation is true; Christological interpretations, for example, they rejected. Greenstein speaks of choices based on people's ''personal or ideological or spiritual needs.'' But what about those who approach texts, Scripture or other, in hope of finding out what their needs really are? What about Jews and Christians who read their respective Bibles in quest of self-definition and not simply in the hope of imposing their current self-definition on the text? Greenstein tells us ''that modern critical approaches are no more or less than our own midrash." But where is the *peshat*, the plain sense? And if we were to inflate the term "midrash" to the point that it denotes all types of interpretation, would we not still be faced with the task of distinguishing good midrashim from poor ones, worthy communities of interpretation from less worthy?

Several times in his essay Greenstein pointed out that our interpretations are a function of our mental templates; "scholars shape the data into configurations of their own imagination," he said. I agree, but I would point out that the templates themselves, the scholars' imaginations, are also partly shaped by the data, and this is why the models change in response to new data, and more persuasive construals appear. Greenstein is surely right in his attack on naive empiricism, the idea that scholars just relay the facts, but I would add an attack on the a priorism that holds that we never transcend our biases. Such a view confuses two similar-sounding statements. The first is, "We all have biases"; the second, "All we have is biases." The first is true; the second is false. If all we had were biases, argument would be foredoomed to failure, and scholarship would be incorrigible. But such is not the case. True, consensus is rare and fleeting, but the absence of consensus is no indication of the absence of truth, nor is agreement proof of the validity of what is agreed on.

The great need in Biblicial scholarship today is to find a way to reject both the absolutism that says the text has only one meaning and the relativism that puts all interpretations on the same footing.[12] The challenge to Biblical studies is a particular instance of the challenge to the humanities in general and to society at large: how can we affirm pluralism without stepping onto the slippery slope that leads to the black void of relativism?

Notes

1. Since *Tsafenat Pa'aneah* is not available to me, I have translated this sentence from the citation of it in Moshe Greenberg, *On the Bible and Judaism*, ed. Abraham Shapira (Tel Aviv, 1984), p. 276.

2. Franz Rosenzweig, *Briefe* (Berlin, 1935), p. 582.

3. An example is Nahum M. Sarna, "The Modern Study of the Bible in the Framework of Jewish Studies," in *Proceedings of the Eighth World Congress of Jewish Studies* (Jerusalem, 1983), esp. pp. 20, 27.

4. Benjamin Jowett, "On the Interpretation of Scripture," in *The Interpretation of Scripture and Other Essays* (London, n.d.), p. 36.

5. *Num. Rab.* 13:15. See also Moshe Idel, "Infinities of Torah in Kabbalah," in *Midrash and Literature*, ed. Geoffrey H. Hartman and Sanford Budick (New Haven, Conn., 1986), pp. 141–57.

6. John Barton, *Reading the Old Testament* (Philadelphia, 1984), p. 172.

7. Hans W. Frei, *The Eclipse of Biblical Narrative* (New Haven, Conn., 1974), passim. See also Barton, *Reading*, p. 161.

53

Ancient Judaism

5

THE MODERN STUDY OF ANCIENT JUDAISM

Shaye J. D. Cohen

Scholarship on the Judaism of the Greco-Roman period has enjoyed explosive growth in the past twenty years. The number of books and articles that have appeared is so staggering that one person cannot read them all, let alone survey their contents and assess their relative contributions. Each of the major bodies of literary evidence—the later books of the Tanakh, the Qumran scrolls, the works of "the Apocrypha" and "the Pseudepigrapha," the New Testament, Greco-Jewish literature (especially Philo and Josephus), rabbinic texts, pagan and Christian references to Jews and Judaism—has been the subject of numerous studies large and small. New editions, translations, commentaries, concordances, and dictionaries make these texts more accessible than ever. The nonliterary evidence—archaeology, numismatics, and epigraphy—has not enjoyed quite the same lavish attention, but the number of works in these fields, too, is considerable. In addition to these specialized studies of individual documents or bodies of evidence, numerous large-scale syntheses have appeared that integrate the data provided by diverse sources. Guidance through this luxuriant scholarly overgrowth is provided by several excellent bibliographical guides.[1] In this essay I shall discuss three themes or concerns that characterize much of this scholarship.

Shaye J. D. Cohen

Polemics and Apologetics

History, like most of the humanities, is art, not science. Its results are conditional, not inevitable; conjectural, not empirical. Historical truths are not "discovered" so much as "created" by the interpreter—"une fable convenue" Voltaire called it. "Bias-free" or "dispassionate" scholarship is an unattainable goal. These truisms apply with special force to ancient Judaism, a field that has ideological relevance to many different groups.

Perhaps no other area of Jewish history has as much importance for Christianity as does the Judaism of Greco-Roman antiquity, for the obvious reason that this Judaism provides the matrix for the birth and growth of early Christianity. In the German universities of the nineteenth century, ancient Judaism was the domain of the faculty of *Theologie,* not *Geschichte* or *klassische Philologie.* These professors of Lutheran or Catholic theology (mostly the former) had a vested interest in proving that Christianity was the legitimate and authentic expression of all that was good and enduring in the Hebrew Bible (the universal ethics and the spirituality of the prophets); that the triumph of "the Law" was a relatively late development in Israelite religion (a reaction to the destruction of the Temple in 587 B.C.E.); and that the Judaism Christianity left behind was a sterile, empty, and "legalistic" religion. This perspective is manifest in the works of the greatest scholars of the period, notably Schürer, Bousset, Wellhausen, and Harnack, who took Christian theology and transcribed it in historical form.[2] For a long time Christian scholarship accepted this perspective and saw nothing wrong with denigrating the subject it was trying to explain.

Since World War II, and especially in the last twenty years, this perspective has been in clear remission. Pietist and fundamentalist scholars may still accept as "gospel truth" the New Testament portraits of the Pharisees and the Jewish authorities, but in liberal and academic circles the signs of change are evident. The denigrating epithet "late Judaism" (*Spätjudentum*), the German appellation for the Judaism after Ezra or after the Maccabees, has been replaced by "early Judaism," which paradoxically is its exact equivalent.[3] Many Christian authors and publishing houses routinely publish books and articles that use "B.C.E." and "C.E." as the religiously neutral equivalents of "B.C." and "A.D." Perhaps under the impact of the Qumran scrolls, there is greater acknowledgment than ever that early Christianity was a Jewish movement and that most of its formative ideas developed from a Jewish context. There is greater attention to "Jesus the Jew," a real effort to understand Jesus in his Jewish context ("the Jesus of history") and not just as the focal point of Christian theology ("the Christ of faith"). Even the gnostic speculations about two gods, which previous scholars had regarded as an extreme manifestation of Christian anti-Judaism, have recently been shown to be of Jewish origin.[4]

"Anti-Semitism" in the New Testament and in Christianity has been treated several times in recent years, especially in the wake of the Second Vatican Council. These discussions manifest not only an apologetic tone but also a strong desire to show that Paul was not "anti-Semitic." This goal is achieved by an ecumenical reading of the famous chapters in Romans 9–11 on the status of Israel and the Jews, and by arguing that Paul rejected Judaism not because he found it inadequate but because he believed that God had recently revealed something better (Sanders). Others have argued that Paul preached freedom from the law only to gentiles who wished to accept faith in Christ, and had no objection if native Jews wished to continue observing it (Stendahl, Lüdemann, and many others).[5] Christian scholarship on Jews and Judaism in antiquity is displaying a sensitivity and a sympathy that was conspicuously absent (with a few exceptions such as George Foot Moore) in earlier generations.[6]

There is one area of scholarship, however, that in novel form sometimes revives the anti-Jewish animus of the nineteenth century. Many Christian feminists, adopting a "liberation theology," argue that Jesus came to free women (and other powerless groups) from their oppression. In Judaism women are impure, are segregated from positions of power, and are not regarded as full members of the cultic community, but the original Jesus movement accorded women status and prestige. (The fact that not long after Jesus, Christianity, too, regarded women as impure and segregated them from positions of power is either ignored by these critics or explained as a deviation from the original message of the church). In this conception Christianity represents liberation for women, Judaism represents their oppression.[7] Similarly, in some feminist scholarship Israelite religion, too, is seen as oppressive, because the God of the Hebrew Bible, by triumphing over pagan gods and goddesses, removed an outlet for religious expression for women and ensured the establishment of patriarchal religion and society. Here the old Christian animosity toward Judaism has resurfaced in a new form.

Jews, too, have a large ideological and religious stake in ancient Judaism. Jewish scholars of previous generations were eager not only to refute the Christian denigration of Judaism in general and rabbinic Judaism in particular but also to legitimate their own expressions of Judaism by appeal to the normative precedents of antiquity.[8] Some Jewish scholars in both Israel and the diaspora, at both seminaries and universities, are still engaged in these activities,[9] but many, perhaps most, are not. For them the study of Judaism is the secular equivalent to *talmud tora*—the duty to study Torah. Not only does it provide the existential satisfaction that is supposed to derive from all humanistic study but it also allows the scholar to "be" Jewish, to express his or her Jewish identity in a nonreligious way. If this is true for Jewish studies (or, as some would have it, Judaic studies) in general, it certainly is true for the study of the formation of classical Judaism in late antiquity.

Separators and Unifiers

The abandonment of the frames of reference erected by Jewish and Christian ideology has been accompanied by a heightened awareness of the manifold nature of ancient Judaism. Indeed, the words "diversity," "variety," "varieties," and "complexity" are commonly encountered in studies of ancient Judaism. Even "Judaisms" regularly makes an appearance. There is now wide agreement that the terms "Hellenistic Judaism" and "Palestinian Judaism" are not antonyms. Valid distinctions can be drawn between the Greek-speaking Judaisms of the diaspora and the Greek- , Hebrew- or Aramaic-speaking Judaisms of the Land of Israel,[10] but all the Jews of Greco-Roman antiquity, no matter what language they spoke or where they lived, were "hellenized' to some degree. "Hellenism" and "Judaism" (or, in the language of Matthew Arnold, "Hebraism") are not mutually exclusive categories, and "Hellenistic Judaism" is neither an anomaly nor an oxymoron. Further, even the defenders of the distinction between "Hellenistic Judaism" and "Palestinian Judaism" generally concede that these constructs are far more complex than previously believed. Philo cannot be taken as *the* representative of Greek-speaking Jewry, because not all "Hellenistic Jews" were determined allegorists like Philo, and even those who were did not necessarily allegorize in a Philonic manner or reach Philonic conclusions. The identity and social status of the Pharisees remain obscure, but even if they were an "elite" rather than a "sect," they were neither the exclusive leaders of Palestinian Judaism nor the sole arbiters of Jewish opinion.

Another construct that has come under increased attack in the last twenty years is the notion of "orthodox" or "normative" Judaism, and its antonyms "heterodox" or "heretical" Judaism.[11] Most of those in antiquity who identified themselves as *Jews* and were known as *Jews* to their neighbors shared certain important beliefs and practices. For example, they believed in a supreme God who created the world, chose the Israelites/Jews to be his people, revealed his Torah to his servant Moses, and rewards the righteous and punishes the wicked. They also practiced the laws of the Torah of Moses, most conspicuously circumcision, Sabbath, and abstention from certain foods. Jews interpreted these beliefs and practices in numerous and diverse ways, but it is not for the historian to determine which of these ways is right or "orthodox." The appropriate term for this regimen of belief and practice, and the social structures created by its adherents, is not "orthodox Judaism" but simply "Judaism."[12]

Rather than speak glibly about "Hellenistic Judaism," "orthodoxy," "apocalyptic Judaism," contemporary scholars are more comfortable with a minimalist approach. The argument that ancient Judaism was diverse and multiform has led to a readiness to read each document of ancient Judaism independently, to emphasize its distinctive characteristics, and not to homogenize it with other, related documents. Documents that previously had been read in the light of one another are now read as autonomous works endowed with their own peculiar viewpoint. Not only have the documents been separated one from the other, they also have been dissected. Texts that previously had been read as organic compositions are now shown to be composite and stratified. The goal of this research is to deconstruct the large structures and to look at each of their constituent elements separately. The results of the analysis are minimalistic. As scholarship increases, ancient Judaism progressively but retrospectively becomes more and more complex and diverse.[13]

In its most extreme form this approach is reminiscent of one school of literary critics in antiquity. Most of the ancients believed that the author of the *Iliad* was identical with the author of the *Odyssey* and that the two poems together formed one perfect organic whole. Hence, contradictions and other inconsistencies between the two had to be reconciled through exegesis. However, some ancient critics, known as the *chôrízontes*, the "separators," argued that the two poems were so distinct in their diction, content, and other characteristics, that they must have been composed by separate authors.[14] The debate between "separators" and "unifiers" (if I may call them that)[15] has been a constant in the field of literary criticism and has close analogues in some contemporary scholarship on ancient Judaism. Discussion has been aroused most sharply by the work of Jacob Neusner on rabbinic texts, but the point is illustrated in numerous other areas as well, and it is to these that I turn first.

Philo, Josephus, and Paul are three Jewish writers of the first century C.E. There is near universal consensus on the identification of the genuine and the spurious works of each author,[16] but there is far from universal consensus on the extent to which the works of each author constitute a unified canon. Philo, probably the most consistent and uniform author of the three, wrote works in different genres for different audiences. David Winston's anthology of topically arranged selections from Philo's works, published in 1981, is very similar in conception and design to Hans Lewy's, published in 1945. Both assume that Philo's works reflect a basically coherent and consistent mind; Winston states explicitly that the task of the commentator on any given passage of Philo is to assemble as many Philonic parallels as possible, thereby demonstrating the fundamental unity of Philo's thought. But if Philo is primarily a scriptural exegete who does philosophy rather than a philosopher who does scriptural exegesis, a position defended by Valentin Nikiprowetzky, then this approach will invariably lead to a distortion of Philo's message. Without their exegetical context Philo's remarks cannot be properly interpreted, nor can a distinction be made between an argument that is essential to Philo's purpose and an argument that is peripheral.[17]

In Josephan studies the debate between the separators and the unifiers is more pointed. Under the influence of Richard Laqueur and Morton Smith I argued in my book *Josephus in Galilee and Rome* (Leiden, 1979) that in numerous important matters the *Jewish War* and the *Jewish Antiquities* (with its appendix, the *Vita*) reflect different viewpoints. They differ in their explanations for the origins of the war of 66–70 C.E., in their attitudes toward the revolutionaries, in their assessment of Josephus's own actions in the war, in their perceptions of the Pharisees, in their attitudes toward the Romans, and much else. I concluded that these contradictions and contrasts reflect not Josephus's discovery of new sources[18] but different stages in Josephus's own development as Jew and historian. In contrast, in her book *Josephus the Historian and His Society* (London, 1983), Tessa Rajak argues that Josephus is basically a truthful historian whose works reflect uniformity in style and purpose. Although the *Jewish War* and the *Jewish Antiquities* belong to a single canon and were written by a single author within the span of twenty years, I hold that the works are sufficiently distinct that they should not be harmonized. Rajak, however, is unwilling to separate the works of the Josephan canon; for her the distinctions merely reflect differences in genre and audience.[19]

A similar methodological problem is apparent in the interpretation of Josephus's data on the revolutionaries. For Martin Hengel and his followers, "Zealot" is a generic term for "revolutionary." All those who rebelled against Rome were Zealots who belonged to *the* Zealot movement. But an increasing number of studies has attacked this unifying approach, arguing instead that Zealot is the name not of a united revolutionary movement but of a single particular revolutionary party; that there were many other revolutionary parties as well; and that these parties differed from one another in social composition, political orientation, and religious practice. In this debate the separators have clearly emerged victorious.[20]

The theme "Paul and the Law" has been treated exhaustively in two major studies in English, and some of the differences between them reflect the tension between separators and unifiers. E. P. Sanders is a unifier. Out of the mass of Jewish literature of first-century Palestine Sanders has attempted to extract a single unifying theology, dubbed "covenantal nomism," and to show that Paul's theology, as exemplified by his attitude toward the Law, is a departure from it. Sanders finds uniformity not only in Palestinian literature but also in Paul; various passages from the Pauline epistles are combined to yield a portrait of Paul's attitude toward the Law. Heikki Räisänen, in contrast, argues that Paul's view of the Law is fundamentally incoherent and inconsistent, because each of the epistles presents a different part of the argument and employs distinctive terminology.[21]

Most of the extant works produced by ancient Judaism are not attributable to named individuals such as Philo, Josephus, and Paul, but are either anonymous, pseudonymous, or the result of collective enterprise ("school literature"). These books have been gathered together in various collections: the Bible (or Tanakh), the Apocrypha, the Pseudepigrapha, the Qumran scrolls, the New Testament, and rabbinic literature. These collections are of different sorts. The Tanakh remains an authoritative document for both Jews and Christians, whereas the New Testament is authoritative only for the latter and rabbinic literature only for the former. All three of these collections are "canons" and contain "canonical" works. If we knew how the Qumran collection was assembled and what role its books played in the life of the community, we would know whether this collection, too, was a canon or merely a library. The remaining two collections, the Apocrypha and the Pseudepigrapha, are not the products of Jewish antiquity at all and tell us nothing as collections about ancient Judaism. The church fathers spoke of "apocryphal" books and "pseudepigrapha," but used the terms to designate only a book's lack of authoritative status. "Apocrypha" did not designate a collection of books until the sixteenth century, "Pseudepigrapha" the eighteenth or nineteenth. The Apocrypha and the Pseudepigrapha represent neither the canon nor the library of any Jew in antiquity.[22] Consequently, although I applaud the immensely useful new edition of *The Old Testament Pseudepigrapha* edited by James H. Charlesworth, I deplore its perpetuation of the concept "the Pseudepigrapha" as if such a collection ever existed before modern scholars invented it, and as if the term did not have a useful meaning of its own. (A pseudepigraph is any work that bears a false ascription.)[23]

I am interested here in the Qumran library and the rabbinic canon. How do the diverse works within these collections relate to one another? Do in fact the works of one collection cohere more closely than those of the other? Until recently scholars spoke of "the Essene library of Qumran," as if all the previously unknown texts discovered there were of Essene provenance. Even in the earliest stages of Qumran research scholars recognized that the collection was quite diverse, but at first there was more interest in recovering the theology and history of the Qumran group than in determining the provenance and setting of each of the works of the library. Now, however, there is general agreement that the Qumran library contains works of three sorts: (1) works that were widely read and widely available in Jewish society; (2) works that originated in esoteric, pietistic, or sectarian circles outside of Qumran; and (3) works that were the product of the Qumran sect itself. The simplest category is (1), which includes the works of the Tanakh and books like Ben Sira and Tobit. The distinction between categories (2) and (3) is more difficult and is just now attracting detailed attention. *Jubilees, Testament of Levi,* and *Enoch* probably belong to category (2): they are esoteric or pietistic works but give no indication of having been composed at or for the Qumran group. Category (3) consists of works of two types, those which reflect the distinctive history and ideology of the Qumran group and have a marked sectarian character (for example, *The Rule of the Community, The Damascus Covenant, The War of the Sons of Light against the Sons of Darkness,* the *Pesharim*), and those which do not (for example, the *Hymns,* the angelic liturgy). Whether the *Temple Scroll* belongs to the second or the third category is the subject of contemporary debate. Complicating the matter even more is the literary history of the documents. *Enoch, The Temple Scroll, The Damascus Rule, The Rule of the Community*—all these and no doubt many other Qumran documents are composite, the result of a long period of editing and redacting. The provenance and setting of the various sources must be distinguished from the provenance and setting of the works in which these sources are now embedded.[24]

Although we are still far from a complete classification of all the works discovered at Qumran, not least because many important texts remain unpublished, scholars now agree that the Qumran scrolls constitute a library, a collection of works of diverse origins that cannot be combined to yield a uniform and ready portrait of the Essenes. Obviously the best way to interpret the Qumran scrolls is from the scrolls themselves; in particular, the distinctively "Essene" works can only be understood in the light of one another. But at the same time the scrolls are now being treated also as independent works.

In sum, much of the research on the Jewish literature of the Second Temple period reflects a tension between unifiers and separators. The two approaches are complementary rather than contradictory, and a fully convincing interpretation of the material will require some attention to each.

I turn now to the corpus of rabbinic literature. The tension between the unifiers and the separators is particularly evident here, although the distinction between the positions is not always as clear as sometimes suggested. All scholars agree that the numerous and diverse works of the rabbinic canon cohere much more closely than the works of the Qumran library,[25] but the same question needs to be asked of each corpus: to what extent can or must each work be read as an autonomous document separate from its associated literature? The most prominent and extreme of the separators is Jacob Neusner, who has spent the past twenty years disassembling the rabbinic canon and defending a minimalist approach in the historical use of rabbinic materials.

In his voluminous writings Neusner has made three methodological contributions that will endure as significant advances in research on rabbinics. First, he interprets rabbinic texts as independent wholes, as distinctive literary units with their own interests and concerns. Second, he attempts to uncover the meanings that are immanent in the texts rather than collect anthologies of rabbinic dicta on diverse subjects. Third, he devalues rabbinic "history" and emphasizes instead "historiography," the development of rabbinic ideas and traditions. Each of these contributions, however, involves difficult questions that need to be addressed.[26]

First, Neusner interprets rabbinic texts as independent wholes. Traditional Jewish scholarship has always emphasized the interconnectivity of the rabbinic texts, and it is in reaction to this approach that Neusner has attempted to disassemble the rabbinic canon. He argues that the Mishna is an independent text and that later rabbinic literature (the Tosefta, the two Talmudim, the Sifra and the other tannaitic midrashim) comments on and reacts to the Mishna but preserves no pre-Mishnaic texts. The Mishna and the Tosefta are not synoptic texts because there is no common source linking them together; the Tosefta is entirely subordinate to the Mishna. Therefore, the Tosefta and the other rabbinic works of antiquity are primary evidence only for their own concerns and issues, and are secondary evidence at best for the interpretation of the Mishna.[27]

This approach is very attractive but is not without its problems. The links between the Mishna and the Tosefta cannot be ignored so easily. Some tractates of the Tosefta are nothing more than commentaries on the Mishna, but others assuredly derive from the same sources as the Mishna and preserve the remains of those sources.[28] Furthermore, while we interpret the rabbinic texts as wholes, we must also inquire how these wholes assumed their current form. Neusner argues that because the Mishna is such a highly edited and stylized document we cannot "get behind" the text as it currently stands, but this argument ignores the possibilities of source criticism, redaction criticism, and the analysis and reconstruction of recensions and versions. (Witness the important work that has been done with these methods in recent years, most famously in connection with the Babylonian Talmud, by David Weiss Halivni and Shamma Friedman.)[29]

In sum, many of the rabbinic texts are composite works whose diverse parts are conjoined to form wholes. Many of the rabbinic texts are synoptic works, and synoptic works must always be studied synoptically. But these facts hardly mean that rabbinic works are mere anthologies with no individual identity or distinctive characteristics. A full interpretation of rabbinic literature requires an assessment of both sets of facts: the distinctive characteristics of each rabbinic work, and the points at which they intersect and cohere to create the system we call "rabbinic." Such research remains for the future.[30]

Second, Neusner argues that we should study the message that is immanent in the text, rather than compile anthologies of rabbinic statements about this or that topic. He argues that the Mishna is not a book of law but a book of "philosophy," in which the rabbis address the existential needs of their age. In the wake of the destruction of the Temple, the Mishna states that Jews can sanctify creation through their actions and that the harmony of the cosmos, once guaranteed by the temple, can now be guaranteed by human actions and intent. This interpretation is very attractive but, again, is not without its problems. The immanent message of a text is always elusive; different interpreters will find different messages. Neusner argues that the Mishna's distinctive message is its "philosophy," its utopian vision of a perfect world. Halivni argues that what makes the Mishna distinctive is its predilection for apodictic law, law that commands obedience but offers no rationale or justification. Elsewhere I have argued that the Mishna is an implicit reflection of a new type of society previously unattested in Jewish history, a society that consciously allows individuals the freedom to disagree on matters of law and practice. E. P. Sanders argues that the Mishna spells out the details of the covenantal relationship between God and Israel. In addition to whatever philosophy it might advocate, the Mishna is also a book of law, or at least a source of law (see below on the parallel with the Digest). All of these views are right, to one extent or another, but in accordance with modern literary theory, none of them is any more correct, or more inherent in the text, than any other. All of these meanings allegedly immanent in the Mishna have been brought to the Mishna by its contemporary interpreters. The method has value, but it also has its limits.[31]

Last, Neusner argues that we should not study rabbinic history, because the rabbis were not historians and do not provide reliable historical data. Individual historical narratives are unreliable; ascriptions of dicta to named authorities are not necessarily reliable, and even if they are, they preserve only the gist of the sages' remarks, not their actual words. Consequently, Neusner argues, we can study only the history of rabbinic ideas, not the biography of rabbinic sages or the history of rabbinic "events." If this minimalist logic were pushed to its maximal limit, we would conclude that the rabbinic texts are primary sources for the Judaism of their final redactors and editors, and nothing more. That is, the Mishna reveals the interests of Judah the Patriarch and his time (c. 200 C.E.), not those of R. Aqiba and his time (c. 100 C.E.); the Babylonian Talmud reveals the interests of R. Ashi, Rabina, and the "stamma'im" (the late fifth century C.E.), not those of Abbaye, Rava, R. Judah, and others. We might even conclude that all rabbinic texts are pseudepigraphs, filled with stories and sayings of people who never existed or, at least, who never did and said any of the things that were attributed to them.[32] Neusner, however, does not draw these conclusions. Even he admits (implicitly, to be sure) some degree of reliability in the rabbinic texts. For example, in his study of the Mishna he analyzes the contribution of each generation of sages to the unfolding of law; even if individual ascriptions are inaccurate, they are at least attributed to figures of the appropriate generation. In other words, even Neusner assumes some degree of fidelity and historical accuracy in the rabbinic texts, and this fidelity differs in degree, not in kind, from that assumed by the most fundamentalist and gullible of scholars.[33]

Neusner has sounded a salutary warning against the facile use of rabbinic texts for the writing of the history of pre– and post–70 C.E. Judaism.[34] But we must distinguish between skepticism and nihilism; we still need to discover firm criteria by which we can determine how and why the rabbinic texts are reliable for some things but not for others.[35]

I turn now to one last area in which the impact of the separators has been evident. Our knowledge of the archaeological remains of ancient Judaism has increased enormously in the past twenty years. In the diaspora, the synagogue of Sardis and the (synagogue?) inscription of Aphrodisias are spectacular discoveries. The Sardis synagogue was a municipal building before being given or sold to the Jews. It is a magnificent structure, the size of a football field. The Aphrodisias inscription is a long list of names of members of, or donors to, some Jewish body; after the Jewish names come the names of pagan "God-fearers," as the inscription calls them, and these include several town councilors of the city of Aphrodisias. Here is new and unexpected evidence for the power and prosperity of the Jews of western Asia Minor in the Roman period. In the Land of Israel, of course, the archaeological record is much richer. Among the most important discoveries are the seemingly endless numbers of synagogues and synagogue inscriptions that have been found throughout the land from south to north, even in the Golan heights, which, it is now revealed, was a major area of Jewish settlement in the late Byzantine period. The synagogues were built in a large number of styles, decorated in a bewildering array of motifs and designs, and outfitted with inscriptions in Hebrew, Aramaic, or Greek.[36]

Until the work of E. R. Goodenough a generation ago, archaeologists routinely tried to harmonize the archaeological evidence with the literary, especially the rabbinic. Although few scholars have followed Goodenough's suggestion that the archaeological discoveries be read in the light of Philo rather than the rabbis, almost everyone now concedes that the archaeological evidence must be allowed to speak for itself. How the archaeological discoveries from "the rabbinic period"—with their mosaics, paintings, reliefs, zodiacs, and scant mention of rabbis or displays of rabbinic piety,— are to be squared with the literary tradition is a difficult question, one that remains open. One important discovery, the synagogue inscription of Rehov (near Bet Shean), containing a long excerpt of the Talmud Yerushalmi, shows by contrast how "nonrabbinic" the other synagogue inscriptions are.[37] The rabbinic and the archaeological evidence seem almost unrelated.[38]

Furthermore, the archaeological discoveries have led to the complete abandonment of the old monistic view of the development of the architecture of the synagogue. No longer do scholars speak of a monumental Galilean style, which led to a transitional broadhouse style, which finally graduated to the Byzantine style; rather, there is a growing consensus that regional variation, personal preference, and varied religious needs led to a wide variety of synagogue styles that cannot be homogenized or made to fit a single linear progression. Here again the separators have triumphed.

Jewish Antiquity versus Ancient Judaism

To some extent ancient Judaism was simply a local variation of the common culture of the Greco-Roman world, and to some extent it was unique. Many studies of Judaism in antiquity focus on its interactions with its ambient cultures, while others adopt an "internal" perspective. What has not yet been achieved is a synthesis of these two approaches. Here are three examples.

In their search for the roots of Jewish apocalyptic literature and eshatological speculations, some scholars have argued that these are the natural and organic outgrowths of Biblical ideas, whereas others have sought parallels and sources in non-Jewish contexts, especially Egypt and Persia. In recent years, alongside the attempt of the separators to interpret each apocalypse as an independent literary work, there has risen the tendency to see the Jewish developments within their larger context. The goal is not to identify sources so much as to understand the meaning and function of the literature through the study of parallel phenomena in the ancient world.[39] The Jews were not the only ethnic group in the East to be stirred by nationalist sentiment in the second century B.C.E. and to turn to dreams of the end-time and glorious conquests.

The great rebellion against the Romans (66–73/74 C.E.) is often regarded as a product of uniquely Jewish circumstances: messianic speculations, Jewish nationalism, loyalty to Torah, and the like. But the war can also be interpreted as a "normal" phenomenon within early Roman imperial history. It was a native rebellion, led first by the aristocracy and later by more radical elements, and was provoked by Roman misrule. Marxists emphasize that the war was, in many of its phases, primarily an internal struggle of "oppressed" groups against their oppressors. Eschatological speculations and radical politics often figure in revolutions and rebellions, both ancient and modern.[40] In sum, the war is both a uniquely Jewish phenomenon and a normal reaction to political and economic pressures.

Some aspects of rabbinic creativity too are "normal" phenomena in antiquity. The rabbis are scholars and jurists. As scholars they used a literary form that ancient scholars often used, the scriptural commentary. As jurists they wrote the Mishna, a peculiar work that has a close analogue in the Digest of Justinian, published in 530 C.E. (but surely not influenced by the Mishna!):

> It was certainly a strange idea of the Emperor or his counsellors to construct a code of existing law by compiling passages written three to five centuries before. . . . The compilers, moreover, did not restrict themselves to collecting legal rules and formulations of a general character: they copied passages with historical reminiscences, etymological observations, quotations taken from Homer, polemics and divergent opinions, precious of course from a historical point of view, but superfluous and embarrassing in a work which according to a strict order of Justinian should have been a codification, since the jurists' opinions were to be considered as current and valid law.[41]

With a few slight modifications (for example, change "Homer" to "the Torah"), this description of the Digest could as easily apply to the Mishna. (And perhaps the Mishna, too, for all of its peculiarities, should be regarded like the Digest as a work of law.) The place of rabbinic Judaism within Hellenistic culture remains an open question.

These three illustrations show how difficult it is to determine the "Jewish" component of various Jewish phenomena. I am not suggesting that the Jews who wrote apocalypses, rebelled against the Romans, or joined the rabbinic estate thereby consciously imitated their neighbors or realized that what they were doing was typical for people in their situation. Insofar as the actors in these situations were Jews that which they were doing was Judaism, but insofar as what they were doing was the common culture of the ancient world it is not "Jewish," or at least not distinctively Jewish, at all. Contemporary scholarship has yet to balance these two approaches, the "internal" and the comparative or "external."

67

Shaye J. D. Cohen

Concluding Reflections

I have discussed three aspects of modern scholarship on ancient Judaism. I conclude with some reflections derived from each of these aspects.

The demise, or at least the diminution, of polemics and apologetics should provide an opportunity for the emergence of new methods and new questions. In particular, social anthropology, folklore, the "new" archaeology,[42] women's studies (if pursued without the malice and prejudices discussed above)—all these have yet to make their full contribution. Undoubtedly other and newer disciplines will make contributions as well.

The publication of the Qumran scrolls and the triumph of the separators should lead to the dissolution of the Tanakh, the Pseudepigrapha, and the New Testament as canonical categories for the study of Second Temple Judaism. To a great extent these canons are meaningful only in religious contexts and are an obstacle to scholarship. The earliest of the Qumran texts predate the later books of the Tanakh, just as the earliest texts of the Nag Hammadi library and the apostolic fathers predate the later books of the New Testament. The separation of the Qumran scrolls from the Pseudepigrapha is particularly lamentable and unjustifiable because it erects artificial barriers between works that are of the same or similar genre or that are nearly equal in date. In the case of rabbinic literature we await an interpretation that will treat both the distinctive characteristics of each work and the points that unite it to other distinctively rabbinic works. Similarly, the interpretation of the literature of the Second Temple period requires a balance between the two approaches, but that balance is hampered by the erection of artificial categories.

Last, scholars must always pay attention to the context of each text, institution, and idea, not just the intra-Jewish context but also the setting within the larger world. If Jewish studies are indeed to be part of the humanities, the humanistic setting of Judaism must always be considered, even if Judaism loses something of its uniqueness as a result.

Notes

1. The most important large syntheses are *Compendia Rerum Judaicarum ad Novum Testamentum,* sec. 1: *The Jewish People in the First Century,* ed. S. Safrai and M. Stern (Philadelphia, 1974–76), 2 vols., and sec. 2, vol. 2: *Jewish Writings of the Second Temple Period,* ed. M. Stone (Philadelphia, 1984), with several other volumes scheduled to appear; Martin Hengel, *Judaism and Hellenism* (Philadelphia, 1974); Jacob Neusner, *History of the Jews in Babylonia* (Leiden, 1965–70), 5 vols.; Emil Schürer, *The History of the Jewish People in the Age of Jesus Christ,* rev. and ed. Geza Vermes, Fergus Millar, et al. (Edinburgh, 1974–87), 4 vols.; E. Mary Smallwood, *The Jews under Roman Rule* (Leiden, 1976; reprint, 1981); *The World History of the Jewish People,* vol. 6: *The Hellenistic Age,* ed. A. Schalit (New Brunswick, N.J., 1972), vol. 7: *The Herodian Period,* ed. M. Avi Yonah and Zvi Baras

(1975), and vol. 8: *Society and Religion in the Second Temple Period*, ed. Michael Avi Yonah and Zvi Baras (1977). The most important bibliographies and bibliographical surveys are Louis H. Feldman, *Josephus and Modern Scholarship (1937–1980)* (New York, 1984), with the reviews of H. Schreckenberg, *Gnomon* 57 (1985), pp. 408–15, and Menaham Mor and Uriel Rappaport, *Jewish History* 1/2 (Fall 1986), pp. 67–78; Baruch M. Bokser, "Recent Developments in the Study of Judaism 70–200 C.E.," *Second Century* 3 (1983), pp. 1–68; Menahem Mor and Uriel Rappaport, *Bibliography of Works on Jewish History in the Hellenistic and Roman Periods 1976–1980* (Jerusalem, 1982) and *Bibliography of Works on Jewish History in the Hellenistic and Roman Periods 1980–1985* (Jerusalem, 1987); idem, "A Survey of 25 Years (1960–1985) of Israeli Scholarship on Jewish History in the Second Temple Period," *Biblical Theology Bulletin* 16 (1986), pp. 56–72; Jacob Neusner, ed., *The Study of Ancient Judaism* (New York, 1981), 2 vols.; Robert Kraft and George W. E. Nickelsburg, eds., *Early Judaism and Its Modern Interpreters* (Atlanta, 1986); and the numerous survey articles in *Aufstieg und Niedergang der römischen Welt*, ed. W. Haase, pt. 2, vols. 19 (1979), 20 (1987), and 21 (1983–84).

2. See esp. Wellhausen's dating of P: "ritualism," legalism, and institutionalized worship belong to the latest strata of the Hebrew Bible and represent the Jewish rejection of the prophetic message (Christianity). See my essay in Kraft and Nickelsburg, eds. *Early Judaism*, pp. 34–35.

3. For example, Christian Wolff, *Jeremia im Frühjudentum und Urchristentum* (Berlin, 1976), bore as its original title *Jeremia im Spätjudentum*. The origins of the term *Spätjudentum* are obscure.

4. Daniel J. Harrington, "The Jewishness of Jesus," *Catholic Biblical Quarterly* 49 (1987), pp. 1–13. On the gnostic speculations, see Alan F. Segal, *Two Powers in Heaven* (Leiden, 1977), with the review article by van den Broek, *Vigiliae Christianae* 37 (1983), pp. 41–71.

5. E. P. Sanders, *Paul and Palestinian Judaism* (Philadelphia, 1977); K. Stendahl, *Paul among Jews and Gentiles* (Philadelphia, 1976); Gerd Lüdemann, *Paulus und das Judentum* (Munich, 1983). Cf., too, John G. Gager, *The Origins of Anti-Semitism* (New York, 1983); A. T. Davies, ed., *Anti-Semitism and the Foundations of Christianity* (New York, 1979); and Norman A. Beck, *Mature Christianity: The Recognition and Repudiation of the Anti-Jewish Polemic of the New Testament* (London, 1985).

6. Connected with this development is the now widespread view of Judaism's *vitality* in late antiquity, even after 70 C.E. Judaism did not retreat from the world; much of Christian "anti-Semitism" was provoked precisely by Judaism's continuing success and attractiveness. This thesis was first articulated by Marcel Simon, *Versus Israel* (Paris, 1948; H. McKeating, trans., New York, 1986).

7. See Ross Kraemer's review of Elisabeth Schüssler Fiorenza's *In Memory of Her*, in *Religious Studies Review* 11 (1985), pp. 6–9, esp. p. 7. For a recent example of Christian feminist polemic masquerading as scholarship, see Marla Selvidge, "Mark 5:25–34 and Leviticus 15:19–20," *Journal of Biblical Literature* 103 (1984), pp. 619–23. The same perspective sometimes appears in prefeminist or nonfeminist scholarship; see, e.g., Joachim Jeremias, *Jerusalem in the Age of Jesus* (Philadelphia, 1969), pp. 375–76.

8. This is particularly evident in the work of Abraham Geiger; see *New Perspectives on Abraham Geiger: An HUC-JIR Symposium* (1975) and Daniel R. Schwartz, " 'And You Shall be to Me a Nation of Priests' as a Pharisaic Slogan," *Zion* 45 (1980), pp. 96–117 [in Hebrew]. See Emil Schürer's disparaging words about Jewish scholarship of this kind in his *Geschichte des jüdischen Volkes* 2:427. Many nineteenth-century Jewish scholars "cleansed" rabbinic Judaism of its magic and mysticism because classic rabbinic Judaism had to appear respectable.

9. For the characteristics of much (not all!) of Israeli historiography, see my essay in Kraft and Nickelsburg, eds. *Early Judaism and Its Modern Interpreters*. Lest I appear to find

Shaye J. D. Cohen

fault only with the work of others, I briefly analyze some of my own. In two articles I present a diaspora Jew's evaluation of the rebellion against Rome and its "heroes": "Josephus, Jeremiah, and Polybius," *History and Theory* 21 (1982), pp. 366–81, and "Masada: Literary Tradition, Archaeological Remains, and the Credibility of Josephus," *Journal of Jewish Studies* 33 (1982) = *Essays in Honour of Yigael Yadin*, pp. 385–405. My "The Significance of Yavneh: Pharisees, Rabbis, and the End of Jewish Sectarianism," *Hebrew Union College Annual* 55 (1984), pp. 27–53, can be read as a plea for pluralism in the contemporary American Jewish community; the article is criticized by Jacob Neusner, *Reading and Believing: Ancient Judaism and Contemporary Gullibility* (Chico, Calif., 1986), pp. 82–89, but Neusner neglects its central thesis.

10. For example, Jewish writers in Greek were much more willing to claim authorship for their work than were their Aramaic- and Hebrew-writing counterparts. Philosophical allegory is known only in the Greek literature of the diaspora.

11. See the debate between Neil J. McEleney, "Orthodoxy in Judaism of the First Century," *Journal for the Study of Judaism* 4 (1973), pp. 19–42, and David Aune, "Orthodoxy in First Century Judaism?" *Journal for the Study of Judaism* 7 (1976), pp. 1–10. Rather than speak of "the formation of orthodoxy," E. P. Sanders and colleagues prefer to speak of "normative self-definition." See *Jewish and Christian Self-Definition*, ed. E. P. Sanders et al. (Philadelphia, 1980–82), 3 vols.

12. Indeed, only few Jews in antiquity can be shown not to have shared these basic points. The new Schürer, and other modern works beholden to nineteenth-century conceptions, still use "orthodoxy," "Pharisaic orthodoxy," "strict Pharisaism," and the like. The immense authority of these works guarantees that these terms, in spite of their ambiguity and inappropriateness, will not disappear from the scholarly lexicon. Note, however, that even the new Schürer recognizes that "the old distinction between Palestinian and Hellenistic Judaism . . . is no longer acceptable" (3:v).

13. I am describing this approach, not criticizing it. After all, I have contributed to it myself (see below).

14. Rudolf Pfeiffer, *History of Classical Scholarship* (Oxford, 1968), pp. 230–31.

15. I do not know what the opponents of the separators were called in antiquity.

16. The authenticity of Philo's *De Vita Contemplativa* is no longer in doubt. Of the Philonic works preserved in Armenian alone, some are genuine (the *Quaestiones* on Genesis and Exodus; the *De Animalibus* edited by Abraham Terian [Chico, Calif., 1981]), some not (see Folker Siegert, *Drei hellenistisch-jüdische Predigten* [Tübingen, 1980]). There is universal agreement on the identity of the genuine works of Josephus, even if the manuscript tradition and many church fathers ascribe to him a wide variety of additional works as well; see Heinz Schreckenberg, *Die Flavius Josephus Tradition in Antike und Mittelalter* (Leiden, 1972), and *Rezeptionsgeschichtliche and textkritische Untersuchungen zu Flavius Josephus* (Leiden, 1977). The identification of the genuine Pauline letters is secure even if the Pauline content of the deutero-Pauline letters is still debated.

17. David Winston, *Philo: Selections* (New York, 1981); Hans Lewy, *Philo* (1945), reprinted in *Three Jewish Philosophers* (New York, 1969); Valentin Nikiprowetzky, *L'Éxegese de l'écriture chez Philon* (Leiden, 1977). On the methodological problems in the study of Philo, see D. T. Runia, "How to Read Philo," *Nederlands Theologisch Tijdschrift* 40 (1986), pp. 187–98.

18. As argued by Daniel R. Schwartz, "Josephus and Nicolaus on the Pharisees," *Journal for the Study of Judaism* 14 (1983), pp. 157–71. Schwartz practices source criticism with a fervor and a certainty seldom seen outside of German dissertations of the nineteenth century.

19. See my review of Rajak in *Journal of Biblical Literature* 105 (1986), pp. 350–352.

20. Martin Hengel, *Die Zeloten* (Leiden, 1961; 2nd ed., 1976). Against Hengel, see esp. Morton Smith, "Zealots and Sicarii: Their Origins and Relation," *Harvard Theological Re-*

view 64 (1971), pp. 1–19. Hengel responds to Smith in an addendum to the second edition of his book (pp. 387–412). In other historical questions, too, the separators have emerged victorious. The unifiers still speak of "the Biblical canon" and "the Biblical text" (or "the Massoretic text" or "the pre-Massoretic text"), but the separators speak instead of various Biblical canons (different Jewish communities had different canons) and various Biblical texts (according to Frank M. Cross, "local" texts).

21. Sanders, *Paul and Palestinian Judaism;* Heikki Räisänen, *Paul and the Law* (Tübingen, 1983; Philadelphia, 1986). For the debate, see E. P. Sanders, *Paul, the Law and the Jewish People* (Philadelphia, 1983), pp. 88–89, n. 25, p. 91, n. 58, p. 163, n. 14, and cf. pp. 144–49.

22. But they do represent at least in part the canons of certain Christian churches. The Christian adoption and adaptation of the Jewish Pseudepigrapha await detailed study. See James H. Charlesworth, "Christian and Jewish Self-Definition in Light of the Christian Additions to the Apocryphal Writings," in Sanders, ed., *Jewish and Christian Self-Definition,* vol. 2: pp. 27–55. For a detailed study of a specific text, see H. W. Hollander, *The Testaments of the Twelve Patriarchs* (Leiden, 1985), pp. 67–82. Various rabbinic texts refer to "outside books" and recommend the "hiding away" of various books, but neither phrase denotes a specific collection.

23. James H. Charlesworth, *The Old Testament Pseudepigrapha* (New York, 1983–85), 2 vols. Charlesworth, of course, is following the path laid out by R. H. Charles, *The Apocrypha and Pseudepigrapha of the Old Testament* (Oxford, 1912–13), 2 vols. The inappropriateness of the term and the concept can be seen from the futile efforts of Charles and Charlesworth to define the limits of the canon they have created. Charles includes the Mishnaic Sayings of the Fathers, Charlesworth a medieval *hekhalot* text. Two other anthologies assiduously avoid the term: *The Apocryphal Old Testament,* ed. H. F. D. Sparks (Oxford, 1984), and the German series *Jüdische Schriften aus hellenistisch-römischer Zeit.*

24. For a fine detailed survey of the Qumran texts, see the chapter by Deborah Dimant in *Jewish Writings of the Second Temple Period* (see n. 1), pp. 483–550, and Schürer, *History of the Jewish People,* vol. 3, pp. 380–469. For examples of attempts to recover pre-Qumranic sources from Qumranic documents, see for example Philip R. Davies, *The Damascus Covenant* (Sheffield, 1983), and M. Hengel, J. H. Charlesworth, and D. Mendels, "The Polemical Character of 'On Kingship' in the Temple Scroll," *Journal of Jewish Studies* 37 (1986), pp. 28–38.

25. Cf. Jacob Neusner, *Judaism: The Classical Statement: The Evidence of the Bavli* (Chicago, 1986), p. 137: "The [rabbinic] documents all together flow together. They constitute a canon and not merely a library. . . . They form a single canon, the authoritative and harmonious statement of the theology and law of a coherent religious group. That the Essene library constitutes a library while the rabbinic documents form a canon, seems to me self-evident."

26. On the distinctiveness of Neusner's contribution to Jewish scholarship, see my article "Jacob Neusner, Mishnah, and Counter-Rabbinics," *Conservative Judaism* 37 (1983), pp. 48–63.

27. All this is implicit in *Judaism: The Evidence of the Mishnah* (Chicago, 1981). The point is argued explicitly in "The Synoptic Problem in Rabbinic Literature: The Case of Mishna, Tosepta, Sipra and *Leviticus Rabba,*" *Journal of Biblical Literature* 105 (1986), pp. 499–507; "The Synoptic Problem in Rabbinic Literature," *Proceedings of the American Academy for Jewish Research* 53 (1986), pp. 111–45; and *Canon and Connection: Intertextuality in Judaism* (Lanham, Md., 1987).

28. The situation is well summarized by Peter Schäfer, "Research into Rabbinic Literature: An Attempt to Define the *Status Quaestionis,*" *Journal of Jewish Studies* 37 (1986), pp. 139–52: "Although it can be shown that, for the main part of the material, the Tosefta

presupposes the Mishnah, and is to be understood as its very first commentary, this result cannot be applied to all the tractates. There appear to be Mishnah tractates which presuppose the Tosefta, and above all there are Tosefta tractates which identify it as an independent 'work' vis-à-vis the Mishnah, in which the Tosefta does not refer to the Mishnah, at least not the one extant today. Finally, certain Tosefta tractates suggest that they appeal to another (earlier?) Mishnah than the one which became normative through the final redaction'' (pp. 147–48).

29. Ibid., p. 146.

30. "Synoptic texts must always be studied synoptically" does not mean that synoptic texts must *only* be studied synoptically. For Neusner the Mishna and *Leviticus Rabba* are *either* "synoptic documents," mere anthologies of words from the seamless Oral Torah, *or* original documents, independent compositions with their own distinctive points of view. The contrast is false, however, because even anthologies and commentaries can have their own distinctive agenda and interests. For example, The *Yalqut Shimoni*, the *Midrash Hagadol*, and the *Pitron Tora*, are all medieval anthologies of rabbinic midrashim on the Torah, but the three works differ from one another in flavor, character, and interests. Even synoptic works can have independent points of view; cf. Matthew and Luke.

31. See the debate between Sanders and Neusner in *Approaches to Ancient Judaism*, ed. W. S. Green (Chico, Calif., 1980), vol. 2, pp. 43–79; David Weiss Halivni, *Midrash, Mishnah and Gemara* (Cambridge, Mass., 1986); Cohen "Significance of Yavneh." Cf. the work of Max Kadushin a generation ago. Neusner also insists on methodological exclusivity when he argues that documents must be analyzed only according to the categories of thought found in the documents themselves, but here, too, interpreters routinely bring their own questions and categories to the texts they seek to interpret. When seeking the historical context of the Mishna and of Leviticus Rabba (see *Judaism and Scripture: The Evidence of Leviticus Rabbah* [Chicago, 1986]), Neusner employs data derived from other texts; no interpreter can remain bound by the horizons of the text that is being interpreted.

32. Jean Hardouin (1646–1729) argued that the bulk of extant Greek literature was forged by Byzantine monks. See the entries for Hardouin in the *Oxford Dictionary of the Christian Church*, ed. E. A. Livingstone, and the *New Catholic Encyclopedia*. Without physical evidence from antiquity (for example, papyri and inscriptions) for the Greek texts that were preserved through the medieval manuscript tradition, it is difficult to disprove this argument no matter how improbable it may be.

33. Cf. Halivni, *Midrash, Mishnah*, pp. 19–21, a critique of Neusner.

34. For an excellent application of Neusner's skepticism to a historical problem, see Peter Schäfer, *Der Bar Kokhba Aufstand* (Tübingen, 1981), with my review in *Second Century* 4 (1984), pp. 118–20.

35. For example, Neusner argues that the Mishna became the central canonical text in rabbinic Judaism because it was produced under the aegis of the patriarch and served as the law book for a court system, thus making it a text that had to be confronted by later rabbis. See *Judaism: The Classical Statement: The Evidence of the Bavli*, p. 234. But these historical facts about the Mishna are derived not from the Mishna but from the Talmudim.

36. For a good survey of the archaeological evidence, see the chapter by Eric M. Meyers and A. Thomas Kraabel in *Early Judaism and Its Modern Interpreters*, pp. 175–210. The Aphrodisias inscription has now been published by Joyce Reynolds and Robert Tannenbaum, *Jews and God-fearers at Aphrodisias* (Cambridge, Mass., 1987). On the archaeological evidence for ancient synagogues, see the two recent volumes edited by Lee Levine, *Ancient Synagogues Revealed* (Israel, 1981) and *The Synagogue in Late Antiquity* (Philadelphia, 1987), and the anthology *Synagogues in Antiquity*, ed. Aryeh Kasher et al. (Jerusalem, 1987).

37. The first edition of the inscription is Yaakov Sussman, "A Halakhic Inscription from the Valley of Beth Shean," *Tarbiz* 43 (1974), pp. 88–158 [in Hebrew].

38. Thus in Levine, *The Synagogue in Late Antiquity* (the proceedings of a symposium), the rabbinic and other literary evidence is treated separately from the archaeological.

39. See esp. the proceedings of the symposium *Apocalypticism in the Mediterranean World and the Near East*, ed. D. Hellholm (Tübingen, 1982).

40. Rajak, *Josephus*, pp. 104–43; Heinz Kreissig, *Die sozialen Zusammenhänge des judäischen Krieges* (Berlin, 1970); and my essay in Kraft and Nickelsburg, eds., *Early Judaism and Its Modern Interpreters*, pp. 43–44.

41. *Oxford Classical Dictionary*, 2d ed., p. 342, s.v. "Digesta" (by Adolf Berger and Barry Nicholas).

42. That is, archaeology that seeks to recover not just the beautiful and the important (in our case, for example, synagogues and Herodian buildings) but also evidence for patterns of life in a community as a whole (in our case, for example, Jewish villages in Galilee).

I am grateful to my friends Baruch M. Bokser, Richard Sarason, and Burton Visotzky for their comments and suggestions.

6

RESPONSE

Richard S. Sarason

Since I broadly agree with Cohen's characterization of recent trends in the study of ancient Judaism, the following remarks are intended as amplifications and, in some instances, refinements of the major points he made.

Obviously no scholarship is done in a vacuum, and no methodology is without its culturally determined presuppositions. Precisely because the academic humanistic study of Judaism in the Greco-Roman period and late antiquity encompasses the origins and early development of both rabbinic Judaism and Christianity, about which *both* religious traditions have developed and maintained "ecclesiastical historiographies" with normative implications,[1] there have been more heated controversies in our field than in most other areas of Jewish studies, where the stakes for adherents are not deemed to be so high. Academic humanistic learning—at least in theory if not always in practice—does not privilege any particular culture, religion, or society vis-à-vis the others. It is fundamentally comparativist (even when focused on a particular society or period) because it is predicated on an underlying concept of a human nature that is capable of innumerable variations and cultural expressions within the finite parameters set by genetics, biology, and physical environment.[2] We may well note that this kind of interpretive stance admirably fits, and obviously reflects, a pluralistic society in which difference and "otherness" must somehow be tolerated. For humanistic learning, Judaism and the Jews are simply another instance of human creativity, resourcefulness, and pathos in the face of ubiquitous finite constraints.[3] It is also the case, as Cohen remarks, that academic learning is at base secular. When approaching the data of religious traditions and experience, it tends to be reductive—at least it phenomenologically brackets the question of God and nonimmanent causality. Yet this stance need not be hostile—indeed, it may remain sympathetic—to the underlying concerns of religious traditions. The academic study of ancient Judaism, then, is not value-free, and it is easy to understand why its practice is so frequently tinged with the residues of Jewish and Christian apologetics: the practitioners, too, are human. Critical self-consciousness in research and openness to other interpretive possibilities are the only effective—if necessarily partial—antidotes.

Judaism in Greco-Roman antiquity increasingly has been, and must continue to be, interpreted in the larger context of Greco-Roman culture, particularly in the hellenized eastern Mediterranean basin and Mesopotamia. The interpretive pitfalls here lie in the extremes of parallelomania on the one hand and apologetics on the other. Not all vaunted parallels between Greco-Roman and Jewish cultural forms are equally significant or convincing. Substantive, as opposed to superficial or unusually arcane, parallels must involve similarities of form, function, and context. The work here must be nuanced and precise. It must be cognizant, when relevant, of differences as well as similarities. At the same time, "where Judaism differed" must not lapse into apologetics. The best, most nuanced, and interpretively richest modern research has repeatedly shown that, more often than not, where Judaism most differed from the surrounding culture(s) in content, it was most like them in form, particularly in form of response to common problems. Once again, nuance, precision, and contextual sensitivity are mandatory.

It is a commonplace of responsible historical scholarship that sources cannot be taken at face value but must be read with a discerning eye. The question "Cui bono?" is part of a larger hermeneutic of suspicion. To be skeptical of quasi-historical reports in Jewish, Christian, and pagan literature from antiquity (particularly when that literature is avowedly didactic or hortatory), to construe these reports not as brute facts but as perspectives—interpretations—is simply sound historical method. To be sure, when applied *in extremis* in Cartesian fashion this method can leave us with very little that is historically certain. But strong statements, such as those of Neusner, at least serve to focus the attention of practitioners in the field on the underlying issues. There *is* a difference between plausibility and factuality, between verisimilitude and veracity. These cautions are necessary precisely because statements in rabbinic literature—but also in other sources from the period—too frequently have been used for historical reconstruction without sufficient attention to the question of their typicality, point of

75

view, possible idealization, didactic or hortatory function, literary context, and the like. The ultimate aim should not be nihilistic (though, to be sure, some previous scholarly conclusions may be vitiated) but, rather, careful, balanced, nuanced, and precise claims based on critical self-awareness. It is by no means the case that all rabbinic statements thereby lose their evidentiary value. It is simply that conclusions frequently must be more modest, more tentative, less certain. Scholars may reasonably disagree on the likelihood that a particular plausible statement in the sources may *also* be factual. The point is that this move can no longer be made automatically or without considerable reflection. If this is labeled "minimalism" in comparison with the approaches of previous generations of scholars, so be it. With increased recognition of the complexity, diversity, and sometimes outright incommensurability of all of our evidence from Greco-Roman antiquity, both literary and nonliterary, and the acknowledgment that the surviving evidence is only partial and incomplete must come the willingness to scale down our assured results accordingly. Some perennial questions, such as the origin and nature of the Pharisees before 70 C.E. and their relation to the post-70 rabbis, under these circumstances are incapable of probative solutions; our assertions, therefore, must be put forth in more tentative language.

Given the fact that our evidence is partial, it is methodologically appropriate to distinguish among documents in a nuanced fashion and to construe statements in their immediate literary contexts before juxtaposing them (or, worse, harmonizing them) with statements from other literary contexts. In actual fact, however, no document is ever read in total isolation from all others, since the identity and singularity of each can only be established through comparison with the rest. With respect to the rabbinic sources specifically, Cohen is correct to maintain that "a full interpretation of rabbinic literature requires an assessment of both sets of facts: the distinctive characteristics of each rabbinic work and the points at which they intersect"—though I believe that "the distinctive system we call rabbinic" is sometimes less a matter of the coherence of the documents than of *our* abstraction and generalization from them and of the way in which the documents are read "canonically," that is, as part of a larger normative construct, internal to Jewish tradition. This caution notwithstanding, the problem of "parallels" cannot be so neatly resolved as Neusner has maintained. The systematic and nuanced comparison of intersecting documents—for example, Mishna with Tosefta, Mishna and Tosefta with the so-called "halakhic" midrashim (and these midrashim with one another), the Palestinian Talmud with the early aggadic midrashim (and these with each other)— while by no means giving us a clear picture of the nature of common, antecedent sources, nonetheless strongly indicates the existence of such antecedents (in whatever form) and sheds light on editorial decisions made in the formulation and construction of each document.

Let me give two salient examples, the first dealing with Mishna and Tosefta, the second with the early aggadic midrashim.

a. While it is clear on literary grounds that the Tosefta as a document is post-Mishnaic, there are also literary indicators that some of the materials in the Tosefta are contemporaneous with materials in the Mishna. Neusner himself allows that the relatively small proportion of Toseftan materials that are completely autonomous in content from the Mishna—that is, that are not in any way Mishna commentary—can in principle have come from the period in which the Mishna took shape (though he also points out, correctly, that these do not constitute *parallels* to Mishnaic materials).[4] But there *is* one type of material in the Tosefta that, while not making up a large portion of the document, *does* parallel the Mishna and logically must be contemporaneous with Mishnaic materials. I refer to those instances in which a ruling that is unattributed in the Mishna is found attributed in the Tosefta followed by a disputing, also attributed, opinion. Unless we regard this material as totally spurious and pseudepigraphic, it must, on logical grounds alone, be as old as the materials in the Mishna and would give us sufficient reason to claim that the Mishna is a *selectively* edited document. That claim, in turn, both underscores the importance of the editorial role in shaping the Mishna and, at least somewhat, relativizes the primacy of the Mishna as the sole literary encapsulation of early rabbinic materials.[5] If I wish to adhere to my own methodological caveat about a nuanced, finely tuned reading of the texts, then I cannot generalize on this basis beyond this particular type of Toseftan material.[6] But here is an instance in which reading the Mishna and the Tosefta in tandem indeed "present[s] important insight into the character of the documents at hand."[7]

b. The same kind of insight can sometimes be obtained through the study of parallels in the aggadic midrashim and between them and the Palestinian Talmud. In particular, parallels to *petiḥtot* in the midrashim frequently show how editors reshaped these materials to fit specific literary contexts. The order of materials internal to the *petiḥta* will be rearranged so that the appropriate prooftext appears at the end. In some instances it is possible to show (or at least strongly suggest) on the basis of parallels that serial exegeses of particular verses that originally were not *petiḥtot* have been made into *petiḥtot* by editors who nonetheless have retained all of the exegetical materials that are extraneous to the new literary context.[8] Once again, such observations focus our attention on both the work of the editors and the prior existence of at least some materials—in whatever form. They also suggest, as Cohen maintains, that the distinction between "anthology" and "original work" should not be overdrawn,[9] since a document such as

Leviticus Rabba may display both sorts of characteristics. But—and here I agree with the thrust of Neusner's work—we must be very careful in juxtaposing texts and drawing generalized conclusions about what lies behind them. We cannot simply replicate the assumptions of the traditional approach to the texts.

We must even be cautious, as Cohen suggests, in generalizing about a single text such as the Mishna, whether we are pursuing a topical-thematic inquiry or are attempting to make sense out of the entire document. In dealing with a text so richly complex and so full of discrete, disparate rulings as this one, no single generalization will capture the sense of the whole (if indeed one can even speak of the sense of the whole).[10] Generalizations—essentializations—by their very nature tend to obscure distinctions. Virtually every larger interpretive pattern suggested by, for example, the Mishna's discrete rulings will bear some exception. These exceptions must not be disposed of too quickly. The "meaning" of any text is overdetermined (using the Freudian sense of that term) and will indeed permit a number of valid noncontradictory interpretations, each of them only partitive, illuminating a particular facet of the text.

If my remarks put me squarely in the camp of the separators in regard to the interpretation of the literary (and nonliterary) evidence for ancient Judaism, so be it. I believe that stance is mandated by the peculiar characteristics of the sources themselves. Nineteenth-century scholarship in our field, in its flush of optimism, not infrequently harmonized sources and imaginatively filled in gaps in pursuit of the larger picture. We, no less, are interested in the larger picture but, chastened both by the experiences of our century and the maturation of scholarly epistemology and hermeneutics, must pursue it with requisite attention to nuance, differentiation, and context—in short, with restraint.

Notes

1. In rabbinic Judaism, the various "chains of tradition" and histories of the Oral Torah (e.g., Sherira's 'Iggeret, Abraham ibn Daud's *Sefer haqabbala,* Maimonides' introduction to the *Mishne Tora*—all, to be sure, dating from the Islamic period and responding in some measure to the rabbinite-Karaite controversy). Tractate Abot, from the Greco-Roman period, while not fully comparable to the foregoing, is nonetheless a rudimentary "ecclesiastical history."

2. Cf. Wilhelm Dilthey, "The Understanding of Other Persons and Their Life-Expressions," in Patrick Gardiner, ed., *Theories of History* (New York, 1959), pp. 213–25.

3. Although Jacob Neusner indeed has been the most vocal and consistent advocate of this position, as Cohen notes, he has by no means been the only one. The Association for Jewish Studies was founded nineteen years ago out of precisely the same concern for professionalism and the maintenance of recognized disciplinary standards by practitioners of the then newly burgeoning field of Jewish studies in the academy. Arnold J. Band in particular had

much to say on this subject (see early issues of the *AJS Newsletter*). Many of Neusner's polemical remarks in the 1960s and 1970s were directed to the issue of the disciplinary location of Jewish studies within the academy. (Similar concerns were being voiced at the same time by others with respect to black studies, American studies, women's studies, and other "area studies" then blossoming in the academy of the late 1960s.) Within the (multidisciplinary) field of religious studies, whose morphology and concerns have been heavily influenced in this country by those of mainline Protestantism, Neusner correctly argued that the serious integration into academic religious studies of data from Judaism must necessarily have a reciprocal effect on the construction of both. See Neusner, *The Academic Study of Judaism: Essays and Reflections* (New York, 1975), and Jonathan Z. Smith, *Imagining Religion: From Babylonia to Jonestown* (Chicago, 1982), p. 36. That Neusner sometimes may have overstated his case in no way vitiates its basic correctness to my mind.

4. J. Neusner, "The Synoptic Problem in Rabbinic Literature," *Journal of Biblical Literature* 105 (1986), pp. 501–2.

5. Neusner in fact treated the Tosefta at great length in tandem with the Mishna in his *History of the Mishnaic Law of Purities* (Leiden, 1974–77). The analysis of Tosefta became less extensive in his treatment of other orders, particularly Nashim, Moed, and Neziqin, a regrettable loss.

6. Peter Schäfer's characterization of Mishna-Tosefta relationships, cited by Cohen, also appears to me to be oversimplified. I am not aware of any entire tractates that are characterized consistently and exclusively by the types of literary relationships catalogued here. (Indeed, I am unaware of any Tosefta tractate that does not cite and gloss our Mishna inter alia.) Rather, these kinds of relationships usually obtain between units of materials within chapters of Mishna and Tosefta. Neusner's analysis of Mishna-Tosefta relationships in *Purities* nicely illustrates this point.

7. Neusner, "Synoptic Problem," p. 500. In regard to the relationship between the Mishna and the "halakhic" midrashim, the literary indicators suggest that the edited midrashim are post-Mishnaic (cf. E. Z. Melamed, *Hayahas sheben midreshe hahalakha lamishna welatosefta* [Jerusalem, 1967]). The fairly consistent use of *mikkan ʾameru* to introduce a Mishnaic ruling is suggestive in this regard—although the Mishna itself contains some halakhic midrash, and in this context uses *mikkan ʾameru* to introduce rulings that obviously are *not* Mishna citations (see M. *Maʿaser Sheni* 5:14 and M. *Sanhedrin* 10:5–6). So the genre clearly *is* contemporary with Mishnaic materials.

8. See my article "The *Petiḥot* in Leviticus Rabba: 'Oral Homilies' or Redactional Constructions?" *Journal of Jewish Studies* 33 (1982) = *Studies in Honor of Yigael Yadin,* pp. 557–67.

9. Cf. Neusner, "Studying Synoptic Texts Synoptically: The Case of Leviticus Rabba," *Proceedings of the American Academy for Jewish Research* 53 (1986), pp. 115–16.

10. Cf. my remarks on the difficulties of thematic-topical inquiries involving the Mishna, in "The Significance of the Land of Israel in the Mishnah," in *The Land of Israel: Jewish Perspectives,* ed. Lawrence A. Hoffman (Notre Dame, Ind., 1986), pp. 109–36, esp. pp. 110–11.

7

TALMUDIC STUDIES

Baruch M. Bokser

I. Introduction

In the period 1967–87 Talmudic studies underwent significant developments; the field is currently on the threshold of even greater advances. Using David Goodblatt's classic 1979 essay on the Babylonian Talmud as a point of departure,[1] this essay will explain: how the field has received firmer foundations; how higher literary and historical criticism can now be approached with greater assurance than ever before; and how rabbinic sources can more effectively be studied for the world-view they project, the corresponding way of life they prescribe, and the social order they reflect.

As Goodblatt noted, despite numerous advances in Talmudic studies through the 1970s, the lack of a scientific commentary to the Talmud and the scholarly divisions over the use of higher source criticism point to the lack of firm philological, lexicographical, and historical assessment of the sources as well as the lack of detailed text-critical research. To be sure, by 1979, (a) the work of Jacob Epstein, Saul Lieberman, Hyman Klein, Abraham Weiss, and others, despite their differences, provided models of how to tackle higher- and lower-critical issues; (b) several projects analyzing the history of amoraic teachings and their transformations as they were transmitted and incorporated into the gemara, in particular by David Weiss Halivni and Shamma Friedman, had started; (c) the Herzog institute had made some progress in fully collating manuscript readings; and (d) important research, especially the publications of Jacob Neusner, had illuminated the historical background of Babylonian Jewry. The issue is, therefore, how these initial efforts have advanced to provide a solid foundation for composing scientific commentaries, using higher criticism, and investigating broader issues.

II. A Review of Scholarship

1. Babylonian Talmud and Palestinian Talmud Text and Text Criticism

Because the current printed texts of the two Talmuds (hereafter BT and PT) are the result of a long process of transmission, corrections, and copy editing, by both printers and scribes who introduced minor and major changes, students of the Talmud have assessed the manuscript evidence as well as the printed editions and early witnesses to the text. Despite the long tradition of scholarship in this area, several significant new trends have emerged.

First, it is now physically easier to examine the evidence. Reprints of many important manuscripts to the Mishna, BT, PT, and midrashic texts appeared in the late 1960s and early 1970s. To these we should add, for example, several collections of Geniza fragments, including Russian fragments gathered by Katsh; several fragments to the PT; and most important, the Escorial Manuscript to PT *Neziqin*.[2] Of related importance is Sokoloff's collection of Geniza fragments to *Genesis Rabba*, which provides a model of how to assess and publish a full corpus of fragments.[3]

The very fact that Safrai's semischolarly, semipopular volume *The Literature of the Sages*[4] includes several excellent articles by Michael Krupp, who briefly characterizes and systematically lists the manuscripts to rabbinic works,[5] indicates the projected use of such information. The publication of the more important manuscripts has democratized scholarship by making these resources available to those who may not be at major research institutions. It has furthermore contributed to a consensus, on the one hand, that the citation of a rabbinic text must be informed by manuscript testimony and, on the other hand, that the goals of scholarship must center on not merely the listing of variants but rather the ability to categorize, use, and build on the variant readings.

For the same reason, scholars have decided to confront the problem of manuscript testimony on a large scale. For example, drawing on technical advances, Friedman has initiated a project to put Bavli Talmud manuscripts on computer and Schäfer has started a synopsis of Yerushalmi manuscripts and fragments. Even if Friedman and Schäfer publish in accessible book and computer formats the heretofore unpublished fragments and new readings of previously published manuscripts, we will still need an assessment of all the manuscripts and Geniza fragments to the Talmud according to the standard set by Sokoloff.[6] Sussmann has promised such a review, and Friedman's analysis of the manuscripts to tractate *Bava Metsia* exemplifies how it can be done.[7] Moreover, if the data base of the *Comprehensive Aramaic Lexicon* and especially of the *Dictionary of Jewish Palestinian Aramaic* and the *Dictionary of Jewish Babylonian Aramaic* are distributed on compact disk, their on-line texts of the two Talmuds will become available, though at this point it is unclear what manuscripts were used for text entry.[8]

Assessing Early Editions. Epstein's and Lieberman's concern to delineate the character of early editions has been carried forward by the work of Feintuch, Ta-Shema, and Dimitrovsky, who published fragments of Spanish incunabula that represent a textual and manuscript tradition considerably different from the Franco-German texts that have shaped the textual tradition to modern times.[9] Sussmann and Assis, building on Lieberman, have made comparable advances in analyzing the PT textual tradition.[10] Kahana's prolegomenon to a new edition of midrash *Sifrei Numbers*[11] provides a model of how to apply these concerns to edit a text.

Early Witnesses to the Text. We also find systematic text-critical analysis of early medieval works (Rishonim) that provide witnesses to the text of the two gemarot, for example: Natan b. Yehiel of Rome's *Aruch* by Abramson; the *Sefer ha-Ittur* by Glatzer; the novellas and forthcoming edition of *responsa* of the Rashba by Dimitrovsky; the Alfasi by Friedman; and the forthcoming edition of *Halakhot Pesuqot* by Neil Danzig.[12] These improve our understanding of early medieval study and text criticism of the two Talmuds. Likewise, several broader works offer a wider view of medieval rabbinic exegetical and textual activities, including the revised edition of Urbach's *Baale hatosafot* (1980), studies by Benedict (1985), and the investigation by Grossman (1981) of Franco-German rabbinic circles (and a forthcoming study of Spanish authorities).[13] Because these diverse analytical and comprehensive inquiries should make possible better interpretive-historical work, especially regarding medieval handling, copy editing, and correcting of earlier rabbinic texts, they will lay firm foundations for tracing the history of the text's transmission and interpretation and for the eventual production of definitive editions.[14]

2. Collation of Manuscripts and Critical Editions

Collating Manuscript Readings. Some modest advances have taken place in editing classical rabbinic works, though we still lack proper editions of the Talmud. The traditional collation of readings has continued and remains useful, especially since scholars, in assuming that variants preserve important early readings that may provide a key to early recensions of the text, do not want an eclectic, leveled text. Such collations, keyed to the traditional Vilna Texts, are found, first, in the supplements to Rabbinovicz's unfinished *Diqduqe Soferim* to the Bavli, by Feldblum to *Gittin* and by the Makhon haTalmud, *Complete Diqduqe Soferim* by the Israeli Talmud Institute of the Rav Herzog Foundation.[15] To be sure, even with the addition of insightful notes, in merely listing variants without differentiating them by family, these volumes leave it to the reader to consider the significance of the variants for understanding the text. Volume two of *Gemara Shelema*[16] provides one model of how to evaluate variants from manuscripts and early medieval witness, though it, too, does not offer a corrected text. For the Yerushalmi, two projects indicate that the work can be done. Goldman edited PT *Rosh Hashana* with a full listing of variants from manuscripts and fragments, and Sussmann comprehensively and insightfully analyzed variants to PT *Sheqalim*.[17]

Toward Critical Editions. The long-awaited critical text edition of *Pesaḥim* by Rosenthal has not yet appeared. To judge from Rosenthal's introduction to the Sassoon manuscript,[18] however, it will comprehensively confront the complex textual history, with the particular object of clarifying how different manuscripts and early commentaries preserve distinct recensions that may have become conflated in later texts. Friedman has published a preliminary model of a series of critical commentaries to the Talmud text, undertaken by him, his students, and associates. Depending on the parameters of the finished products, this project may represent a new era in Talmudic study.

In the interim, we find models for preparing a critical text in several completed projects on related documents. First, those on the Mishna and Tosefta, though generally eschewing higher-critical issues, have systematically taken up the lower-critical matters so well grasped and laid out by Epstein.[19] These include: the two volumes on Mishna *Zeraʾim* in the Herzog Foundation Talmud series, which lists variants (with, however, no collation by families); individual German treatises such as the one on Mishna *Yoma*, which is interested in parallels and realia, and the series of Tosefta tractates, with variants and translations, edited by Rengstorf; Goldberg's volumes on *Shabbat* and *ʿEruvin*, which go considerably beyond his earlier work on *ʾOhalot* in tracing the manuscript traditions, the layers in the Mishna (which are seen as a key to the Mishna's formation), and the history of interpretation in the two Talmuds; and David Rosenthal's edition and study of the manuscript traditions of Mishna *ʿAvoda Zara*.[20] Even the last item, with its interest in philology and manuscript families, generally focuses neither on higher-critical matters nor on the meaning of the text. Of greatest importance, of course, is Lieberman's critical edition and commentary on the Tosefta, which primarily, from the perspective of the history of the halakha, treats lower text-critical issues, the purported literary, historical, and cultural context, and the implications for understanding the BT and

PT. The posthumous volumes on the first part of *Neziqin* provide an important supplement.[21]

Second, additional models are represented by recent works on several midrashim such as Kahana's aforementioned prolegomenon to a new critical edition to *Sifrei Numbers;* Tabory's discussion of the textual history of *Esther Rabba;* Shinan's critical edition and brief commentary on *Exodus Rabba,* somewhat patterned after Margulies's *Leviticus Rabba* with, however, added attention to newer literary concerns; and German treatises or fascicles on different pesiqtot of *Pesiqta Rabbati.*[22]

A different type of model relevant to the preparation of a critical edition is provided by the series of higher-critical studies by Friedman, Halivni, Neusner, and others. In focusing on the transmission of teachings, their place in the *sugya,* and the role of both in the composition of the gemara, they illuminate traditional philological issues as well as the text's wider meaning, as we shall see from the discussion of these approaches, below.

The Yerushalmi. PT with its own special problems requires much work to effectuate Lieberman's program for text criticism, for clarifying the character of old PT commentaries, and for identifying the relationship of the manuscripts to their urtexts and to the several printed editions.[23] I have set out elsewhere the current state of scholarship and the issues, and we should note in particular Goldman's fresh transcription of manuscripts and fragments to *Rosh Hashana,* and Asiss's and Sussmann's systematic analysis of scribal and printers' corrections to PT, especially *Sheqalim.*[24] As we will see below, traditional philological lower-critical work will gain much if it is combined with higher criticism. In that way we may be able to trace how the materials were orchestrated to compose larger statements transcending their individual parts.

Original Text and Additions. Acting on the current consensus for scientific editions of individual recensions or text types accompanied by a collation of variant readings may elucidate the longstanding and difficult problem of the nature of the Talmud's original text. On the one hand, there is much truth, as we shall see, in the claim that "since these texts are compilations of discrete traditions with only a loose external framework, additions or deletions are not felt by the reader [and] thus every copyist can edit the text anew if he so wishes. This makes it almost impossible to recover the *Urtext* as it left the hands of the original editor."[25] On the other hand, despite the numerous additions in the BT, the use of manuscripts and other early testimonies can often reveal what is secondary. Friedman, in fact, has set out criteria to identify such additions;[26] for example, the presence of numerous variants to a given phrase or passage may indicate that that portion of the text is secondary or later than the adjoining material.

84

Moreover, because the Bavli's editing makes sources subservient to their new context, we can probe what does and does not appear to fit within its context.[27]

Accordingly, the Talmud represents a text that has in certain respects remained elastic or free floating. Our challenge is to define its contours more precisely.[28] In this regard, it is worth noting Ta-Shema's suggestion that some of the fluidity in the textual history of the Talmud may be characteristic of one family of manuscripts and editions originating in a particular historical and social milieu, such as the German twelfth-century pietists (the Ḥaside Ashkenaz), who altered texts more than Spanish authorities.[29] This issue may be illuminated by its analogue in the PT, in which numerous *sugyot* have duplicates elsewhere in the Yerushalmi. Lieberman, Rosenthal, Epstein, Melammed, and Assis[30] differ over whether the repetitions were introduced by text editors/redactors, by scribes who later transferred the material, or by some combination of the two. We obviously need to learn more about the nature of the Talmud text as well as late antique and medieval editing, redacting, and scribal practices.[31]

Hence, until further philological and comparative research yields a consensus on a definition of the gemara's text, scholars, while agreeing on the importance of manuscripts, will diversely employ them in their textual work. Those interested in the Talmud's circulation in the medieval period will not find the current situation overly problematic, but those probing the earlier state of the material will confront the possibility that the process of editing may have entailed leveling one recension in favor of another one or integrating some materials into the body of the text tradition.

3. Languages of Rabbinic Documents

Kutscher's Firm Foundation and Program. The work of Kutscher, who led the recovery of the dialects of rabbinic literature, provides linguistic and philological precision to the earlier work by Epstein, Yalon, and Lieberman that had isolated distinguishing features of different layers of Hebrew and Aramaic. Kutscher refined their work from the obfuscation caused by anachronistic corrections and distortions. Though his initial work was published in 1951–52 ("Studies in Galilean Aramaic"), the bulk appeared from 1966 to the early 1970s. His work has been continued in that of his students, especially Bar-Asher and Moreshet, who studied the distinctive linguistic features of BT *beraitot*.[32] Bar-Asher, identifying three principal traditions of Mishnaic Hebrew and early Mishna manuscripts, recently called for even greater precision and the study of each manuscript's characteristics and overall system.[33] Several studies had already taken up this task.[34] The most recent research may be found in a collection recently edited by Bar-Asher containing many important articles that treat, among other subjects, the Hebrew of Babylonian amora'im; they also provide up-dated bibliographies.[35]

New Tools. A firm scientific basis now exists for studying rabbinic dialects. We should expect grammars going beyond existing ones, including the posthumously published *Grammar of Galilean Aramaic* by Levias,[36] and lexicons and dictionaries. As the concordance to the Babylonian Talmud has finally been completed, with a five-volume set of names added, a *Concordance to the Talmud Yerushalmi* has started to appear, with three volumes of word entries and a volume of names, to date.[37] Sperber, has turned to Greek and Latin loanwords, analyzing, first, the methodological issue, and then legal and nautical terms.[38] Specialized studies have elucidated such matters as fauna, especially flora of the Talmud, and the terms for workers and artisans.[39] Much work remains to be done on the Iranian impact on Babylonian Aramaic and culture, as Rosenthal's modest though very detailed study of several words illustrates.[40]

Perhaps most revolutionary will be the three publications mentioned above: Sokoloff's *Dictionary of Jewish Palestinian Aramaic,* whose computer base may be used to produce a grammar; Sokoloff's recently initiated *Dictionary of Jewish Babylonian Aramaic* and the grammars it will spin off; and Hillers's comprehensive Aramaic lexicon, with separate demarcations of each dialect. Despite the progress in the study of Aramaic, we lack, however, even the promise of comparable lexicographical advances in the analysis of the Hebrew dialects of rabbinic literature. The only comprehensive works are Moreshet's *Lexicon of the New Verbs in Tannaitic Hebrew* and the several Kasowski concordances to the Midreshe Tora, which supplement the earlier ones to the Mishna (1927) and the Tosefta (1933–61).[41]

The creation of these secondary tools will allow nonphilologists to make use of modern linguistic advances and as a result to have their research evaluated on its own terms, without issues of translation getting in the way. To be sure, it will still be necessary to apply philological expertise to analyze newly published documents and, for all documents, to choose the proper rendering, in particular the appropriate nuance for each context and its substance.[42] In addition, the publication of the secondary resources may facilitate the study of the cultural and historical significance of the linguistic data, as Sperber aptly points out.[43] Several works provide models of how to approach the problem. Lieberman, in 1962, discussed the technical philosophical terminology, claiming rabbinic literature did not borrow such loanwords; the revised *History of the Jews* by Schürer assesses the repertoire of loanwords by subject and the amount of loanwords in different documents; and Avery-Peck, who in comparing Mishna *Zera'im* with other ancient works on agriculture, notes how the former exhibits distinctive elements fitting overall rabbinic interests.[44]

4. Higher Criticism

Introduction and New Developments. The specific modes of analyzing the Talmud from the perspective of its "sources," "forms," or "redaction" are interrelated, though for the sake of discussion it will be useful to address each area individually. Before we can proceed, it is necessary to clarify certain general advances in understanding the transformations that amoraic traditions underwent and that have affected every reading of the text. Most scholars agree that traditions may have been adapted by amora'im, who cited and applied them, and by later circles, who arranged them and composed them into *sugyot* and then the entire Talmud text, often adjusting them in the process to new contexts or new uses. The latter stage in particular entailed redacting and embedding the material in what is now generally agreed to have been an artificially created anonymous framework aimed at integrating the divergent earlier amoraic traditions and at employing them for theoretical discussions. While an impetus of literary enrichment has been widely attributed to the Bavli, some type of analogous process would seem to have held to some degree, as well, for the Yerushalmi.[45]

The Talmud is not merely the record of discussions between masters, but rather a sophisticated literary orchestration of sources, exegeses, traditions, and narrative accounts integrated and organized formally around the Mishna (with some subunits, as discussed below, structured around topical, formal, or exegetical rubrics). At one point the earliest amoraic teachings responded to the Mishna, though subsequently they became in their own right the point of departure for other comments, as I have argued elsewhere.[46] Accordingly, the traditions to some degree may have originated as teachings that masters directed at students and other Jews, but later they became the subject of study. As Halivni notes, some forms of nondiscursive teachings such as individual dicta (which he calls "apodictic" statements) patterned after the Mishna, could be readily memorized, as could stories about a given master, though the discussion or argumentation that accompanied or explained a tradition might not.[47] Such groupings of teachings—perhaps in sets of three traditions or sets of stories about an individual master or sets of exegesis of a given Biblical pericope—were integrated with other traditions or comments on similar matters, as Neusner emphasizes.[48] It is this process that created the impression of an actual give and take.

The need to accept such a theory becomes compelling in light of Goodblatt's research, which cogently argues that a social context in which Babylonian rabbis could have regularly faced one another did not exist. This is so because instruction in Babylonia primarily took place not in an academy (an institution that transcends the personality of a single master and outlives the life of that individual) but rather in disciple circles where individual masters, even those associated with a particular location, taught a circle of students.[49]

Scholars have speculated on why at one point discussions were preserved and presented in the BT and what differentiates them from discursive material that is found, for example, in the Sifra or that may actually date back to a preredacted amoraic state, whether from the time of Abaye and Rava or other masters.[50] In moving beyond the notion that the anonymous parts are generally late, the research suggests that, on the one hand, earlier examples of discussions sought to prove rhetorically the correctness of an interpretation or the need for Scripture in addition to logic; while, on the other hand, the later type of discussion—making up the characteristically anonymous "Talmudic dialectic"—formed an analytical inquiry in several tiers on the consistency of opinions, logic, and legal principles, and aimed at correlating and integrating sources and approaches.[51]

Future Research. Where will (or should) research now turn? When the character of the anonymous discussion within the dynamic of redaction is considered, two areas, at least, deserve renewed interest. First, the earlier model of the anonymous framework in the PT needs further clarification.[52] Halivni, for example, recognizes that:

> There are some layers of stam even in the Yerushalmi (less so—almost none—in the older parts of the Yerushalmi, that of Tractates Baba Kama, Baba Metzia, and Baba Bathra). . . . [But the PT's stam differs from BT's because it represents the PT's editors' own comments when they] decided to close the development of the text and to "freeze" it into a book . . . [creating] an anonymous ring around the attributed material. But the ring was thin and not always significant; it was the result of a technical decision to record the "present speakers' " ideas anonymously. In contrast, the anonymous sections of the Babylonian Talmud are rich, multi-tiered and comprehensive, the result of a new awareness of the importance of the "give and take" and a desire to preserve and develop it. The difference is a qualitative one.[53]

Without minimizing the qualitative distinction between the Yerushalmi's and Bavli's anonymous material, ongoing research suggests that we should appreciate the role that even the PT anonymous material (or "ring") plays in orchestrating, integrating, and commenting on traditions.[54]

Second, the transition from oral to written forms of the Talmud deserves investigation. One factor that has not been explored is the possible impact of the process of writing down the gemara. For example, perhaps once traditions were arranged in sequence, their very writing down (in

Babylonia, ca. 425?) may have produced a text or corpus that could then be analyzed through diverse logical principles.[55] A comparative study would be in order along the lines suggested by C. M. Brown's comments regarding the Hindu tradition:

> Perhaps writing stimulates certain kinds of reflective speculation and analysis, while orality, with its relative lack of distancing between knower and known, encourages in some circumstances a meditative inwardness less tied to reflection on written words and more oriented to the direct interpretation of immediate experience. We can say with [W. J.] Ong [*Orality and Literacy* (London, 1982)], at least, that *in both the Buddhist and Hindu cases, the more self-conscious, analytical philosophies, and theologies developed after writing had become widely accepted.*[56]

5. Source Criticism

"Early" Palestinian Sources, in Particular Regarding the BT. It is not surprising that for a long time scholars have inquired into the Talmud's sources. The Talmud itself calls attention to sources by alternating the use of Hebrew and Aramaic, by using terminology introducing purported quotations, and by the attribution—or nonattribution—of traditions. As Goodblatt indicates, earlier scholarship had focused on what sources were "known" to the Babli (or Yerushalmi) and the relation between the citations and the corpora out of which they ostensibly were quoted. This includes Palestinian tannaitic teachings, whether from the Mishna or *beraitot* and Palestinian amoraic traditions. Melammed[57] carefully lays out the diverse phenomena discussed by Epstein, Albeck, and others. Goodblatt's observation remains to the point: "Whether or not the Babylonian Amoraim knew the extant Tannaitic collections, they obviously had at their disposal compilations of Tannaitic sources."[58]

The PT. A comparable question exists for the Palestinian Talmud. Materials may possibly be considered "earlier sources" where they have analogues in the Tosefta or Midreshe Tora or in *beraitot* cited in the Bavli, or where the PT designates them as Babylonian imports. The problem is compounded, however, because the Yerushalmi at times lacks quotational terminology and, as Epstein and Lieberman note, both amora'im and scribes who copied the gemara digested and abbreviated citations.[59]

Assessment. Scholars have responded to the presence of these sources from different perspectives. Some, like Albeck and especially Epstein, took up the challenge of traditional source criticism to evaluate and identify the "sources." Some, like Rosenthal in particular, have stressed the difficulties and subjectivity in this task.[60] More recently, scholars have redefined the project. Halivni, investigating what happened to sources in the course of their transmission and use, probes how divergent versions of sources may have caused individual amora'im to interpret earlier traditions differently and how, in the course of transmission, the knowledge or lack of knowledge of those initial sources may have affected the subsequent assessment of those interpretations.[61] Others have analyzed how the purported sources may have been revised to fit their new context. Goldberg[62] thus appropriately differentiates between the editing of the sources, their mode of circulation among amora'im, and the nature and purposes of the gemara's *sugya,* which might require a source to be manipulated. Neusner argues that however the parallel materials originated, they have been transformed to become an integral part of their new context in the BT.[63]

Yet Kraemer suggests that the gemara's having chosen to identify sources explicitly might play a rhetorical role in the *sugya* as well. That is, the analytical discussion might be designed not only to test the sources or to show that a given view or notion can withstand the citation of earlier views (or sources) but to highlight a dialectic or religious tension or issue. This suggestion would provide an additional means to appreciate the final redacted text if it could be proven systematically for large blocks of material, and if we could be confident that the terminology pointing to the citation of a source and the actual quotation of that source—beyond merely alluding to it—derives from the Talmud's redactional circles and not simply from later scribes.[64]

Amoraic Sources. Babylonian Sources in the BT. Even more intractable are the sources used by amora'im and out of which the literary gemara was woven. These consist not only of citations of individual Babylonian teachings but also of edited pericopae or discussions that may have been quoted, used, or adapted within their location or reused in a secondary location,[65] especially as part of the anonymous framework and discussion in which the attributed material is embedded. The evaluation of these materials, even more than possible Palestinian sources, is dependent on redaction criticism, for the use of traditions is more and more seen as affecting the formulation and wording of material, though the date of these transformations remains problematic. Some, like Rosenthal, suggest that later alternate versions of pericopae tend to be imposed on earlier versions, which end up developing into longer conflated passages.[66]

Palestinian Sources in the PT. The comparable issue regarding the Palestinian Talmud has received additional interest since Epstein's posthumously published rejection of Lieberman's explanation of the distinctive character of PT *Neziqin,* to wit, that its briefer composition and style and distinctive features—such as choice of terminology, vocabulary, and roster of names—represent not an earlier editing of the material from Caesarea but a different recension, incompletely edited, contemporary with the remaining Tiberian gemara. Despite Lieberman's published rejoinder, the problem has reemerged as the result of the publication of the Escorial Manuscript. In part it continues distinctive PT *Neziqin* characteristics, but in some ways it lacks some of the supposed evidence to which Lieberman had earlier pointed.[67] Hence, irrespective of where the PT *Neziqin* material originated, since a comparison of the parallel pericopae, set out graphically by Lieberman by 1931, demonstrates that the non-PT *Neziqin* versions are more developed than the PT *Neziqin* parallels, the PT clearly presents us with two divergent recensions of the Talmud, one briefer than the other. It is therefore beyond speculation that there are (at least) two distinct options for how to interpret and edit Palestinian materials and how to cast them into the literary form of a *sugya* and of a gemara. Each alternative is characterized by an orchestration of traditions, additions of questions at key points, and the inclusion of a possibly anonymous framework, though in comparison with the other, one version remains considerably briefer, with less anonymous material, and closer to the Mishna and to the issues raised in *beraitot* that are attested in the Tosefta.[68]

The question, therefore, becomes, can we discern within the rest of PT other alternate editings of materials that have been combined, as Lieberman and others had pointed to long ago?[69] Significantly, comparable recensions are attested in the parallels between PT and *Genesis Rabba*, for *Genesis Rabba* contains *sugyot* of the Palestinian gemara that appear somewhat less worked than those of the PT; that is, the material in the PT gemara seems more integrated into its context than that of the gemara assumed and quoted in *Genesis Rabba*.[70] Additional indirect attestation to the joining together of PT pericopae and of the adaptation or expansion of the PT text may be found in the synagogue inscription at Rehov, which directly or indirectly quotes and makes use of Toseftan and two Yerushalmi *sugyot* (from *Demai* and *Shevi'it*), to set out forbidden and permitted fruits and vegetables in particular locations in the seventh year.[71]

Recensions in the BT. Scholars have proposed that the BT took shape in several recensions. Although many scholars have associated different recensions with divergent contemporary or near-contemporary amoraic circles,[72] the discovery and dating of the fifth-century or later "stam" has led some to apply this term to the form of the gemara prior to its mostly anonymous literary embellishment and reworking. Some in fact believe that the Yerushalmi provides a model of what an early Bavli gemara recension may have resembled.[73] Additional illumination might come from further analysis of the so-called five and a half BT tractates—*Nedarim, Nazir, Me'ila, Keritut, Tamid*, and the portions of *Temura* introduced with the superscription *lishna 'ahrina*—whose brief and rudimentary form of discussion, lack of stylistic polish (which today might be associated with the gemara rather than the later anonymous literary embellishment), and archaic Aramaic differ from the rest of BT.[74]

Anonymous Sources. The considerable amount of anonymous material—or sources—that is not attributed to a named individual has been heavily scrutinized in recent years, and its assessment has led to significant developments in BT research. Since we discussed the emerging consensus above, I shall now highlight three points.

First, the discursive material in its own right makes up a "late" source. Just as systematic analysis of the complete corpus of the Mishna has led Neusner to conclude that the Mishna's anonymous material is generally late and not "early," so a careful examination of the Talmud text by Klein, Weiss, Feldblum, and, more recently and more extensively, Halivni and Friedman has led to the analogous argument that the anonymous gemara is generally late.[75]

Because the discursive anonymous material has its own characteristics, it can be characterized as a distinctive "source." Foremost is its rhetoric of dialectic, which appears to analyze problems by presenting one master responding to another master with a series of questions and answers. This rhetoric arranges divergent traditions and sources so that they arrive at a point that may have been predetermined before the discussion was initially structured. As noted by Friedman (working independently of Halivni), this composition exhibits various literary features, including a contrived tripartite arrangement of material. Halivni redefined his source-critical commentary to separate the discursive stam from the amoraic teachings—in 1975 for the latter half of the order of *Mo'ed,* and then more extensively in 1982 for tractates *Shabbat, 'Eruvin,* and *Pesahim.* Other scholars have employed these methods to illuminate legal, literary, historical, and conceptual developments.[76]

Second, to evaluate the date of this source, scholars have sought to differentiate between the "late" long-winded analytical materials and "earlier" anonymous discussions.[77] Their dating varies, however, depending on their differing views of the editing history of individual tractates and on their theories as to the authorities who provided the literary enrichment. On the one hand, Halivni and Friedman believe it generally derives from the stamma'im, which Halivni dates to the fifth century. Kalmin's initial research likewise points to this date for the beginning of the phenomenon, though his subsequent work, raising complications, argues that much of it may be later.[78] On the other hand, Goldberg holds that it primarily comes from the Savora'im.[79] In the absence of more research, objective criteria, and a theory attuned to the social context of these developments, all of these theories remain provisional.

Third, early redacted *sugyot* or discussions, if they existed (as noted in my discussion of "Recensions in the BT"), would constitute a possible additional anonymous source. It is clear that where BT and PT have parallel *sugyot* consisting of similar traditions, stories, or discussion, someone transmitted them in a patterned or fixed manner, though the differences indicate that they subsequently underwent additional development. The question is, therefore, whether anyone arrayed these individual discussions around a structured framework such as the sequence of *mishnayot*, producing an "ur" form of gemara.[80] Weiss and Rosenthal make that claim, suggesting that such early "editions" received additional supplements by later masters. Others suggest that although individual *sugyot* may have been remembered, they were not fully structured around a complete tractate of the Mishna until a later period.[81]

6. Form and Subject Matter

Brief and Discursive Material. Because we can separate the earlier amoraic "strata" from a possible later editing by distinguishing between brief independent statements and longer discursive discussions, we can define these genres as two major forms of Talmudic material. But we should speak not only in terms of stam/unattributed material versus attributed—as important as this distinction may be—but also in terms of a brief or simple statement or teaching over against a lengthy discursive analysis of logical principles.

Other Forms. The recognition that other building blocks or compositional organization units or forms are present in the Talmud further highlights the way in which some gemaraic material was composed even though such material was *not* chosen to constitute the main framework of the Talmud, as emphasized by Neusner.[82] Weiss's by now classic classification of the three categories has greatly contributed to the study of these materials as units.[83] Adapting his categories, we have: (1) collections, assemblages of series of three or more traditions in their own structure, such as traditions attributed to an individual master, or questions, or contradictory sources, legal decisions; (2) midrashic compilations structured around successive verses or sections in a Biblical book, such as Esther[84] or Ruth, or aggadic themes heavily tied to verses, such as prayer,[85] works of the chariot, and legends concerning the Temple's destruction;[86] and (3) treatises extensively treating individual themes, such as Hanukkah, dreams, the evil inclination, and (depending on one's classification) perhaps some of the items listed under midrashic units. The problem of interpreting the significance of these patterned and arranged materials likewise applies to whatever subunits we can add to the above list, such as queries, sermon forms, cases, or story forms.[87]

Issues. The issues include: whether such collections or units existed outside their present context; if so, the degree to which they have been integrated and revised in the course of transmission and integration into their present context; and whether or to what degree they represent *literary* forms, that is, a literary means by which to shape the materials that prior to this stage did not circulate in that fashion.[88] It is reasonable to assume that the collections identified by Weiss may have originally served to transmit some of the materials but, as Neusner observes,[89] they did not make up the structures by which the gemara as a whole was organized. To further clarify the various uses of such collections we need, as Goodblatt notes,[90] more research on the life settings of the amoraic sources—and of the redaction of the Talmud.

7. Redaction Criticism

A New Perspective. One of the most important developments of recent research is that it concentrates on the redaction process of the gemara in terms not merely of who edited the Talmud but of how the process of editing and redaction affected the contents. Whatever sources contributed to the Talmud and whatever forms they took (or into which they were cast), the contours of the Talmud itself shaped the result. It is this notion that justifies speaking of the Talmud as a single unit, as though it were authored by a single "individual," giving testimony of one "textual" community or circle of rabbis. We have already repeatedly drawn on Halivni, Friedman, and Neusner to support this proposition.

Halivni believes that the stam's discursive analysis even completed missing discussions; emended earlier sources; integrated the whole text into a flowing discourse; and prefaced, correlated, and interpolated amoraic comments. Sabora'im later added more material to this existing "text."[91] To gain greater chronological precision, we still require further assessment of the dates for this literary embellishing. In particular, if the rise of anonymous teaching, analysis, and glossing was accompanied by the waning of autonomous teaching attributed to named masters, we need some sense of the social context behind these intellectual developments.[92] It is insufficient, for example, merely to say that masters, considering themselves subservient to their predecessors, chose no longer to identify themselves by name. Other possibilities exist, as I demonstrated in my discussion of "Future Research." Keeping in mind that we speak not merely of anonymity but of a shift in the mode of analysis, let me build on that suggestion. If, for the sake of discussion, at the time of "the end of *hora'a* (instruction)," which has been associated with R. Ashi,[93] someone consciously orchestrated the teachings (in accord with the process already attested in the PT), and then wrote this structure down, the presence of such a written structure (or "text") could account for later authorities seeing themselves as glossators and for their being able to study this document analytically.

8. Implications

Literary Aesthetics and Transcending the Discursive Veneer. Although much still needs to be elucidated, we have a working basis for using the Talmud in an unprecedented fashion. Earlier scholarship had already begun to avoid harmonizing and anthologizing rabbinic comments on given topics by systematically treating each subject and by taking into account the aesthetics and interests of each document. With this method, the Talmudic sources may be compared with the results of analysis of the Mishna, Tosefta, and the Midreshe Tora, as well as the other midrashim, so as to illuminate and then interpret diverse stages in the history of rabbinic Judaism.[94] Some research has already indicated that a global perspective and a concern for literary aesthetics are very rewarding. These include, in addition to Neusner's assessment of the Bavli as a whole, the more limited studies by Bokser, on the amoraic response to M. *Berakhot;* Eisen, on the images of the gentile in M. *ʿAvoda Zara* and its companion gemarot; and Jaffee, on the contrasting images of the judicial branch of government in Mishna and BT *Horayot.*[95] Recent Talmudic research promises to enhance the subtlety of this effort for we can now trace the dynamic of the gemara in treating given issues, specifically seeing how it orchestrated, embellished, and expanded traditions, and, where other versions of those traditions exist either in earlier corpora or in the other gemara, how it shaped materials to make new points. Although any inquiry ultimately remains speculative regarding the original context and function of amoraic teachings, we may still get beyond the editors' embellishments, possible revisions, and theoretical analysis to see, if only in gross terms, what different amoraic circles may have believed and to evaluate more precisely divergent Talmudic treatments of issues.[96]

An Emerging Picture. To provide an example of current results, I now describe the picture of Talmudic Judaism that is emerging. The Mishna reflects a two-pronged response to the Temple's loss and the Bar-Kokhba fiasco. Providing a theoretical and ahistorical view of religious life, it suggests that, despite the recent upheavals, Judaism remains intact and the experience of holiness previously tied to the Temple remains accessible. In addition, it anachronistically provides a precedent for extracultic forms of religiosity. Amoraʾim, who did not feel threatened by the earlier disruption and who therefore no longer had the need to prove that religious life is viable, interpret and adapt the earlier program in light of a realistic view of life under Roman and then Byzantine rule in Palestine, or under Iranian rule in Babylonia. In seeking to justify Mishnaic law on the basis of Scripture (as noted by Neusner and Halivni), they acknowledge that the Mishna forms not an independent Torah but rather part of an overall revelation in which it is distinct yet dependent on the written Scripture.[97]

Although features of the above scheme should be further elaborated, the divergent Palestinian and Babylonian amoraic applications of this program in particular need clarification. Literary-historical analysis will be helpful in this regard and can build on recent research on historical background. For the Bavli, it can supplement the important older research of Neusner with more recent publications by, among others, Beer, Goodblatt, Gafni, Rosenthal, and Oppenheimer.[98] The comparable analysis of the Yerushalmi must rely on individual studies, which provide a less comprehensive picture in need of constant revision due to new archaeological discoveries.[99] Neusner's assessment of the self-image of the Palestinian rabbinic circles[100] exemplifies how a literary-historical approach can yield meaningful results, though even it will need some revisions on the basis of the redactional analysis discussed here (and which Neusner himself subsequently advocated)[101]—though for now these studies offer the tentative picture necessary before any interpretive effort can begin.

The program that I envision would succeed in producing contrastive pictures of the Bavli and Yerushalmi rabbinic circles and perhaps, by extension, Babylonian and Palestinian society and culture. Ginzberg had made an admirable attempt to draw such distinctions; even before Goldberg followed them up, Lieberman showed they were problematic, at least regarding beliefs in magic, astrology, and superstitions.[102] While Neusner insightfully contrasts overall BT and PT treatments of the Mishna and Scriptures as well as the portrayal of sages, various scholars have undertaken more limited studies.[103] Consequently, with redaction-critical tools we can now more effectively examine how Babylonian and Palestinian editorial authorities employed traditions from each of the two rabbinic centers.

Cultural Interpretation. The new and emerging developments in the study of the Talmud will likewise affect the interpretation of the Talmud's cultural significance. Scholars have already made imposing gains in transcending the text and in making "thick" descriptions of rabbinic Judaism and its society and institutions.[104] Several authors have recently sought to apply modern literary criticism to rabbinic literature. Despite the stimulating insights they provide, they have not yet sufficiently taken into account the literary and historical contexts of the sources.[105] For the cultural and literary studies, the challenge is not merely to become more precise in applying anthropological, sociological, literary, religio-historical, and other methodologies to the Talmud, but to pose questions appropriate to the nature of the evidence, in particular the aesthetics of the individual documents. As Lawrence Hoffman, who is interested in rabbinic rituals, observes: "What we have is less an ordered interpretation arranged to suit our enquiries then it is a random recounting of signification contained within a literary corpus *that was designed with wholly other rules of organization.*"[106] It is for this reason, for example, that we must consider whether the particular Talmudic text reflects the thoughts of individuals responding to an actual life situation or whether it reflects a literary, dynamic process and a theoretical expansion of earlier teachings. As I have argued in a study of the ritual expansion of the seder,[107] we can make that distinction. But even if the development or articulation of an idea is shaped by the literary process that created the Talmud, this intellectual activity is still subject to cultural interpretation.

These considerations apply equally to the practice of literary criticism. Deconstructionists might insist that by definition the context is secondary, but it is possible that in a given culture a text reflects or is shaped by its particular historical context. The critic must prove that the materials incorporated into and worked over to make up the text were composed as a result of textual or scriptural interpretation or in a scribal process, and not as a result of some other activity, such as teaching. Green notes that since some rabbinic circles held that reverence for "the book" transcends its content, not all rabbis saw themselves primarily as expounders of that content and thus interpreters of a text.[108] Although the later analytical expansion of the Talmud, which spread a veneer over the earlier materials, may appropriately be explained in literary terms, that process and stage of development does not represent all of rabbinic Judaism. Indeed, as we have seen, advances have been made to take account of and at times to penetrate that veneer.

Creating New Commentaries. My review of current scholarship indicates that exegesis can be expanded in three directions. First, to clarify the textual tradition we require theories to assess the significance of variants. Rosenthal has begun to discuss this and should explore it further in his model edition of BT *Pesaḥim.* New tools, such as computers, may facilitate this task; Friedman's project for critical commentaries and editions of Bavli chapters is predicated on their use. Second, new linguistic and lexicographical advances, informed by actual usage and alternative manuscript readings, can put the explication of the text on a firm foundation. Third, lower-critical exegesis must be attentive to higher-critical issues. The current larger projects by Neusner, Halivni, and Friedman recognize the importance of these concerns, though each treats a different part of the problem.[109] Let me give some concreteness to this observation.

The commentaries and translations of the Mishna, the Talmud, and Midrashim initiated by Neusner,[110] who has been joined by a series of other scholars, address a set of issues often treated in modern Bible commentaries. Among other things, they pay attention to: (a) manuscript variants;

(b) the interconnections between literary formulation, patterned language, and content;[111] (c) the repertoire of literary units throughout a document and the implications for the composition of the work; (d) the stages of legal and conceptual development assumed in each generation; (e) the relation between Scripture and the Mishna; and (f) a tractate's place in early rabbinic Judaism. Although these studies differ considerably from work to work and author to author, of the volumes by Neusner himself those on the Mishna, especially to *Tohorot*,[112] are the most detailed, those on the Yerushalmi pay considerable attention to the flow of the discussion and its constituent parts, and those on the Bavli tend to be briefer. On the other hand, structured as a translation and commentary (many actually a ''preliminary explanation'') to the complete text, they assess each individual corpus as a whole.

Halivni (whose work is discussed above) analyzes in depth certain selected, difficult passages in the Bavli—to date covering over half the Talmud—so as to trace the transformations of the traditions and, especially since 1975, the anonymous later circles' (the stam's) reworking of the earlier sources and teachings. Friedman, ostensibly the most comprehensive in commenting on everything within his purview, tries to take stock of complete units, their component parts, and their place within the larger composition. Because in its thoroughness his work necessarily limits itself to individual Bavli chapters, it will not be able to assess the chapter's role within the whole tractate and thus the general response of the amora'im and stamma'im to the Mishna and its issues.

These three projects, as a result of their differing concerns, have different priorities. Whereas Neusner seeks to provide a cultural interpretation of the materials, Halivni and Friedman focus more on legal history. Halivni discusses the halakha only as it relates to the local textual and literary problems. Friedman discusses the full Talmudic rabbinic tradition and notably the ancient Near Eastern legal background.[113] But Halivni and Friedman, in contrast to Neusner, pay less attention to the rhetorical designs of the text and to how the meaning is projected and manipulated through the use of different literary devices. The work of Yona Fraenkel on literary hermeneutics of rabbinic *aggadot* underscores the need to consider these dynamics.[114]

Examples. Let me now exemplify how combining the several methodologies and analyzing each source or document in its own right illuminates the transformations of the common heritage in different circles and generations, in particular in the response of the amora'im to the Mishna. The examples, moreover, illustrate the need to place lower criticism within a larger context and to consider the cultural significance of variant readings to the Mishna and gemara.[115]

First, M. *Pesaḥim* 10:3, which speaks of the elements of the seder, mentions (after the bitter herbs, unleavened bread, and *ḥaroset*) that "in the temple precincts they bring the carcass of the Passover sacrifice." The addition of this clause, describing an item that would be brought before those who happened to be in the Temple, draws a contrast with the standard, presumably contemporary, practice outside the precincts. As Epstein and Lieberman noted,[116] later printed editions transform the clause to past tense and add an auxiliary "used to," to wit: "they used to bring the carcass of the Passover offering," which contrasts a post-70 and a pre-70 practice. It is only by recognizing the overall design of the Mishna, however, that we appreciate the significance of the original reading (without the "used to") and its essential role in the Mishna. The Mishna anachronistically projects backward to pre-70 times a precedent for celebrating Pesaḥ without the sacrificial cult.

The addition of the auxiliary verb "used to" in M. 10:3 reflects the later mentality attested in amoraic circles, which, in contrast to the Mishnaic authorities, openly acknowledge the break from pre-70 days. In making that acknowledgment, amora'im empowered themselves to overcome the loss of the Temple. For example, they added symbolic reminders of the cultic rite or imparted symbolic significance to neutral features of the meal. We find this very "ritualizing" process in amoraic comments that led to the post-Mishnaic addition of the gloss "two cooked foods" to M. 10:3. Although these words appear, in printed editions of the Mishna, amid the list of objects to be brought to the table, they break the flow of the Mishna and are not attested in the manuscripts or in the Tosefta analogue that quotes the Mishna. They apparently were generated by the amoraic discussion of a *beraita*, which mentions this phrase and was understood to connote objects in memory of the lost Passover sacrifices. Being sensitive to such religious implications makes us appreciate not only what is secondary to the Mishna but also the distinctive amoraic (and post-amoraic) developments.

A second example, from M. *Pesaḥim* 10:4, highlights the need to consider higher-critical interests relating to the formation of the gemara. It deals with one of the series of three (later expanded to four) "children's questions," which notes that "on all the nights we dip once, this night twice." Since the amoraic authorities (BT *Pesaḥim* 116a) assume in Babylonia that it was no longer customary daily to dip even once, they revise this question, ostensibly differing on whether to say "on other nights it is not even required to dip once" or "on other nights one does not even dip once." Upon closer analysis we find that these authorities may actually differ over the very nature of the recitation of the questions. Those who held that it has become a ritualized text to be recited by anyone (and not just a child) could speak of a "requirement," whereas those who believed it represents a typical set of questions presented to a child who does not know how to ask would find the notion of a requirement inappropriate. The gemara's editor, however, has created a *sugya* out of both opinions by casting one as the answer to a question posed on the other.

A third example illustrates how divergent theories or levels of interpretation may explain why the stam introduced a new rhetoric and reinterpreted materials. Halivni believes that forced reasoning was employed by later anonymous circles to make sense out of the received traditions, not so much for programmatic purposes. The question remains, however, why the conceptualization took the direction that it did. This applies even if we hold, as suggested above, that the very process of the transformation from oral to written study and teaching contributed to the rise of discursive analytical probing of earlier material and the derivation of conceptual principles.[117] To answer this question, I suggest we consider the possibility that later authorities manifest a distinctive stage of intellectual development. It is this dynamic that may explain BT *Pesaḥim* 120's expansion of the requirement to eat unleavened bread post-70 C.E.

The gemara correlates a set of amoraic views with a series of verses, purported tannaitic sources (*beraitot*), and its own Biblical exposition. As Halivni notes,[118] the BT interprets that a certain authority (R. Aḥa bar Yaʿaqov) applies the obligation to eat unleavened bread even to those who are on a journey or unclean (exempted by Numbers 9 from participating in the Passover sacrifice on its appointed time), who might otherwise in the absence of a Passover offering be assumed to be exempt. But this representation of R. Aḥa bar Yaʿaqov is not in accord with the cited *beraitot's* extant tannaitic analogues (from midrash Mekhilta de Rabbi Ishmael and Mekhilta de Rashbi), which present two alternative views on the matter. According to both of these sources, in the absence of a Passover sacrifice, the class of individuals in question would *not* be required post-70 to eat unleavened bread.

What led to the reinterpretation? It is possible, as Halivni implies, that the *sugya* reinterpreted R. Aḥa's position because of the nature of its sources. Since it did not have the full range of the relevant Mekhilta de R. Ishmael passages, it believed that R. Aḥa was confronted with two ostensibly contradictory verses in need of harmonization and for which an analogue existed regarding a different class of special individuals who were required to eat unleavened bread. I suggest, however, that the *sugya's* editor may have acted, as well, on the basis of the well-attested heightened importance that amoraʾim ascribed to the unleavened bread, which became the holiday's central symbol instead of the Passover offering.[119] The revised reading would then reflect the vital importance of the *matsa* and the assumption that all parties must have held that it is essential under all circumstances. If this factor played a part, the reinterpretation gains significance as part of wider amoraic and stammaitic intellectual and religious developments.

III. Conclusions

Let me summarize and highlight my results.

1. Research from 1967 to 1987 has developed programs set by earlier scholars.

2. Talmudic scholarship is becoming the domain of ever wider circles, reflecting perhaps the overall rise in Jewish studies in Israel and the United States.

3. Some scholars have turned to new questions and methodologies that had not generally been taken up in the earlier period. Many of these concerns form part of wider trends in the study of literature and history, in particular in the United States. As Tzvee Zahavy notes,[120] this may reflect, among other things, the general shift in the traditional role of philology in all the humanities, for scholars in many fields no longer see their goals restricted to lower-textual linguistic matters. That is, as the need for a careful philological approach based on critical editions and manuscripts has become widely recognized among all those who employ rabbinic sources, more and more scholars pursue redaction and other forms of higher criticism and seek to answer questions originating in fields such as the history of religion, sociology, and literary criticism.

4. Although scholars have reached a consensus on how to use rabbinic sources from a text-critical perspective, they remain divided on many other methodological and substantive matters, in particular over the nature and date of the late discursive, literary embellishing of the gemara.

5. Current research suggests areas that need to be addressed in the coming years. These include not only the production of Hebrew lexicographical tools and more comprehensive commentaries, but also, in particular: the precise dating of the analytical discursive stam portions of the Talmud and an assessment of the causes for its emergence; the impact of the transition from the oral to the written forms of the Talmud; the analysis of the Yerushalmi's stam, its role in orchestrating traditions and editing the Palestinian Talmud, and its implications regarding the nature of the Bavli's stam; the investigation of conceptual and institutional contributions that the later stam authorities made to the earlier amoraic intellectual heritage; and the significance of the contrasting Bavli and Yerushalmi treatments of issues and themes.

These results have at least four major implications for the interpretation of Talmudic sources.

1. Because the very composition of the documents and their editing significantly shaped their contents, the substance of a work is represented by more than its sources.

2. Because we can evaluate the impact of, or reasons for, the reworking of text material, we can correlate divergent redactional perspectives.

3. Because the sources are shaped by literary and rhetorical considerations, we cannot blindly employ them for information as to what they purportedly claim.

4. The analaysis of given themes within several documents as well as efforts at interpreting the cultural significance of the material must consider the literary and aesthetic traits of each document.

Notes

1. David Goodblatt, "The Babylonian Talmud," *Aufstieg und Niedergang der römischen Welt* 2:19/2 (1979), pp. 257–336. My discussion and references, especially for the Mishna, Tosefta, and midrashic literature, which are only peripherally treated, may be supplemented by H.L. Strack, *Einleitung in Talmud und Midrasch*, 7th ed., rev. G. Stemberger (Munich, 1982); Baruch M. Bokser, "An Annotated Bibliographical Guide to the Study of the Palestinian Talmud," *Aufstieg und Niedergang der römischen Welt* 2:19/2 (1979), pp. 139–256; idem, "Recent Developments in the Study of Judaism 70–200 C.E.," *Second Century* 3 (1983), pp 1–68, which suggests literary and substantive ways in which tannaitic sources differ from amoraic ones; Anthony Saldarini, "Reconstructions of Rabbinic Judaism," in *Early Judaism and Its Modern Interpreters*, ed. Robert A. Kraft and George W. E. Nickelsburg (Atlanta, 1986), pp. 437–77; Isaiah Gafni, "The Historical Background," and Abraham Goldberg, "The Mishna," "The Tosefta," "The Palestinian Talmud," and "The Babylonian Talmud," all in *The Literature of the Sages*, ed. S. Safrai (Philadelphia, 1987), pp. 1–34 (Safrai), and 211–51, 283–301, 303–19, 323–45 (Goldberg).

2. A. I. Katsh, *Ginze Talmud Babli* (Jerusalem, 1975–79) 2 vols.; Moshe Assis, "A Fragment of Yerushalmi Sanherdrin," *Tarbiz* 46 (1977), pp. 29–90, [in Hebrew]: other fragments listed in Bokser, "Palestinian Talmud"; and E. S. Rosenthal, ed. and "Introduction," *Yerushalmi Neziqin* from the Escorial Manuscript (Jerusalem, 1983).

3. Michael Sokoloff, *The Geniza Fragments of Bereshit Rabba* (Jerusalem, 1982; in Hebrew). See also Z. M. Rabinovitz, *Ginze Midrash* (Tel Aviv, 1976); Judah Goldin, *The Munich MS to Mekilta* (Baltimore, 1980); various fragments including Menahem Kahana, "New Fragments of the Mekilta on Deuteronomy," *Tarbiz* 54 (1985), pp. 485–551 [in Hebrew], and Mark Bregman, "An Early Fragment of Avot deRabbi Natan from a Scroll," *Tarbiz* 52 (1982–83), pp. 201–22 [in Hebrew].

4. Shmuel Safrai, *The Literature of the Sages* [Compendia Rerum Iudaicarum ad Novum Testamentum 2:3.1] (Philadelphia, 1987).

5. Michael Krupp, "Manuscripts of the Mishnah," "The Tosefta Manuscripts," "Manuscripts of the Palestinian Talmud," and "Manuscripts of the Babylonian Talmud," in Safrai, *Literature*, pp. 252–62, 301–2, 319–22, 346–66.

6. Sokoloff, *Fragments*.

7. Jacob Sussmann, "Talmudic Fragments in the Geniza," *Teudah* 1 (1980), pp. 21–31 [in Hebrew]; Shamma Friedman, "Early Manuscripts to Tractate Bava-Metsia," *Alei Sefer* 9 (1981), pp. 5–55 [in Hebrew], and "Le'Elu Yoḥasin shel Nushe Bava Metsia—pereq beḥeqer nusaḥ haBavli," in *Meḥqarim beSifrut haTalmudit* (Jerusalem, 1983), pp. 93–147.

8. Delbert R. Hillers, "A Comprehensivce Aramaic Lexicon" (in preparation); Michael Sokoloff, *A Dictionary of Jewish Palestinian Aramaic of the Byzantine Period* (Ramat Gan, 1989); idem, *A Dictionary of Jewish Babylonian Aramaic* (Ramat Gan, in press). The Bar-Ilan Responsa Project reportedly has put the Babylonian and Palestinian Talmuds and the midrashic literature on line, though they have used the traditional Vilna editions.

9. Israel Zvi Feintuch, *Versions and Traditions in the Talmud. Studies* (Bar-Ilan, 1985; in Hebrew); Israel Ta-Shema, "Sifriyatam shel ḥakhme ᵓAshkenaz bene hameᵓa ha -11-12," *Kiryat Sefer* 60 (1984–85), pp. 298–309; Haim Z. Dimitrovsky, *Sŕidei Bavli. Spanish Incunabula Fragments of the Babylonian Talmud, with an Historical and Bibliographical Introduction* (New York, 1979).

10. Jacob Sussmann, "Mesorat limud umesorat nusaḥ shel talmud hayerushalmi," in *Meḥqarim besifrut hatalmud* (Jerusalem, 1983), pp. 12–43; Moshe Assis, "R. Elijah of Fulda's First Recension of Tr. Shekalim," *Teudah* 3 (1983), pp. 57–70 [in Hebrew]; idem, "On the Glosses of the Gaon of Vilna on Tractate Shekalim," *Tarbiz* 53 (1983), pp. 97–115 [in Hebrew]; idem, "Concerning the Commentary Attributed to the Disciple of R. Samuel B. Shneur on Tractate Shekalim," *Teudah* 4 (1986), pp. 129–36 [in Hebrew].

11. Menahem Kahana, *Prolegomena to a New Edition of the Sifre on Numbers* (Jerusalem, n.d. [1982?]; in Hebrew).

12. Shraga Abramson, "On the ʿAruk of R. Natan," *Leshonenu* 36 (1972–74), pp. 122–49; 37, pp. 26–42, 253–69; 38, pp. 91–117 [in Hebrew]; Mordechai Glatzer, *ᵓIttur soferim (Sefer haᶜittur) of R. Isaac B. Abba Mari* (Jerusalem, 1985; in Hebrew), 2 vols.; Shamma Friedman, *Halakhot Rabbati of R. Isaac Alfasi*, Ms. Jewish Theological Seminary of America Rab. 692, Facs. and Intro. (Jerusalem, 1974).

13. E. E. Urbach, *The Tosaphists: Their History, Writings and Methods*, 4th ed. (Jerusalem, 1980; in Hebrew), 2 vols.; Benyamin Z. Benedict, *Merkaz hatora biprovants* (Jerusalem, 1985); Avraham Grossman, *The Early Sages of Ashkenaz* (Jerusalem, 1981; in Hebrew).

14. See my discussion below of "Original Text and Additions," and, in general, Ivan Marcus, "Review of Abraham Grossman, *The Early Sages of Ashkenaz*. Jerusalem, 1981," *AJS Newsletter* 33 (Winter 1983), pp. 4–7, 9.

15. M. S. Feldblum, *Dikduke Sopherim, Tractate Gittin* (New York, 1966); Moshe Hershler, Joshua Hutner, and Moshe Liss, *The Babylonian Talmud with Variant Readings Collected from Manuscripts, Fragments of the "Genizah" and Early Printed Editions*, Institute for the Complete Israeli Talmud, Rav Herzog Foundation, (Jerusalem, 1972–), 7 vols. [*Nedarim, Ketubot, Sota, Yebamot*] to date.

16. Baruch Naeh, *Gemara shelema* (Jerusalem, 1986; in Hebrew), vol. 2.

17. E. A. Goldman, "A Critical Edition of Palestinian Talmud Tractate Rosh HaShanah," *Hebrew Union College Annual* 46–49 (1973–78); and Sussmann, "Mesorat limud."

18. E. S. Rosenthal, "Introduction to the History of the Text to Tractate *Pesaḥim*" [in Hebrew], in *The Pesahim Codex Babylonian Talmud* [Sassoon 594] (London, 1985), pp. 5–59.

19. J. N. Epstein, *Mavo lenusaḥ hamishna*, 2d ed. (Jerusalem, 1964); see Baruch M. Bokser, "J. N. Epstein's Introduction to the Text of the Mishnah," in *The Modern Study of the Mishnah*, ed. Jacob Neusner (Leiden, 1972), pp. 13–36.

20. Nissan Sacks, ed., *The Mishnah with Variant Readings Collected from Manuscripts, Fragments of the Genizah and Early Printed Editions*, Institute for the Complete Israeli Talmud, Rav Herzog Foundation (Jerusalem, 1971–75), 2 vols.; Gören Larsson, *Der Toseftatraktat Jom hak-Kippurim, Text, Übersetzung, Kommentar, 1. Tiel* (Lund, 1980); K. H. Rengstorf, ed., *Rabbinische Texte. Erste Reihe: Die Tosefta* (Stuttgart, 1960–) (which notably includes *Tohorot* and portions of *Neziqin* not covered in Lieberman's edition); Abraham Goldberg, *The Mishnah Treatise Ohaloth* (Jerusalem, 1955; in Hebrew); idem, *Commentary to the*

Baruch M. Bokser

Mishna Shabbat (Jerusalem, 1976; in Hebrew); idem, *The Mishna Treatise Eruvin* (Jerusalem, 1986; in Hebrew); and see Goldberg's own characterization of his work, in Goldberg, "The Mishna"; David Rosenthal, *Mishnah Aboda Zara—A Critical Edition* (Jerusalem, 1981; in Hebrew), 2 vols.

21. Saul Lieberman, *The Tosefta* [in Hebrew], 4 vols. in 5 parts, and the companion *Tosefta Ki-fshutah* (New York, 1955–88; in Hebrew), 10 vols.; on which see E. S. Rosenthal, "HaMoreh," *Proceedings of the American Academy for Jewish Research* 31 (1963), Hebrew section, pp. 1–71, and Peter Schäfer, "Research into Rabbinic Literature: An Attempt to Define Status Quaestionis," *Journal of Jewish Studies* 37 (1986), pp. 139–52.

22. Kahana, *Prolegomena;* Joseph Tabory, "Some Problems in Preparing a Scientific Edition of Esther Rabbah," *Sidra* 1 (1985), pp. 145–52 [in Hebrew]; Avigdor Shinan, *Midrash Shemot Rabbah: Chapters I–XIV* (Tel Aviv, 1984); and for *Pesiqta Rabbati,* see the list in Strach, *Einleitung in Talmud und Midrasch,* pp. 273–74.

23. Saul Lieberman, *On the Yerushalmi* (Jerusalem, 1929; in Hebrew); idem, "The Old Commentators of the Yerushalmi," in *Alexander Marx Jubilee Volume,* ed. Saul Lieberman (New York, 1950; in Hebrew), Hebrew section, pp. 287–336; idem, "Yerushalmi *Horayot,*" in *Sefer hayovel leRebbi Ḥanokh Albeck* (Jerusalem, 1963; in Hebrew), pp. 283–305.

24. Bokser, "Palestinian Talmud"; Goldman, "A Critical Edition"; Assis, "Fulda," "Gaon," "Disciple"; Sussmann, "Mesorat limud."

25. Goodblatt, "Babylonian Talmud," p. 272, paraphrasing Mordecai Margulies, *Midrash Wayyikra Rabbah* (Jerusalem, 1960), vol. 5, p. xl.

26. Shamma Friedman, "A Critical Study of Yevamot X with a Methodological Introduction," *Meḥqarim Umeqorot* (New York, 1978), pp. 277–441.

27. Jacob Neusner, *The Bavli and Its Sources* (Atlanta, 1978).

28. Cf. Steven Fraade, "Interpreting Midrash. 1: Midrash and the History of Judaism," *Prooftexts* 7 (1987), pp. 179–94; idem, "Sifre Deuteronomy," *Hebrew Union College Annual* 54 (1983), pp. 245–301 (on the application to Sifre Deut., to which cf. Kahana "Fragments"); and Schäfer, "Research."

29. Ta-Shema, "Sifriyatam," p. 309, See Goodblatt, "Babylonian Talmud," p. 272, nn. 28–30; Elazar Touitou, "Concerning the Presumed Original Version of Rashi's Commentary on the Pentateuch," *Tarbiz* 56 (1987), pp. 236–42, esp. pp. 240–41 [in Hebrew], and the references, esp. to D. Rosenthal (I thank Moshe Idel for this reference); cf. Yosef Dan, "Review. Peter Schäfer. *Geniza Fragmente zur Hekhalot Literatur,* Tübingen 1984," *Tarbiz* 56 (1987), pp. 433–37 [in Hebrew]. This may affect our assessment of Sussmann, "Mesorat limud," regarding the origins of the additions to PT *Sheqalim.*

30. Bokser, "Palestinian Talmud," p. 178–82; Strack, *Einleitung in Talmud und Midrasch,* pp. 166–67.

31. Charles Rosen, "Romantic Originals," *New York Review of Books,* December 17, 1987, pp. 22–31, illustrates how modern editors must consider these matters before they edit a text.

32. See Eduard Y. Kutscher, *Hebrew and Aramaic Studies* (Jerusalem, 1977; in English and Hebrew); idem, *A History of the Hebrew Language* (Jerusalem, 1982); Moshe Bar-Asher, ed., *Qovets ma'amarim bilshon ḥazal,* vols. 1–2 (Jerusalem, 1972, 1980); idem, *The Tradition of Mishnaic Hebrew in the Communities of Italy [according to Ms. Paris 328–329],* Edah veLashon 6 (Jerusalem, 1980; in Hebrew); Menahem Moreshet, *A Lexicon of the New Verbs in Tannaitic Hebrew* (Ramat-Gan, 1980; in Hebrew).

33. Moshe Bar-Asher, "The Different Traditions of Mishnaic Hebrew," *Tarbiz* 53 (1984), pp. 187–220, [in Hebrew].

34. E.g., Moshe Bar-Asher, "Mishnaic Italy"; Gideon Haneman, *A Morphology of Mishnaic Hebrew According to the Tradition of the Parma Manuscript (De-Rossi 138)* (Tel Aviv, 1980).

35. Moshe Bar-Asher, *Language Studies*, vols. 2–3 (Jerusalem, 1987; in Hebrew). Joseph Naveh and Shaul Shaked, *Amulets and Magic Bowls* (Jerusalem, 1985), and J. N. Epstein, *Studies in Talmudic Literature and Semitic Languages*, 1 (Jerusalem, 1983; in Hebrew); are important resources as well.

36. Casper Levias, *A Grammar of Galilean Aramaic*, intro. Michael Sokoloff (New York, 1986; in Hebrew).

37. H. Y. Kasowski and B. Kasowski, *ʾOtṣar leshon haTalmud* (Jerusalem, 1954–82), 41 vols.; B. Kasowski, *ʾOtṣar hashemot laTalmud haBavli* (Jerusalem 1976–83), 5 vols.; Moshe Kosovsky, *Concordance to the Talmud Yerushalmi* [in Hebrew], 3 vols. to date, and *Onomasticon: Thesaurus of Proper Names* (Jerusalem 1979–).

38. Daniel Sperber, "Greek and Latin Words in Rabbinic Literature," *Bar-Ilan Annual* 14–15 (1977), pp. 9–60; 16–17 (1977), pp. 9–30; idem, *A Dictionary of Greek and Latin Legal Terms in Rabbinic Literature* (Ramat Gan, 1984); idem, *Nautica Talmudica* (Ramat Gan, 1986).

39. See, e.g., Yehuda Feliks, *Talmud Yerushalmi. Tractate Sheviit. Critically Edited. A Study of the Halachic Topics and Their Botanical and Agricultural Bakground* (Jerusalem, 1979–86), 2 vols.; Meir Ayali, *A Nomenclature of Workers and Artisans in the Talmud and Midrashic Literature* (Israel, 1984; in Hebrew).

40. E. S. Rosenthal, "For the Talmudic Dictionary—Talmudica Iranica," in *Irano-Judaica*, ed. Saul Shaked (Jerusalem, 1982; in Hebrew), pp. 38–134. See also Baruch M. Bokser, "Talmudic Names for Iranian Festivals," *Journal of the American Oriental Society* 95 (1975), pp. 261–62, revised in Jacob Neusner, *Talmudic Judaism in Sasanian Babylonia* (Leiden, 1976), pp. 178–80.

41. Moreshet, *Lexicon*; B. Kasowski, *ʾOtṣar leshon haTannaim: Mekhilta d'Rabbi Ishmael* (Jerusalem, 1965–66), 4 vols.: *Sifra-Torat Kohanim* (Jerusalem, 1967–69), 4 vols.: *Sifrei Numeri et Deuteronomium* (Jerusalem, 1971–75), 5 vols.

42. Friedman's forthcoming index of studies of Talmudic terms and passages (Shamma Friedman, "New Bibliographic and Textual Tools for Talmudic Research," *Proceedings of the Ninth World Congress of Jewish Studies* [1986], Division C, pp. 31–37) will supplement whatever bibliographical references the new Aramaic dictionaries and lexicons may contain.

43. Sperber, *Legal Terms*, p. 18.

44. Saul Lieberman, "How Much Greek in Jewish Palestine" (1962), reprinted in his *Texts and Studies* (New York, 1974), pp. 216–34; Emil Schürer, *The History of the Jewish People in the Age of Jesus Christ (175 B.C.–A.D. 135). A New English Version*, rev. and ed. Geza Vermes, Fergus Millar, and Matthew Black (Edinburgh, 1979), vol. 2, esp. pp. 52–80; Alan J. Avery-Peck, *Mishnah's Division of Agriculture* (Chico, Calif., 1985). See also Moshe Assis, "On the Question of the Redaction of Yerushalmi Neziqin," *Tarbiz* 56 (1987), pp. 162–65 [in Hebrew], on loanwords in PT *Neziqin*; and Bokser, "Recent Developments," p. 7.

45. See, e.g., Saul Lieberman, *Talmud of Caesarea* [suppl. to *Tarbiz* 2] (Jerusalem, 1931; in Hebrew); Rosenthal, "Hamoreh"; Jacob Neusner, *The Talmud of the Land of Israel*, vol. 35, *Introduction: Taxonomy* (Chicago, 1983); Baruch M. Bokser, "Yerushalmi Pesaḥim. An Annotated Translation" (Chicago; forthcoming).

46. Baruch M. Bokser, *Samuel's Commentary on the Mishnah: Its Nature, Forms, and Content* (Leiden, 1975); idem, *Post Mishnaic Judaism in Transition* (Chico, Calif., 1980).

47. See also Dov Zlotnick, "Memory and the Integrity of the Oral Tradition," *Journal of the Ancient Near Eastern Society* 16–17 (1984–85), pp. 229–41 [printed in 1987].

48. See also Shamma Friedman, "Some Structural Patterns of Talmudic Sugyot," *Proceedings of the Sixth World Congress of Jewish Studies* (1977), vol. 3, pp. 389–402; Jacob Neusner, *Judaism: The Classical Statement. The Evidence of the Bavli* (Chicago, 1986); idem, *The Oral Torah* (San Francisco, 1986); Abraham Weiss, *Studies in the Literature of the Amoraʾim* (New York, 1962; in Hebrew); Goldberg, "Babylonian Talmud."

Baruch M. Bokser

49. David Goodblatt, *Rabbinic Instruction in Sasanian Babylonia* (Leiden, 1975); and idem, "New Developments in the Investigation of the Babylonian Yeshivot," *Zion* 46 (1981), pp. 14–38 [in Hebrew], which was initially rejected by Isaiah Gafni, "Yeshiva and Metivta," *Zion* 43 (1978), pp. 12–37 [in Hebrew], but then basically accepted in Gafni, "The Babylonian Yeshiva as Reflected in *Bava Qamma* 117a," *Tarbiz* 49 (1980), pp. 292–301 [in Hebrew] (on Geonic patterns affecting the understanding and reporting of amoraic materials), and in Gafni, "On the Talmudic Chronology in *ʾIggeret Sherira Gaon*," *Zion* 52 (1986), pp. 1–24 [in Hebrew] (on Geonic chronicles anachronistically treating the institutional framework of the sages). This position receives further support from Daniel Sperber, "On the Unfortunate Adventures of Rav Kahana," in *Irano-Judaica*, ed. Shaul Shaked (Jerusalem, 1982), pp. 83–100 [and xi], which argues that a Bavli account of a purported Palestinian academic setting is postamoraic and reflects post-Talmudic Babylonian practices. Cf. Isaiah Gafni, "The Historical Background," in *The Literature of the Sages* (Philadelphia, 1987).

50. Richard Kalmin, "Relationships among Diverse Groups of Amoraim during the Amoraic Period" (paper presented at annual meeting of the Association for Jewish Studies, December 1987); David Kraemer, "Compositional Intent and Meaning in the Bavli" (paper presented at annual meeting of the Society of Biblical Literature, December 1987).

51. See esp. Rosenthal, "History of the Text"; Goldberg, "Babylonian Talmud."

52. Cf. the attempt by David Kraemer, "Stylistic Characteristics of Amoraic Literature" (Ph.D. diss., Jewish Theological Seminary of America, 1984).

53. David (Weiss) Halivni, *Midrash, Mishnah, and Gemara* (Cambridge, Mass., 1986), p. 142, n. 16.

54. See Bokser, "Yerushalmi *Pesaḥim*."

55. See, in particular, Goldberg, "Babylonian Talmud," pp. 330–31, on the gemara's use of abstract concepts and categories. Cf. the oral dimension of tannaitic teachings, discussed in Jacob Neusner, *The Memorized Torah: The Mnemonic System of the Mishnah* (Chico, Calif., 1985); Zlotnick, "Oral Tradition."

56. C. Mackenzie Brown, "Purana as Scripture: From Sound to Image of the Holy Word in the Hindu Tradition," *History of Religions* 26 (1986); p. 85, n. 69. Cf. Robert W. Thompson, "The Reception of Greek Literature in Armenia," in *Greek Connections*, ed. John T. A. Koumoulides (South Bend, Ind., 1987), on the impact of the *fifth-century* fashioning of an Armenian script that enabled a small group of scholars rapidly to write down Armenian literature and compose original works in Armenian; and Werner H. Kebber, "Biblical Hermeneutics and the Ancient Art of Communication: A Response," and Herbert N. Schneidau, "Let the Reader Understand," both in *Semeia* 30 (1987), pp. 99 (Kebber), 144 (Schneidau).

57. E. Z. Melammed, *An Introduction to Talmudic Literature* (Jerusalem, 1973; in Hebrew).

58. Goodblatt, "Babylonian Talmud," p. 287.

59. Epstein, *Nusaḥ*, pp. 782–801; Saul Lieberman, *Hellenism in Jewish Palestine* (New York, 1950), pp. 97–99. See, e.g., PT *Pesahim* 4:3. Goldberg, "Palestinian Talmud," p. 311, in this regard is thus perplexing.

60. Ḥanokh Albeck, *Introduction to the Talmud, Babli and Yerushalmi* (Tel Aviv, 1969; in Hebrew); Epstein, *Nusaḥ*; idem, *Introduction to Tannaitic Literature* (Jerusalem, 1957; in Hebrew), Rosenthal, "Hamoreh."

61. David (Weiss) Halivni, *Sources and Traditions: A Source Critical Commentary* [in Hebrew]: *Seder Nashim* (Tel Aviv, 1968), *Seder Moed from Yoma to Hagiga* (Jerusalem, 1975), *Tractate Sabbath* and *Tractates Erubin and Pesahim* (Jerusalem, 1982). See also, e.g., Israel Francus, "Additions and Parallels in T.B. *Bava Qamma* VII," *Bar-Ilan Annual* 12 (1974), pp. 43–63 and ix [in Hebrew]; Noah Aminoah, *The Redaction of the Tractate Qiddushin in the Babylonian Talmud. Compilation, Redaction, Textual Readings, Parallel Sugyot* (Tel Aviv,

1977; in Hebrew); idem, *The Redaction of the Tractate Betza, Rosh-Hashana and Taánith in the Babylonian Talmud* (Tel Aviv, 1986); I. D. Gilat, "Lo Titgodedu," *Bar-Ilan Annual* 18–19 (1981), pp. 79–98 [in Hebrew].

62. Goldberg, "Babylonian Talmud," p. 334.

63. Neusner, *Sources*: cf. Arnold Goldberg, "Der Diskurs in babylonischen Talmud. Anregungen fuer eine Diskursanalyse," *Frankfurter judäistische Beiträge* 11 (1983), pp. 1–45, on which see Schäfer, "Research," p. 145.

64. See David Kraemer, "Compositional Intent and Meaning in the Bavli"; cf. Epstein, *Nusaḥ*, pp. 817–76; Shamma Friedman, "TNY' and TNN" (forthcoming). See also Bokser, "Palestinian Talmud," pp. 173–78 and references there, esp. to Lieberman; Judy Hauptman, *The Development of the Talmudic Sugya: Relationship between Tannaitic and Amoraic Sources* (Lanham, Md., 1988).

65. Goodblatt, "Babylonian Talmud," speaks of "variant versions," "quotations," "parallel pericopae," and "inconsistencies within a pericope."

66. Rosenthal, "History of the Text." Two BT *Pesaḥim* traditions exemplify the subtle dynamics and problems. First, at BT *Pesaḥim* 109a a tradition stating when women do or do not recline during the Passover evening meal seems to be the result of the conflation of two alternative explanations of an originally briefer tradition; yet the PT contains one version of the expanded tradition. Does this mean that in amoraic times, the conflation had already taken place, or that the PT merely attests an early date for an interpretation (and expansion) of the original briefer comment, or that the PT text was corrupted based on the BT? Second, at 119b a problematic text defining the term *'afiqomen* is clearly an expanded text and the briefer version, attested in the Columbia Manuscript and elsewhere, accords with the version in the PT and the social use of the foods in question. Apparently a scribe (?) who noted BT *Berakhot* 47a's mention of these same foods misunderstood the import of that reference and corrupted the BT *Pesaḥim* passage.

67. Saul Lieberman, *Siphre Zutta* (New York, 1968; in Hebrew); idem, "A Few Words by Julian the Architect of Ascalon. The Laws of Palestine and Its Customs," *Tarbiz* 40 (1971), pp. 409–17 [in Hebrew]; E. S. Rosenthal, ed. and "Introduction," *Yerushalmi Neziqin from the Escorial Manuscript* (Jerusalem, 1983; in Hebrew). See Bokser, "Palestinian Talmud," pp. 192–94; Assis, "Redaction"; Jacob Sussmann, "Yerushalmi *Neziqin*" (paper delivered at the Ninth World Congress of Jewish Studies, Jerusalem, August 1985); Gerd A. Wewers, *Probleme der Bavot-Traktate* (Tübingen, 1984); Saul Lieberman, "Introduction and Commentary" to *Yerushalmi Neziqin*, ed. E. S. Rosenthal (Jerusalem, 1983); cf. Goldberg, "Palestinian Talmud," pp. 313–14.

68. See, in particular, Neusner, *Taxonomy*; Sussmann, "Neziqin."

69. Lieberman, *On the Yerushalmi*; idem, *Caesarea*; see esp. Rosenthal, "HaMoreh."

70. Ḥanokh Albeck and J. Theodor, eds. *Bereschit Rabba*, 2d ed. (Jerusalem, 1965), 3 vols., conveniently assembles these parallels. See Baruch M. Bokser, "A Minor for Zimmun and Recensions of Yerushalmi," *AJS Review* 4 (1979), pp. 1–25; idem, *Post Mishnaic*, pp. 92–102.

71. Jacob Sussmann, "A Halakhic Inscription from the Beth-Shean Valley," *Tarbiz* 43 (1974), pp. 88–158 [in Hebrew]; idem, "The Boundaries of Eretz-Israel," *Tarbiz* 45 (1976), pp. 213–57 [in Hebrew]; idem, "The Inscription in the Synagogue at Rehob," in *Ancient Synagogues Revealed*, ed. Lee Levine (Jerusalem, 1981), pp. 146–53.

72. E.g., Weiss, *Studies*; J. N. Epstein, *Introduction to Amoraitic Literature* (Jerusalem, 1962; in Hebrew); Rosenthal, "History of the Text"; David Rosenthal, "Ancient Redactions in the Babylonian Talmud," *Proceedings of the Ninth World Congress of Jewish Studies* 9 (1986), Division C, pp. 7–14; Aminoah, *Betza*; see Goodblatt, "Babylonian Talmud."

73. See esp. Abraham Goldberg, "The Sources and Development of the *Sugya* in the Babylonian Talmud," *Tarbiz* 32 (1962–63), pp. 143–52 [in Hebrew]; David Rosenthal, "Pirqa

Baruch M. Bokser

de'Abbaye (TB *Rosh Ha'Shana*) II," *Tarbiz* 46 (1977), pp. 97–109 [in Hebrew]; Aminoah, *Betza.*

74. See Goodblatt's important observation on this point; "Babylonian Talmud," pp. 304–7.

75. Jacob Neusner, *A History of the Mishnaic Law of Purities* (Leiden, 1974–77), 22 vols.; Hyman Klein, *Collected Talmudic Scientific Writings of Hyman Klein* [from 1947–48, 1952–53, 1959–60, 1960–61], ed. and intro. Abraham Goldberg (Jerusalem, 1979); M. S. Feldbium, "The Impact of the Anonymous Sugyah on Halakhic Concepts," *Proceedings of the Armerican Academy for Jewish Research* 38 (1986), pp. 19–28; Halivni, *Sources and Traditions* (1975, 1982); idem, *Midrash;* Friedman, "Structural Patterns"; idem, "Critical Study." Goodblatt, "Babylonian Talmud," pp. 291–318, extensively discusses this development.

76. E.g., Aminoah, *Qiddushin;* idem, *Betza;* Francus, "Additions"; Baruch M. Bokser, "Maᶜal and Blessings Over Food: Rabbinic Transformations of Cultic Terminology and Alternative Modes of Piety," *Journal of Biblical Literature* 100 (1981), pp. 557–74; David Kraemer, "The Scientific Study of Talmud," *Judaism* 36 (1987), pp. 471–78.

77. Kraemer, "Stylistic," and Richard Kalmin, *The Post-Rav Ashi Amoraim: Transition or Continuity? A Study of the Role of the Final Generations of Amoraim in the Redaction of the Talmud* (Ann Arbor, 1985) [summarized in *AJS Review* 11 (1986), pp. 157–85], dissertations written under Halivni, aimed at refining and proving these points; see also Richard Kalmin, *Late Amoraim and the Redaction of the Babylonian Talmud* (Cincinnati, 1989), where he makes important revisions, such as those he suggested in "Relationships among Diverse Groups of Amoraim during the Amoraic Period."

78. Halivni, *Sources* (1975), "Introduction" (1982): idem, *Midrash*; Friedman, "Critical Study"; Kalmin, *Post-Rav Ashi*; idem, *Late Amoraim.*

79. Goldberg, "Babylonian Talmud." See, on the Savora'im, Jacob E. Ephrati, *The Savoraic Period and Its Literature* (Petaḥ Tikva, 1973; in Hebrew), and Jacob S. Spiegel, "Comments and Late Additions in the Babylonian Talmud," *Te'uda* 3 (1983), pp. 91–112 [in Hebrew]; and in general, Melammed, *Introduction,* and Goodblatt, "Babylonian Talmud."

80. Cf. Martin S. Jaffee, "The Babylonian Appropriation of the Talmud Yerushalmi," *New Perspectives on Ancient Judaism*, vol. 4, ed. Alan J. Avery-Peck (Lanham, Md., 1989), pp. 3–27.

81. See Goldberg, "Babylonian Talmud," which suggests that the middle part of discussions were deleted when they were transported to Babylonia.

82. Neusner, *Classical;* idem, *Oral.*

83. Weiss, *Studies.*

84. Cf. Eliezer L. Segal, "The *Petiḥta* is Babylonia," *Tarbiz* 44 (1984), pp. 177–204 [in Hebrew], for the beginning of such a project; and idem, "The TB Megillah Esther Midrash and the Study of Babylonian Aggadah" (paper delivered at Association for Jewish Studies annual conference, December 1987), on redactional adaptations of the traditions, though Segal's theory of the text remains unclear; cf. Tabory "Esther Rabbah."

85. See Baruch M. Bokser, "Maᶜal"; idem, "The Wall Separating God and Israel," *Jewish Quarterly Review* 73 (1983), pp. 349–74.

86. David J. Halperin, *The Merkabah in Rabbinic Literature* (New Haven, Conn., 1980); Anthony Saldarini, "Varieties of Rabbinic Responses to the Destruction of the Temple," *Society of Biblical Literature Seminar Papers* 21 (1982), pp. 437–58; Robert Goldenberg, "Early Rabbinic Explanations of the Destruction of Jerusalem," *Journal of Jewish Studies* 33 (1982), pp. 517–25. Texts on the chariot or the destruction might be catalogued as part of the third unit.

87. See, on cases, Jacob Neusner, *A History of the Jews in Babylonia* (Leiden, 1966–70), vols. 3–5, whose results are confirmed by Isaiah Gafni, "Maᶜaśe bet-din beTalmud ha-

Bavli," *Proceedings of the American Academy for Jewish Research* 49 (1982), Hebrew section, pp. 23–40; and, on narratives, in particular Yonah Fraenkel, "Hermeneutical Problems in the Study of the Aggadic Narrative," *Tarbiz* 47 (1978), pp. 139–72 [in Hebrew]; and idem, *Studies in the Spiritual World of the Aggadic Tale* (Tel Aviv, 1981; in Hebrew). See Baruch M. Bokser, "Wonder-Working and the Rabbinic Tradition," *Journal for the Study of Judaism in the Persian, Hellenistic and Roman Period* 16 (1985), pp. 42–92; Joseph M. Davis, "Literary Studies of Aggadic Narrative. A Bibliography," in *New Perspectives on Ancient Judaism*, vol. 3, ed. Jacob Neusner and E. S. Frerichs (Lanham, Md., 1987), pp. 185–218; and cf. Goldberg's review of these forms, in "Babylonian Talmud."

88. Cf. the situation regarding the midrashic *petiḥtot*, which scholars today recognize as literary creations; Richard Sarason, "The Petiḥtot in Leviticus Rabba: 'Oral Homilies' or Redactional Constructions?" *Journal of Jewish Studies* 33 (1982), pp. 557–67, and the literature cited there; Jacob Neusner, *From Tradition to Imitation: The Plan and Program of Pesiqta Rabbati and Pesiqta deRab Kahana* (Atlanta, 1987).

89. Neusner, *Oral;* idem, *Sources.*

90. Goodblatt, "Babylonian Talmud."

91. Halivni, *Sources* (1982), "Introduction," and *Midrash.* Some scholars such as B. M. Lewin, *Rabbanan Savoraʾei we-talmudam* (Jerusalem, 1937), and Goldberg, "Babylonian Talmud," suggest that Saboraʾim introduce the tractates with an opening long *sugya.*

92. Cf. Goldberg, "Babylonian Talmud," which repeats the "persecution" theory.

93. See Goodblatt, "Babylonian Talmud"; Halivni, *Midrash.*

94. For the aesthetics of these corpora and attempts to identify their perspectives, see Baruch M. Bokser, "Rabbinic Responses to Catastrophe," *Proceedings of the American Academy for Jewish Research* 50 (1983), p. 47, n. 21; idem, *The Origins of the Seder: The Passover Rite and Early Rabbinic Judaism* (Berkeley, 1984); idem, "Approaching Sacred Space," *Harvard Theological Review* 78 (1985), pp. 279–99; idem, "Recent Developments" (note esp. Lieberman, *Zutta*), to which add Abraham Goldberg, "The Repeated Expositions in *Mekhilta deMilluʾim*," *Sinai* 89 (1981), pp. 115–18 [in Hebrew]; Saldarini, "Responses"; idem, *Scholastic Rabbinism* (Chico, Calif., 1982); Fraade, "Sifre"; Norman J. Cohen, "Analysis of an Exegetic Tradition in the *Mekhilta de-Rabbi Ishmael*: The Meaning of 'Amanah' in the Second and Third Centuries," *AJS Review* 9 (1984), pp. 1–25; Noam Zohar, "The Living and the Dead in the March of Redemption—Editing and Meaning in *Mekhilta de-Rabbi Yishmaʾel*—an Interpretation of the First *Parshah* of 'Massekhet Beshalah," *Jerusalem Studies in Jewish Thought* 4/3–4 (1984–85), pp. 223–36, xxvii–xxviii [in Hebrew]; Jacob Neusner, *Sifra: Parshiyyot Negaim and Mesora* (Chico, Calif., 1985); idem, *Sifre to Numbers: An American Translation and Explanation* (Atlanta, 1986), 2 vols.; idem, *Sifre Deuteronomy* (Atlanta, 1987), 3 vols.; Jacob Elbaum, "From Sermon to Story: The Transformation of the Akedah," *Prooftexts* 6 (1986), pp. 97–116; Howard Eilberg-Schwartz, *The Human Will in Judaism* (Atlanta, 1986); and Baruch M. Bokser, "Messianism, the Exodus Pattern, and Early Rabbinic Judaism," in *The Messiah in Early Judaism and Christianity*, ed. J. Charlesworth (forthcoming).

Not only sophisticated students of the halakha—such as Gilat, "Titgodedu"; Zvi Arie Steinfeld, "Towards Understanding the Prohibition of 'Foods Cooked by Gentiles," *Sidra* 2 (1986), pp. 125–43 [in Hebrew]; Francus, "Additions"; and Halivni—but also those interested in nonlegal materials—such as the accounts of the "four who entered *Pardes*," the "escape of Yohanan ben Zakkai," or the "rise of Hillel"—have seen the need to compare divergent versions of a pericope or set of traditions. The focus on a document's literary characteristics, however, is necessary to harness critical work for historical interpretation. See, e.g., W. S. Green, "Palestinian Holy Men: Charismatic Leadership and Rabbinic Tradition," *Aufstieg und Niedergang der römischen Welt* 2:19/2 (1979), pp. 619–47; esp. idem, "What's

Baruch M. Bokser

in a Name?'' *Approaches to Ancient Judaism* 1 (1980), pp. 77–96; Bokser, "Ma'al"; idem, "Responses"; "Wonder-Working"; idem, "Changing Views of Passover and the Meaning of Redemption according to the Palestinian Talmud," *AJS Review* 10 (1985), pp. 1–18; idem, "Todos and Rabbinic Authority in Rome," in *New Perspectives on Ancient Judaism*, vol. 1: *Religion, Literature, and Society in Ancient Israel, Formative Christianity and Judaism*, ed. Jacob Neusner and E. S. Frerichs (Lanham, Md., 1987), pp. 117–30; idem, "Reasons and Rationales for the Commandments," *Proceedings of the Rabbinical Assembly* 49 (1989), pp. 235–44. See also Jacob Neusner, *Messiah in Context* (Philadelphia, 1984); idem, *Torah: From Scroll to Symbol in Formative Judaism* (Philadelphia, 1985); and the programmatic idem, *Canon and Connection* (Lanham, Md., 1987); Richard Sarason "The Significance of the Land of Israel in the Mishnah," in *The Land of Israel: Jewish Perspectives*, ed. Lawrence A. Hoffman (Notre Dame, Ind., 1986), pp. 109–36. This approach provides a new means to evaluate the longstanding issue of the parallels between Josephus and rabbinic literature, as demonstrated by Shaye J. D. Cohen, "Parallel Tradition in Josephus and Rabbinic Literature," *Proceedings of the Ninth World Congress of Jewish Studies* 9 (1986), Division B, pp. 7–14. Cf. also idem, *From the Maccabees to the Mishnah* (Philadelphia, 1987).

95. Neusner, *Classical*; Bokser, *Post Mishnaic*; Arnold M. Eisen, *Galut* (Bloomington, Ind., 1986), pp. 35–56, to which cf. Luipold Wallach, "A Palestinian Polemic Against Idolatry," *Hebrew Union College Annual* 19 (1946), pp. 389–404, and Gary G. Porton, "Forbidden Transactions: Prohibited Commerce with Gentiles in Earliest Rabbinism," in *"To See Ourselves as Others See Us"*, ed. Jacob Neusner and E. Frerichs (Chico, Calif., 1985), pp. 317–35; Martin S. Jaffee, *The Talmud of Babylonia: An American Translation*, vol. 26: *Tractate Horayot* (Atlanta, 1987).

96. Cf. Abraham Goldberg, "Palestinian Law in Babylonian Tradition, as Revealed in a Study of *Pereq ʿArvei Pesaḥim*," *Tarbiz* 33 (1963–64), pp. 337–48 [in Hebrew]; idem, "Rabbi Zeira and Babylonian Customs in Palestine," *Tarbiz* 36 (1966–67), pp. 319–41 [in Hebrew]; Bokser, "Wall," which attempts to assess such a problem; esp. David Goodblatt, "The Story of the Plot against R. Simeon b. Gamaliel II," *Zion* 49 (1984), pp. 349–74, [in Hebrew].

97. Cf. Jacob Neusner, *Judaism: The Evidence of the Mishnah* (Chicago, 1981); Martin Goodman, *State and Society in Roman Galilee* (Totowa, N.J., 1983); Saldarini, "Reconstructions"; Gafni, "Background"; S. Cohen, *From the Maccabees*.

98. Neusner, *Babylonia*; Moshe Beer, *The Babylonian Exilarchate in the Arsacid and Sassanian Periods* (Tel Aviv, 1970; in Hebrew); idem, *The Babylonian Amoraim: Aspects of Economic Life* (Ramat Gan, 1974; in Hebrew); idem, "Notes on Three Edicts against the Jews of Babylonia in the Third Century C.E.," in *Irano-Judaica*, ed. Shaul Shaked (Jerusalem, 1982; in Hebrew), pp. 25–37; Goodblatt, *Instruction;* idem, "The Poll Tax in Sasanian Babylonia," *Journal for the Economic and Social History of the Orient* 22 (1979), pp. 233–95; Isaiah Gafni, *Babylonian Jewry and Its Institutions in the Period of the Talmud* (Jerusalem, 1976; in Hebrew); idem, "Babylonian Yeshiva"; idem, "Nestorian Literature as a Source for the History of the Babylonian Yeshivot," *Tarbiz* 51 (1981–82), pp. 567–76 [in Hebrew]; Rosenthal, "Talmudica Iranica"; Aharon Oppenheimer, *Babylonia Judaica in the Talmudic Period* (Wiesbaden, 1983), a study of the Talmudic geographical references.

99. See the works listed in Bokser, "Palestinian Talmud," pp. 195–99, to which add the studies by Strange, drawing on archaeological discoveries illuminating Judaism; the revised Schürer on the cultural setting of Palestine; Baras's collection of studies on Palestine— esp. vol. 2 on art and archaeology; Dan, on the city; Levine on the status and role of Palestinian sages (with extensive bibliography); and Yahalom, on Byzantine Palestine. See J. F. Strange, "Archaeology and the Religion of Judaism in Palestine," *Aufstieg und Niedergang der römischen Welt* 2:19/1 (1979), pp. 646–85; Schürer-Vermes, Millar, Black, *History,*

110

vol. 2, pp. 1–84; Z. Baras et al., *Eretz Israel from the Destruction of the Second Temple to the Muslin Conquest* (Jerusalem, 1982–84; in Hebrew); 2 vols.; Yaron Dan, *The City in Eretz-Israel during the Late Roman and Byzantine Periods* (Jerusalem, 1984; in Hebrew); Lee Levine, *The Rabbinic Class in Palestine during the Talmudic Period* (Jerusalem, 1985; in Hebrew [English ed. forthcoming]); Yosef Yahalom, *Poetic Language in the Early Piyyut* (Jerusalem, 1985; in Hebrew), pp. 31–40.

100. Jacob Neusner, *Judaism in Society* (Chicago, 1983).

101. Neusner, *Canon.*

102. Louis Ginzberg, *A Commentary on the Palestinian Talmud,* vol. 1 (New York, 1941; in Hebrew, with Hebrew and English Introductions); Goldberg, "Babylonian Talmud"; Saul Lieberman, *Greek in Jewish Palestine* (New York, 1942), pp. 110–11.

103. Neusner, *Classical*; and, e.g., Sperber, "Rav Kahana"; David Goodblatt, "Towards the Rehabilitation of Talmudic History," in *History of Judaism: The Next Ten Years,* ed. Baruch M. Bokser (Chico, Calif., 1980), pp. 31–44; idem, "Plot"; Bokser, "Todos"; esp. idem, "Wonder-Working," and the literature cited there.

104. For earlier efforts in this regard, see the diverse works by Neusner, esp. *The Religious Study of Judaism: Description. Analysis, Interpretation* (Lanham, Md., 1986), 3 vols.; and idem, *Canon*; Bokser, *Origins*; Eilberg-Schwartz, *Human-Will*; Harvey E. Goldberg, *Judaism Viewed from Within and from Without* (Albany, 1987), esp. "Introduction," and Zvi Zohar, "The Consumption of Sabbatical Year Produce in Biblical and Rabbinic Literature," pp. 75–106; Reuven Kimelman, "The Šemaʿ and Its Blessings: The Realization of God's Kingship," in *The Synagogue in Late Antiquity,* ed. Lee Levine (Philadelphia, 1987). pp. 73–86.

105. In addition to the older studies collected in Fischel, *Essays in Greco-Roman and Related Literature* (New York, 1977), in particular the one by the editor, see the discussions in David Stern, "Moses-cide, Midrash, and Contemporary Literary Criticism," *Prooftexts* 4 (1984), pp. 193–203; idem, "Literary Criticism or Literary Homilies," *Prooftexts* 5 (1985), pp. 96–103; Fraade, "Interpreting Midrash," pp. 179–94, 284–300; Howard Eilberg-Schwartz "Where the Reader Is in the Write," *Prooftexts* 7 (1987), pp. 194–205; and esp. W. S. Green, "Romancing the Tome: Rabbinic Hermeneutics and the Theory of Literature," *Semeia* 40 (1987), pp. 147–68.

106. Lawrence A. Hoffman, *Beyond the Text* (Bloomington, Ind., 1987), p. 16.

107. Baruch M. Bokser, "Ritualizing the Seder," *Journal of the American Academy of Religion* 56 (1988), pp. 443–71.

108. See Green, "Romancing"; Richard G. Martin, "Text and Contextuality in Reference to Islam," *Semeia* 40 (1987), pp. 125–45.

109. See also Aminoah, *Qiddushin*; idem, *Betza;* and cf. Jacob E. Ephrathi, *The Trial of the Akedah* (Petaḥ Tiqva, 1983; in Hebrew), on analogous problems in *Genesis Rabba.*

110. These projects cover the Mishna and Tosefta, the Yerushalmi (Chicago, 1982–), and the Bavli (Chico, Calif., 1984–), in addition to various midrashic texts; see the list in Neusner, *Oral*, pp. 217–21. Reflecting a similar desire to make rabbinic works more accessible are translations to midrashic works by Goldin, Saldarini, Braude, and Hammer. Most relevant for this study is the German Yerushalmi translation project *Übersetzung des Talmud Yerushalmi* (Tübingen), ed. Martin Hengel, Jacob Neusner, Hans Peter Rüger, and Peter Schäfer. Other than *Berakhot,* which was translated by Charles Horowitz, in 1975, the remaining eight volumes to date were translated by Gerd A. Wewers: I/2, *Pea* (1986); I/6 *Terumot* (1985); II/1, *Ḥagiga* (1983); IV/1–3, *Bavot* (1982); IV/4, *Sanhedrin* (1981); IV/5–6, *Makkot and Shevuʿot* (1983); IV/7, ʿ*Avoda Zara* (1980); IV/8, *Horayot* (1984).

111. Of special interest is how a formulation may suggest that different literary components derive from different sources and how these sources have been combined to form new units; and how patterned language may be superimposed on these new larger units.

112. Neusner, *Purities.*

113. See also Shamma Friedman, "The Woman with Two Husbands in the Talmud and in Ancient Near Eastern Law," *Shenaton haMishpat ha'Ivri* 2 (1975), pp. 360–82 [in Hebrew].

114. Fraenkel, "Hermeneutical Problems"; idem, *Studies.* The failure in this regard by Yochanan Breuer, "Perfect and Participle in Description of Rituals in the Mishnah," *Tarbiz* 56 (1987), pp. 299–326 [in Hebrew], flaws an otherwise excellent article on narratives; cf. Bokser, *Origins.* See also Wallach, "Idolatry"; Fischel, *Essays,* pp. 443–72.

115. Bokser, *Origins,* and idem, "Ritualizing," provide full documentation for these examples. See also the more general "Recent Developments."

116. Epstein, *Tannaitic,* p. 334; Lieberman, *Tosefta Ki-fshuṭah,* vol. 4, p. 654.

117. Cf. Goldberg. "Babylonian Talmud."

118. Halivni, *Sources, Pesaḥim,* pp. 590–92.

119. See Lawrence A. Hoffman, "A Symbol of Salvation in the Passover Haggadah," *Worship* 52 (1979), pp. 519–37; Bokser, *Origins;* idem, "Ritualizing."

120. Tzvee Zahavy, "Recent Methodological Advances in the American School of Talmudic Scholarship," Dworsky Center for Jewish Studies, *Occasional Paper* 1 (Minneapolis, 1987).

I thank Shaye Cohen, David Goodblatt, and Richard Kalmin for their comments on earlier drafts of this paper.

Medieval Judaism

8

MEDIEVAL JEWISH STUDIES: TOWARD AN ANTHROPOLOGICAL HISTORY OF THE JEWS

Ivan G. Marcus

Approaching the end of the twentieth century, we find ourselves increasingly aware of living in a postmodern time. Ironically, at this very same time there is a new appreciation for the premodern or medieval past. In an "op-ed" piece in late 1978, the eminent American architect Philip Johnson, writing about shifting styles in architecture, said: " 'Modern' hated history, we love it. 'Modern' hated symbols, we love them. . . . Why the new interest in Eastern religion and in all religions? Maybe reason itself isn't the only solution. Maybe tradition, maybe things of the heart count. Maybe progress isn't the only way. The whole world ideology is making a subtle shift."[1]

And medieval studies are flourishing as never before. In addition to the annual meetings of a few hundred of the more senior fellows and fellow travelers of the august Medieval Academy of America, each May thousands of enthusiastic medievalists from all over North America and even Europe go on pilgrimages to Kalamazoo, Michigan, the Jerusalem of American medievalists today.

Not long ago, the host institution of that conference, the Medieval Institute of Western Michigan University, published a book detailing the growth of medieval studies especially since the late 1960s. *Medieval Studies in North America: Past, Present, and Future*[2] surveys the field from the time President Eliot of Harvard appointed the young Henry Adams assistant professor of medieval history in 1870 to the year of publication, 1982.

When that first academic appointment was made, Adams later recalled, he protested his lack of competence. President Eliot replied, "If you will point out to me any one who knows more, Mr. Adams, I will appoint him."[3]

The book goes on to chart the gradual growth of the field over its first hundred years, and its extraordinary takeoff in the last twenty. Some 250 pages list the hundreds of journals and newsletters, regional conferences, associations, and academic programs in medieval studies in North America, most of which have come into existence in recent years. Indeed, the book documents the striking fact that more activity in medieval studies has occurred in the last twenty years than in the previous hundred. This pattern argues for a cultural shift today that is fostering a renewed interest in things medieval, a hunger for premodern roots and values partly channeled into academic pursuits. It may not betoken another Decline of the West but rather a dissatisfaction with the recent, modern West, and a search for an earlier, medieval one. Postmodernism has another name—neomedievalism.

The Jewish academic world has not been immune to these trends in the general culture. Even as punctilious a scholar as the late, great S. D. Goitein recalled his early traditional Jewish background as an aid in helping him study medieval religions with the remark "I, too, once was a medieval man; now, I am a medievalist, which is, of course, quite a different matter."[4]

Medieval studies have been a staple of Jewish scholarship from the early nineteenth-century beginnings of *jüdische Wissenschaft*. Outstanding pioneering efforts include the biographical research essays by Galician rabbi Solomon Judah Leib Rapoport (Shir) of Geonic figures (such as Saadia and Hai), and of the prolific liturgical poet Eliezer Kallir and of Nathan ben Jehiel of Rome, author of the *Arukh* dictionary.[5] In so doing, Rapoport stimulated the methodologically sound study of medieval rabbinic literature. He also traced the two fundamental cultural transmission routes of medieval Judaism, that of Palestine-Italy-Germany-Western Europe—(Ashkenazic Judaism)—on the one hand, and of Babylonia-North Africa-Spain—(Sephardic Judaism) on the other.[6] He also set in motion a preference for historical biography—or, more accurately, for history written as biography—a pattern that persists to our own day.

In the works of Zunz, Rapoport, Graetz, Güdemann, among many others, the basic historical picture of Jewish life and letters was reconstructed and, with it, a decided preference for the Gaonic-Sephardic cultural sphere emerged. With the notable exception of Zunz's biography of Rashi[7] and of Moritz Güdemann's great history of Jewish culture,[8] the lure of Baghdad and Cordova was greater than that of Mainz and Troyes, in the West, and of Cracow and Vilna, in the East. This preference for what I have referred to as the Sephardic Mystique[9] has colored Jewish culture and medieval Jewish scholarship to this day. It is reflected, for example, in the extraordinary number of conferences held to mark the 850th anniversary of the traditional birth date of the avatar of the Sephardic Mystique—Maimonides;[10] and it will be even more noticeable in the conferences, volumes, and exhibitions that are being planned to mark the year 1992, the five hundredth anniversary of the expulsion of the Jews from Christian Spain. Granted that Maimonides and medieval Spanish Jewry were of extraordinary historical importance, the degree of their present cultural significance says as much about those who celebrate as it does about the past. Clearly the Sephardic Mystique is alive and well and is meeting contemporary needs for collective celebration and identification with the Spanish-Jewish past, real and imagined.

Rather than review in detail the major and minor scholarly writings about medieval Jewish history, literature—sacred and profane—law, exegesis, philosophy, mysticism, and the like from the early nineteenth-century beginnings, I focus on how the field is being defined and worked today and propose a new program for future study. I refer the curious and industrious to earlier historiographic and bibliographic essays that colleagues and I have written in recent years.[11] These present the critical assessments of the details from which patterns can be discerned.

The Current State of the Field

Although there are various conventions as to what defines the Jewish Middle Ages as a useful historical period,[12] I propose we use a basic politico-cultural definition. Regardless of the dates, Jews lived in a medieval setting when they were organized as a self-governing religious minority within a dominant host society that was monotheistic in religious ideology, usually either Christian or Muslim. According to this construct, when Jews lived under pagan regimes, even though organized as a self-governing religious polity, they lived in antiquity; when they achieved or sought to achieve a footing of political and social equality as individual citizens or subjects alongside Christians or Muslims, they lived in a modern society, even though they lived among a Christian or Muslim majority. Schematically, antiquity in Jewish history involves conditions of corporate equality; modernity, of individual equality; the Middle Ages, of corporate subordination to a dominant monotheistic and, hence, exclusivistic religious majority in power over them. That's a working definition.

Recently, there are signs that the early Middle Ages, especially Christian Roman or Byzantine times up to the Muslim Conquest, are being defined as a distinct premedieval period called late antiquity. Similarly, at the other end, one hears references to early modern Jewish history from the Spanish Expulsion down to the late seventeenth or early eighteenth century.

These newer periods reflect a realignment of general historians' interests in transition periods in general, a reflection of our own sense of being post-modern and uncertain of the future of Western culture.

Although there is some merit in being sensitive to these newer boundaries, they overlap the larger construct offered here as the Jewish Middle Ages. The implications for the proposed wider definition are that much of what we call classical Judaism, documented almost entirely by post-fourth-century sources, should properly be viewed as part of Byzantine or early medieval Jewish history. That includes the Jerusalem Talmud and all early midrash collections. If we include Zoroastrian influence on late Sassanian Persia as parallel to Christian and Muslim hegemony, the Babylonian Talmud can also be said to derive from an early medieval religious society as well. I do not want to press this too far. But the degree that Jewish experience fundamentally altered when Jews went from living under relatively benign and supportive pagan regimes to the theoretically less tolerant and challenging monotheistic religious ideologies of Christianity and Islam, at least, should always be kept in mind.

On the other hand, it is not clear what fundamentally changed for most Jews in the sixteenth and seventeenth centuries such that we should lop off those centuries from the Jewish Middle Ages and treat them as a separate period called early modern. Clearly, there was a major disruption of Iberian Jewish life, and some individuals of the so-called Marrano diaspora were torn between Christianity and Judaism, to allude to Joseph Kaplan's recent book on seventeenth-century Dutch Jews.[13] But there was much continuity in central Europe, and an entirely new medieval experience got under way in eastern Europe and the Ottoman Empire. To end the Middle Ages with the expulsion of Iberian Jewry is, once again, to be unduly influenced by the Sephardic Mystique and its claim that the Spanish-Jewish experience is central and supremely significant in Jewish history.

All of which is to emphasize that there is need for flexibility in considering the field of medieval Jewish studies. But some coherence can be achieved, despite newer boundaries at the beginning and end, by adopting the functional working definition outlined earlier. When the corporate Jewish religious polity becomes a group of individual Jews living on a par with Christians and Muslims, then Jews shifted from a medieval to a modern setting. This would mean, for English Jews, a long process over the seventeenth to nineteenth centuries; for French Jews, the legislation accompanying the French Revolution; for German Jews, much of the eighteenth and nineteenth centuries; and for east European and Mediterranean Jews, World War I, the Russian Revolution, and even through World War II.

Despite the breadth of the time and space embraced by even the least imperialistic definition of medieval Jewish culture, it is remarkable how research is divided today into highly specialized spheres of influence. In the area of Jewish legal studies, for example, research is concentrated on what is called Jewish jurisprudence (*mishpat ivri*), and on the history of Jewish religious law (halakha). Israeli scholars tend to dominate the field of Jewish jurisprudence, in which the standard has been set by Menahem Elon.[14] Students of Jewish religious law are scattered about in several academic institutions in Israel and North America, but some of the most interesting work on the history of Jewish religious law has been done by the Israeli social historian Jacob Katz and his former student Haym Soloveitchik.[15] There is much to be done in both fields, and research has been stimulated by a data bank of *responsa* (religious legal decisions) and a series of indices to that literature appearing slowly in printed form.

The field of medieval Hebrew poetry is also largely based in Israel, especially at the Hebrew University of Jerusalem. Ezra Fleisher[16] and Yosef Yahalom, among others, are reconstructing the poetry of medieval Judaism largely on the basis of information provided by the Cairo Geniza. The same is true of the history of Jewish art and material culture in which Bezalel Narkiss, also of Jerusalem, has led the way.[17]

In an even more dramatic vein, the entire field of Jewish mysticism has been cultivated largely in Jerusalem, this time in the wake of the prodigious achievements of the late Gershom Scholem. In the generation now at work, the voluminous writings of Joseph Dan and Moshe Idel, among many others, have set the pace for scores of new studies, text editions, and translations, and recently the appearance of an international newsletter of works in progress called *Kabbalah*. There is a seemingly insatiable appetite for the fruits of scholarly efforts in this field not only in Israel but also in Europe—especially France—and in North America among specialists and nonspecialists alike.

The recent opening to the scholarly world of the Gershom Scholem Memorial Library, built around Scholem's personal research library of some twenty-five thousand volumes, housed in a special room in the Jewish National and University Library in Jerusalem, only adds to Jerusalem's already considerable assets for serious scholars of the history of Jewish mysticism. Today, both Dan and Idel are engaged in writing their own revisions of the entire field, building on all earlier work, to be sure, but offering fresh reconstructions of wide scope and great promise.

Medieval Jewish philosophy has had an even more international flavor, if that is imaginable, perhaps because this field is usually approached within the context of the history of general philosophy. Since Harry Austryn Wolfson, at least, scholars have faced the challenge of studying medieval Jewish philosophy not only within the framework of ancient philosophy but also that of medieval Christian and Muslim theology, from "Philo to

Spinoza,'' as Wolfson put it. Today, the field lacks that magisterial focus. Although many able and talented scholars in Israel, North America, and Europe are at work on specific thinkers and problems, Wolfson's synthesis still remains in place for many or, for others, the notion of working within a new synthesis has lost its attraction.

Before looking at recent trends in Jewish history, it should be noted that traditionally all of the areas discussed thus far can be subsumed under a historical-philological perspective. That is, the student of Jewish law, literature (whether poetry or liturgy or narrative), mysticism, and religious philosophy generally has been concerned with establishing and interpreting texts and of looking at the history of those texts. In this sense, it is correct to say that medieval Jewish history, viewed at least as the history of medieval Jewish high culture, includes all of the above. Scholars of Jewish law, poetry, mysticism, and philosophy have often been students of the history of those subjects.

What of the field of Jewish history as generally thought of as the political, social, economic, and cultural history of the Jews? Here two giants have generated and inspired two generations of students—the late Yizhak Baer, in Jerusalem, and Salo Baron, in New York. Despite several important differences, they have in common a holistic view of Jewish history and a fundamentally comparative approach. Both consider it impossible to talk about Jewish history outside of a Christian or Muslim comparative framework. The seminal work of Zvi Ankori on the Karaites and of Gerson D. Cohen on the rabbinic elite of Andalusian Spain[18] are outstanding examples of the comparative, social-intellectual history that can result from these perspectives. Another creative direction in medieval Jewish history has been offered by Jacob Katz, a pioneer in the sociological history of the Jews[19] and of Jewish law.[20]

Although many students of medieval Jewish history today have sought to continue and develop further the kinds of comparative approaches that these masters have stimulated, others have limited their focus of medieval Jewish history to one kind of Jewish culture and show little or no interest in either Jewish social contexts or non-Jewish society or culture. This alternative within the study of medieval Jewish history is a continuation of the very early trend to focus on rabbinic culture and to do so within a biographical framework. Such was the case for many years at Yeshiva University under the example and direction of Irving Agus, who tended to concentrate on rabbinic figures from northern Europe.[21]

A biographical focus is also true of Isadore Twersky and his students and colleagues at Harvard on Provençal or Spanish figures such as Rabad of Posquières, Radak or Meir Abulafia.[22] The emphasis is on Jewish legal figures and their works. Twersky's achievement is broader and more sophisticated than Agus's, but his erudite and rich studies generally ignore non-Jewish contemporary culture and to some degree even nonelite Judaism or even nonhalakhic Jewish religious culture.

An underlying biographical, religious approach is also evident in the work in Jerusalem of Ephraim E. Urbach on the Tosafists (Talmud glossators) and in the work of his student and colleague Abraham Grossman on early European rabbinic culture.[23] Although neither scholar has worked on biographies as such, both define part of their research as what might be called collective biographies of rabbis, the influences on them from Palestine or Babylonia, their teachers, their works, their approaches, and their students.

New Perspectives in the Humanities

Although historical perspectives and interests have dominated not only history per se but also the study of medieval Jewish law, literature, mysticism, and philosophy as well, recent trends in the humanities indicate that two other related disciplines are emerging to challenge Clio's rule. They are the application of literary criticism and cultural anthropology to several areas of humanities research. I will concentrate on these related trends and outline the significance of this potentially revolutionary development for the field of medieval Jewish studies as a whole. At the end of this essay I propose that cultural anthropology in particular offers new ways to complement the disparate specialized areas of historically oriented research with a more holistic methodology that takes account of the vast territory the field embraces and its multidisciplinary character.

The influence of literary criticism not only on the study of literature but on many other subjects, such as the social sciences, including anthropology, is an important recent development in the humanities. In his essay "Blurred Genres,"[24] Clifford Geertz has noted that metaphors of social analysis are being taken increasingly not from the natural sciences, themselves beholden to mechanical analogies, but from the performative areas of theater, painting, grammar, law, play, and literature. Some of the signals of the influence of metaphors from literary theory include a new sense of culture as a text to be read and decoded and a formalistic attention to multivalence and symbolism in these "texts," which include societies and cultures.

This shift is beginning to have an impact on Judaica research in general and on medieval Jewish studies in particular. The two traditional scholarly approaches in medieval Jewish studies—the philological interpretation of single classical texts and the overall historical approach—are directly challenged by this turn away from history as cultural and social causality to culture as meaning.

One area of medieval Judaism in which the literary bent has had an impact is in Jewish Bible commentary, a field that bridges the interests of Bible scholars and medievalists in whose domain medieval authors might logically belong. Despite the existence of many commentaries that play havoc with the plain sense or surface meaning of the Bible, the vast majority of scholarship on Jewish Bible commentary has traditionally focused on those exegetes who were concerned with the plain sense, the Geonic-Spanish-Provençal-northern French exegetes whose commentaries could be of aid in fathoming the original meaning and implication of the Biblical narrative itself. In part, this preference reflects once again the Sephardic Mystique. (The attention paid to French exegetes does not contradict this because they are prized to the degree that they resemble the Spanish ones, that is, those who quest after the plain sense.) In part, this emphasis is the result of the professional interests of the Bible scholars themselves. After all, they study the medievals in order to understand better their center of attention, the Bible, not necessarily to place the medieval writers in their own conceptual and comparative contexts. This is all understandable.

More recently, under the influence of the new literary model of humanities research, scholars have begun to focus primarily on the Bible as a literary document and to ask of it literary, not genetic, questions; not what are the sources from which the text is built up but how does the text as composed or edited or redacted work as a complex multivalent narrative. A distinct sign of this shift in Bible scholarship is the attention being paid to the Bible by literary scholars such as Northrop Frye and Robert Alter.[25]

A corollary of a literary approach to the Bible is a renewed interest in Bible commentators insofar as they are sensitive to nuances and ambiguity in the original text, not just to the philological meaning of the plain sense. A new respect for what I would call surface bumpiness, rather than smoothness of the text, has led to a renewed interest in this aspect of Rashi, for example. Still relatively ignored, despite offering great promise in this direction for students of medieval culture, are other groups of commentators such as the so-called Tosafists or the German pietists and their followers or the anthologizing Yalqut collections or the exegetical presuppositions and techniques of the medieval poets, philosophers, and mystics. As long as Bible commentaries are primarily the concern of Bible scholars and not of medievalists as well, only those commentaries will be studied that reflect the changing interests of Bible scholarship. There need to be more medievalists working here in a fruitful, symbiotic relationship with Biblicists. Each group is dependent on the other.

Related to the growth of literary models of discourse in Judaica research is a second, cultural anthropology, itself influenced by the performative metaphors about which Geertz wrote. If the effect of literary questions on, say, Jewish Bible exegesis has been, in part, to dehistoricize the text, to set aside questions of time and place in favor of the world within the literary text, so too anthropology is challenging the field of Jewish history itself. Following accepted trends in general history, Jewish history has usually been concerned with what Ranke referred to as determining "what actually happened" and the causes that brought it about. The new cultural anthropology challenges all historians to consider an alternative approach by treating society as a culture to be read.

In part, general historians have already been broadening their canvas by looking at descriptive rather than explanatory grids especially since 1929, when Marc Bloch and Lucien Febvre founded the journal *Annales*. Over the past several decades the work of Fernand Braudel and more recently Georges Duby and Jacques Le Goff have anticipated a self-conscious anthropological approach to history that they called *histoire totale*, focused less on political history and more on society and most recently on mental constructs or *mentalités*.

As the *New York Times Magazine* recently noted, the Department of History at Princeton University, near Clifford Geertz at the Institute for Advanced Study in Princeton, New Jersey, has a number of distinguished practitioners of the new anthropological history. And it is at Princeton, thanks in no small measure to the collegial presence of the medieval Jewish historian Mark R. Cohen, that a scholar such as Natalie Zemon Davis has developed an interest in how her approach to history might apply to the history of the Jews in early modern Europe.[26]

In other respects, the writings of such dominant cultural anthropologists as Mary Douglas and the late Victor Turner have scarcely begun to be applied to medieval and early modern Jewish studies. The approach that I would call an anthropological history of the Jews is just aborning today, and I will now explore what this might entail and also raise some questions as to its relationship to more traditional philological and historical perspectives.

An Anthropological History of the Jews

I am not certain when I caught the anthropology bug. It was, as they say, in the air, but there are precipitating events that make one aware of something already there and known to others. I do recall being at the first Lionel Trilling Symposium at Columbia University some years ago at which Clifford Geertz and Victor Turner participated. At the time I knew neither name, as understandably is the case with most Judaica scholars today, at least until the recent *New York Times Magazine* article. They are original and creative cultural anthropologists, Turner, alas, gone; both prolific and highly influential. Geertz's essay "Religion as a Cultural System"[27] is arguably one of the most influential essays in the humanities in the last half of the twentieth century, along with Thomas Kuhn's monograph on shifting paradigms in scientific revolutions.[28]

I do not recall what either said that night in detail, but what struck me was that they offered a new way of thinking about medieval Jewish studies. For Geertz kept using such terms as "thick description" and the metaphor of reading a culture in order to elicit from it various layers of interwoven meanings. His approach to any one culture was to treat it in its peculiarities as unique, not universal, yet through its parochial uniqueness, as an emblem of multivalent, complex meanings of general significance. As I listened, I kept thinking of premodern Judaism, its uniqueness, its richness, its multifaceted layers of meaning. I also kept saying to myself, This sounds very midrashic.

Above all, it was the specificity or what I would call the weirdness of a particular cultural phenomenon that lent itself to the approach of cultural anthropology. The more bizarre the behavior and its ritual vocabulary of gesture, the more one was tempted to try and decipher or decode it and milk its riches. Surely, I thought, the otherness of medieval Jewish religious movements—like the ascetic and extremist Jewish pietists of medieval Germany on which I was working, as well as all or most of premodern Judaism—could be subjected to a similar reading. When looked at without the modern rationalist biases of the Sephardic Mystique as to what Judaism is supposed to be like, how very "other" traditional Judaism appears to be, with its celebratory and highly articulated life-cycle rites of passage, yearly and weekly cycles, food taboos, pollution taboos, customs, laws, songs, jokes, curses, gestures.

This is a far cry from the theological definition of Judaism as a creed, as in some of the medievals like Maimonides or of liberal nineteenth-century movements and thinkers who invented a private, creedal Judaism. Ironically, if we call Judaism a religion today, that label still evokes the liberal nineteenth-century construct of a private religious creed, so much narrower than traditional Judaism's character as the public culture of a self-governing minority and religious polity. Yet when anthropologists speak about Judaism as a "religion," or as a "religious culture," they mean not a body of doctrines but a complex, richly textured public civilization.

Mordecai Kaplan's claim that Judaism is a civilization receives new meaning this way but in a context that respects the religious claims of that historical civilization. It is sometimes said that Kaplan's reconstructionism holds to the creed "There is no God and Mordecai Kaplan is his prophet." Today, the anthropological history of the Jews would understand itself not as presupposing that Judaism is a failed traditional religious culture for a posttraditional modern secular age. Rather, it would seek to understand it in its own terms—including claims about God—and not force it into a secular Procrustean bed for reformist purposes.

When I returned from the Trilling session, I made up my mind to find out about Turner and Geertz and read their work. I found their theoretical discussions about religion very stimulating, even though Turner tended to use words in unfamiliar ways or even invent new ones. Neither discussed Judaism—Geertz had done fieldwork in Muslim cultures in Morocco and Indonesia, Turner among the the Ndembu in central Africa. But both had used concrete data from their unique cultural fieldwork to build enticing theoretical models and a vocabulary that would be useful—mutatis mutandis—in investigating any culture, including historical Judaism.

A second, longer exposure to Victor Turner occurred in Jerusalem during a sabbatical year I spent there in 1979–80. That winter Harvey Goldberg, an American anthropologist who has made his career at the Hebrew University, invited Victor Turner and his wife and co-worker, Edith, to Jerusalem, where Turner was to participate in a series of symposia on anthropology and the Jews. During the three days I attended Turner delivered a major paper and there were a series of presentations by Israeli anthropologists, mostly on Jewish subjects, on which Turner commented. In wisdom and wit, Turner's remarks were a delight. He welcomed the various papers on Judaism, about which he professed great ignorance. They included such subjects as the greater worldliness of Jewish Hasidic women in Meah Shearim compared to their husbands; a symbolic interpretation underlying the laws of forbidden mixtures in Jewish law; a reading of the similarity of gestures in the ways Jews treat the Torah scroll and their young children, among others. Many of these papers have now appeared in print as the first book in a new series on anthropology and Judaic studies, edited by Walter Zenner and published by SUNY Press, as *Judaism Viewed from Within and from Without: Anthropological Studies,* edited by Harvey E. Goldberg.[29]

Since the early 1980s, a few Jewish historians and folklorists have begun to explore how the models and constructs of cultural anthropology could lead to new questions and types of studies of premodern Jewish culture and society. Among these are Reuven Bonfil, of the Hebrew University, and Elliott Horowitz, trained at Yale and now at Beer Sheva University. Bonfil's recent work on the culture and collective memory of early medieval southern Italian Jewry, as reflected in the eleventh-century rhymed narrative Hebrew text *Book of Genealogies of Ahimaaz ben Paltiel,*[30] offers a new method for treating familiar sources. It looks at the document as preserving a collective memory of the cultural shift that occurred in the late ninth century from Palestinian to Babylonian cultural hegemony in southern Italy. It promises to open up the vast and still largely unexplored territory of the formation of early Jewish culture in Europe, and it complements Abraham Grossman's other pioneering studies approached from different historical perspectives.

Elliott Horowitz has worked on early modern Italian Jewish history and is pushing forward his own research agenda on several fronts, including the Jewish treatment of death in early and later times. His recent review essay "The Way We Were," on Thérèse and Mendel Metzger's art book *Jewish Life in the Middle Ages*,[31] is solid and stimulating and calls for a wedding of textual study and the use of illuminations or other nonverbal sources to reconstruct Jewish life as lived in all classes of Jewish society. It is also informed by several categories from cultural anthropology.

Others such as Chava Weissler, Yael Zerubavel, and Yedida Stillman, trained in folklore and related disciplines, have been working on various aspects of Jewish popular and learned culture in eastern Europe or the Mediterranean. Moshe Idel, a dynamic and protean scholar in the history of Judaism, has opened our eyes to myriad new possibilities by placing the history of ecstatic mysticism and magic at the center of many groups in elite Judaism.

In my own case, I rewrote my doctoral dissertation entirely and introduced frames of reference from Geertz and Arnold van Gennep, among others, and published it in 1981 as a preliminary foray by a medievalist into new conceptual turf.[32] Since then, I have also become interested in topics related to the European Jewish rite of passage at which a Jewish boy is taken to school for the first time and initiated into the learning of the Torah. This research has taken me far afield into a number of new areas.

One of them is the history of how early classical Judaism, an oral as well as written culture, dealt with the problem of memorizing its sacred texts, as compared to the Greco-Latin method, described by Cicero, of picturing a memory palace of several rooms in which are different objects. The speaker mentally walks through the palace and thinks of the consecutive topics in his talk by means of associations with the objects in the rooms.[33] Until the Renaissance, when Jews learned about this method for the first time, they used verbal not visual mnemonic techniques. This story needs to be explored further.

Related to it is how groups of Jews have chosen what to remember as a culture. Collective memory is not a uniform matter. Rather, it is made up of many different communities who sift their past critically and selectively and choose what to forget and what to remember—sometimes commemorating it by inscribing it into the liturgy and custom. It treats not the mnemonic mechanism of individual scholars who have to remember sacred texts, but how communities remember and fashion a sacred past.[34]

Another connected research area is how thinkers in Jewish culture from earliest rabbinic times picture Moses and Torah teachers as mothers giving suck to students. Study of rabbinic commentaries on the Song of Songs, for example, reveals that the erotic female lover is transformed into a maternal, nurturing figure who, in turn, is glossed as a teacher of Torah. What can we learn about the male culture of the history of Jewish education, the family, and the symbols of gender from the ways Jews have associated Torah with one's mother's milk?

Above all, the rite of passage includes an incantation to ward off the demon of forgetfulness, and the entire field of the history of Jewish magic beckons.

Despite these tempting directions, a key question remains. How does this approach affect earlier ones? It should be emphasized that this method is not limited to so-called popular culture—ceremonials, rituals, customs—thereby bypassing the conventional subjects of medieval Jewish studies discussed earlier. Rather, the whole power of this approach lies in its treatment of a historical culture as a unit: it asks how any surviving source sheds light on the whole. It is meant to open up interrelationships among medieval thinkers and the common man and woman and child by focusing on the meanings that permeate the whole or about which groups in it are divided.

This approach can be used to explore the symbols of elite rulers as well as the mentality of the ordinary folk.[35] All subjects within the more conventional areas of medieval Jewish studies are grist for the mill of the anthropological historian. All aspects of the historical culture are texts to be read. And this returns us, in some sense, to where we began, with medieval Jewish studies as the subject of philologians and historians. Indeed, Geertz has referred to this new kind of reading as the New Philology. It is also a new kind of history, one informed by anthropology now extending its insights to the so-called civilized cultures of history and the present.

And we need not hesitate to associate this method previously reserved for so-called primitive or nonliterate peoples with one of the most highly literate cultures in history—Judaism. In the course of one of his remarks in Jerusalem, Victor Turner noted that there are two kinds of peoples: tree peoples, like those in nonliterate Africa that he and others have studied, and book peoples, like the Jews. At this point someone in the audience disagreed by saying that Judaism, too, is a tree religion since Scripture says about wisdom—that is, the Torah—"She is a tree of life to those who grasp her, and whoever holds on to her is happy" (Prov. 3:18).

Notes

1. *New York Times,* December 28, 1978.

2. Francis G. Gentry and Christopher Kleinhenz, eds., *Medieval Studies in North America: Past, Present, and Future* (Kalamazoo, Mich., 1982).

3. *The Education of Henry Adams* (1907; reprint, New York, 1931), pp. 293–94, quoted in William J. Courtnay, "The Virgin and the Dynamo: The Growth of Medieval Studies in North America 1879–1930," in Gentry and Kleinhenz, eds., *Medieval Studies*, p. 5.

4. S. D. Goitein, "Religion in Everyday Life as Reflected in the Documents of the Cairo Geniza," in Goitein, ed., *Religion in a Religious Age* (Cambridge, Mass., 1974), p. 3.

5. Most of the articles first appeared in *Bikkurei ha-Ittim* in 1828–31 and were reprinted as *Yeriot Shelomo* (Warsaw, 1904).

6. For a reassessment of the Palestinian and Babylonian influences on early European Jewish culture, see Abraham Grossman, "The Ties of the Jews of Ashkenaz to the Land of Israel," in Richard I. Cohen, ed., *Vision and Conflict in the Holy Land* (New York, 1985), pp. 78–101; and Reuven Bonfil, "Between Eretz Israel and Babylonia," *Shalem* 5 (1987), pp. 1–30 [in Hebrew, with English abstract]. An earlier version appeared as "Tra due mondi," in *Italia Judaica: Atti del I Convegno internazionale, Bari 18–22 maggio 1981* (Rome, 1983), pp. 135–58.

7. Leopold Zunz, "Salomon ben Isaac genannt Raschi," *Zeitschrift für die Wissenschaft des Judenthums* (Berlin, 1822–23), pp. 277–385, on which see Ismar Schorsch, "From Wolfenbüttel to Wissenschaft: The Divergent Paths of Isaak Markus Jost and Leopold Zunz," *Leo Baeck Yearbook* 22 (1977), pp. 109–28, esp. pp. 124–25.

8. Moritz Güdemann, *Geschichte des Erziehungswesens und der Cultur der abendländischen Juden* (Vienna, 1880–88).

9. Ivan G. Marcus, "Beyond the Sephardic Mystique," *Orim: A Jewish Journal at Yale* 1:1 (Autumn 1985), pp. 35–53.

10. That the date should be revised to 1138, see the remarks of S. D. Goitein, "Moses Maimonides, Man of Action: A Revision of the Master's Biography in Light of the Geniza Documents," in Gerard Nahon and Charles Touati, eds., *Hommages à Georges Vajda* (Louvain, 1980), p. 155.

11. See, in particular, the essays by Kenneth R. Stow, Mark R. Cohen, Lawrence V. Berman, Jochanan H. A. Wijnhoven, and myself in *Bibliographical Essays in Medieval Jewish Studies* (New York, 1976) and the magisterial essay by Gerson D. Cohen on Geonic scholarship, "The Reconstruction of Gaonic History," published as a new introduction to Jacob Mann, *Texts and Studies in Jewish History and Literature* (New York, 1972).

12. See my essay in *Bibliographical Essays*, pp. 19–20. Cf. Haim Z. Dimitrovsky, "Is There a Jewish 'Middle Ages'?" in *Mehqarim be-Mada'ei ha-Yahadut* (Jerusalem, 1986; in Hebrew), pp. 257–65, with references to Dinur, Baer and Ben-Sasson, as well as a definition based on the dominance of the Talmud from Gaonic times to the Emancipation. I am grateful to Menahem Schmelzer for calling this article to my attention.

13. Joseph Kaplan, *From Christianity to Judaism* (Jerusalem, 1982; in Hebrew).

14. See his *Jewish Law: History, Sources, Principles*, 2d ed. (Jerusalem, 1978; in Hebrew), 2 vols., and the English collection of *Encyclopedia Judaica* articles, *The Principles of Jewish Law* (Jerusalem, 1975).

15. Jacob Katz, *The Sabbath Gentile* (Jerusalem, 1983; in Hebrew; English edition: Philadelphia, 1989); Haym Soloveitchik, *Pawnbroking: A Study in the Inter-Relationship between Halakhah, Economic Activity and Communal Self-Image* (Jerusalem, 1985; in Hebrew) and also his "Pawnbroking: A Study in Usury and of the Halakhah in Exile," *Proceedings of the American Academy for Jewish Research* 38–39 (1972), pp. 203–68.

16. See Fleisher's *Hebrew Liturgical Poetry in the Middle Ages* (Jerusalem, 1975; in Hebrew).

17. See his *Hebrew Illuminated Manuscripts* (Jerusalem, 1969), and *The Journal of Jewish Art* (1974–). See Chapter 14 of this book by Joseph Gutmann.

18. Zvi Ankori, *Karaites in Byzantium: The Formative Years, 970–1100* (1959; reprint, New York, 1968); Abraham Ibn Daud, *Sefer ha-Qabbalah,* ed. and trans. Gerson D. Cohen (Philadelphia, 1967).

19. See Jacob Katz, *Tradition and Crisis* (New York, 1961), and his methodological essay "The Concept of Social History and Its Possible Uses in Jewish Historical Research," *Scripta Hierosolymitana* 3 (1955), pp. 292–312.

20. See above, n. 15.

21. See Irving Agus, *Rabbi Meir of Rothenburg* (1947; reprint, New York, 1970).

22. See Isadore Twersky, *Rabad of Posquières* (Cambridge, Mass., 1962); *Introduction to the Code of Maimonides* (New Haven, Conn., 1980); Frank Talmage, *David Kimhi: The Man and the Commentaries* (Cambridge, Mass., 1975); Bernard Septimus, *Hispano-Jewish Culture in Transition: The Career and Controversies of Ramah* (Cambridge, Mass., 1982).

23. Ephraim E. Urbach, *The Tosaphists: Their History, Writings and Methods,* 4th ed. (Jerusalem, 1980; in Hebrew), 2 vols.; Abraham Grossman, *The Early Sages of Ashkenaz* (Jerusalem, 1981; in Hebrew).

24. Clifford Geertz, "Blurred Genres," *American Scholar* 49/2 (Spring 1980), pp. 165–79.

25. See Northrop Frye, *The Great Code: The Bible and Literature* (New York, 1982); Robert Alter, *The Art of Biblical Narrative* (New York, 1981) and *The Art of Biblical Poetry* (New York, 1985). See Chapter 3 by E. Greenstein in this volume.

26. Mark Silk, "The Hot History Department," *New York Times Magazine* April 19, 1987, pp. 42ff. See Mark R. Cohen, trans. and ed., *The Autobiography of a Seventeenth-Century Venetian Rabbi* (Princeton, 1988).

27. Clifford Geertz, "Religion as a Cultural System," in Michael Banton, ed., *Anthropological Approaches to the Study of Religion* (London, 1966), pp. 1–46; and more recently, see Robert L. Moore and Frank E. Reynolds, eds., *Anthropology and the Study of Religion* (Chicago, 1984).

28. Thomas S. Kuhn, *The Structure of Scientific Revolutions,* 2d ed. enl. (Chicago, 1970).

29. See, too, Harvey E. Goldberg, "Anthropological Perspectives on the Study of Jewish Society and Culture," a paper presented at the conference "The Study of the Jews," University of Indiana, November 1987.

30. See above, n. 6, and also Robert Bonfil, "The Historian's Perception of the Jews in the Italian Renaissance: Towards a Reappraisal," *Revue des études juives* 143/1–2 (Jan./June 1984), pp. 59–82.

31. Elliott Horowitz, "The Way We Were," *Jewish History* 1/1 (Spring 1986), pp. 75–90, a review of Thérèse and Mendel Metzger, *Jewish Life in the Middle Ages: Illuminated Hebrew Manuscripts of the Thirteenth to the Sixteenth Centuries* (New York, 1982).

32. Ivan G. Marcus, *Piety and Society: The Jewish Pietists of Medieval German,* (Leiden, 1981).

33. See the summary in Frances A. Yates, *The Art of Memory* (Chicago, 1966), chap. 1.

34. See Yosef Hayim Yerushalmi, *Zakhor: Jewish History and Jewish Memory* (Seattle, 1982) and the essay in n.9 above.

35. See S.R.F. Price, *Rituals and Power: The Roman Imperial Cult in Asia Minor* (Cambridge, Mass., 1984); and Mary R. O'Neil, "From 'Popular' to 'Local' Religion," *Religious Studies Review* 2/3–4 (July/Oct. 1986), pp. 222–26.

9

RESPONSE

Hava Tirosh-Rothschild

In response to Marcus's lucid presentation I will begin by discussing the strength of medieval studies in both America and Israel. I will then survey some of the major breakthroughs in the various disciplines of medieval Jewish studies and conclude by reflecting on Marcus's proposal to apply cultural anthropology to the study of medieval Jewish history. I hope that Marcus's essay and my response will answer the questions set before us by the editors of this volume: to what extent has the enormous growth of Judaic scholarship in recent years been occasioned by major new discoveries, major methodological breakthroughs, or a real increase in knowledge? Is the old consensus in the field still in place? If not, what has replaced it? What are the major areas that remain to be explored, and what are the major issues that need to be resolved? Let us keep these questions in mind as we continue to explore the state of medieval Jewish studies.

I

Marcus begins his presentation by stating the objective growth of medieval studies in America. He views this growth as a testimony to a more sympathetic attitude toward symbolism and "things of the heart" in American culture, clearly reversing rationalist tendencies of previous decades. Indeed, no one can deny the impressive number of professional medievalists registered at the Medieval Academy of America (3,060 in 1982), or the existence of numerous academic programs, associations, research centers, and scholarly journals devoted to the Middle Ages. These facts, documented in *Medieval Studies in North America: Past, Present, and Future*,[1] might promote contentment and optimism about the strength of the field. Nevertheless, I cite two leading medievalists, Joseph R. Strayer and David Herlihy, who differ in their assessment of the field.

On November 15, 1969, Joseph R. Strayer addressed the Midwest Medieval Conference at the University of Illinois at Champaign:

> Medieval history is facing a time of troubles. In many colleges, course enrollments are declining. In many universities few students begin graduate work in medieval history, and even fewer finish it; they drift into other fields. The decline is gradual, not abrupt; we can keep going at close to our present rate for another decade or so. But I wonder if the teachers of medieval history who are just beginning their careers will have as many excellent students as my contemporaries did, and indeed, if they will have any students at all by the year 2000.[2]

Strayer cited the steady decline of the classics and the lack of linguistic competence in Latin, Greek, and the European languages as causes of the dwindling enthusiasm for medieval history as a graduate career. A more serious peril to medieval history, he observed, was the attack on the validity of history as a discipline. The radical version of the attack came from militant students arguing that the rapid change of modern society made the past irrelevant and incomprehensible. A milder form of the assault on history came from those who, according to Strayer, "value the study of past societies, but minimize observations of continuity and growth." Those who study history "in slow motion under extreme magnification" highlight structures at the expense of causal explanation—the backbone of history. Strayer did not name the advocates of this ahistorical approach to the past, but one can surmise that he had in mind both Marxist historians and the contributors to the *Annales* school, notwithstanding their differences. To counteract the impact of structuralism on the study of the past, Strayer went on to reaffirm the validity of traditional approaches to medieval history and mapped out the desiderata for the field. He called for rigorous use of quantification in the exploration of pending questions in social and economic history, greater attention to collective biographies of a class or a social group, and a contextual approach to the study of intellectual trends.

It is too early to tell whether Strayer's prophecy of doom has already come true, or whether it was but a false alarm. If Strayer is right, then what appears to us as growth in American medievalism[3] is, in fact, but the waning of the discipline, which today still reaps the harvest of previous growth.

Recently, David Herlihy shared some of Strayer's concerns. On April 9, 1983, Herlihy addressed the annual meeting of the Medieval Academy of America at the University of California, Berkeley, with a lecture titled "The American Medievalist—a Social and Professional Profile."[4] Herlihy analyzed the membership lists of the academy in 1973 and 1982, from which he generalized about the field. He presented three major findings that are relevant to us: first, in the period under consideration there was a decline in the number of professional medievalists in America. Second, diminishing numbers of medievalists hold stable academic jobs. Third, whether we like it or not, "we are witnessing a major increase in the proportion of women among medievalists in this country." The trend is especially visible in art history, Romance languages, French literature, and music, but it affects other disciplines as well, such as philosophy and history. Herlihy explained this fact by changing expectations of women who are no longer satisfied "with marriage and family but no life outside the home." He by no means suggested that the increase of women lowered the standards of medieval studies, but he related the changing sex ratio to the declining numbers of medievalists and the increasing difficulties in obtaining academic positions. Medieval studies, and the humanities in general, no longer attract males, who instead flock to professional and technical schools "in evident search of money making skills." Medieval studies, like other fields in the humanities, attract women, who are less deterred by the insecurity of the field, perhaps because they expect to be second income earners in a two-career family. Herlihy urged the members of the academy to ask themselves "Why is it more difficult to attract men to medieval studies?" so that the trends he had observed could be carefully monitored.

I cite Strayer and Herlihy in order to suggest that the reality of medieval studies in America is more complex than the picture depicted by Marcus. Furthermore, I doubt the causal relationship between the postmodernist trends in the West and the growth of medieval Jewish studies implied in Marcus's statement "The Jewish academic world has not been immune to these trends in the general culture." It seems to me that the development of medieval Jewish studies and that of American medievalism were two parallel processes occasioned by the immigration of European intellectuals to America during the first half of this century. The growth of medieval Jewish studies has less to do with postmodernism and more to do with the growing acceptance of Jewish studies in American universities. The liberalization of American universities during the 1960s and 1970s, and the identity crisis of American Jewry after the Six-Day War, brought about the proliferation of Jewish studies programs all over America, primarily for undergraduates.

Yet I urge us to take a close look at these programs before we draw conclusions about the state of medieval Jewish studies. Despite the proliferation of Jewish studies programs, I am skeptical about real growth for this field. The strength of a given field can be assessed by looking at graduate programs in it. How many graduate programs offer training in medieval Jewish studies? How many graduate students, enrolled in Jewish studies programs or in graduate school in general, declare medieval studies as their field of concentration? Among those who intend to become medievalists, how many successfully complete their graduate work and remain in academe? Finally, among those who specialize in medieval Jewish studies, how many are tenured, or with a tenure prospect, and how many are on the verge of drifting to other fields? If the professional profile of the Jewish medievalist is ever compiled (an essential task of the Association of Jewish Studies), I suspect that it will confirm Herlihy's findings and Strayer's fears. Even an impressionistic examination of the list of doctoral dissertations written in America between 1977 and 1984[5] suggests that the field of medieval Jewish studies is not in the forefront of Jewish studies in America.

A much brighter picture has been projected from Israel, where academic research has been progressing vibrantly and unabatedly for the last sixty years. The resources of the National Library with its dynamic Microfilm Institute, the enthusiastic reading public that eagerly follows scholarly discoveries and controversies on the pages of daily newspapers, and the large pool of students interested in Jewish studies have already secured Israel the lead in Jewish studies. This too might not last forever, and the current fiscal crisis of Israeli academe (along with other changes) might force scholars to find their future abroad. For the meantime, an interesting symbiosis between the Israeli and the American scholarly communities is taking place. Technical research is published in Hebrew in Israel, whereas synthetic overviews are published in English by American publishers. Therefore, despite the growing internationalization of all academic fields, we should be careful to separate the Israeli and American academic communities when we consider the state of medieval Jewish studies. Never-the-less, the future of the field depends on close cooperation and joint enterprises.

II

Let me now respond to the second part of Marcus's essay, namely, the survey of the various disciplines of medieval Jewish studies. Marcus distinguishes between jurisprudence (halakha), poetry, mysticism, philosophy, and Biblical exegesis on the one hand, and history on the other. The first five disciplines, according to Marcus, have been dominated by the

131

"philological-historical" perspective, whereas history has been studied from the "comparative" perspective. Instead, I prefer to discuss the first five disciplines under the rubric of intellectual history and reserve the term "history" for political, social, and economic history. Like all classifications, of course, this one is but a methodological tool and should not be used with rigidity.

I fully agree with Marcus's assertion that until recently intellectual history was the major interest of Jewish scholarship on the medieval period. I believe that this overemphasis on Jewish thought and literary activity led Marcus to develop the concept of the Sephardic Mystique first in a programmatic essay,[6] and then throughout his essay in this volume. Given the centrality of this notion to Marcus's view of medieval Jewish studies and Jewish history in general, let me respond to his survey by using the same construct.

If I understand the notion of the Sephardic Mystique correctly, it stands for three different, though related, things: (a) an exaggerated preoccupation of Jewish scholars with Sephardic Jewry at the expense of Ashkenazic Jewry; (b) a mistaken periodization of Jewish history in which the Expulsion from Spain looms large as a major turning point in Jewish history; and (c) a fascination with the rationalist and secularist sensibilities of the Sephardic courtier class resulting from its high degree of acculturation in Muslim society. All three components of the Sephardic Mystique reflect a pro-Sephardic bias among Jewish historians, inadvertently revealing overt or covert assimilationist and reformist tendencies. The preoccupation with Sephardic Jewry is alleged to have created a myth of a golden age that never was, and a misconception of medieval Jewry as a monolithic and unanimously traditional society.

Marcus charges that such a view of medieval Jewish society is both inaccurate and misleading. He therefore calls on Jewish historians to relinquish the Sephardic Mystique in order to better understand the diversity of Jewish religious cultures in the Middle Ages. If Jewish historians go beyond the Sephardic Mystique, they will both liberate medieval Jewish studies from debilitating myths and attain the correct balance between their scholarly and communal endeavors.[7]

I am ready to accept Marcus's assertion that a pro-Sephardic sentiment was dominant in nineteenth-century *Wissenschaft des Judentums*. Still, I am very hesitant to endorse his claim that "the Sephardic Mystique is alive and well and is meeting contemporary needs for collective celebration and identification with the Spanish-Jewish past, real or imagined."[8] Such a claim could involve Marcus in self-contradictions, and the developments in medieval Jewish studies during the last five decades do not support it. Let me make myself clear.

To begin with, a preoccupation with Sephardic Jewry has been occasioned not by a conscious or unconscious mystique, but by the simple fact that from the seventh to the twelfth century the bulk of world Jewry resided in the geographic area from Baghdad to Cordoba, and that this Jewry had benefited from the material advances and cultural creativity of Muslim civilization. The Jewish Middle Ages in the Latin West is clearly a phenomenon of the High Middle Ages, resulting from the awakening of Europe by the eleventh century, the success of the Christian Reconquista, and the decline of the Muslim East after the Mongol Invasion. The Jewish scholars who chose to focus on the High and late Middle Ages did not do so as a result of Sephardic favoritism. During the twentieth century, at least as far as I can judge, Ashkenazic Jewry has not been undervalued by Jewish historians. Hence, I doubt that the Sephardic Mystique can mean a preoccupation with Sepharad at the expense of Ashkenaz.

To the extent that the scholarly preoccupation with Oriental Jewry has a basis in reality, it has resulted from another objective factor—the discovery of the Cairo Geniza. That Geniza scholarship has changed medieval Jewish studies is well known and need not be repeated here. Not only did the Geniza facilitate research on the so-called Sephardic Jewry, especially in North Africa, Palestine, and Yemen, but it also shifted the concerns of medieval Jewish studies from intellectual history to social and economic history. Goitein's masterpiece, *Mediterranean Society,* is unprecedented in its reconstruction of the daily life, economic practices, individual personalities, communal institutions, family life, and ritual and religious customs of a vibrant, diversified, and colorful Oriental Jewry. Goitein and other Geniza researchers, such as E. Ashtor, M. Gil, M. Cohen, and N. Stillman, have taken medieval Jewish studies far from the intellectual interests of *Jüdische Wissenschaft.*

The revolutionary impact of the Geniza on medieval Jewish studies has been somewhat matched by another important archival resource made available to Jewish scholars in recent years, the Archives of the Ottoman Empire, including the records of the religious court (the *sijill*) in Jerusalem. The pathbreaking research of A. Cohen, U. Heyd, and B. Lewis, followed by a younger generation of scholars, yielded a much more accurate knowledge of legal status, taxation, demography, communal organization, and other aspects of the social history of Ottoman Jewry. The new archival material has been studied in conjunction with *responsa* literature, which, as Marcus has noted, has been increasingly utilized for historical documentation. The new research on Ottoman Jewry challenges some long-held views as fanciful myths, for example, the notion that the Jews were part of the so-called *millet* system under the jurisdiction of a chief rabbinate. Concomitantly, the uncritical glorification of another alleged golden age was replaced with a more realistic portrayal of this immigrant society in which Romaniots, Ashkenazim, Italiani, and Sephardim struggled to coexist through bitter factionalism and communal tension. Ironically, one aspect of Ottoman Jewry that has been understudied is intellectual history. The initial work of J. Hacker has suggested that, contrary to accepted notions, Ottoman Jews in the sixteenth century were deeply involved in the study of philosophy and the sciences rather than kabbala.[9]

A third objective factor that might have contributed to scholarly interest in Oriental Jewry, but that I do not interpret as a Sephardic Mystique, is the rise of Israel as the leading center in medieval Jewish studies. The knowledge of Arabic and Muslim culture is much more prevalent in Israel than it was among the European scholarly community, notwithstanding the great Orientalists Steinschneider and Goldziher. Arabic is no longer a language known to a handful of Orientalists, philologists, and bibliographers, but the language that holds the key to the survival of the State of Israel in a hostile Middle East. The new generation of Israeli Orientalists consists of trained social historians, and political scientists, interested in the Middle East as a geopolitical unit and the presence of the Jews in it from time immemorial. There has been an immense surge of studies devoted to the Land of Israel, for example, the multivolume *History of Eretz Israel* and *The History of the Jews in Jerusalem.*[10] The sixth volume of the first series, *The Land of Israel under Moslem and Crusader Rule (643–1291),* integrates philology, economic history, political history, art history, demography, geography, and archeology for the express purpose of reconstructing the vibrant Jewish Land of Israel.

If there is a mystique in modern scholarship of the Jewish Middle Ages, it is not Sephardic but Zionist, a focus on the centrality of the Land of Israel in the national history of the Jews. Such a Palestino-centric perspective was a conscious program of the founding editors of *Zion,* Y. Baer and B. Z. Dinur, as recently acknowledged by S. Ettinger.[11] *Zion* was conceived, in Ettinger's words, as an antithesis to the emancipationist and apologetic tendencies of *Wissenschaft* scholarship. In their programmatic statement, the editors declared the objectives of their historical research to be an examination of "the politico-religious goals to which our people aspired during the various epochs, as well as the factors which frustrated the attainments of these goals. . . Naturally, in the center of such studies stands the Land of Israel."[12] Nevertheless, despite the editors' agenda, *Zion* took other directions and became the major scholarly publication about the history of the Jews in both the Land of Israel and the diaspora. To the best of my knowledge, there has not been a pro-Sephardic bias among Israeli scholars of medieval Jewry.

I suggest that perhaps the Zionist outlook underlies the periodization of Jewish history in which the Expulsion from Spain marks the end of the Middle Ages. This periodization has been given an almost canonical status by Scholem's reconstruction of Jewish history. I concur with Marcus's probing analysis of Scholem's reconstruction and its impact on younger generations of Jewish historians,[13] but I fail to see it as a Sephardic Mystique.

In contrast, I understand Scholem's periodization to be guided by a need to prove the inevitable breakdown of diaspora-centered traditional Judaism. The dialectic of Jewish history in its unyielding Hegelian logic had to culminate in secular Zionism, the only possible existence for a modern Jew. Thus the demise of Sephardic Jewry through expulsion, Marranism, and heretical messianism stands as a symbol of *Galut* for which Lurianic kabbala was, in Scholem's view, the only reasonable explanation. I share Marcus's call to challenge Scholem's periodization, even though I believe that there is sufficient justification to talk about the sixteenth to the eighteenth centuries as the early modern period in Jewish history.

Scholem's monumental enterprise brings us back to the domain of intellectual history. Within this framework, Marcus is correct to note a fascination with Maimonides and the medieval Jewish philosophers. Nobody disputes the fact that Maimonides has generated more scholarship than any other medieval Jewish intellectual, and possibly more controversy. I also grant that nineteenth-century scholars were attracted to the Jewish philosophers of Spain, Provence, and Italy because they viewed their medieval predecessors as models of what they themselves desired to become: Jewish intellectuals at home in an enlightened society. I agree that the emphasis on the philosophers reflects a pro-Sephardic bias for assimilationist purposes. One could justifiably argue that such emphasis has obscured the fact that the philosophers were a tiny minority even in Sephardic Jewry, and that their literary productivity did not overshadow other, nonrationalist forms of Jewish spirituality such as pietism, mysticism, and theurgy. There is, however, a difference between a preoccupation with Maimonides and a rationalist bias. The latter is the result of German idealism to which *Jüdische Wissenschaft* was indebted; the former has to do with the internal development of medieval Jewish philosophy.

Interestingly, the one who, more than any other, attempted to debase the rationalist agenda of *Jüdische Wissenschaft* was Scholem, the alleged proponent of the Sephardic Mystique. One result of Scholem's rewriting of Jewish history has been the reorientation of scholarship from philosophy to mysticism, the very anathema of *Wissenschaft*. Scholem not only erected the scientific study of kabbala but also popularized kabbala by making it accessible to the international scholarly community, which now reads Scholem in lieu of kabbalistic texts. We should admit, however, that regardless of Scholem's critique of *Wissenschaft des Judentums*,[14] his own research of kabbala and Jewish mysticism was greatly determined by the intellectual sensibilities and philological techniques of his despised teachers.

Recently, Scholem's enterprise has been further advanced in the work of M. Idel. His recently published *Kabbalah: New Perspectives* is clearly a breakthrough in this field, and perhaps in Jewish studies at large. Idel's reconstruction of Jewish mysticism and theurgy will probably deal the final blow to the rationalist agenda of earlier scholarship. Though Idel challenges many assertions of Scholem, he continues in Scholem's footsteps by viewing kabbala as mainstream Judaism from which Maimonides and the philosophers deviated. Idel is a master of manuscript literature, and his revolutionary concepts are well substantiated by painstaking research. Yet the fact that his synthetic overviews are published in English and French will again yield an unwanted result—the overview will be studied instead of the primary sources. By situating kabbala in the context of phenomenology of religion, Idel opens the field to a different segment of the scholarly world. Kabbala has recently become a very sought after commodity not only by scholars of religion but by poststructuralist literary critics. Poststructuralists have been attracted to kabbalistic symbolism and theory of language to support their deconstructionist enterprise. Before long, kabbala will be removed from the intellectual context in which it developed and will become but another form of midrash, another expression of the infinity of language and the multiplicity of meaning. "The stone rejected by the builders" indeed has become a "cornerstone," but to a very different structure than the one envisioned by Scholem.

The enterprise of Scholem and his many disciples has been successful—perhaps too successful. Too little is done today in the field of Jewish philosophy, and I wonder how many students will study it by the turn of the century. As much as I welcome the study of kabbala as essential to our understanding of Judaism, I lament the diminishing interest in philosophy, at least in this country. If such a decline is due to postmodernism, which shuns systematic thinking, or rather to Jewish particularism, which avoids openness to broader cultural trends, I would view the new trends with regret.

The rising interest in kabbala has gradually come at the expense of medieval Jewish philosophy. This field experienced its major growth during the 1940s, 1950s, and 1960s under the leadership of H. A. Wolfson, S. Pines, A. Altmann, and G. Vajda. Their outstanding erudition in European culture, Arabic, Latin, and Greek philosophy, in addition to their thorough knowledge of Judaism and sustained philological research, put the field on a sound scholarly foundation. As historians of philosophy they impartially studied all intellectual trends. The Kalam school, the Neoplatonists, and the Aristotelians all received unbiased treatment. Major and minor philosophers were all deemed worthy of study from the point of view of the history of Jewish philosophy. To these scholars Maimonides was perhaps the major Jewish philosopher, but they by no means equated medieval Jewish philosophy with Maimonidean studies. G. Vajda and A. Altmann in particular have contributed to our understanding of the interplay between philosophy and kabbala and the indebtedness of Jewish thinkers to the non-Aristotelian trends of Muslim philosophy and theology.

Within the Aristotelian tradition, Maimonides has reigned supreme from the thirteenth to the end of the sixteenth century, because of his ingenious and comprehensive synthesis of Greek philosophy and Jewish Law. During the twentieth century, the enigmatic legacy of Maimonides has been probed and debated as historians and theologians search for contemporary solutions to the dilemma of Jewish existence.[15] Earlier in our century, S. Pines and L. Strauss revolutionized the study of Maimonides by situating it in the context of Platonic political theory and explaining Maimonides' esotericism as an exponent of a literary genre typical of political thinkers writing under the threat of persecution. Pines's and Strauss's collaboration on the English translation of *The Guide of the Perplexed* was essential to the proliferation of Maimonidean studies worldwide. During the 1970s and the early 1980s, their approach to Maimonidean interpretation was challenged by I. Twersky and D. Hartman, who proposed a harmonistic reading of the relationship between Maimonides the halakhist and Maimonides the philosopher. In the most recent scholarship on Maimonides there is an attempt to go even further and reconcile the two approaches by integrating Maimonides' political philosophy with his halakhic stance. Both W. Z. Harvey and G. Blidstein have taken this fruitful direction.[16]

Most important, the work of Pines and Strauss initiated a new field of research in medieval Jewish studies, namely, Jewish political science. This young field has witnessed the blurring of conventional boundaries between intellectual and social history. Studies in the history of Jewish Law, *responsa* literature, and legal theory coexist with studies in philosophy of law, political theory, and political ideology. D. Elazar has been instrumental in the consolidation of this field as exemplified in a recent anthology of studies, *Kinship and Consent: The Jewish Political Tradition and Its Contemporary Uses*. The title itself suggests that the very existence of the State of Israel, and the new reality of Jewish power, have some relevance to the emergence of this field.

Other research in medieval Jewish philosophy has contributed to the expansion of the field beyond Maimonideanism. First, more attention has been given to the critics of Maimonides, notably Gersonides and Crescas, although the former was within the Maimonidean tradition, whereas the latter attempted to debunk it. Second, the pioneering work of S. Rosenberg on the fourteenth-century Provençal logicians opened new vistas in the application of analytic philosophy to medieval Jewish texts. Third, G. Sermonetta almost single-handedly uncovered the hitherto little studied Thomist school among the Jewish Aristotelians. Fourth, new research in fifteenth-century Jewish philosophy has clarified the interplay of philosophy with both kabbala and anti-Christian polemics. Finally, recent studies of Italian Jewry by D. Ruderman, R. Bonfil, A. Melamed, A. Lesley, and M. Idel have deepened our knowledge of Jewish thought during the Renaissance, especially its relationship to Renaissance humanism, Platonism, and Hermeticism.

In order to ensure the continued growth of research in medieval and Renaissance Jewish philosophy, we need to insist not only on fluency in classical and European languages but also on knowledge of both history of philosophy and analytic philosophy. To me, this sort of openness to non-Jewish culture is a necessity for first-rate quality in medieval Jewish studies.

A final comment on Jewish intellectual history refers to the important growth in the study of Jewish-Christian relationships. This field is dominated by scholars in America and France, including some non-Jews, for understandable reasons, thereby providing a counterbalance to the Palestino-centric interests of Israeli scholars. The works of S. Grayzel, B. Blumenkrantz, G. Kisch, F. Talmage, A. Funkenstein, D. Berger, J. Cohen, R. Chazan, K. Stow, J. Rembaum, and D. Lasker have all brought real increases in knowledge. Their contributions may be summarized under the following categories: (a) clarification of church policies and ideologies toward the Jewish minority in the Latin West; (b) delineation of the major themes of the Jewish-Christian debate in public disputations and polemical literature; (c) integration of polemical literature with other modes of Jewish self-expression, primarily Biblical exegesis and philosophy; and (d) presentation of the Jewish-Christian relationship within the larger scope of European society. This new research has successfully integrated Jewish studies into the broader context of medieval studies.

What is left for medieval Jewish intellectual historians to do? We need to do more of the same and get better at it by refining our methods and sharpening our analytical tools. We need to continue the philological research of the German founding fathers of Jewish studies by publishing critical editions of primary sources and subjecting texts to minute thematic analysis. Our energies should be directed to works preserved in manuscript, of which only a small portion is thoroughly understood. We need to acquire basic competence in paleography and look for the application of new computerized technology to the study of manuscripts. We need to continue to study Jewish intellectual trends in their broad cultural context in both Islam and Christendom. To do so we need to keep abreast with research in the various disciplines of medieval studies and the humanities. The contextual approach to intellectual history will necessitate an integration of the various modes of Jewish self-expression: halakha, poetry, philosophy, mysticism, Biblical exegesis, and polemics. Instead of compartmentalizing the various modes of Jewish thought, we should seek to understand their interplay in the writings of one individual or in the intellectual climate of a given period. In other words, whether we study Ashkenazic or Sephardic Jewry, our approach should be contextual and interdisciplinary. No better model for this approach can be found for Jewish medievalists than Salo Baron's *A Social and Religious History of the Jews.* Let us follow in his footsteps to the extent we can.

III

In the last part of my response, I will consider Marcus's proposal to study medieval Jewish history from the perspective of cultural anthropology. I welcome this new direction as a major breakthrough in medieval Jewish studies. Marcus's own research in German Hasidism has demonstrated the merits of cultural anthropology in the study of one religious culture. Cultural anthropology can help render intelligible rituals, religious customs, symbols, patterns of conduct, and attitudes of all segments of a given society, from aristocratic elites to the ordinary folk. Undoubtedly, medieval Jewish studies could benefit from the new approach, and thus grow beyond the parameters of *Wissenschaft* scholarship.

Yet Marcus's proposal leaves me uneasy. Although he insists that the new approach will not bypass "the conventional subjects of medieval Jewish studies," I fear that it will substitute structural analysis for causal explanations. Furthermore, even though Marcus invokes the motto of the French *Annales* school—*histoire totale*—as a warranty for considering all conventional aspects of medieval history, I doubt whether cultural anthropology can address the concerns of political, social, and economic history.

From another perspective, I am uncomfortable with the insufficient differentiation between the methods of cultural anthropology and those of the various trends of the *Annales* school. Indeed, cultural anthropology is close to the history of *mentalités,* which is but one trend within the *Annales* school.[17] Nevertheless, there is still a difference between Geertz's interpretation of the "ritual vocabulary of gestures," as Marcus puts it, and the claim of Marc Bloch and Lucien Febvre—the founders of the *Annales*— that consciousness is reflected in material culture. At its best, the history of mentalities is successful because it utilizes research done by the other trend of the *Annales*, the one based on the claim that structure is quantitative and relatively independent of human action. In its less successful forms, the history of mentalities is impressionistic and conjectural, open to conflicting interpretations, as R. Darnton has convincingly argued in his critique of Philip Aries.[18] Elsewhere, Darnton put it succinctly: "Despite a spate of prolegomena and discourses on method, however, the French have not developed a coherent conception of *mentalités* as a field of study."[19] In any case, we should be wary of generalizations about the *Annales* school and, instead, differentiate among the various approaches of its major contributors.

I cannot discuss the history of the *Annales* in this context, but let me briefly talk about the direction the school took after World War II, especially under the directorship of Fernand Braudel.[20] From 1956 to 1972 Braudel headed the Sixth Section of the École Pratique des Hautes Études, a teaching and research institute funded by the ministry of education, outside the framework of the French universities. Under Braudel's leadership, the *Annalistes* studied agrarian structure, the interaction of technology, science and mentalities, changes in structure and function of social groups, and the development of early capitalist business practices. Land registers, tax records, parish records—all were combed for the purpose of reconstructing the material past. History of material culture thus considered biological, geographical, and climatic factors. Hence, the contributors to the *Annales* studied harvests, epidemics, nutrition, clothing, fashion, means of production, and distribution of commodities by means of rigorous statistical analysis and quantification methods. The massive information was organized in three historical durations: the long duration of social institutions, the middle range of conjunctures (namely, the interplay of trend and cycle), and the short duration of events. The shared premise of the numerous studies was that social history is the most relevant history, and that in social history structures and conjunctures, not actions of individuals, were most important. Political and intellectual events were viewed as dependent on long-range cyclical oscillations, though the correlation of the three historical durations was never made sufficiently clear.

Marcus is right to urge medieval Jewish historians to be conversant with the research of the *Annales* school. My point is that the historian should be familiar not only with the history of mentalities but also with the quantification of material culture. We are coming to realize that the material life of the Jews was not significantly different from that of the society at large. Since Jewish historians cannot reconstruct the material culture of medieval Jews solely on the basis of Jewish records, it is incumbent upon them to study Jewish history against the background of the social practices and norms of the non-Jewish majority.

In fact, Jewish historians have already begun to do precisely that. Jewish social history has made great advances in using halakchic sources, especially *responsa* and communal ordinances, for its raw material. The pioneering studies of I. Agus, J. Katz, and H. Soloveitchik taught us how to cull historical information from legal sources despite their inherent limitations.[21] The future of Jewish social history in the medieval period lies in juxtaposing information gleaned from internal Jewish sources with documentary evidence taken from non-Jewish sources, whether they are the files of the Inquisition, the archives of the Ottoman Empire, the records of Spanish civil courts, or the reconstruction of material life by *Annales* historians. When Jewish daily life is studied against the norms and prevalent practices of the society at large, we can expect to find that in certain cases the Jews exemplified the dominant trends of the majority, whereas in other cases they deviated from them. Explaining Jewish conduct in either case is the task of the social historian. An illuminating example of medieval Jewish social history is Y. T. Asis's study of criminal behavior in Sephardic society during the late Middle Ages.[22] This realistic depiction of violent and deviant conduct among Jews takes the field farther away from the glorification of the Sephardic Mystique of *Wissenschaft* scholarship. A similar approach has been taken by K. Stow in his study of Jews in Roman jails during the sixteenth century.[23]

These two studies demonstrate that Jewish social historians can, and indeed should, be well-trained medievalists intimately familiar with recent scholarship in European social history. They also make it abundantly clear that Jewish historians need a solid foundation in both traditional sources and in the quantification methods of the social sciences. Most important, these studies demonstrate the need to improve our knowledge of Jewish demography and Jewish family history, a need recognized a long time ago by Salo Baron. To the best of my knowledge, however, most programs that train medieval Jewish historians do not prepare their graduates for research in the social sciences. So far, medieval Jewish studies still concentrate on the literary and intellectual dimensions of the Jewish past, not unlike the dominant trend in *Wissenschaft* scholarship.

In short, if medieval Jewish history is to adopt new trends, I suggest that we look to the social sciences rather than to the humanities to find our new models and research tools. And if we are to adopt the achievements of the *Annales* school, we need to study not only mentalities but also material culture. The French school can provide us as well with an organizational model for a research center in which teams of scholars collaborate on the search for solutions to shared historical problems. We need to encourage joint enterprises among scholars and institutions so that scholarship can take place beyond individual book-lined cells.

Notes

1. Francis G. Gentry and Christopher Kleinhenz, *Medieval Studies in North America* (Kalamazoo, Mich., 1982).

2. Joseph R. Strayer, "The Future of Medieval History," *Medievalia et Humanistica* 2 (1971), p. 179.

3. See Karl F. Morrison, "Fragmentation and Unity in American Medievalism," in M. Kammen, ed., *The Past Before Us: Contemporary Historical Writing in the United States* (Ithaca, N.Y., 1980), pp. 49–77.

4. David Herlihy, "The American Medievalist—a Social and Professional Profile," *Speculum* 58 (1983), pp. 881–90.

5. See Nehama Glogower, ed., "Jewish Studies—Selected Collection of Doctoral Dissertations 1977–1984" (Ann Arbor, Mich., 1984).

6. Ivan Marcus, "Beyond the Sephardic Mystique," *Orim* 1 (1985–86), pp. 35–53.

7. Ibid., pp. 50–52.

8. This statement was included in the version submitted to me prior to the conference.

9. See Joseph Hacker, "The Intellectual Activity among the Jews of the Ottoman Empire during the 16th and 17th Centuries," *Tarbiz* 53 (1974), pp. 569–603 [in Hebrew].

10. Jacob Shavit, ed., *The History of Eretz Israel* (Jerusalem, 1981–85); Benjamin Z. Kedar, ed., *Jerusalem in the Middle Ages* (Jerusalem, 1979).

11. Shemuel Ettinger, "*Zion* and the Historical Research in the Present," *Zion* 50 (1986), pp. 8–15 [in Hebrew].

12. Ibid., p. 12, excerpted from *Zion* 1 (1936), p. 1.

13. See Marcus, "Beyond the Sephardic Mystique," p. 46.

14. See Gershom Scholem, "Mitokh Hirhurim al Ḥokhmat Israel," in his *Devarim Bego, Pirkey Morasha u-Tehiya* (Tel Aviv, 1975), pp. 385–403.

15. See Warren Z. Harvey, "The Return to Maimonideanism," *Journal of Jewish Studies* 42 (1980), pp. 249–68.

16. Warren Z. Harvey, "Political Philosophy and Halacha in Maimonides," *Iyyun* 29 (1980), pp. 198–212 [in Hebrew]; Gerald Blidstein, *Eqronot Mediniyyim be-Mishnat ha-Rambam: Iyyunim be-Mishnato ha-Hilchatit* (Ramat Gan, 1983).

17. See Georg G. Iggers, "The Annales Tradition—French Historians in Search of a Science of History," in his *New Directions in European Historiography* (Middletown, Conn., 1975), pp. 43–79.

18. See Robert Darnton, "The History of Mentalités: Recent Writings on Revolution, Criminality and Death in France," in Richard H. Brown and Stanford M. Lyman, eds., *Structure, Consciousness and History* (Cambridge, Mass., 1978), pp. 106–36.

19. Robert Darnton, "Intellectual and Cultural History," in Kammen, ed., *The Past Before Us*, p. 346.

20. See Jack H. Hexter, "Fernand Braudel and the Monde Braudelien . . . ," in his *On Historians* (Cambridge, Mass., 1979), pp. 61–145.

21. See H. Soloveitchik, "Can Halachic Texts Talk History?" *AJS Review* 3 (1978), pp. 153–96.

22. Yom Tov Asis, "Crime and Violence among the Jews of Spain (13th–14th Centuries)," *Zion* 50 (1986), pp. 221–40 [in Hebrew].

23. Kenneth Stow, "Crime and Punishment in the Papal States: Jews in Roman Jails, 1572–1659," *Italia Judaica* 2 (Rome, 1987). Stow kindly shared with me the yet unpublished English version of this study.

Modern Jewish History

10

THE IDEOLOGICAL TRANSFORMATION OF MODERN JEWISH HISTORIOGRAPHY

Paula E. Hyman

The historiography of modern Jewry has been particularly sensitive to the ideological, political, and cultural trends of modern Jewish life, even as it has become firmly anchored in the academy. This is not surprising, for in the study of the recent past the issue of subjectivity is difficult to mask. As modern historians, we are ourselves directly influenced by the historic forces and events we seek to analyze. We lack the distance from events that enables our colleagues studying other periods to approach their subjects with ostensible objectivity. Further, in the modern period the study of history plays a major role in the self-understanding of Jewish intellectuals. As Yosef Yerushalmi has recently noted in *Zakhor,* his reflection on Jewish historiography and collective memory, for many modern Jews (and especially for intellectuals), the study of Jewish history is a substitute for the religious myth that had traditionally shaped Jewish memory.[1]

Although modern Jewish historiography was a product of the birth of Jewish scholarship in the *Wissenschaft des Judentums* movement of the early and mid-nineteenth century, the ideological presuppositions and goals of *Wissenschaft* scholars led them to pay little attention to their own time, the modern period. Concerned with proving the worthiness of Jews for emancipation and their potential contribution to the larger society, they studied the past with apologetic purposes. Thus they focused on such periods as the golden age of Spanish Jewry, which demonstrated the cultural creativity and political talents of a Jewry fully integrated in the larger milieu. Concerned as well with providing an intellectual rationale for religious reform, they explored the early development of rabbinic Judaism—at first solely to justify contemporary reforms and to understand what had gone wrong in the past, later (most notably in the case of Abraham Geiger) to claim the rabbis as their predecessors in adjusting Judaism to new circumstances.[2]

For *Wissenschaft* scholars the beginning of the modern period could be easily identified. The rise of the Enlightenment, with its rationalism and tolerance, signaled a new age, which offered Jews the opportunity to enter into the life of the surrounding society. Moses Mendelssohn, who responded so brilliantly to that opportunity, became the symbol of the modern Jew.[3] Because they saw their own era as a radical break with the past and because they devalued the traditional Jewish culture of their own time, *Wissenschaft* scholars viewed what we now call the "early modern period" as the nadir of Jewish history, as the end of the Middle Ages, and as a period characterized by the internal corruption of the Jewish community.[4]

Sharing in the emancipationist ideology that defined Judaism solely as a creed and denied the existence of its national/political elements, most *Wissenschaft* scholars explored Jewish religious, philosophical, and literary texts and illuminated the history of Judaism rather than the history of the Jews. Heinrich Graetz's multivolume Jewish history was an exception to the rule, for it was imbued with distinct ethnic pride. Indeed, it was this quality that evoked the vitriolic criticism of a German nationalist scholar such as Heinrich von Treitschke.[5]

By the end of the nineteenth century and the beginning of the twentieth, the Jewish nationalist spirit, which characterized so many of the contemporary ideologies of Russian Jewry—from Bundism to Zionism to diaspora national autonomism—found its way into the writing of the history of modern Jewry. Viewing communal institutions as the vehicle of Jewish political as well as religious and cultural expression, Simon Dubnow, a secularist and staunch promoter of Jewish national cultural autonomy in the diaspora, deliberately wrote the history of the Jews as a people, culminating in his magisterial ten-volume *Weltgeschichte des jüdischen Volkes.*[6] For Dubnow religion was, in premodern times, the essential defense mechanism of the Jewish nation in exile and thus a tool for Jewish survival. With the emancipation of the Jews into a modern secular and nationalist world, however, religion became largely irrelevant to the Jewish future.

Although he scorned the German *Wissenschaft* scholars' failure to recognize the ongoing vitality of the Jews as a people, Dubnow shared their celebration of the diaspora. Whereas many *Wissenschaft* figures justified the diaspora through the mission theory—which saw the dispersion as a God-given opportunity for Jews to spread the truth of ethical monotheism—

144

Dubnow saw the diaspora as having enabled the Jews to develop the most advanced (that is, nonterritorial) form of nationalism.

By the turn of the century the center of modern Jewish historiography had moved eastward. To be sure, Jews in western and central Europe and in the United States continued to engage in scholarly research. Most of their forays into the realm of history, however, were concerned with demonstrating the longevity of the Jewish presence in a particular place, celebrating the local Jewish community, or touting the contributions of Jews to the national culture. Although some of these studies were valuable, many were clearly the work of amateurs. Historical research was thus mobilized to serve the needs of communal apologetics. Moreover, their emancipated status persuaded most Jews in the West that they had no distinctive history in the modern period, for they were integrated into the larger society.[7]

In eastern Europe, on the other hand, Jewish historians, aware of the linguistic, economic, and cultural barriers that separated Jews from the larger society and largely drawn to nationalist definitions of Jewry, suffered from no such illusion. Steeped in the culture of the Jewish masses and concerned with the interaction of the Jews with broad social forces, the new generation of Jewish historians in early twentieth-century Poland pioneered in the writing of Jewish social and economic history. Thus the major work of the Galician-born historians Ignacy Schiper and Meir Balaban focused on Jewish economic life, communal self-government, and popular culture in Poland. Emerging from the same Galician milieu a generation later, Raphael Mahler added a Marxist materialist orientation to the prevailing socioeconomic focus. Some of the younger historians—including Elias Tcherikower, Jacob Shatzky, and Abraham Menes, as well as the master Dubnow—were supported by the YIVO institute for Jewish Research, founded in 1925 and headquartered in Vilna. The YIVO promoted research in which the tools of the social sciences were mobilized to explore such issues as the development and nature of modern Jewish identity and culture, Jewish political behavior, and the socioeconomic conditions of the Jews. At the same time, it also conducted sociological research on twentieth-century Jewry.[8] The contemporary political and cultural concerns of Jewish intellectuals in Poland and Lithuania thus shaped their definition of what issues were of historical significance and suggested how those issues should be addressed. In this they were similar to the *Wissenschaft* scholars.

With the mass migration of east European Jews to the West, the historiography of modern Jews and Judaism, largely ignored by *Wissenschaft* scholars, attracted academic attention reflecting the same presuppositions as east European Jewish historical writing. In interwar France, for example, émigré scholars associated with the YIVO produced the first studies of the socioeconomic characteristics of the immigrant Jewish masses of Paris. The children of those immigrants themselves, graduates of French universities, rejected the notion that French Jews had no postemancipation history and conducted valuable investigations of the process of emancipation and its impact on French Jewish life.[9]

Combining the legacies of *Wissenschaft* and east European scholarship, Salo Baron has defined the parameters of modern Jewish historiography in the diaspora for two generations. His early work on the nature and consequences of political emancipation in Europe served to establish that topic, in its broadest conceptualization, as a primary subject for historical investigation.[10] No longer dazzled by the glories of the Enlightenment period and sensitive to socioeconomic as well as intellectual currents, Baron rethought the periodization of Jewish history. Rejecting the vision of the seventeenth and early eighteenth centuries as a period of decline or stagnation, he located the beginning of the modern era in the mid-seventeenth century, when new economic and intellectual currents in European society and the impact of returning Marranos in Jewish society set in motion the changes that would result in the modernization of the Jews. In determining this periodization, he demonstrated his sensitivity—a hallmark of all of his work—to the interplay of factors within the Jewish community and outside it, in the larger society.[11]

Indeed, Baron's major contribution to modern Jewish historiography has been his emphasis on the need to place the Jewish community and its development within a wider historical context and to explore fully the relations of Jews with the non-Jewish environment. In his battle against "the lachrymose view of Jewish history," he has pointed out that the relations of gentiles and Jews cannot be reduced to those of oppressor and victim. Rather he has illuminated elements of mutual, and beneficial, influence. Because of his interest in the larger context and in long-term historic processes, he has brought to bear in his own multivolume history, far more than was the case with his predecessor Dubnow, innovative analyses of the role of demographic and economic factors in Jewish development. The very title of the work, *A Social and Religious History of the Jews*, reflected his interdisciplinary and interactive approach as well as his synthesis of the interests of *Wissenschaft* and east European Jewish historians.

Baron's contemporary in Israel, Jacob Katz, has, in his work in modern Jewish history, explored themes similar to Baron's. Although he has rejected Baron's early dating of the beginning of the modern period in favor of the more traditional Enlightenment era, he has investigated the processes of Emancipation in western and central European societies. Trained in Germany as a sociologist as well as a historian, he has focused in such books as *Out of the Ghetto* and *Jews and Freemasons in Europe* on the interplay of political, intellectual, and socioeconomic factors in the transformation of Jewish civil status and Jewish consciousness and behavior in the modern period.[12]

Perhaps because he entered the academy relatively late in his career, Katz pioneered in areas that have only recently become fashionable. As early as 1944 he published an important essay on the Ashkenazi family in the early modern period.[13] Similarly, his typological study of Ashkenazi society of the sixteenth to eighteenth centuries, *Tradition and Crisis,* dealt with such unusual (for the time) issues as kinship responsibilities, social stratification, and the interplay of religion and economics.[14] Although the book can be criticized on several grounds, its broad sociological perspective and innovative use of rabbinic *responsa* and commentary for historical purposes were noteworthy.[15] Although most modern Jewish historians have devoted their attention to those who broke with rabbinic Judaism and entered wholeheartedly into modern society—perhaps because they assumed that such a break was both inevitable and desirable—Katz has attempted to understand those who rejected modernity as well as those who carried its torch. Long before the resurgence of fundamentalism made it fashionable to study religious orthodoxies of all sorts, Katz addressed himself to the activity of the Hatam Sofer of Hungary, the foremost leader of the Orthodox resistance to modernity. More recently, in his *Goy shel Shabbat,* he has explored the adaptation of halakha to changing economic conditions and conceptions.[16]

Katz is unusual among Israeli historians in that his choice of subject matter as well as his analysis do not appear to have been highly influenced by his personal commitment to Zionism. Most of his studies focus on European Jewry, whose intellectual, social, and political development he treats as worthy of consideration in their own right and not simply as a prelude to the Zionist enterprise.

This is not the case with many Israeli historians of the modern Jewish experience, who often force the diverse trends found in the modern Jewish world into a Procrustean bed of Zionist analysis. Viewing modern Jewish history in teleological terms, they see the purpose of all trends in this era as leading to the restoration of a third Jewish commonwealth in the Land of Israel. Indeed, the "transcendent meaning" of this era is the return of the Jews to their homeland. Thus the Israeli historian Ben-Zion Dinur dated the beginning of the modern period from the year 1700, when Rabbi Yehudah HeHasid, a crypto-Sabbatean, led a small band of followers to the Land of Israel. For Dinur, this act, which had no discernible influence on the Jewish world, was a symbolic statement of the ultimately correct direction (in both geographic and ideological terms) of modern Jewish history. Moreover, the choice of this symbolic act suggested that the primary thrust in modern Jewish history was, as Gershom Scholem's important work on Jewish messianism and Sabbateanism had indicated, internal to the Jewish community rather than external to it.[17]

Zionist ideology weighs heavily as well upon the ways in which some Israeli historians (and others in the diaspora) have analyzed the Emancipation and assimilation of Jews in the Western diasporas. Perhaps the most influential example is Shmuel Ettinger's contribution to the massive volume *A History of the Jewish People*. Responsible for the modern period in its entirety, Ettinger analyzes the forces, both external and internal, that led to the changed status, consciousness, and role in society of Western Jews. The modern period is implicitly organized according to three overarching categories—emancipation, failure of emancipation, and Zionism. Because Ettinger presumes that emancipation has always failed and must everywhere fail, it is difficult for him to fit the American Jewish community into his schema. He solves this dilemma by according the history of American Jews a mere handful of pages in his several-hundred-page discussion of the modern era.[18]

If it is easy to criticize the excesses of Zionist ideology in the writings of some Israeli historians of modern Jewry, it is important to acknowledge the positive influences of Zionism in the development of modern Jewish historiography. Since Zionism stressed the need for self-emancipation in the broadest terms and defined the Jews as a people who had always had political interests, it is not surprising that Israeli historians have developed the field of Jewish political history (though diaspora historians have also played a part). The works of Jonathan Frankel and Ezra Mendelsohn on Polish and Russian Jewry are an important case in point.[19] The settlement of Jews from Arab lands in Israel has also led Israeli historians to recognize their Ashkenazi-centrism and to acknowledge that the *edot hamizrah* (the Oriental communities) also had a history worth exploring (and not simply a traditional culture to be left to the anthropologist). Thus the Ben-Zvi Institute sponsors research on the Jews of Arab lands in their countries of origin as well as on their immigration to Palestine. Important studies of the Jews of Yemen, Iraq, Algeria, and Morocco have helped to fill the lacunae in modern Jewish history and to illustrate that such issues as modernization and migration occur within contexts other than the Western. The Zionist renaissance has thus introduced a truly international and comparative focus to modern Jewish historiography.[20]

Not surprisingly, the subject that dominates in Israeli historiography is the history of Zionism and the Yishuv (the modern Jewish community of Palestine). Israeli historians have explored the ideological roots and branches of Zionism, the central political figures of the Yishuv, the Arab question in Zionist thought and action, and the building of Zionist institutions in Palestine.[21] Although Zionist leaders of the Second and Third Aliya excoriated the old Yishuv as a community dependent on charity from the diaspora, a revisionist trend in Zionist historiography has now documented the contributions made by this population to the building of a stable Jewish settlement in modern Palestine.[22] What would be useful for modern Jewish historiography is the integration, through comparative study, of the Jewish experience in Palestine with the history of Jews in the diaspora. Such subjects as the impact of migration, socioeconomic stratification, religious thought, and political expression would lend themselves to fruitful comparative analysis.

Within the diaspora, and particularly in North America, modern Jewish historiography has benefited from the flourishing of Judaic studies within the university. A younger generation of Jewish historians of the modern period has emerged that has been rigorously trained in the regnant methodologies of historical study. These scholars, who are open to the uses of the social sciences in historical writing, have introduced a new emphasis on social history to complement the more traditional focus on intellectual history and have thus incorporated the experience of ordinary men and women into modern Jewish historiography. They have also developed an agenda that is distinctly oriented toward diaspora conceptions of Jewry. In fact, the shift of general historiography from its traditional emphasis on the exercise of political power, diplomacy, and the study of "great men" to social history and the study of "mentalities" has made it easier to pursue the history of the Jews and to incorporate that scholarship within a general historiographic framework.

Following in the footsteps of Baron and Katz, the current generation of historians of modern Jewry has chosen to study the variegated patterns of the adaptation of Jews to the societies in which they lived. Eschewing all-inclusive models of social change, they have demonstrated the importance of local context—political, economic, and ideological—in Jewish responses to Emancipation. Thus, for example, Todd Endelman has illustrated how liberal British society of the eighteenth and early nineteenth centuries fostered a gradual accommodation by Jews of all social levels to English mores of their respective classes; Phyllis Cohen Albert has demonstrated how the institutional structure imposed by Napoleon on the French Jewish community shaped the religious expression of French Jewry; Monika Richarz, Steven Lowenstein, and I have explored the persistence of traditional patterns of culture and economics among rural and village Jews in both Germany and France.[23] Painting on a broader canvas, Michael Meyer has examined the influence of new intellectual, political, and social conditions on movements for religious reform, and Ismar Schorsch has placed the *Wissenschaft des Judentums* movement within the cultural and political climate of central Europe of the nineteenth century.[24] In their studies of diverse

149

contexts, all these scholars have focused on the subject that remains central to modern Jewish historians in the diaspora—Emancipation (or in eastern Europe, modernizing social and political currents) and its long-term impact on the socioeconomic behavior, institutional structure, religion, culture, and self-definition of modern Jews.

The American Jewish experience as well as new currents of American historiography have left their mark on the agenda of modern Jewish historians at work in the United States. Thus perhaps because of the dominance of religion in the self-definition of Jews in the West, American-trained historians have paid considerable attention to the emergence of varieties of modern Judaism in Europe and America.[25] Their research, however, draws on the perspectives of contemporary religious studies, especially sociology and intellectual history, rather than the older philological approaches. The impact of the immigrant experience and its importance for the self-concept of American Jews has led to serious investigation of Jewish immigration not only to the United States but also to France, England, and Germany (despite the fact that the latter countries have never seen themselves as nations of immigrants).[26] The predominance of American Jewry in the international Jewish world, as well as the development of Judaic studies in American universities and the recognition of ethnic pluralism within American history, has resulted, for the first time, in professional scholarship of a high order on the American Jewish community.[27] This new historiography has replaced the hagiography of earlier local community studies with sophisticated examination of urban residential development, social mobility, patterns of Jewish political participation, institutional growth, and transformations of Jewish religio-ethnic self-definitions. Such new fields as urban history and family history have also emerged recently in modern Jewish historiography.[28] Indeed, scholars in these areas have suggested that the inclusion of Jews within the parameters of the field has much to offer the general historian as well as the specialist in Jewish history, for the Jews often provide an example of a "deviant case" whose distinctive experience reflects on the norm.

One of the most striking developments in scholarship of the past century, including Jewish scholarship, has been the entry of women into a society that was exclusively male. Although this social change within the academy is a relatively recent one, its impact can be discerned in the realm of scholarship as well as that of sociology. This history of Jewish women is no longer a blank page, and it is widely recognized that the experience of women can no longer simply be subsumed in that of their husbands or brothers. In addition to beginning the process of recovering the history of one-half of all Jews, scholars who are focusing on Jewish women's history have introduced the analytical category of gender into Jewish historiography. When applied to such issues as assimilation, popular religion, and definitions of community and politics, the analytical tool of gender suggests that Jewish historians will have to revise some of their dearly held assumptions about the nature of Jewish behavior in the modern world. To give but one example: Marion Kaplan's analyses of German Jewish women in the Second Reich challenge the view of extremely high levels of assimilation among urban German Jews at the end of the nineteenth century and the beginning of the twentieth.[29]

Although Kaplan's work is influenced primarily by developments in the general fields of European social and women's history, it also reflects a trend currently visible among a broad segment of modern-Jewish historians trained in the United States. In their explorations of the social, cultural, and political accommodations of Jews to the new conditions of modern Western societies, these diaspora historians have tended recently to "rehabilitate" the very "assimilationists" so often condemned by nationalist and Zionist historians.[30] In part this process was a necessary corrective to the value-laden way in which the terms "assimilation" and "assimilationist" were used—that is, as an insult. In part, this process may reflect the interest of diaspora historians in legitimating the continuity and value of Jewish life in the diaspora. During the past generation Jewish historians and sociologists have analyzed with greater precision the different processes that make up assimilation and have suggested that a high degree of assimilation to the culture and mores of the larger society was not inconsistent with an equally high degree of Jewish identity and commitment to Jewish survival. For example, Ismar Schorsch's work on the assimilated leadership of German Jewry's major defense organization, the Centralverein, demonstrates the political assertiveness and Jewish consciousness of the elite stratum of the German Jewish population.[31] This tendency to stress the Jewish concerns of Jews seeking both acculturation and integration into the larger society may lead to an understatement of the assimilatory pressures within nineteenth- and twentieth-century European societies in particular, and to a failure to take seriously the extent of alienation of Jews from the organized Jewish community.

Despite its importance in the contemporary Jewish consciousness, the Holocaust has not yet had any particular impact on modern Jewish historiography. To be sure, scholars have addressed themselves in both general studies and monographs to the Nazi extermination of European Jewry and to the variety of Jewish responses to Nazi persecution.[32] The Holocaust has also stimulated scholarly interest in the question of anti-Semitism and in Jewish reactions to it, both political and cultural.[33] It has, however, led to no thoroughgoing revision of our understanding of modern Jewish history. Zionist historians were convinced well before the Nazi rise to power that Jewish life and culture in the diaspora were untenable. Diaspora historians, on the other hand, remain convinced that the Holocaust was neither inevitable nor the sinister underside of Emancipation.

If the Holocaust has not caused a rethinking of the fundamentals, it has inspired a modulation in tone, a reevaluation of the costs and benefits of Emancipation. It is likely that a contemplation of the indifference of most European and Americans, liberals included, to the destruction of European Jewry led Arthur Hertzberg, for example, to study Enlightenment attitudes toward the Jews and to conclude—wrongly, I think—that there is a straight line between Voltaire and Auschwitz.[34] Jacob Katz also revised his early description of the space created by the Enlightenment for the meeting of Jews and gentiles as the "neutral society." In his later study of the process of Emancipation he qualified his assessment and was willing to characterize the meeting ground only as the "semineutral society."

As a discipline modern Jewish history, during the past century, has both reflected developments within the field of history and mirrored the ideological currents in the Jewish world. Thus the declining acceptance of the Emancipationist definition of Jews as simply adherents of a particular creed has led to a concept of modern Jewish historiography that embraces both the history of Judaism and the history of the Jews in all their political, socioeconomic, and cultural dimensions. With the growing acceptance of Judaic studies in the university and the increasing sense of security of both American and Israeli Jews, it is no wonder that contemporary Jewish historiography is far less apologetic than its predecessors in both western and eastern Europe. Still, although it is less open about its assertions of ideology, its choice of subject matter and treatment of the major theme of Jewish accommodations to the conditions of modernity reflect an implicit ideological conceptualization of the nature of Jewish identity and the issue of Jewish survival in modern times.

Like other fields within the discipline of history, modern Jewish historiography has become increasingly specialized. Contemporary Jewish historians firmly locate the Jews that they study within a particular geographic and chronological context and emphasize the links between Jews and the surrounding society (which they must also know well). Confronting a proliferation of sources, they are therefore less prone (and less well equipped linguistically) to write the overarching multivolume history of the Jews that culminated the life's work of so many of their predecessors. In choosing to specialize and to avoid the comprehensive work of synthesis, they also declare that they lack the certitude of the scholars of prior generations as to whether finding such a unifying principle would be consonant with good scholarship. Their work thus reflects the geographical, cultural, religious, and ideological diversity (or fragmentation) of the contemporary Jewish world as well as the professionalization of the field of history.

The historiography of modern Jewry has been immeasurably enriched by the entry of Judaic studies within the academy, as the *Wissenschaft* scholars knew it would. The contact with scholars in cognate disciplines, the acceptance of the undesirability of "special pleading," and the contextualization of Jewish historic experience have enabled the modern Jewish historians of today to investigate the Jewish past and present their findings to a broad, and nonsectarian, academic community. If, as Yosef Yerushalmi has persuasively argued, Jewish historians have failed to provide the Jewish community with a collective memory to replace the shattered collective myth of religious tradition, that is not their task.[35] With their scholarship, they have nonetheless contributed to the dispassionate understanding of the modern Jewish condition and to the place of Jews and Judaism within the humanistic academic tradition.

Notes

1. Of course, scholars of all periods bring their values and culture-bound perspectives to their work. It may simply be easier to identify these values when they are addressed to recent developments whose repercussions are still being felt. For Yerushalmi's comments, see his *Zakhor: Jewish History and Jewish Memory* (Seattle, 1982), p. 86.

2. On the ideology of *Wissenschaft* scholars, see Ismar Schorsch, "From Wolfenbuettel to Wissenschaft: The Divergent Paths of Isaack Markus Jost and Leopold Zunz," *Leo Baeck Institute Yearbook* 22 (1977), pp. 109–28, "The Emergence of Historical Consciousness in Modern Judaism," *Leo Baeck Institute Yearbook* 28 (1983), pp. 413–37, and "Ideology and History in the Age of Emancipation," in Heinrich Graetz, *The Structure of Jewish History and Other Essays*, trans., ed., and introd. Ismar Schorsch (New York, 1975), pp. 9–31; Michael A. Meyer, *The Origins of the Modern Jew* (Detroit, 1967), pp. 144–82, and "Jewish Religious Reform and Wissenschaft des Judentums: The Positions of Zunz, Geiger and Frankel," *Leo Baeck Institute Yearbook* 16 (1971), pp. 19–41; Yosef Yerushalmi, *Zakhor*, pp. 83–85, 88–89. For the results of Abraham Geiger's appropriation of the rabbis in the cause of reform, see his *Das Judentum und seine Geschichte* (Breslau, 1865–71), 3 vols.

3. For an example of this periodization, see Heinrich Graetz, *Geschichte der Juden von den ältesten Zeiten bis auf die Gegenwart* (Leipzig, 1870), vol. 11. I. M. Jost devotes considerable attention to Mendelssohn but dates the beginning of the contemporary period to the French Revolution. See his *Allgemeine Geschichte des Israelitishen Volkes,* (Berlin, 1832) vol. 2, pp. 486–557.

4. Graetz, *Geschichte*, vol 10, esp. chap. 10 and 11; Jost, *Allgemeine Geschichte,* vol. 2, pp. 421, 467–76.

5. On the Graetz-Treitschke controversy, see Michael A. Meyer, "Great Debate on Antisemitism: Jewish Reactions to New Hostility in Germany 1879–1881," *Leo Baeck Institute Year Book* 11 (1966), pp. 137–70.

6. Simon Dubnow, *Weltgeschichte des juedischen Volkes* (Berlin, 1925–30), 10 vols.

7. For a fine study of the state of American Jewish scholarship and the role of apologetics at the turn of the century, see Shuly Rubin Schwartz, "The Coming of Age of Jewish

Paula E. Hyman

Scholarship in America: The Making of the Jewish Encyclopedia'' (Ph.D. diss., Jewish Theological Seminary, 1987).

8. A history of YIVO is a desideratum.

9. See, for example, M. Dobin, ''Yiddishe immigrantn arbeter in Pariz, 1923–1928,'' *YIVO Bleter* 3/4–5 (Apr./May 1932), pp. 385–403, and ''Di professies fun di yiddishe emigrantn in Pariz,'' *YIVO Bleter* 4/1 (August 1932), pp. 22–42; S. Fridman (Zosa Szajkowski), *Di professionelle bevegung tsvishn di yiddishe arbeter in Frankraykh biz 1914* (Paris, 1937); A. Menes, ''Yidn in Frankraykh,'' *YIVO Bleter* 11/5 (May 1937), pp. 329–55; Baruch Hagani, *L'Émancipation des Juifs* (Paris, 1928); and Boruch Szyster, *La Révolution française et les juifs* (Toulouse, 1929).

10. Salo Baron, ''Ghetto and Emancipation,'' *Menorah Journal* 14 (June 1928), pp. 515–26, and ''Newer Approaches to Jewish Emancipation,'' *Diogenes* 29 (Spring 1960), pp. 56–81.

11. For Baron's consideration of the beginnings of the modern period, see his *A Social and Religious History of the Jews,* 1st ed. (New York, 1937), vol. 2, pp. 164–65. Building on Baron's evaluation of the Marranos as agents of modernity are Yosef Hayim Yerushalmi, *From Spanish Court to Italian Ghetto* (New York, 1971), and Yosef Kaplan, *Minatsrut leyahadut* (Jerusalem, 1982).

12. Jacob Katz, *Out of the Ghetto* (Cambridge, Mass., 1973), *Jews and Freemasons in Europe, 1723–1939* (Cambridge, Mass., 1970), *Emancipation and Assimilation* (Westmead, England, 1972).

13. Jacob Katz, ''Marriage and Sexual Life among the Jews at the End of the Middle Ages,'' *Zion* 10 (1944), pp. 21–54 [in Hebrew].

14. Jacob Katz, *Tradition and Crisis: Jewish Society at the End of the Middle Ages* (New York, 1961). The book was first published in Hebrew as *Masoret umashber* (Jerusalem, 1958).

15. The greatest weakness of the book is its treatment of Ashkenazi Jewry from Alsace in the West to Poland and Russia in the East as one undifferentiated cultural unit. The vast differences in the socioeconomic and political status of Western Ashkenazi and Eastern Ashkenazi Jews are thereby ignored. Moreover, Katz argues for the structural parallel of Hasidism and Enlightenment in undermining the bases of traditional Jewish society, a dubious contention at best.

16. Jacob Katz, ''Contributions towards a Biography of R. Moses Sofer,'' in *Studies in Mysticism and Religion Presented to G. G. Scholem,* ed. E. E. Urbach, R. J. Zwi Werblowsky, Ch. Wirszubski (Jerusalem, 1967 [in Hebrew]), pp. 115–61; *Goy shel shabbat* [The Sabbath Gentile] (Jerusalem, 1983).

17. For a classic example, see Ben-Zion Dinur, *Bemifne hadorot* (Jerusalem, 1955). Gershom Scholem, *The Messianic Idea in Judaism* (New York, 1971), pp. 78–141, and *Sabbatai Zevi,* trans. R. J. Zvi Werblowsky (Princeton, 1973), also stresses an internal dynamic for the development of modern Jewish history. It should be stressed that not all Israeli historians are ''Zionist historians'' and not all Zionist historians place their research within a strict ideological framework.

18. *A History of the Jewish People,* ed. S. Safrai, H. H. Ben-Sasson, and S. Ettinger (Cambridge, Mass., 1976). The ''Jewish centre'' in the United States is discussed on pp. 984–85, 1066–67.

19. See, for example, Jonathan Frankel, *Prophecy and Politics: Socialism, Nationalism, and the Russian Jews* (Cambridge, England, 1981); Ezra Mendelsohn, *Class Struggle in the Pale* (Cambridge, England, 1970), *The Jews of East Central Europe between the Wars* (Bloomington, Ind., 1983), and *Zionism in Poland: The Formative Years* (New Haven, Conn., 1981); and Jacob Toury, *Die politischen Orientierungen der Juden in Deutschland* (Tübingen, 1966).

20. For recent scholarship on the Jews in Arab lands, see, in particular, the journals *Pʿamim* and *Sefunot,* both published by the Ben-Zvi Institute.

21. For new work on Jews in Palestine, Zionism, and the Yishuv, consult the journals *Cathedra* and *Baderekh* and such books as Yosef Gorni, *Aḥdut Ha Avodah, 1919–30* (Tel Aviv, 1973) and *Hashe'ela ha'aravit vehabe'aya hayehudit* (Tel Aviv, 1985); Israel Kolatt, *Avot umyasdim* (Jerusalem, 1975); Anita Shapira, *Berl Biografia* (Tel Aviv, 1980) 2 vols.; David Vital, *The Origins of Zionism* (Oxford, 1975) and *Zionism: The Formative Years* (Oxford, 1982).

22. See, for example, Mordechai Eliav, *'Erets Yisrael veyishuva bamea ha-19, 1777–1917* (Jerusalem, 1978).

23. Todd Endelman, *The Jews of Georgian England: Tradition and Change in a Liberal Society* (Philadelphia, 1979); Phyllis Cohen Albert, *The Modernization of French Jewry: Consistory and Community in the Nineteenth Century* (Hanover, N.H., 1977); Monika Richarz, "Emancipation and Continuity: German Jews in the Rural Economy," in *Revolution and Evolution: 1848 in German-Jewish History,* ed. W. Mosse, A. Paucker, and R. Rürup (Tübingen, 1981), pp. 95–115; Steven M. Lowenstein, "The Pace of Modernization of German Jewry in the Nineteenth Century," *Leo Baeck Institute Year Book* 21 (1976), pp. 41–56, "The Rural Community and the Urbanization of German Jewry," *Central European History* (Sept. 1980), pp. 218–36, "Jewish Residential Concentration in Post-Emancipation Germany," *Leo Baeck Institute Year Book* 28 (1983), pp. 471–95; Paula E. Hyman, "Emancipation and Cultural Conservatism: Alsatian Jewry in the Nineteenth Century," *Umah vetoldoteha* 2 (Jerusalem, 1984), pp. 39–48 [in Hebrew]. Other significant works on European Jewry include Mikhael Graetz, *Haperiferya hayeta lemerkaz* [The Periphery Became the Center] (Jerusalem, 1982); Frances Malino, *The Sephardic Jews of Bordeaux: Assimilation and Emancipation in Revolutionary and Napoleonic France* (University, Ala., 1978); Michael Marrus, *The Politics of Assimilation: French Jewry at the Time of the Dreyfus Affair* (New York, 1971); Uriel Tal, *Christians and Jews in Germany* (Ithaca, N.Y., 1975); the series of books on German Jewry published by the Leo Baeck Institute; Immanuel Etkes, *Rav Yisrael Salanter vereshitah shel Tenuat hamusar* (Jerusalem, 1982); Michael Stanislawski, *Tsar Nicholas I and the Jews* (Philadelphia, 1983); and Steven Zipperstein, *The Jews of Odessa: A Cultural History* (Stanford, Calif., 1985).

24. Michael A. Meyer, "Jewish Religious Reform," *Leo Baeck Institute Year Book* 16 (1971), pp. 19–41, "The Religious Reform Controversy in the Berlin Jewish Community, 1814–1823," *Leo Baeck Institute Year Book* 24 (1979), pp. 139–55; Schorsch, "From Wolfenbuettel to Wissenschaft," "The Emergence of Historical Consciousness," and "Ideology and History in the Age of Emancipation."

25. See, for example, Robert Liberles, *Religious Conflict in Social Context* (Westport, Conn., 1985) and "The Origins of the Jewish Reform Movement in England," *AJS Review* 1 (1976), pp. 121–50; David Ellenson, "Rabbi Esriel Hildesheimer and the Quest for Religious Authority: The Earliest Years," *Modern Judaism* 1 (1981), pp. 279–97, "The Development of Orthodox Attitudes to Conversion in the Modern Period," *Conservative Judaism* 36/4 (Summer 1983), pp. 57–73, and "The Role of Reform in Selected German-Jewish Orthodox Responsa: A Sociological Analysis," *Hebrew Union College Annual* 53 (1982), pp. 357–80; Leon Jick, *The Americanization of the Synagogue, 1820–1870* (Hanover, N.H., 1976); Arnold Eisen, *The Chosen People in America* (Bloomington, Ind., 1983).

26. Paula E. Hyman, *From Dreyfus to Vichy: The Remaking of French Jewry, 1906–1939* (New York, 1979); David Weinberg, *A Community on Trial* (Chicago, 1977); Nancy Green, *The Pletzl of Paris* (New York, 1986); Lloyd Gartner, *The Jewish Immigrant in England* (Detroit, 1960); Steven Aschheim, *Brothers and Strangers* (Madison, Wis., 1982); Jack Wertheimer, *Unwelcome Strangers* (New York, 1987).

27. See, for example, Naomi Cohen, *Encounter with Emancipation* (Philadelphia, 1984); Arthur Goren, *New York Jews and the Quest for Community* (New York, 1970); Jeffrey

Paula E. Hyman

Gurock, *When Harlem Was Jewish* (New York, 1979); Stephen Hertzberg, *Strangers within the Gate City: The Jews of Atlanta, 1814–1915* (Philadelphia, 1978); Jenna Weissman Joselit, *Our Gang* (Bloomington, Ind., 1983); Thomas Kessner, *The Golden Door* (New York, 1977); Deborah Dash Moore, *At Home in America* (New York, 1980); Moses Rischin, *The Promised City* (New York, 1962); Jonathan Sarna, *Jacksonian Jew* (New York, 1980); William Toll, *The Making of an Ethnic Middle Class: Portland Jewry over Four Generations* (Albany, 1982).

28. See, in addition to the works cited above, Marsha Rozenblit, *Assimilation and Identity: The Jews of Vienna, 1867–1914* (Albany, 1984); *The Jewish Family: Myths and Reality*, ed. Steven M. Cohen and Paula E. Hyman (New York, 1986); *Modern Jewish Fertility*, ed. Paul Ritterband (Leiden, 1981).

29. Marion Kaplan, "For Love or Money: The Marriage Strategies of Jews in Imperial Germany," *Leo Baeck Institute Yearbook* 28 (1983), pp. 263–300, "Priestess and Hausfrau: Women and Tradition in the German-Jewish Family," in Cohen and Hyman, *The Jewish Family*, pp. 62–81, "Tradition and Transition: The Acculturation, Assimilation and Integration of Jews in Imperial Germany—a Gender Analysis," *Leo Baeck Institute Year Book* 27 (1982), pp. 3–35, and *The Jewish Feminist Movement in Germany* (Westport, Conn., 1979). Other examples include Paula E. Hyman, "Immigrant Women and Consumer Protest: The Lower East Side Kosher Meat Boycott of 1902," *American Jewish History* 70 (Sept. 1980), pp. 91–105, and "Culture and Gender: Women in the Immigrant Jewish Community," in *The Legacy of Mass Migration: 1881 and Its Impact*, ed. David Berger (New York, 1983), pp. 157–68; and Chava Weissler, "The Traditional Piety of Ashkenazic Women," in *Jewish Spirituality*, ed. Arthur Green (New York, 1987), vol. 2. pp. 245–75, and "The Religion of Traditional Ashkenazic Women: Some Methodological Issues," *AJS Review*, 12 (1987), pp. 73–74.

30. See, for example, Rozenblit, *Assimilation and Identity;* Ismar Schorsch, *Jewish Reactions to German Anti-Semitism* (New York, 1972); and Marjorie Lamberti, *Jewish Activism in Imperial Germany* (New Haven, Conn., 1978).

31. Schorsch, *Jewish Reactions*, pp. 117–48.

32. Major books on the Holocaust include Raul Hilberg, *The Destruction of the European Jews*, rev. ed. (New York, 1985) 3 vols.; Lucy Dawidowicz, *The War against the Jews* (New York, 1975); Yehuda Bauer, *The Holocaust in Historical Perspective* (Seattle, 1978) and *A History of the Holocaust* (New York, 1982); Helen Fein, *Accounting for Genocide* (New York, 1979); Y. Trunk, *Judenrat* (New York, 1972); Y. Gutman, *The Jews of Warsaw, 1939–43* (Bloomington, Ind., 1982); Bernard Wasserstein, *Britain and the Jews of Europe* (New York, 1979); Michael Marrus and Robert Paxton, *Vichy France and the Jews* (New York, 1981); Richard Cohen, *The Burden of Conscience* (Bloomington, Ind., 1987); Meir Michaelis, *Mussolini and the Jews* (New York, 1978); Henry Feingold, *The Politics of Rescue* (New Brunswick, N.J., 1970); David Wyman, *The Abandonment of the Jews* (New York, 1984); and Deborah Lipstadt, *Beyond Belief* (New York, 1986).

33. The literature on anti-Semitism and the Jewish responses it evoked is voluminous. For general histories of modern European anti-Semitism, see Hannah Arendt, *The Origins of Totalitarianism* (Cleveland, 1958); Leon Poliakov, *The History of Anti-Semitism* (New York, 1965–85), 4 vols.; Jacob Katz, *From Prejudice to Destruction* (Cambridge, Mass., 1975). On German anti-Semitism; see Paul Massing, *Rehearsal for Destruction* (New York, 1949); Eva Reichmann, *Hostages of Civilization* (1951; reprint, Westport, Conn., 1970); Fritz Stern, *The Politics of Cultural Despair* (Berkeley, 1961); George Mosse, *The Crisis of German Ideology* (New York, 1964); Richard Levy, *The Downfall of the Anti-Semitic Political Parties in Imperial Germany* (New Haven, Conn., 1975); Geoffrey Field, *Evangelist of Race* (New York, 1981); and Jacob Katz, *The Darker Side of Genius: Richard Wagner's Anti-Semitism* (Hanover, N.H., 1986). On French anti-Semitism, see Robert Byrnes, *Antisemitism in Modern France* (New Brunswick, N.J., 1950), and Stephen Wilson, *Ideology and Experience: Anti-Semitism in*

156

France at the Time of the Dreyfus Affair (Rutherford, N.J., 1982). On Jewish responses to anti-Semitism, see Schorsch, *Jewish Reactions;* Jehuda Reinharz, *Fatherland or Promised Land* (Ann Arbor, Mich., 1975); Lamberti, *Jewish Activism;* S. Ragins, *Jewish Responses to Anti-Semitism in Germany, 1870–1914* (Cincinnati, 1980); and Marrus, *The Politics of Assimilation.*

34. Arthur Hertzberg, *The French Enlightenment and the Jews* (New York, 1968).

35. Yerushalmi, *Zakhor,* pp. 93–94. Yerushalmi acknowledges that Jewish collective memory never depended on historians.

11

RESPONSE

Todd M. Endelman

At the heart of Hyman's analysis of modern Jewish historiography is the astute observation that the writing of Jewish history has become "normalized"—normalized in the sense that the enterprise is conducted more or less in the same spirit and by the same standards that characterize other fields of historical inquiry. Today's historians of the modern Jewish experience, Hyman notes, are not concerned, at least in their published work, with the overarching questions of Jewish existence and destiny that troubled earlier generations. Unlike their predecessors, they do not feel that they have a special responsibility for creating an ideologically correct, politically viable historical memory. Indeed, specifically Jewish ideological commitments play little, if any, role in shaping the outcome of their research and writing.

This transformation—the "normalization" of modern Jewish historiography—is the outcome of two critical developments in the larger context in which Jewish historical scholarship is conducted. First, its practitioners, whether here or in Israel, feel "at home"—secure both culturally and politically—in the larger communities in which they live and thus feel no pressing need to engage in "special pleading" in their work. At the same time, they are increasingly part of secular, nonparochial scholarly communities and exposed to the same intellectual currents and methodological trends as other men and women in those communities, regardless of their field of inquiry. This kind of acculturation is due, as Hyman explains, to the recent incorporation of the study of Jewish history into the academy and its subsequent professionalization. In North America, these two developments are linked, since the recognition of Jewish history as a legitimate field of scholarly inquiry by the secular university and the sense of security felt by the younger generation of historians are part and parcel of the more general improvement in Jewish status that has occurred in America since the end of World War II.

It would be wrong, however, to infer from the increasing normalization of Jewish historical scholarship that extrascholarly concerns are absent in recent work. To be sure, historians of modern Jewry are no longer concerned with demonstrating Jewish "contributions" to the larger society nor with proving the "antiquity" of Jewish settlement in a particular locale. But there are ways in which larger Jewish concerns still impinge on the writing of Jewish history. Hyman has touched on some of these, pointing out, for example, how feminist commitments have not only opened up new areas of inquiry but have also led to the revision of previous assumptions about the nature of assimilation, popular religion, and political activism. Still, I do not believe she has sufficiently emphasized the impact of contemporary concerns on modern Jewish historiography and so I want to extend the discussion in this direction.

Toward the end of her essay, Hyman asserts that the Holocaust has not yet had a significant impact on modern Jewish historiography in the sense that it has not caused a fundamental rethinking of the course of modern Jewish history. She reminds us that the belief that Jewish life in the diaspora was doomed, either by persecution from without or decay from within, was a stock notion of classical Zionist ideology and predated the Nazi seizure of power by several decades. I agree with Hyman that, in this sense, awareness of the Holocaust has not yet generated a fundamentally new rereading of the emancipation epoch, but I would also suggest, to a greater extent than she, that it has generated new emphases in, and new understandings of, basic historiographical issues, although in ways that are not always immediately apparent.

My starting point for this assertion is the public furor that has raged since the early 1960s over the adequacy of Jewish responses to Nazi persecution. The question of Jewish behavior in crisis and extremity became a matter of widespread public debate following the publication of the highly tendentious works of Raul Hilberg, Bruno Bettelheim, and Hannah Arendt.[1] This debate, aside from inspiring more balanced historical accounts of Jewish behavior during the Holocaust, also led historians of prewar European Jewry to consider, perhaps for the first time, the character of Jewish responses to anti-Semitism in earlier, less acute situations. Some, like Michael Marrus,[2] following in the footsteps of Hannah Arendt, con-

159

demned assimilationist Jews for their timidity and naivete, whereas others, like Ismar Schorsch,[3] reacted strongly to such accusations and instead hailed them for their sagacity and assertiveness. Most reacted negatively to the sweeping, ahistorical accusations of Arendt et al, and tended to "defend" the behavior of the assimilated Jewries of western and central Europe. That is, instead of judging the behavior of such Jewries in the light of what later transpired, they sought to demonstrate that these assimilationist Jews acted reasonably, intelligently, and honorably, in light of their own previous historical experience and the regnant political and social assumptions of the age.

The urge to present Jewish behavior in the face of hostility in a more positive manner has corrected an imbalance in the portrait of pre-Holocaust assimilationist Jewry drawn by the Arendt camp and by historians imbued with the assumptions of classical Zionist ideology. But it also has had an unfortunate, though unintended, consequence. By focusing attention on the behavior of communal agencies and activists, whose work can legitimately be interpreted in a heroic light, it has blunted interest in reactions outside the political arena and outside those circles that took an active role in communal affairs. It thus has led historians to ignore ways in which anti-Semitism unsettled the lives of ordinary Jews—disrupting careers, breeding insecurity and anxiety, shattering cherished hopes, poisoning relationships—and how they responded to defamation and discrimination at the personal level. In fact, when one begins to examine the responses of these Jews, one discovers that their behavior tended to be more opportunistic and accommodationist than heroic or defiant.[4] In western and central Europe, it should be remembered, more Jews abandoned Judaism than took an active role in communal defense activities.

Hyman reminds us that there is another dimension to this reevaluation of Jewish consciousness and behavior in pre-Holocaust Europe. Historians in both Israel and the United States have reacted strongly in recent years to the crude manner in which an earlier generation of largely nationalist historians used the term "assimilation" to describe the acculturation, secularization, and integration of Western Jews. As Hyman rightly stresses, for them the term was one of abuse and condemnation, and not a finely honed, value-free conceptual tool. A new generation of historians, influenced in part by the work of American social scientists on ethnicity and intergroup relations, have analyzed these social processes in far more sophisticated terms than anything attempted previously, and they have convincingly demonstrated that a high level of Jewish consciousness and social solidarity were compatible with a high level of cultural assimilation and religious indifference. Hyman suggests that this "rehabilitation" of Western Jewry is largely a product of diaspora historiography and attributes this tendency, in part, to a natural interest on the part of diaspora historians in demonstrating the possibility of Jewish continuity and vitality outside the Land of Israel. That this has been an unconscious motive on the part of diaspora historians is no doubt true, but it is not true that this effort at "rehabilitation" is an exclusively diaspora phenomenon. In tone and mood, the work of such Israeli historians as Shulamit Volkov and Henry Wassermann on Germany closely resembles that of such American historians as Marion Kaplan, Ismar Schorsch, and Jack Wertheimer on Germany, Marsha Rozenblit on Austria, and Deborah Dash Moore, Naomi Cohen, and Jonathan Sarna on America.[5] Both groups celebrate the tenacity of Western Jews in preserving their Jewishness in the face of overwhelming pressures working to dissolve it, largely through the evolution of new forms of Jewish identity.

The tendency to stress the Jewishness of assimilationist Jews troubles Hyman, for she believes it may lead us, first, to underestimate the pressures for cultural and religious conformity that operated in Western society and, second, to misgauge the extent to which Western Jews were alienated from communal and religious concerns. Her reservations about this historiographical trend are well founded. A reading of Marsha Rozenblit's study of fin-de-siècle Viennese Jewry or of Deborah Dash Moore's study of interwar New York Jewry, for example, would not suggest that these were communities whose health would one day be endangered by widespread disaffiliation and defection (in the former case) and indifference and drift (in the latter).

The problem with works such as these is twofold. First, the authors are primed, even before the enterprise commences, to see the glass as half full rather than half empty. They begin with a commitment to, in Hyman's words, "legitimating the continuity and value of Jewish life in the Diaspora," even if they frequently do not appear to be aware of the strength of their commitment and its impact on their work. Second, the methods they employ to study assimilation obscure the full extent to which drift and defection have weakened Western Jewry in the last two hundred years. The abandonment of Jewish attachments is a cumulative, multigenerational process, with each succeeding generation becoming progressively more distant from traditional practices and loyalties. Most recent studies have taken too narrow a slice of the historical continuum—three or four decades at the very most—to assess a process whose impact is most adequately measured only after the passage of several generations. Most studies also mask the extent of drift and defection by examining the process of disaffiliation in the aggregate—that is, by portraying the losses sustained by diaspora communities in the West in terms of annual rates of conversion and intermarriage for the entire community. This method does not take into consideration the fact that Jews in the West who abandoned their community of origin were continually being replaced by immigrants from the great reservoir of traditional Jewry in the Russian and Habsburg empires. Successive waves of newcomers periodically swelled the size of Western communities, thereby offsetting the losses occurring among families long settled there. If the Holocaust had not brought an abrupt end to the assimilatory process within the Jewries of continental Europe, it is doubtful that historians would today assess the Jewishness of the prewar communities in the way so many of them do. For these communities would undoubtedly have followed the same demographic trajectory as English Jewry (which escaped physical devastation) since the end of eastern European immigration, that is, shrinking slowly year by year, as intermarriage, conversion, and sheer indifference have made growing headway.[6]

Among the other major shifts in the literature on the modern period that Hyman highlights is the increasing attention being paid to Jewish communities once outside the scope of the historiographical mainstream. The most obvious example is the appearance of major studies on Jewish communities in Muslim lands. There remains, however, the question of whether historians have really shed their Ashkenazi-centric orientation and begun to incorporate the experiences of these communities into their thinking about and teaching of the modern period. I would venture a guess that most surveys of modern Jewish history being taught in American universities today do not attempt to include, even in a cursory fashion, the history of the Jews of the Middle East and North Africa.

Oddly enough, a somewhat analogous situation exists in regard to American Jewish history. As Hyman notes, for nationalist historians such as Shmuel Ettinger, for whom the failure of emancipation is a matter of faith, the American Jewish experience is a historiographical stumbling block, for it does not fit into the overarching scheme he employs for the modern period. (I might add parenthetically that the dean of modern Jewish historians, Jacob Katz, also fails to incorporate the experience of American Jews—or, indeed, the experience of Jews in any English-speaking lands—into his accounts of either the origins of Jewish modernity or the development of anti-Semitism.) In the case of historians such as Katz and Ettinger, it is not ideology alone that accounts for this neglect; there is another reason as well. Ettinger, Katz, and many others of their generation were raised and schooled in Europe at a time when educated Europeans were largely uninterested in events, historical or contemporary, across the Atlantic. If European historians believed that American history was uninstructive or irrelevant or unchallenging, why should Jewish historians have been any different?

Surprisingly, it is still possible to encounter similar attitudes among American-born Jewish historians today. There is an unarticulated bias at work that views the writing of American Jewish history as a less serious endeavor than the writing of European Jewish history. Some of this bias derives from the false belief that the writing of American Jewish history does not require mastery of foreign languages and hence is easier; some undoubtedly can be traced to a cultural snobbery frequently found in academic circles. Whatever the reason, the result has been that American Jewish history has not received the serious attention it merits. Although Hyman is undoubtedly correct that much progress has been made—after all, the field is no longer dominated by well-meaning amateurs—it is nonetheless true that far too little energy and talent are being devoted to the history of what is now the largest and richest Jewish community in the world. The best and the brightest of our graduate students, for example, are channeled into earlier fields and more exotic climes—medieval Spain, renaissance Italy, tsarist Russia, imperial Germany. The centennial of the Jewish Theological Seminary makes clear to all that American Jewry is no longer a brash, uncultured, developing community. The time has come to mark its maturation by treating its history with the respect it warrants.

Notes

1. Raul Hilberg, *The Destruction of the European Jews* (Chicago, 1961); Bruno Bettelheim, *The Informed Heart: Autonomy in a Mass Age* (New York, 1960); idem, "The Ignored Lesson of Anne Frank," *Harper's* (November 1960), pp. 45–50; Hannah Arendt, *Eichmann in Jerusalem: A Report on the Banality of Evil* (New York, 1963).

2. Michael R. Marrus, *The Politics of Assimilation: A Study of the French Jewish Community at the time of the Dreyfus Affair* (Oxford, 1971).

3. Ismar Schorsch, *Jewish Reactions to German Anti-Semitism, 1870–1914* (New York, 1972); idem, *On the History of the Political Judgment of the Jew*, Leo Baeck Memorial Lecture, no. 20 (New York, 1977).

4. Todd M. Endelman, "Conversion as a Response to Antisemitism in Modern Jewish History," in *Living with Antisemitism: Modern Jewish Responses*, ed. Jehuda Reinharz (Hanover, N.H., 1987), pp. 59–83.

5. Shulamit Volkov, "The Dynamics of Dissimilation: *Ostjuden* and German Jews," in *The Jewish Response to German Culture from the Enlightenment to the Second World War*, ed. Jehuda Reinharz and Walter Schatzberg (Hanover, N.H., 1985); eadem, "Zehihut hada'at vesin'a atsmit: yehudim germanim bitehilat hame'a ha'esrim" [Pride and Self-Hate: German Jews at the Beginning of the Twentieth Century], *Zemanim*, no. 14 (Winter 1984), pp. 28–41; eadem, "Yihud utemi'a: paradoqs hazehut hayehudit baraykh hasheni" [Distinctiveness and Assimilation: The Paradox of Jewish Identity in the Second Reich], in *Crises of German National Consciousness in the Nineteenth and Twentieth Centuries*, ed. Moshe Zimmermann (Jerusalem, 1983), pp. 169–85; Henry Wassermann, "Tarbutam ha'intimit shel yehudei germanyah" [The Intimate Culture of German Jewry], in *Crises of German National Consciousness*, pp. 187–198; Marion Kaplan, "Tradition and Transition: The Acculturation, Assimilation and Integration of Jews in Imperial Germany—a Gender Analysis," *Leo Baeck Institute Year Book* 27 (1982), pp. 3–35; Jack Wertheimer, *Unwelcome Strangers: East European Jews in Imperial Germany* (New York, 1987); Marsha L. Rozenblit, *The Jews of Vienna, 1867–1914: Assimila-*

Modern Jewish Literature

12

JEWISH LITERARY SCHOLARSHIP AFTER THE SIX-DAY WAR

David G. Roskies

If scholarship can be likened to an ancient city where one builds and rebuilds on existing foundations of knowledge, then the study of modern Jewish literature can be likened to condominiums constructed along a geological fault. Whatever formidable buildings had existed there before have already been razed by a series of earthquakes. Only the blueprints remain. Meanwhile, those who inhabit the ultramodern structures nervously monitor the Richter scale.

As I see it, there are three reasons for the discontinuity in the study of modern Jewish literature. The first is the general revolution in the study of literature. As everyone who reads *Newsweek* and the magazine section of the *New York Times* knows, the once stodgy and static field of literary criticism has been taken over by a dizzying array of literary theories, each with its own European hinterland, competing departments of literature, and specialized journals. Where once professors of English could comfortably dedicate their lives to a single author and not worry about anything more ominous than the "intentional fallacy," nowadays they need to negotiate among Russian formalists, Czech and French structuralists, the deconstructionists, the German reception-theorists, the feminists, and poststructuralists—taking care, all the while, to pronounce their names correctly! Where once the objects of literary scholarship were self-evident, now one must begin by asking (with Paul Ricoeur), What is a text?; (with Michel Foucault) What is an author?; (with Wolfgang Iser and Umberto Eco) Who is the reader? And since one center of this worldwide upheaval is Tel Aviv University, it is no wonder that the field of *Jewish* literary scholarship is in perpetual turmoil.[1]

The second reason is familiar to all students of Jewish culture. As a result of the mass immigration to America, the Bolshevik Revolution, two world wars, and the return to Zion, the old heartlands of the culture have been abandoned; the old ideologies have been rendered obsolete either by failure or success, and, most important for the study of literature, the multilingual character of Jewry has been replaced almost everywhere by monolingualism, often to the accompaniment of functional Jewish illiteracy. Whereas the founders of *Wissenschaft des Judentums* had the good sense to conduct their research in German, a language that enjoyed some currency both in Jerusalem and on American college campuses, there was hardly a place to go after the war where one could study Hebrew and Yiddish, Polish and Russian, French and German, even before embarking on graduate work in the field of modern Jewish literature. To be sure, both in Israel and America there were still a few survivors—both actual and vicarious—who bridged the historical and cultural abyss and who tried to reshape Jewish literary scholarship for a postwar generation. But whatever personal integration such men as Simon Halkin, Dov Sadan, and Barukh Kurzweil achieved between their severed past and their present situation, between literary scholarship and cultural politics, could not be translated into a methodology that their students were willing or able to follow. Instead, these bridge figures became the measure of the break.

Third, the object of study—modern Jewish literature—was itself an ongoing chronicle of all the ruptures that had taken place. Here the concept of deconstruction comes in especially handy, in the sense that modern Jewish literature willfully and systematically *decentered* the civilization of the Jews. Since this literature was coterminous with the Emancipation and its checkered career, everything that was up for grabs in life was only magnified on the page of prose, poetry, or drama. One school of writers refracted all experience through the individual consciousness rather than through the life of the collective; another placed work on the land over life in the city and created a gallery of down-to-earth heroes (the *ba'al-guf*, the *ḥaluts*, the *kolkhoznik*) who championed brawn over brain; another school, reacting to the trauma of catastrophe, recast the entire culture into a culture of memorial and disavowed all the achievements of Jewish literary modernism. How, then, could one ever know what the normative culture had looked like in order to gauge the thrust of its literary deconstruction?

Take something as obvious as Tevye's use and abuse of Scripture. Even if one knows that Sholem Aleichem's Tevye belongs to a folk aristocracy discovered by east European Jewish writers in response to romantic nationalism; and even if one can prove, through careful rhetorical analysis, that Tevye's mistakes are all intentional, that he knows precisely what he's doing,[2] we will never know how much of this wordplay originated with the folk and how much was Sholem Aleichem's own invention.[3] Without this data, our theories about Jewish folk irony and about the semiotics of Jewish folklore will forever remain theoretical.[4]

Yet despite all methodological and historical odds, a composite portrait of modern Jewish culture was pieced back together. This is the abridged story of how it was done and of what still remains undone in that well nigh impossible task.

In 1949, Simon Halkin took over the professorship of modern Hebrew literature at the Hebrew University from Yosef Klausner. At that time, the basic tenets of Jewish literary history were the Great Men approach and a periodization lifted out of European textbooks. Klausner had built his *History of Modern Hebrew Literature* on minibiographies of the Haskalah Hall of Fame, then pressed this motley of maskilim into a grand movement from neoclassicism to naturalism—the precise sequence followed by French and Russian literature over a 150-year time span.[5] Halkin, in contrast, saw the struggle for Jewish self-emancipation as the nexus of Hebrew literary creativity in the nineteenth and twentieth centuries. To illustrate this internal dynamic, he focused on the genres and themes, the heroes and antiheroes of modern Hebrew writing. In this scheme, the problems of Jewish existence, of the universal and particular, were to forge the experiential link between the Hebrew Haskalah, the literature of Hibbat Zion and the students in Halkin's seminar. But when, under the influence of New Criticism, French existentialism, and other recent imports, Israeli students stopped reading Hebrew literature as a chronicle of the Jewish collective fate,[6] Halkin's historicism became as great an obstacle as Klausner's biographical and bibliographical data. It would take a whole generation for the first volume of Halkin's *Trends and Forms in Modern Hebrew Literature* to be edited and published by his students.[7]

For Sadan, the What of literature was the language of the text and the How was the closest possible scrutiny to matters of rhyme, rhythm, meter, allusion, and wordplay, aided by the insights of Freudian theory. The heroes were Bialik and Brenner. Unfortunately, for reasons never adequately explained, Sadan disavowed his Freudianism of the late thirties and early forties, never published his magnum opus on Bialik's poetics, and never reprinted his "Chapters on Brenner's Psychology," let alone his more journalistic appreciations of Freud.[8]

What Sadan offered up instead—in response to the Holocaust and the ingathering of Jews to the nascent State of Israel—was a global theory of

167

David G. Roskies

Sifrut Yisrael, a multilingual, ideologically diverse, but internally coherent modern Jewish literature.[9] Countering Klausner's and Halkin's one-track model of Jewish literary history, which legitimated only secular humanism and nationalism as the vehicles of Jewish creativity in the Hebrew language, Sadan proposed a far more complex model in which Hebrew would be viewed as only one axis in a triangular relationship consisting in its other two parts of Jewish diaspora languages (notably Yiddish) and of what Sadan called *la'az,* non-Jewish languages used to address a Jewish reader. Secular humanism, he proposed, should be viewed as only one axis within an ideational triad made up of rabbinic-misnagdic Judaism, Hasidism, and the Haskalah. Since all three movements, to a greater or lesser degree, had recourse to all three linguistic options, the result was a constant dialectical tension that cried out for synthesis.

Despite the great advance that such a theory made in Jewish literary history, tripling its holdings, as it were, in one fell swoop, Sadan himself applied the theory in an idiosyncratic way that required the total recall of all of Jewish culture—ancient, medieval, and modern—in all the languages of the Jewish dispersion. Thus Sadan ultimately defeated his stated purpose, for although both his medium and message projected a sense of wholeness, of cultural integration, the actual effect was to render him obsolete to all but a handful of loyalists.[10]

By default, therefore, the field was left open to Barukh Kurzweil, who was to dominate Hebrew literary criticism throughout the fifties and sixties. As Sadan saw the integration of Jewish culture, both religious and secular, in Hebrew, Yiddish and *la'az,* as the central task of Jewish literary scholarship, Kurzweil dedicated his formidable talents to the crisis of faith and the fragmentation of language that had been left in the wake of modernity.[11] In Kurzweil's scheme, modern Hebrew literature was the detritus of that metaphysical disaster and its major writers were children of the *ḥurban beit hamidrash* (the Destruction of the House of Study). As Sadan looked to Bialik as the arbiter of cultural synthesis, Kurzweil championed the apocalyptic vision of Uri Zvi Greenberg and even devised a periodization of modern Hebrew literature that culminated with Greenberg—its one and only occupant.[12] Though Kurzweil had many disciples and even spawned a school of Hebrew literary studies at Bar-Ilan University, his all-out condemnation of secular Zionism and his appeal to metahistorical issues left no room for the real developments in Israeli poetry, prose, and drama.[13]

To move from the vibrant—and almost violent—literary-critical scene in Israel to the other center of postwar Jewry, America, is to see in bold relief just how little still remained. The world of Yiddish was permanently traumatized by the Holocaust and the revelations of Stalin's terror. Building

168

pious and politically expedient memorials to the past is what the surviving intellectuals saw as their central task. The most prolific among them was still the critic S. Niger, who produced, in short order, an unwieldy survey of Yiddish *Short Story Writers and Novelists* (1946), semicritical biographies of Leivick (1951) and Peretz (1952), plus numerous collections of essays on Yiddish literature old and new.[14] Jacob Glatstein's emergence as the most urbane Yiddish literary critic in America was the one bright light in the immediate postwar era. In the four volumes of *In tokh genumen* [Sum and Substance, 1947–60], Glatstein not only provided contemporary Yiddish literature with its ideal reader but also provided the literary tradition— the *hob un guts,* as he called it—with a much needed critical revision.[15] In a more scholarly vein, Glatstein's former comrade-in-arms, the poet N. B. Minkoff, retrieved the *Pioneers of Yiddish Poetry in America* (1956) and even pieced together a Yiddish critical "tradition" from Alexander Zederbaum to S. Niger.[16] In creating a usable past, albeit for an ever-dwindling group of Yiddishists, these poet-critics carried out almost single-handedly a task that is normally the province of a collectivity of teachers, scholars, students, publishers, journalists, and ordinary readers. Unfortunately, this positive revision did not extend to their own past as leading modernist poets. Glatstein's readers could respond to his defense of beauty in Holocaust poetry,[17] but they could not countenance the cosmopolitan personae of the young Glatstein, just as they had no interest in the modernist poetry and poetic manifestos of A. Glanz-Leyeles.

The rediscovery of *that* past began in a scholarly publication called *The Field of Yiddish* (1954), the brainchild of Uriel Weinreich, who occupied the Atran Chair of Yiddish Language, Literature and Culture at Columbia University. Here Benjamin Hrushovski (Harshav) published the first study in historical poetics in the annals of Jewish literary scholarship. Modestly titled "On Free Rhythms in Modern Yiddish Poetry," Hrushovski began by defining the concept of free rhythms, then proceeded to rewrite the history of Yiddish poetry based on the development of its stanzaic and rhythmic structures.[18] For our purposes, it is important to note that Hrushovski saw the brilliant culmination of this process in the free dynamic and "speaking" rhythms used by the Yiddish modernist poets in America. They alone, Hrushovski demonstrated, fully exploited the rhythmic possibilities inherent in the language.

Even at the risk of disturbing my neat chronology, I must draw out the implications of Hrushovski's achievement. First, his breakthrough was methodological. By charting the evolution of free rhythms from the folk song through modernist poetry, he provided an objective model for others to follow. A Jewish literary phenomenon, in other words, provided a key to the general study of prosody.

His second achievement was cultural. Because Hrushovski later went on to found the first journal and department of poetics in Israel; because he was to write the definitive survey of Hebrew prosody; because he was to make the manifestos and poetry of Jewish modernism accessible to Hebrew and English readers alike, besides issuing his own manifestos in Hebrew, Hrushovski achieved a monumental rescue operation.[19] Thanks to his translations and scholarship, modernism emerged as a grand tradition in Jewish literary history, and Tel Aviv became, for a brief moment in time, the critical heir of St. Petersburg and Prague.[20]

Another closed book of Jewish literary creativity was Soviet-Yiddish culture, which had been strangled and then suppressed under Stalin. Reclaiming that lost legacy was the singular achievement of Khone Shmeruk, who also made his first scholarly appearance in the 1954 volume of *The Field of Yiddish*.[21] Shmeruk's bibliography of Soviet-Yiddish publications and his contribution to *A shpigl oyf a shteyn* [A Mirror on a Stone], a landmark anthology of Soviet-Yiddish poetry and prose, laid the groundwork for all subsequent studies (and translations) of this literature.[22]

Shmeruk reclaimed Soviet-Yiddish culture in the name of Jewish values and in this he proved himself a disciple of Sadan. Just as Sadan opposed the manifest-destiny-of-Hebrew approach to Jewish literary history, Shmeruk rejected all claims (Soviet, Bundist, or otherwise) to the self-sufficiency of Yiddish culture. Shmeruk adapted Sadan's triple-axis model as follows.

Yiddish culture, from the fifteenth century until the twentieth, only flourished when it drew from the wellsprings of the past and remained open to the surrounding non-Jewish environment. By unraveling the textual history of the works that he studied, by focusing on their allusive layers, and by locating each writer within a confluence of three intersecting cultures—the Yiddish, the Hebrew-Aramaic, and the coterritorial—Shmeruk showed how even the most avowedly secular writers were operating within a sanctioned cultural pattern. Thus his pantheon was occupied by those writers who fully exploited the triangular relationship between Yiddish, the religious tradition, and the surrounding cultures and did so often in the face of mounting political pressures. Foremost among them were Soviet-Yiddish writer Der Nister; the classical writers before him—Abramovitsh ("Mendele"), Peretz, and Sholem Aleichem—and a few Polish-Yiddish writers who followed, such as Itzik Manger, Uri Zvi Greenberg, and I. B. Singer.[23] The message of Shmeruk's method was that when Yiddish lost those multiple resources, whether by choice or through coercion, the culture was doomed.[24]

I have chosen to dwell at such length on Shmeruk's scholarly contribution not because it has had so profound an impact on the field as a whole—the Balkanization of Jewish studies at Israel's universities has severely hampered such interpenetration—but because it best illustrates one pole in the methodology and meaning of Jewish literary scholarship since the Six-Day War. The binary opposition that we see at work today is not, as my colleague Alan Mintz has suggested,[25] between poetics and interpretation—that is, between those who are concerned with the universal laws governing the literary text as against those who are concerned with its meaning—but rather between the horizontal and vertical approach to modern Jewish culture. While Hrushovski animates the Jewish literary text horizontally, making it part of a worldwide movement toward greater freedom and complexity, which in turn sheds light on universal laws of poetics, Shmeruk reads the same literature along a vertical line of legitimation, that is, in terms of Jewish tradition.

Squared off in one corner are the modernists—many, but not all, associated with the Tel Aviv School of Poetics—who are concerned with the exact nature of the Mendele persona, with semantic dynamics in the text continuum of Bialik's poetry, or with unreliable narrators in Agnon's fiction.[26] Facing them in the other are the traditionalists, concerned with Abramovitsh's translations of psalms, with folkloristic elements in Bialik's poetry, or with the midrashic layering in *Agunot*.[27] What makes the present moment in Jewish literary scholarship so exciting is that the binary opposition has broken down, that one increasingly finds the same scholar engaged on both fronts simultaneously. Whether because the modernist revolution has run its course, with everyone now seeking a traditional anchor in a secular world gone awry, or because its impact has been so pervasive that even the most conservative minds have adapted its teaching—whatever the reason, the combination of forces has made possible for the first time the reintegration of modern Jewish culture, if not in life, then at least in scholarship.

For the remainder of this essay I will describe and evaluate the various methodologies currently in use that create a semblance of wholeness, and I will point to the one area of Jewish literary scholarship that persists in its glorious isolation from the larger concerns of the field—American Jewish literature.

The most ambitious and potentially most productive scheme to create order out of chaos is Itamar Even-Zohar's theory of the literary polysystem.[28] Acknowledging his debt to Russian formalism, Even-Zohar views literature as a coherent system that always combines a center, or canonized literature, with a periphery, or popular literature. The former is the seat of innovation and the latter is the seat of preservation, but one cannot exist creatively without the other. Applying this theoretical construct to modern Hebrew literature, Even-Zohar discovers it to be—the phrase is positively barbaric—a "defective polysystem." That is to say, until World

War I, Hebrew lacked a popular or noncanonized literature of its own and therefore maintained its symbiotic relationship with Yiddish, while even the canonized literature in Hebrew maintained its dependency on Russian and Soviet models well into the period of statehood. This is Sadan's and Shmeruk's theory turned inside out. For whereas they argued that neither Hebrew nor Yiddish culture could be viable unless it continued to draw on all its internal, Jewish resources, Even-Zohar maintains that *every* literature legitimately strives for self-sufficiency. The fact that Israeli Hebrew literature has finally achieved this status is only to be welcomed. As for the idea of a multilingual "Jewish literature," Even-Zohar has this to say:

> Thus, Heinrich Heine, Boris Pasternak, Osip Mandelstam, Jakob Wasserman, Arnold Zweig . . . or Nelly Sachs . . . belong to the very centers of the various national literatures whose languages they use. Only a nationalistic Jewish approach, or a racist antisemitic one, or ignorance . . . would adopt the term "Jewish literature" on the basis of the origin of writers. It is not enough that a writer be a Jew or even use a "Jewish" language to entitle us to speak of a Jewish literature, if we mean a literature whose core has been Hebrew literature. Thus, Shalom Aleichem still belongs to "Jewish literature"; Isaac Bashevis Singer no longer does.[29]

As a tool of *Jewish* literary analysis, then, polysystem theory can be ruthlessly discriminating—in both senses of the word—even as it broadens the field of inquiry to include areas never taken seriously before. Right now it is the latter, integrationist aspect of the theory that I emphasize. Since Even-Zohar first formulated his theory in 1970, it has already inspired research into such diverse areas as Yiddish popular and sensational literature in the nineteenth and twentieth centuries;[30] the development of the Hebrew crime story in the 1930s;[31] Hebrew children's literature;[32] the shifting norms of Hebrew fiction from the Palmach generation to the generation of the sixties;[33] and most notably, the manifold studies of Gideon Toury on the theory and function of literary translation.[34]

Despite the rebuttal polysystem theory delivers to the ideological presuppositions of Sadan and Shmeruk, it can potentially add new methodological rigor to what I view as their central contribution to the field: the study of the Hebrew-Yiddish symbiosis. Thanks primarily to Shmeruk and his students, we can now see how Yiddish and Hebrew-Aramaic were used in all aspects of Ashkenazic literary culture—halakhic, exegetical, ethical, historical, liturgical, poetic, hagiographic, and fantastical—according to clearly defined but highly flexible rules.[35] Polysystem theory may be especially helpful in explaining how the rules and the rationale for this internal

Jewish bilingualism were transformed with the rise of competing ideologies—Haskalah versus Hasidism, Zionism versus the Bund—that effectively broke Jewish society into warring camps. Meanwhile, an impressive modern bilingual corpus has already been retrieved, ranging from Yosef Perl's Hebrew-Yiddish parody of Nahman of Bratslav;[36] to Sholem Aleichem's Hebrew fiction;[37] to the Yiddish prose writings of Agnon, Berdichewsky, Brenner, Gnessin, and Yaakov Steinberg;[38] to the stunning discovery of Uri Zvi Greenberg's Yiddish poetry spanning forty-six years.[39] The most recent contribution to the field—a work unthinkable even fifteen years ago—is Yael Feldman's study of modernist poet Gabriel Preil, subtitled "Gabriel Preil and the *Tradition* of Jewish Literary Bilingualism" (my emphasis).[40]

Polysystem theory is ostensibly impervious to the ideological fallout of battles lost and won. Paradoxically, however, it has done for Jewish literary scholarship of the 1970s and 1980s what Marxism did for the 1930s: it deparochialized some of the most hermetic and anomalous aspects of modern Jewish culture, and it reversed the cultural priorities. Periphery became center, and the structural complexity of the literary "system" became a measure of its greatness. As systemic consciousness replaces class consciousness among scholars of Jewish literature, it remains to be seen what unifying vision will emerge at the other end of time and space.

Another "modernist" horizontal approach to Jewish literary history is the study of genres, since it correlates formal innovations in the Jewish sphere with generic models in the surrounding, dominant cultures. The chief exponent of this approach is Dan Miron, who has written major studies on the emergence of the novel in Hebrew and Yiddish fiction from Abraham Mapu until Berdichewsky and has recently applied genre criticism very productively to a reevaluation of Bialik and Alterman.[41]

Miron has led the way in using genre theory to rescue from oblivion the literature of the Haskalah.[42] Having fallen from its pedestal as the source of everything vital in modern Jewish culture to being a subject of antiquarian research, Haskalah literature needed its prince in shining armor. Despite the tireless efforts of Shmuel Werses and Yehuda Friedlander to keep the interest in Hebrew satire alive,[43] it required scholars of the radical young guard, such as Miron (and Gershon Shaked before him) to effect an aesthetic rehabilitation.[44] Henceforth, whenever a genre is studied—whether historical drama, the novel, the allegorical story, the ballad, the feuilleton, the autobiography—its roots in Haskalah literature are carefully unearthed.[45] The fact that Uzi Shavit, a student of Hrushovski's, has traced the development of Haskalah prosody and, most recently, of its ideological poetry is the surest sign that the subject has "arrived."[46] Aiding in this

David G. Roskies

search for progenitors is the superbly edited series of the Dorot Library that reinstated many Haskalah classics within the larger corpus of Jewish writing.[47]

Thus some of the major advances in the field of Hebrew literary scholarship have come about by dismantling the great theoretical and practical edifices erected by the founding fathers: Klausner, Halkin, Sadan, and Kurzweil. Scholars of the post-1967 generation—except when they're formulating grand theoretical schemes of their own—write "studies in" a particular genre or "a contribution to" a specific period, as if to say: "the time for synthesis is yet to come." Those literary-historical surveys that have been attempted, notably by Shaked and Miron, define their turf accordingly. Gershon Shaked has undertaken to write the history of Hebrew prose fiction from 1880 to 1970; the first volume is situated entirely in "the diaspora," the second primarily in Palestine.[48] Miron has carved out an even narrower turf, subjecting to minute scrutiny the changes that did and did not occur in Hebrew poetry and prose at the turn of the century.[49]

These new, if more modestly conceived, literary-historical reappraisals have come about thanks to two developments in the scholarly arena. The first is that the amount of text-critical and extraliterary material available to the literary historian has increased exponentially over the past few years: the editions of literary correspondence, the descriptive bibliographies of books and journals published in any given period, the comparison with earlier text variants or with uncollected texts, the analysis of essayistic and polemical writings.[50] The second, more profound change, one affecting all aspects of Israeli intellectual life, is the renewed interest in Zionist ideology.[51]

Both published volumes of Shaked's literary history begin with the stern moralist and most anguished critic of modern Jewish culture, Yosef Hayyim Brenner. Brenner's characterization of a literature created ʾaf-ʿal-pi-khen—despite all odds—becomes for Shaked the key to the miracle and the anomaly that is modern Hebrew fiction. Similarly, it is Brenner who bequeathes to Hebrew fiction in Palestine its most enduring legacy: the distinction between the "Palestinian genre" and the "antigenre," that is, between the sentimental and the critical depiction of Jewish life in Palestine. Because it is safe to assume that Shaked's fourth volume will conclude with Amoz Oz and A. B. Yehoshua, two outspoken critics of Israeli society whose careers Shaked has done more to launch than any other writer, we have the makings of a perfectly symmetrical literary history. My point is not to question the validity of this model but simply to note that Brenner could only assume such symbolic status with the coming of age of Israeli culture, with its renewed confrontation between art and politics. If it is now possible, thanks to the explosion of Brenner studies in Israeli academe, to

174

reconstruct almost every day in this tragic writer's life, it speaks volumes about the current generation's own search for a hero.[52]

One measure, then, of cultural reintegration in Hebrew literary scholarship is the degree to which engagé writers are coming back into vogue. Dan Miron has taken this revisionism one step further by constructing a new literary-historical schema out of Zionist politics. Called "From Creators to Builders without a Home of Their Own," his monograph-length essay charts the interplay between Hebrew literature and Zionist politics through seven fairly distinct periods, from 1881 until the present.[53] In Miron's retelling, informed by his own political agenda, some of the old controversies, such as Natan Alterman's "sellout" to David Ben-Gurion, are made to seem as timely as ever.

Like Brenner, Alterman is enjoying a spectacular comeback, both in terms of his modernist poetry (given the New Critical concern with the existential and formal aspects of literary art) and (given the renewed interest in politics) on the basis of his publicistic verse, the famous *Tur hashevi'i* column.[54] Indeed, Alterman's return to eminence augers the formation of a new modern Hebrew literary canon.

Miron, I think, comes closest to articulating the operative criteria. In the preface to *Bo'a, layla,* he introduces his subjects as follows: "Both Bialik and Berdichewsky were, as creative artists, close to the type of the conservative revolutionary or the revolutionary conservative. Both were people who, on the strength of their attachment to [literary] traditions, engaged in an ever fiercer struggle with these very traditions. These they subjected to the most ruthless scrutiny precisely because they valued them so and treated them with the utmost seriousness" (p. 14). This "conservative-revolutionary" formula, reminiscent in its Oedipal overtones of Harold Bloom's *Anxiety of Influence*, explains not only Miron's abiding fascination with such writers as Bialik, Berdichewsky, Gnessin, and Alterman but also the vast output of Agnon studies. The latter were most recently summarized by Shaked in a long chapter that locates the roots of Agnon's writing in "Tradition and Revolution."[55]

Occupying the "center" of the Hebrew literary "system" are those writers schooled in past traditions who abuse that past as an object of parody or use it as intertextual landscape.[56] What makes this sense of pasthood so compelling and useful a measure of greatness to a new generation of Jewish literary scholars is that it comes supported by an impressive body of practical criticism that itself has become a critical tradition. Now, for the first time, there are critical compendia that provide an immediate overview of an author's "reception" over time. The most impressive is the series called *Penei Hasifrut,* twenty-one volumes of which have appeared to date.[57] Each is devoted to criticism and scholarship on a single author, presented in chronological order, with an introductory survey essay and a bibliography. In addition, Miron has shown that one way of entering the closed world of the text is through its critical readings. In some of his best essays,[58] Miron begins by submitting all the critical opinions on a given author or work to minute scrutiny; then he isolates their major assumptions, reveals the contradictions between them, and arrives at a new synthetic reading based on these very same categories. Thus the "revolutionary-conservative" formula works as well for the critic as it does for the writer.

Of the schemes outlined thus far—polysystem theory, genre studies, the history of literature and of criticism—all are grounded in time and place. There is one remaining school, favored by scholars of Jewish literature writing in English, that is thoroughly ahistorical. I speak here of the archetypal school of Jewish literary scholarship that combines Kurzweil's metaphysical concerns with Northrop Frye's theory of modes. Harold Fisch is its most sophisticated exponent. The idea is to find Jewish archetypes that transcend any given period, language, or genre and to see them as the vessels of Jewish distinctiveness and cultural continuity. In Fisch's recent collection of essays, *A Remembered Future,* he argues that Jewish archetypes are ultimately grounded in historical experience as opposed to the myths that Christian writers operate with.[59] More recently, Nehama Aschkenasy has employed the same method to isolate the various archetypes of women that operate in Hebrew literature across time and place.[60]

Archetypal and thematic studies are particularly well suited for the English reader who is generally unacquainted with Hebrew or Yiddish literature either in whole or in part. Perhaps this explains why it is hard to find an English-language work of Jewish literary scholarship that is not thematic, including my own book on responses to catastrophe in modern Jewish culture.[61] One might even argue that the very fragmentation of Jewish culture in the diaspora makes a synthetic approach so necessary. Even when such studies *are* grounded in history, however, there is no guarantee that the thematic connections one finds aren't the thematic connections one seeks.[62]

This brings me, finally, to that hybrid of subfields in Jewish literary scholarship: American Jewish literature. It is a field rich in biobibliographical materials and poor in literary-historical synthesis.[63] Its pantheon of writers is known to any undergraduate major in American literature, yet its place in Jewish cultural history has hardly been examined even by its most celebrated scholars. If we take the Malin and Stark anthology of 1963, which advertised itself as a *breakthrough* at canonization, then the field is barely twenty-five years old.[64]

In the past quarter century little, if anything, has been resolved. There is still no consensus as to what context to study this literature in, whether in terms of "assimilation and the [Jewish] crisis of identity" or strictly in literary terms.[65] If the latter, then to which literature does it belong— American or Jewish? Most scholars, given their particular training, have chosen the American route and have identified Jewish-American literature with the American Left.[66] The first to have taken the Jewish route, given *her* particular training, is Ruth Wisse, who charted the fortunes of the schlemiel from Eastern Europe until America.[67] To succeed, each scheme must also supply its own genealogy. Those who think in sociological categories need not find a literary common ground between Abraham Cahan, Anzia Yezierska, and Mary Antin. It's enough that all these writers started out somewhere in the "ghetto" and reached the shores of America during the period of mass immigration. For those who equate Jewish with leftist, one can either begin or end with the *Partisan Review*.[68] Indeed, the *Partisan Review* provides a sexy myth of origins, for it calls to mind all those bright young men, born out of radical politics, hanging out in the Village with nothing but Dostoyevsky, Freud, and Marx on their minds. But consider the revisionary impact if one were to start with another, equally self-conscious group of Jewish-American intellectuals—with those who grouped themselves in the twenties and thirties around the *Menorah Journal*.[69] This would conjure up an entirely different image: of bourgeois academic types spread out across America who take Zionism and religion seriously. Will the real American-Jewish literature please stand up?

If American-Jewish literary scholarship is having such a hard time defining its center, how much more so if it begins to confront its periphery. It is from the periphery that the most serious challenges have come of late: Canadian-Jewish scholars have rediscovered a major poet-critic in the person of A. M. Klein,[70] and Benjamin Hrushovski-Harshav has issued the first anthology of American-Yiddish modernist poetry.[71] If, until now, the center has been dominated by non-Jewish Jews, it will be extremely difficult to place, on the one hand, a true writer of *laᶜaz*, someone who used English to address a Jewish reader and possessed more Judaic knowledge than all the American-Jewish novelists combined. Perhaps it will be argued that Klein's aborted career is proof that no *real* Jewish writer can survive in an English-language or diaspora environment. If, on the other hand, the argument for beginning the story of American-Jewish literature ex nihilo is based on the view of the Jewish immigrant masses as barbarians, semiliterate butchers, tailors, peddlers, and shopkeepers, then where does one place

177

a Yiddish modernist movement—the child of the same immigration—that was thoroughly in touch with American urban rhythms and with the latest developments on the literary scene? Perhaps it will be argued that we are dealing with two entirely separate organisms—three, if we include American-Hebrew literature as well—and that America is the ultimate burial ground for any global theory of Jewish literature.

It is to this last that I return, in conclusion. As someone who teaches in the first Department of Jewish Literature ever established (in 1975), and as founder and coeditor of a journal of Jewish literary history, I obviously have a vested interest in defending an integrationist viewpoint. I am also the first to admit that I and my colleagues have devoted precious little effort to thinking through the practical and theoretical implications of such a field. How does one go about teaching it? Where does one draw the line? Does every book about the image of the Jews in this literature and in that also constitute a part of the corpus?

It may be that in the end we will discover that there is no connection between Yiddish, Hebrew, and Anglo-Jewish writing in America; that the historical fate of the Jews does not bring the disparate parts of the culture together; that with the fragmentation of modern Jewry, Jewish collective memory has ceased as well. But before we answer all these questions in the negative, there is a larger challenge to confront. Now that we are sophisti-cated enough to study Jewish literature as a system or, better yet, as a polysystem, it behooves us to look at Jewish *culture* as a system, one that includes overt and displaced forms of religious self-expression, not only the avowedly secular forms that have been studied thus far. What Sadan argued for the nineteenth century makes sense all over again for the last quarter of the twentieth. We live at a time when the Lubavitsher Hasidim broadcast their *farbrengen* on cable TV; at a time of messianic upheaval in Israel; at a time when Soviet Jews have become the vanguard of cultural liberation. At such a time, when everything is up for grabs again, the field of Jewish literary scholarship, so long accustomed to building on a geological fault, is ideally situated to create a sturdy, flexible structure to withstand the unfore-seen tremors still to come.

Notes

1. The best anthologies of twentieth-century literary criticism and literary theory are: *20th Century Literary Criticism: A Reader,* ed. David Lodge (London, 1972) and *Critical Theory Since 1965,* ed. Hazard Adams and Leroy Searle (Tallahassee, 1987), a sequel to their *Critical Theory Since Plato* (New York, 1971). The most readable surveys are Jonathan Culler, *Structuralist Poetics: Structuralism, Linguistics, and the Study of Literature* (Ithaca, N.Y., 1975), and Terry Eagleton, *Literary Theory: An Introduction* (Minneapolis, 1983).

2. For a preliminary study in this direction, see Michael Stern "Tevye's Art of Quotation," *Prooftexts* 6 (1986), pp. 79–96. This study informed Hillel Halkin's superb translation of *Tevye the Dairyman and Railroad Stories* (New York, 1987).

3. On this question, see S. Niger, "Elements of Sholem Aleichem's Humor Before Sholem Aleichem," *Pinkes* 1 (1927–28), pp. 1–12 [in Yiddish]; Yudel Mark, "Sholem Aleichem's Sayings—Created or Inherited?" *Di tsukunft* (May 1946), pp. 379–82 [in Yiddish].

4. On Jewish folk irony, see Ruth R. Wisse, *The Schlemiel as Modern Hero* (Chicago, 1971), pp. 47–48. This analysis is based, in turn, on Nokhem Oyslender, *Gruntshtrikhn fun yidishn realizm* [Major Trends in Yiddish Realism] (Vilna, 1928), pp. 24–25. On the semiotics of Jewish folklore, see H. Binyamin [Benjamin Hrushovski], "The Deconstruction of Speech: Sholem Aleichem and the Semiotics of Jewish Folklore," afterword to Sholem Aleichem, *Tevye hehalban vemonologim* (Tel Aviv, 1983; in Hebrew), pp. 195–212.

5. Yosef Klausner, *Historiya shel hasifrut ha'ivrit hahadasha*, 3rd ed. (Jerusalem, 1960), 6 vols.

6. On this generational shift in attitude, see Nurit Gertz, *Hirbat Hiza'a vehaboqer shelemohorat* [Generational Shift in Literary History: Hebrew Narrative Fiction in the Sixties] (Tel Aviv, 1983), esp. chaps. 1, 7. This was originally her doctoral dissertation written for Hrushovski in 1978.

7. Simon Halkin, *Zeramin vetsurot basifrut ha'ivrit hahadasha* [Book 1: Chapters in the Literature of the Haskalah and Hibbat Zion], ed. Zippora Kagan (Jerusalem, 1984). For a preliminary, popular version of Halkin's approach, see *Modern Hebrew Literature from the Enlightenment to the Birth of the State of Israel: Trends and Values* (New York, 1950), based on his doctoral dissertation for Hebrew Union College. See also Gershon Shaked, "The Teller as Critic: On Simon Halkin's Approach to Hebrew Fiction," in *S. Halkin: Mivhar ma'amarim 'al yetsirato*, ed. Dan Laor (Tel Aviv, 1978; in Hebrew), pp. 204–11.

8. On Sadan's Freudianism, see Shmuel Werses, "Our Literature in the Eyes of Dov Sadan," in *Biqqoret habiqqoret* [Criticism of Criticism: Evaluations in Development] (Tel Aviv, 1982; in Hebrew), pp. 235–42. For a complete bibliography of Sadan's writings, see G. Kressel, *Kitvei Dov Sadan: Bibli'ografiya* (Tel Aviv, 1981), and Joseph Galron-Goldschläger, *Kitvei Dov Sadan* [The Works of D.S.: A Bibliography, 1935–1984] (Israel, 1986).

9. Dov Sadan, "On Our Literature: Introductory Essay" [in Hebrew, 1950], reprinted in *'Avnei-bedeq* (Tel Aviv, 1962), pp. 9–66.

10. For the most thorough reappraisal of Sadan's theory to date, see Dan Miron, "The Literatures of the Jews: A Return to Reality," *Im lo tihye Yerushalayim* [If There Is No Jerusalem: Essays on Hebrew Writing in a Cultural-Political Context] (Tel Aviv, 1987; in Hebrew), pp. 143–62. My own essay on the state of Jewish literary scholarship should be read in the light of this debate.

11. See James S. Diamond, *Barukh Kurzweil and Modern Hebrew Literature*, Brown Judaic Studies 39 (Chico, Calif., 1983); Stanley Nash, "Criticism as Calling: The Case of Barukh Kurzweil," *Prooftexts* 5 (1985), pp. 281–87, and *Baruch Kurzweil Memorial Volume: Essays on Criticism*, ed. M. Z. Kaddari et al. (Tel Aviv, 1975).

12. Diamond, *Barukh Kurzweil*, pp. 101–5.

13. On Kurzweil's impact, see Gershon Shaked, "Literature and Its Audience: On the Reception of Israeli Fiction in the Forties and Fifties," *Prooftexts* 7 (1987), pp. 207–23. On his failure vis-à-vis contemporary Israeli literature, see, among others, Dan Miron, "Modern Hebrew Literature: Zionist Perspectives and Israeli Realities," *Prooftexts* 4 (1984), pp. 60–68.

14. S. Niger [Samuel Charney], *Dertseylers un romanistn 1* (New York, 1946) [no subsequent volumes appeared], *H. Leyvik 1888–1948* (Toronto, 1951), and *Y. L. Perets: zayn lebn, zayn firndike perzenlekhkayt, zayne hebreishe un yidishe shriftn, zayn virkung* (Buenos Aires, 1952).

David G. Roskies

15. Jacob Glatstein, *In tokh genumen: eseyen* [Sum and Substance: Essays], 1 (New York, 1947); 2 (New York, 1956); 3–4 (Buenos Aires, 1960).

16. N. B. Minkoff, *Pionern fun yidisher poezye in Amerike: dos sotsyale lid* (New York, 1956), 3 vols.; *Zeks yidishe kritiker* [Six Yiddish Critics] (Buenos Aires, 1954).

17. Jacob Glatstein, "May One Enjoy a Dirge?" *In tokh genumen* (New York, 1947; in Yiddish), pp. 428–34.

18. Benjamin Hrushovski, "On Free Rhythms in Modern Yiddish Poetry," in *The Field of Yiddish: Studies in Yiddish Language, Folklore, and Literature*, ed. Uriel Weinreich (New York, 1954), pp. 219–66 (now available through Lexik House Publishers, Cold Springs, N.Y.).

19. Benjamin Hrushovski, "Prosody, Hebrew," *Encyclopedia Judaica*, vol. 13, pp. 1195–1240. As translator, see, for instance, "The Poetry of the Young Glatstein and the Introspectivist Manifesto," *Siman kri'a* 8 (April 1978), pp. 73–100 [in Hebrew]; "Poetry and Prose from the Expressionist Journal *Albatros* ed. by Uri Zvi Greenberg," *Siman kri'a* 9 (May 1979), pp. 103–43 [in Hebrew]; and, above all, *American Yiddish Poetry: A Bilingual Anthology* (Berkeley, 1986), ed. in collaboration with Barbara Harshav-Hrushovski. As an author of manifestos, see the manifesto to *Liqrat* [Internal Organ for a Group of Young Writers] 1 (1952), reprinted in *Manifestim sifrutiyim* [Literary Manifestos: A Selection of Manifestos from Hebrew Journals and Newspapers in the Years 1821–1981], ed. Nurit Govrin (Tel Aviv, 1984), pp. 122–23, and "A Quarterly for the Study of Literature in Israel," the editorial to the inaugural issue of *Hasifrut* 1 (1968) [in Hebrew].

20. On this link, see Ziva Ben-Porat and Benjamin Hrushovski, *Structuralist Poetics in Israel* (Tel Aviv, 1974); Alan Mintz, "On the Tel Aviv School of Poetics," *Prooftexts* 4 (1984), pp. 215–35; and Yael S. Feldman, "Poetics and Politics: Israeli Literary Criticism between East and West," *Proceedings of the American Academy for Jewish Research* 52 (1985), pp. 9–35.

21. Khone Shmeruk, "The Earliest Aramaic and Yiddish Version of the 'Song of the Kid,' " in Weinreich, *The Field of Yiddish*, pp. 214–18.

22. *A shpigl oyf a shteyn: antologye* [A Mirror on a Stone: Anthology of Poetry and Prose by Twelve Murdered Yiddish Writers in the Soviet Union], ed. Khone Shmeruk, with the collaboration of Benjamin Hrushovski and Abraham Sutzkever (Tel Aviv, 1964); *Pirsumim yehudiyim bivrit hamo'atsot 1917–1960* [Jewish Publications in the Soviet Union 1917–1960], ed. Khone Shmeruk, with intros. by Y. Slutsky and Khone Shmeruk (Jerusalem, 1961).

23. Khone Shmeruk, "Der Nister: His Life and Work," intro. to Der Nister, *Hanazir vehagediya* (Jerusalem, 1963; in Hebrew), pp. 9–52; "Der Nister's 'Under a Fence': Tribulations of a Soviet Yiddish Symbolist," in *The Field of Yiddish: Second Collection*, ed. Uriel Weinreich (The Hague, 1965), pp. 263–87; *Peretses yiesh-vizye* [Peretz's Vision of Despair: An Interpretation of I. L. Peretz's *Bay nakht afn altn mark* and Critical Edition of the Play] (New York, 1971); "Introduction" to Sholem Aleichem, *Ketavim ʿivriyim* [Hebrew Writings], ed. Khone Shmeruk (Jerusalem, 1976), pp. 13–46; "*Medresh Itzik* and the Problem of Its Literary Traditions," intro. to Itzik Manger, *Medresh Itsik*, 3rd rev. ed. (Jerusalem, 1984), pp. v-xxix; "Uri Zvi Greenberg's Yiddish Work in Erez Israel," *Hasifrut* 29 (1979), pp. 82–92 [in Hebrew]; "The Use of Monologue as a Narrative Technique in the Stories of Isaac Bashevis Singer," intro. to Isaac Bashevis Singer, *Der shpigl un andere dertseylungen*, ed. Khone Shmeruk (Jerusalem, 1975), pp. v-xxxv.

24. Khone Shmeruk, "Yiddish Culture in the Soviet Union," *Gesher* 47–48 (1966), pp. 58–80 [in Hebrew]; *Sifrut yidish: peraqim letoldeteha* [Yiddish Literature: Aspects of Its History] (Tel Aviv, 1978); *Sifrut yidish befolin* [Yiddish Literature in Poland: Historical Studies and Perspectives] (Jerusalem, 1981); *The Esterke Story in Yiddish and Polish Literature: A Case Study in the Mutual Relations of Two Cultural Traditions* (Jerusalem, 1985) and "The Jewish Trilingual Press in Warsaw," *Hasifrut* 30–31 (1981), pp. 193–200 [in Hebrew].

25. Mintz, "On the Tel Aviv School of Poetics."

26. Dan Miron, *A Traveler Disguised: A Study in the Rise of Modern Yiddish Fiction in the Nineteenth Century* (New York, 1973); Menakhem Perry, *Hamivne hasemanti shel shirei Bialik* [Semantic Dynamics in Poetry: The Theory of Semantic Change in the Text Continuum of a Poem] (Tel Aviv, 1977); Gershon Shaked, *Omanut hasippur shel Agnon* [Agnon's Narrative Art] (Tel Aviv, 1973), pp. 228–78.

27. Khone Shmeruk, "'Mendele's Translations of Psalms," *Di goldene keyt* 62–63 (1968), pp. 290–312 [in Yiddish]; also in Hebrew in *Hasifrut* 1 (1968), pp. 327–42; Ziva Shamir, *Hatsratsar meshorer hagalut* [Poetry of Poverty: Folkloristic Elements in Bialik's Works] (Tel Aviv, 1986); Gershon Shaked, "Midrash and Narrative: Agnon's 'Agunot,' " in *Midrash and Literature*, ed. Geoffrey H. Hartman and Sanford Budick (New Haven, Conn., 1986), pp. 285–303. Avraham Holtz's work on the Hasidic and folkloristic sources of *Hakhnasat kalla* also belongs firmly in this camp; see *Ma'aseh reb Yudel ḥasid* [The Tale of Reb Yudel Hasid: From a Yiddish Narrative in Nissim V'niflaot to S. Y. Agnon's Hakhnasat Kalla] (New York, 1986).

28. Itamar Even-Zohar, *Papers in Historical Poetics* (Tel Aviv, 1978).

29. Ibid., pp. 80–81.

30. David G. Roskies, "The Medium and Message of the Maskilic Chapbook," *Jewish Social Studies* 41 (1979), pp. 275–90; Khone Shmeruk, "To the History of *Shund* Literature in Yiddish," *Tarbiz* 52 (1983), pp. 325–54 [in Hebrew]; Yaakov Shavit, "Warsaw/Tel Aviv— Yiddish and Hebrew: Between Mass Literature and Mass Culture," *Hasifrut* 35–36 (1986), pp. 201–10 [in Hebrew].

31. Zohar Shavit and Yaakov Shavit, "On the Development of the Hebrew Crime Story during the 1930s in Palestine," *Hasifrut* 18–19 (1974), pp. 30–73 [in Hebrew].

32. Uriel Ofek, *Sifrut hayeladim ha'ivrit: hahathala* [The Beginnings of Hebrew Children's Literature] (Tel Aviv, 1979); idem, *Gumot ḥen* [Dimples: Bialik's Contribution to Children's Literature] (Jerusalem, 1984); Zohar Shavit, "The Function of Yiddish Literature in the Development of Hebrew Children's Literature," *Hasifrut* 35–36 (1986), pp. 148–53 [in Hebrew].

33. Nurit Gertz, *Ḥirbat Ḥiza'ah.*

34. The one most pertinent to Jewish literary studies is *Normot shel targum vehatargum hasifruti le'ivrit bashanim 1930–1945* [Translation Norms and Literary Translation into Hebrew in 1930–1945] (Tel Aviv, 1977).

35. In addition to the studies already mentioned, it is important to add: Alexander ben Yizhak Pfaffenhofen, *Sefer massa umeriva*, ed. with intro. by Chava Turniansky (Jerusalem, 1985); Sarah Zfatman, *Hasipporet beyidish mireishitah 'ad 'Shivḥei haBesht' (1504–1814)* [Yiddish Narrative Prose from Its Beginnings to 'Shivḥei ha-Besht' (1504–1814): An Annotated Bibliography] (Jerusalem, 1985). This bibliography complements Zfatman's doctoral dissertation on the same subject.

36. *Ma'asiyot ve'igarot mitsadiqim 'amitiyim ume'anshe shelomenu* [Joseph Perl: Hasidic Tales and Narratives], ed. Khone Shmeruk and Shmuel Werses (Jerusalem, 1969). See also Shmuel Werses, "Between Three Languages (On Joseph Perl's Yiddish Writings in the Light of New Materials)," *Di goldene keyt* 89 (1976), pp. 150–77 [in Yiddish].

37. Sholem Aleichem, *Ketavim 'ivriyim.*

38. S. Y. Agnon, *Yidishe verk*, with an intro. by Dov Sadan (1977); M. J. Bin-Gorion (Berdyczewski) *Yidishe ksovim fun a vaytn korev*, ed. with an intro. by Shmuel Werses (1981); and Jacob Steinberg, *Gezamlte dertseylungen*, ed. with an intro. by Aharon Komem (1986). These three volumes form part of the series of Yiddish literary texts issued by the Yiddish Department of the Hebrew University. Yitzhak Bakon has also issued two poorly edited and translated volumes published by Ben-Gurion University: Y. H. Brenner, *Haketavim hayidiyim / di yidishe ksovim* (1985) and *Brenner veGnessin kesoferim du-leshoniyim* (1986).

David G. Roskies

39. Uri Zvi Greenberg, *Gezamlte verk,* ed. Khone Shmeruk (Jerusalem, 1979), 2 vols.

40. Yael S. Feldman, *Modernism and Cultural Transfer: Gabriel Preil and the Tradition of Jewish Literary Bilingualism,* Monographs of the Hebrew Union College, no. 10 (Cincinnati, 1986).

41. Dan Miron, *Bein ḥazon le'emet* [From Romance to the Novel: Studies in the Emergence of the Hebrew and Yiddish Novel in the Nineteenth Century] (Jerusalem, 1979); *Kivun orot* [Back to Focus: Studies in Modern Hebrew Fiction] (Jerusalem, 1979), pp. 17–105; *Mipperat el ʿiqqar* [Parts into a Whole: Structure, Genre and Ideas in Nathan Alterman's Poetry] (Tel Aviv, 1981); *Bo'a, layla* [Come, O Night: Hebrew Literature between the Rational and the Irrational at the Turn of the Twentieth Century] (Tel Aviv, 1987).

42. In addition to *Bein ḥazon le'emet,* see "Rediscovering Haskalah Poetry," *Prooftexts* 1 (1981), pp. 292–305; "Between Precedent and Happening: Y. L. Gordon's Epic Poetry and Its Place in Hebrew Haskalah Literature," *Jerusalem Studies in Hebrew Literature* 2 (1983), pp. 127–97 [in Hebrew].

43. Shmuel Werses, *Sippur veshorsho* [Story and Source: Studies in the Development of Hebrew Prose] (Ramat Gan, 1971); *Mimendele ʿad Hazaz* [From Mendele to Hazaz: Studies in the Development of Hebrew Prose] (Jerusalem, 1987); "Echoes of Lucian's Satire in Hebrew Enlightenment Literature," *Biqoret ufarshanut* 11/12 (1978), pp. 119–85 [in Hebrew]. Yehudah Friedlander, *Peraqim basatira haʿivrit* [Studies in Hebrew Satire: Hebrew Satire in Germany, 1790–1797] (Tel Aviv, 1979); *Bemisterei hasatira* [Hebrew Satire in Europe in the Nineteenth Century] (Ramat Gan, 1984).

44. Gershon Shaked, *Bein tseḥoq ledemaʿ* [Between Parody and Pathos: Studies in the Work of Mendele Mokher Sefarim] (Ramat Gan, 1965).

45. Gershon Shaked, *Hamaḥaze haʿivri hahistori bitqufat hattehiya* [The Hebrew Historical Drama in the Twentieth Century: Themes and Forms] (Jerusalem, 1970) (based on his doctoral dissertation for Simon Halkin); Ruth Shenfeld, *Min hamelekh hamashiaḥ ve'ad lemelekh basar vadam* [From King Messiah to the King of Flesh and Blood: The Hebrew Historical Novel in the Twentieth Century] (Tel Aviv, 1986); Uri Shoham, *Hamashma'ut ha'aḥeret* [The Other Meaning: From Allegorical Parable to Pararealistic Story] (Tel Aviv, 1982); Shlomo Yaniv, *Habalada haʿivrit* [The Hebrew Ballad: Chapters in Its Development] (Haifa, 1986); Zvi Karniel, *Hafeliton haʿivri* [The Hebrew Feuilleton] (Tel Aviv, 1981) (based on his dissertation for Hillel Barzel); Ben-Ami Feingold, "Autobiography as Literature: A Study of Moshe Leib Lilienblum's *Ḥat'ot neʿurim,*" *Jerusalem Studies in Hebrew Literature* 4 (1983), pp. 86–111 [in Hebrew]; Alan Mintz, "Guenzburg, Lilienblum, and the Shape of Haskalah Autobiography," *AJS Review* 4 (1979), pp. 71–110.

46. Uzi Shavit, *Hamahapeikha haritmit* [The Rhythmic Revolution: On the Threshold of Modern Hebrew Prosody] (Tel Aviv, 1983); *Shira ve'idiyologiya* [Poetry and Ideology: A Contribution to the Evolution of Hebrew Poetry in the 18th and 19th Centuries] (Tel Aviv, 1987).

47. They are, in alphabetical order: I. Bershadsky, *Be'ein matara,* ed. Yosef Ewen (1967); M. D. Brandstetter, *Sippurim,* ed. Ben-Ami Feingold (1974); R. A. Braudes, *Hadat vehaḥayim,* ed. Gershon Shaked (1974), 2 vols.; Ayzik-Meyer Dik, *Reb Shmʿaya mevarekh hamoʿadot vedivrei sippur 'aḥerim,* ed. and trans. Dov Sadan (1967); Abraham Goldfaden, *Shirim umaḥazot,* ed. R. Goldberg (1970); Ezra Goldin, *Sippurim,* ed. Yosef Ewen (1970); Abraham Baer Gottlober *Zikhronot umasaʿot,* ed. R. Goldberg (1976), 2 vols.; Yosef Ha'efrati, *Melukhat Sha'ul,* ed. Gershon Shaked (1968); Yehudah Leib Levin, *Zikhronot vehegyonot,* ed. Yehudah Slutsky (1968); Moshe Leib Lilienblum, *Ketavim 'otobiyografiyim,* ed. Shlomo Breiman, (1970), 3 vols.; Joshua Heschel Schorr, *Ma'amarim,* ed. Ezra Spicehandler (1972); Peretz Smolenskin, *Qevurat ḥamor,* ed. D. Weinfeld (1968); Eliezer Zvi Hacohen Zweifel *Shalom ʿal yisrael,* ed. Abraham Rubinstein, (1972), 2 vols.; and two anthologies: *Hashira haʿivrit*

bitqufat Ḥibbat Zion, ed. Ruth Kartun-Blum (1969); *Nitsanei hareʾalizem basipporet haʿivrit*, ed. Yosef Ewen (1972).

48. Gershon Shaked, *Hasipporet haʿivrit 1880–1970* [Hebrew Narrative Fiction, 1880–1970], vol. 1: *In Exile* (Israel, 1977); vol. 2: *In the Land of Israel and the Diaspora* (1983).

49. Dan Miron, "Some Background on the Twentieth Century," *Simon Halkin Jubilee Volume*, ed. Boaz Shahevitch and Menahem Perry (Jerusalem, 1975; in Hebrew), pp. 419–87; *Hapereida min ha'ani heʿani* [Taking Leave of the Impoverished Self: Ch. N. Bialik's Early Poetry, 1891–1901] (Israel, 1986); and *Bo'a, layla* (1987). The central figure in all three of these major studies is, of course, Bialik.

50. These are reviewed by Shaked in "The Study of Modern Hebrew Literature," in *Meḥqarim bemadaʿei hayahadut* [Studies in Jewish Scholarship], ed. Moshe Brasher (Jerusalem, 1986; in Hebrew), pp. 294–306.

51. A turning point came in 1980 with the publication of Anita Shapira's two-volume biography of Berl Katznelson. For an English abridgment of this landmark study, see *Berl: The Biography of a Socialist Zionist* (Cambridge, Mass., 1984).

52. These, in chronological order, are the most notable items: Dan Miron, "On Stylistic Problems in Brenner's Fiction" (1961), reprinted in *Kivon 'orot*, pp. 357–68; Gershon Shaked, *Lelo motsaʾ* [Dead End: Studies in Y. H. Brenner, M. Y. Berdichewsky, G. Shoffman and U. N. Gnessin] (Tel Aviv, 1973), pp. 57–118 (articles written over a fifteen-year period); Yitzhak Bakon, *Brenner hatsa'ir* [The Young Brenner: His Life and Works until the Appearance of *Hameʿorer* in London] (Tel Aviv, 1975), 2 vols.; Yosef Ewen, *Omanut hasippur shel Y. H. Brenner* [Y. H. Brenner's Craft of Fiction] (Jerusalem, 1977); Yitzhak Bakon, *Hatsa'ir haboded basipporet haʿivrit 1899–1908* [The Solitary Youth in Hebrew Fiction] (Tel Aviv, 1978); Menachem Brinker, "Y. H. Brenner's Ideology as a Literary Critic: The Emergence of a Genre in Hebrew Criticism," *Hasifrut* 29 (1979), pp. 23–33 [in Hebrew]; Ḥagit Matras, *Hameʿorer: ketav ʿet veʿarikhato [Hameʿorer:* A Journal and Its Editing] (Jerusalem, 1984); Adi Zemach, *Tenuʿa banequda* [A Movement on the Spot: Y. H. Brenner and His Novels] (Tel Aviv, 1984); Nurit Govrin, *Meʾoraʿ Brenner* ["The Brenner Affair": The Fight for Free Speech, 1910–1913] (Jerusalem, 1985); idem, "In Praise of the 'Genre': Brenner as the Supporter of the 'Palestinian Genre,' " *Dappim: Research in Literature* 3 (1986), pp. 97–116 [in Hebrew]. This, in addition to the *Maḥbarot leheqer yetsirato shel Y. H. Brenner* series, 4 vols. (1975-), ed. Yisrael Levin et al.

53. In *ʾIm lo tihye Yerushalayim*, pp. 11–89.

54. See, for example, Boaz Arpaly, *ʿAvotot shel ḥoshekh* [Bonds of Darkness: Nine Chapters in Natan Alterman's Poetry] (Tel Aviv, 1983); Ruth Kartun-Blum, *Bein hanisgav laʾironi* [The Sublime and the Ironic: Trends and Perspectives in the Poetry of Natan Alterman] (Tel Aviv, 1983); Dan Laor, *Hashofar vehaḥerev* [The Trumpet and the Sword: Critical Essays on the Writings of Natan Alterman] (Tel Aviv, 1983); Dan Miron, *Mipperat el ʿiqqar*, and the 4 volumes to date of the impressive *Maḥbarot Alterman*, ed. Menachem Dorman et al. (1977).

55. Shaked, *Hasipporet haʿivrit*, vol. 2, pp. 157–69.

56. On Gnessin as grand master of intertextuality, see Miron's "Hooks in the Nose of Eternity," in *Uri Nissan Gnessin: Meḥqarim uteʿudot* [U. N. Gnessin: Studies and Documents], ed. Dan Miron and Dan Laor (Jerusalem, 1986; in Hebrew), pp. 231–368. Miron dedicated this groundbreaking essay to Shaked.

57. In alphabetical order: S. Y. Agnon (ed. Hillel Barzel, 1982), Natan Alterman (ed. Ora Baumgarten, 1976), Dvora Baron (ed. Ada Pagis, 1974), M. J. Berdichewsky (ed. Nurit Govrin, 1973), I. D. Berkowitz (ed. Avraham Holtz, 1976), Y. H. Brenner (ed. Yitzhak Bakon, 1972), Yehuda Burla (ed. Avinoam Barshai, 1975), Yaakov Fichman (ed. Nurit Govrin, 1971), Amir Gilboa (ed. Avraham Balaban, 1972), U. N. Gnessin (ed. Lily Rattok, 1977), Leah Goldberg (ed. A. B. Yoffe, 1980), Uri Zvi Greenberg (ed. Yehuda Friedlander, 1974),

David G. Roskies

Hayyim Hazaz (ed. Hillel Barzel, 1978), Simon Halkin (ed. Dan Laor, 1978), Yonatan Ratosh (ed. Dan Laor, 1983), Gershon Shoffman (ed. Nurit Govrin, 1978), Shin Shalom (ed. Shraga Avnery, 1981), Yitzhak Shenhar (ed. Hillel Weiss, 1976), Avraham Shlonsky (ed. Aviezer Weiss, 1975), Saul Tchernichowsky (ed. Josef Ha'efrati, 1976), and S. Yizhar (ed. Chayim Nagid, 1972). All the volumes were published by Am Oved, Tel Aviv, under the revolving editorship of Dan Miron, Yehuda Friedlander, and K. A. Bertini. An anthology of critical essays on Bialik, selected according to different criteria, was edited by Gershon Shaked (Jerusalem, 1974).

58. Dan Miron, *A Traveler Disguised; "Fishke the Lame* by S. Y. Abramovitsh: The First Version of the Story, Its meaning at the Time and Its Place in the Controversy over Its Expanded Form," in *Bein ḥazon le'emet*, pp. 335–411 [in Hebrew]; "Bouncing Back: Destruction and Recovery in Sholem Aleykhem's *Motl Peyse dem khazns*," *YIVO Annual of Jewish Social Science* 17 (1978), pp. 119–84.

59. Harold Fisch, *A Remembered Future: A Study in Literary Mythology* (Bloomington, Ind., 1984). For Fisch's view of literary criticism, see "The Transvaluation of Values in Literary Criticism," in *Baruch Kurzweil Memorial Volume*, pp. 128–38 [in Hebrew].

60. Nehama Aschkenasy, *Eve's Journey: Feminine Images in Hebraic Literary Tradition* (Philadelphia, 1986).

61. David G. Roskies, *Against the Apocalypse: Responses to Catastrophe in Modern Jewish Culture* (Cambridge, Mass., 1984).

62. See, on this question, my review essay, "The Holocaust according to the Literary Critics," *Prooftexts* 1 (1981), pp. 209–16.

63. Ira Bruce Nadel, ed., *Jewish Writers of North America: A Guide to Information Sources*, American Studies Information Guide Series, no. 8 (Detroit, 1981); Daniel Walden, ed., *Twentieth-Century American-Jewish Fiction Writers*, vol. 28 of *Dictionary of Literary Biography* (Detroit, 1984).

64. *Breakthrough: A Treasury of Contemporary American-Jewish Literature*, ed. Irving Malin and Irwin Stark (Philadelphia, 1963). Malin also edited the first collection of critical essays on *Contemporary American-Jewish Literature* (Bloomington, Ind., 1973).

65. See Allen Guttmann, *The Jewish Writer in America: Assimilation and the Crisis of Identity* (New York, 1971). The best of the literary-sociological studies I know of is Stephen J. Whitfield, *Voices of Jacob, Hands of Esau: Jews in American Life and Thought* (Hamden, Conn. 1984).

66. Marcus Klein, *Foreigners: The Making of American Literature, 1900–1940* (Chicago, 1981); Mark Shechner, *After the Revolution: Studies in the Contemporary Jewish-American Imagination* (Bloomington, Ind., 1987).

67. Wisse, *The Schlemiel as Modern Hero*. Most recently in *The Shadows Within: Essays on Modern Jewish Writers* (Philadelphia, 1987), Gershon Shaked has looked at American-Jewish writing from a comparativist German-Jewish and Hebrew perspective.

68. Shechner begins with the *Partisan Review;* Klein ends on the eve of its formation.

69. For the first study in that direction, see Elinor Grumet, "The Apprenticeship of Lionel Trilling," *Prooftexts* 4 (1984), pp. 153–73.

70. They are, in order of publication: *The Collected Poems of A. M. Klein*, ed. Miriam Waddington (Toronto, 1974); Usher Caplan, *Like One That Dreamed: A Portrait of A. M. Klein* (Toronto, 1982); A. M. Klein, *Beyond Sambation: Selected Essays and Editorials, 1928–1955*, ed. M. W. Steinberg and Usher Caplan (Toronto, 1982); A. M. Klein, *Short Stories*, ed. M. W. Steinberg (Toronto, 1983); Solomon J. Spiro, *Tapestry for Designs: Judaic Allusions in the Poetry and the Second Scroll of A. M. Klein* (Vancouver, 1984); and A. M. Klein, *Literary Essays and Reviews*, ed. Usher Caplan and M. W. Steinberg (Toronto, 1987).

71. See n. 19 above.

13

RESPONSE

Gershon Shaked

I

The issues I shall raise in response to Roskies's remarkable presentation will be historical, methodological, and metapoetical (''metapoetical'' designates the questions that Jewish literary scholarship should ask here and now in both Israel and America).

Two of the major historical questions Roskies raises are the problem of continuity and revolution in literary scholarship and the polarity of horizontal and vertical research. There are some cross-connections between these two issues; modern scholarship seems to be ''horizontal'' (influenced by ''imported'' disciplines and analyzing the text from a general universal point of view), whereas conventional approaches are ''vertical'' (trying to understand the inner development of Jewish texts). I have reservations about the way the theme of continuity and revolution was handled, but I should emphasize first and foremost that rather than speak of a contrast between horizontal and vertical scholarship, I will speak of a contrast between historical positivism and poetics. Both methods of research and criticism are of foreign origin, and positivism—high and low text criticism, bibliography, and biography—is neither more nor less Jewish than the various systematic and applied theories of poetry in modern Hebrew criticism. For example, M. H. Luzzatto's eighteenth-century introduction to rhetorics, *Leshon Limudim*, was influenced by conceptions of poetics of the late Ital-

ian Renaissance and Baroque. Shlomo Levinson's *Melitsat Yeshurun*, pub
lished at the beginning of the nineteenth century, was influenced by German Romantic poetics, especially by Herder and his contemporaries. The
very sophisticated interpretation of medieval poetry, *Kashoresh 'Etz*, by the
Israeli New Critic Adi Zemah, was influenced by the American New Critics I. A. Richards, W. Empson, and W. K. Wimsatt. Hrushovski's formal-
ist poetics of Hebrew prosody was influenced by the Russian formalists. We
will have to consider the fact that historical positivism, which achieved certain ends in Klausner's history of Hebrew literature and Zinberg's history of
Jewish (Yiddish and Hebrew) literature, is anything but dead. Conservative
or neoconservative positivistic trends exist all over Europe and in the
United States. These trends have become quite sophisticated and are influenced by the theory of reception (for example, H. R. Jauss, W. Iser), neo-
Marxism (W. Benjamin, L. Goldmann, T. Eagleton, F. Jameson), the
sociology of literature (G. Sammons, Duncan), and the "literary" historians (Hayden White).

In modern Hebrew and Yiddish scholarship one finds more and less
sophisticated applications of some of these theories. Werses, Shmeruk,
Szeintuch, Turniansky, Zfatman, Govrin, Shamir, Friedlander, Weiss,
Bakun (compare his volume on Brenner) in Israel, and Barzilay, Holtz,
Peli, Nash, Spicehandler, and Band (in his own way) in the United States,
are adherents of positivistic research. There are some positivistic elements
in most of Dan Miron's and my own work.

Both critical trends have different functions in different times, and
what seems to be a guarding of the walls of the intellectual ghetto in one
time could be an opening up in another time. To give only one example
from a different area: there are few scholars who have used positivist methodology in a more sophisticated way than Gershom Scholem. He himself
commented on the present meaning of his scholarship in his well-known
article "Mitsva haba'a be'avera" [Redemption through Sin, 1937]. Kurzweil, who did not share Scholem's Zionist interpretation of history, actually
followed in Scholem's footsteps by discussing the meaning of the positivistic approach of his *Wissenschaft des Judentums* forerunners.

When we turn to the more concrete side of criticism, by changing our
concepts we may come to appreciate in a less evaluative way different
trends and various trajectories of continuity. We may conclude that Jewish
literary scholarship has been quite traditional. The fact that we still use, by
standards of most Western literary criticism, a somewhat obsolete methodology is not surprising. Israeli and American-Jewish scholarship are both
regressive and progressive. They are at once conventional, according to the
norms just mentioned, and at the forefront of all modern critical trends.

Think for instance of the formalistic Tel Aviv school (Hrushovski, Perry, Even-Zohar), of Miron's modern critical approach, Yosef Ewen's formalistic volume on Brenner, my structuralist book on Agnon, and the psychoanalytic studies of Yehoshua, Feldman, and Ben-Dov. *Midrash and Literature,* published by Yale in 1986, was supposed to be a contribution to deconstructive criticism; according to the Weinreich-Roskies terminology, it was vertical in concept but actually functioned horizontally.

The problem in Jewish criticism, as in Jewish fiction and poetry, is that it did not develop normally. Jewish literary scholarship and criticism always followed Western patterns but did not do so consistently, so that different schools and scholars were influential at the same time. Within their own traditions, Jews had only two major trends of criticism—the contextual commentary of *peshat* and the acontextual or esoteric midrash of *remez, drash,* and *sod.* These modalities found parallels in the Christian and Islamic interpretations of holy texts, but they basically formed an indigenous tradition. The question to be posed, therefore, is not if or when these horizontal influences occurred, or if they enlarged Jews' intellectual horizons, but rather what function these different modes of interpretation had in their specific time and place.

Positivism is a "must" for a scholarly tradition that has not yet created its own classical legacy—for instance, academic publication of the major classics of Hebrew literature. But there are also some scholarly achievements from Mekhon Katz in Tel Aviv, Shmeruk and Werses in Jerusalem, Friedlander at Bar-Ilan, and Holtz in New York, in addition to the publication of bibliographies and literary histories by Shavit, Govrin, Gilboa, and Matres. Of this type, too, are the scholarly editions of the Dorot series of Mossad Bialik and the Yiddish series of the Hebrew University. Positivism enriches the literary repertoire and the stockpile of data, and thus functions alongside and in conjunction with structuralism, New Criticism, and the other critical schools. It has not yet fulfilled its task.

II

Returning to the history of new trends in modern Jewish literary scholarship, we see that Roskies has accepted more or less the mythology created by one of its major exponents, Hrushovski, who, with one of his students, Ziva Ben-Porat, published in 1974 an introduction to a bibliography of structuralism in Israel. The contents of this bibliography blur the borders between pure structuralist essays, prestructuralist New Critical interpretations, and work done on the margins of the "school." Shmeruk, for instance, was mentioned as part of the new tradition of scholarship. The organizational and public effect of the "new" critical establishment is immense. Witness the impact that *Hasifrut* and the department for the theory of literature at Tel Aviv University have had on scholarship and criticism in Israel.

Any history of criticism has to pay tribute to the late Ludwig Strauss, who began New Criticism (the German school) in Israel, and to the remarkable impact of one of those whom Roskies calls the bridging figures: Dov Sadan. Ludwig Strauss, Martin Buber's son-in-law, was a German poet and critic before he immigrated to Israel. He was part of the intellectual establishment in the Weimar Republic. In Israel he taught literature in the town of Ben Shemen and later in the Youth-Aliya teachers seminary. In 1950 he started teaching courses in general literature at Hebrew University. Well-known poets and critics were his formal and informal students, among them Tuvia Rübner, Dan Pagis, and Natan Zach. Strauss's literary analysis of four psalms and poems by Judah Halevi, Bialik, Rahel, and Leah Goldberg created a tradition—a transformation of the traditions he had brought with him from modern German New Criticism (for example, Wolfgang Kaiser and Emil Staiger). He was most influential through his impact on Natan Zach. The poet, critic, and leader of a literary movement, Zach was a member of the "Liqrat" group, which began in 1952 and included Hrushovski, Amichai, Avidan, Sivan, and, at the beginning, myself. Zach used the new theories to open his major struggle against the ruling tradition of Shlonsky and Alterman in modern Hebrew poetry.

Some of Hrushovski's scholarly articles on Hebrew prosody and rhyme, subjects he taught in Jerusalem from 1953, were part of this rebellion, emphasizing the semantic relativity of literary norms. So were Adi Zemah's New Critical interpretations of medieval poetry and my own articles since 1953. By stressing the literary formal aspects of the novel and the short story, I sought to rescue literature from the pathetic claws of thematics and Marxist-thematic interpretation. Scholarship and criticism formed a literary group, and the transformation of critical methods and devices fed the rebellion against the rule of collectivism, ideologism, and other *ism*'s.

The young critics and scholars had yet another godfather: Dov Sadan. The reinterpretation of Sadan's legacy was another act of their rebellion. Sadan's immense output has given to each and every one of his students a point of departure. His explicitly psychoanalytical studies of Brenner and implicitly psychoanalytical studies of Bialik and Agnon were starting points for Adi Zemah's study of Bialik's "the Hidden Lion," and some other metapsychological studies of Agnon and others. His powerful insights into the deep structure of major Hebrew, Yiddish, and even German-Jewish writers was a source of inspiration for Dan Miron and, I believe, for some aspects of my own work. Even Even-Zohar's concept of a polysystem has its "inner" source of influence in Sadan's major introduction to modern Jewish literature, "The Values of Our Literature." His stylistics influenced anyone who was writing on aspects of style, and his positivistic collections of data became standard. Most of the rebellion constituted a "creative betrayal" of some of Sadan's concepts and his philosophy of the history of Hebrew and Yiddish literature. Young Israeli scholars and critics used the psychoanalytical aspects of his work for the reinterpretation and modernizations of the classics and to fight an intellectual war of independence. There is no question that Halkin and Kurzweil, too, have contributed, each in his own way, to the development of "horizontal" and "vertical," or "positivistic" and "poetic," scholarship in Israel.

To sum up: the interrelationship between the generations was much closer than we could learn from Roskies's presentation, and the development of literary scholarship was more an evolutionary process than a revolutionary one. In Israel, as everywhere else, scholarship has been an integral part of the history of belles lettres.

III

Now we come to the major issue of Jewish scholarship in our time: what is the *function* of Jewish literary criticism and scholarship in its different languages and locations? Scholarship and literature have to be understood in a general and a specific social and ideological framework, and the functions of the scholarship in Yiddish, Hebrew, and English differ according to the different functions of these languages in the two major locations of Jewish scholarship.

Methodologies exist to serve a purpose; they do not exist for their own sake. Scholars use methods and are not used by them. History creates historians; historians create a new reading of history according to the issues and conflicts of their present historical situation. In literary scholarship the issues are more complicated because of the interdependence of literary scholarship, literary criticism, and the local trends and values of literature. What is the function of literary scholarship in Israel as it relates to three areas as different as modern Hebrew, modern Yiddish, and modern Jewish literature?

Hebrew in Israel is a living, vibrant, productive language, and there is a natural reading public for criticism and scholarship. The individualistic rebellion of the New Wave in poetry and fiction—from Amichai and Zach to Yehoshua and Oz—was fed by an individualizing deideologization of scholarship and criticism. New Criticism, structuralism, and psychoanalysis liberated literature from Zionist and socialist ideologies and opened the way for a new anticollectivist outlook. Moreover, it facilitated the appearance of

189

a new and modern reinterpretation of the major figures of Hebrew literature from the end of the nineteenth to the middle of the twentieth century. The breakdown of the national consensus, the clash among the major political parties, and the revival of political poetry (Laor, Sharon) and the socially engaged novel (Oz, Orpaz, Kaniuk, Ben Ner, Grossman, and others) and drama (Sobol) have opened the way for a more socially oriented kind of criticism and scholarship (Miron, Shaked, Gertz, Kalderon, Hever). The methodologies used serve the major concerns of the present day.

Yiddish in Israel is a dead language, used mostly in homes for the elderly and as a literary language by a few Holocaust survivors. It exists for the readership in Israel, as in America, in translation only: Sholem Aleichem in the classical translation by I. D. Berkowitz, Peretz in a simple translation by Shimshon Meltzer. The preoccupation of scholarship is to establish the canon and to integrate Yiddish literature into the mainstream of Hebrew letters. If Yiddish is to survive, this is the only way. Most comparative studies and the work of bilingual writers have this function. The concept of one culture and two languages has no practical meaning. It is but a slogan for scholars to reintegrate in their comparative studies these two sisters with different cultural pasts, presents, and futures. This aim has not yet been achieved, and if literary scholars want to effect a new cultural integration of these twin literary traditions, this should be the major orientation of their research.

IV

In America the scholar has to face two facts: Yiddish literature has lost its creative force, and it exists mostly in translations. Some scholars and critics (Howe, Schultz) have made these translations the object of their inquiry, and in their own way they are justified. They know perfectly well that the only way to reintegrate Yiddish literature into American-Jewish society is to translate it—literally and metaphorically. By "metaphor" I mean the critical explication of the text using any methodology that opens up the text for readers who are not interested in its immediate message and meaning but in its more general and universal applications.

Hebrew literature has only a slightly better chance to survive in America. In Yiddish there is almost no new creativity, and even its academic study is dedicated more to research than to teaching. Hebrew has become the language of ethnic identity, Yiddish more an old curiosity. The function of Yiddish scholarship has become to relate a translated canon to a specific ethnic group, to show the group how it could be enriched by this heritage, and to claim that the major figures of the canon—who should be retranslated with comments, introductions, and glossaries—should be integrated into Jewish education. The function of Hebrew scholars is a bit more complicated. The existence of a living and creative center in Israel is a problem for American scholars and critics of modern Hebrew literature. They have responded variously to the challenge, and their actions bespeak different attitudes and approaches. Some have accepted the centrality of Israel and do whatever they do as though they were participating actively in the endeavors of Israeli scholarship; they publish for an Israeli audience. They are, whether by birth or by vocation, Israeli scholars who happen to live in America. They are not messengers of Hebrew to the Jews or non-Jews in the United States, and they are not attempting to reintegrate modern Hebrew in the American-Jewish heritage. Two examples from two different schools are A. Holtz and S. Nash. It would seem that it is easier to partake of the center as a positivist than as a commentator seeking to interpret or interact with an immediate public, but whatever they do is functional and contributes to the ongoing research in the Israel center. There is no question that theoretically they can do here (America) whatever is done there (Israel) so long as they do not lose their immediate contact with the readers' expectations there.

Others have made an attempt to introduce major Hebrew writers to an American reading public. This was, as far as I can tell, Arnold Band's purpose in his book on Agnon, *Nostalgia and Nightmare;* Miron's in *A Traveler Disguised,* his study of Mendele; and Yael Feldman's in her book on Gabriel Preil. Whether they succeeded or not is another question. Still others try to address Hebrew literature from the vantage point of whatever is of interest to the general American reading public. Thus feminist concerns have spawned some books about women in Hebrew literature by Fuchs and Aschkenasy, and following the deep interest of American Jews in the Holocaust, there have been some major contributions to the interpretation of catastrophes in history and literature by Mintz and Roskies.

There is yet one more response. I refer to the outstanding contribution of Robert Alter, as well as some others such as Spicehandler in *The Modern Hebrew Poem Itself.* Alter has become the advocate of Hebrew literature in America and has done for the circulation of Hebrew literature in this country more than any cultural attaché. He and others, having the benefit of knowing the original, are the critical spokesmen for Hebrew translation. Their critical essays have a very important cultural function. They understand Hebrew literature from the point of view of the American-Jewish reading public and explain to American Jews how the literature of their brethren on the other side of the ocean is relevant to their lives.

191

Jewish Art

14

JEWISH ART AND JEWISH STUDIES

Joseph Gutmann

Jewish art, a late and minor offshoot of the nineteenth-century *Wissenschaft des Judentums,* has in the last forty years blossomed and become a legitimate branch of art history. Once cultivated largely as an avocation by a handful of European scholars, Jewish art history is now taught in courses offered at leading universities. An annual scholarly magazine, *Jewish Art,* explores the subject; international congresses are devoted to it; and a Center for Jewish Art has been established in Jerusalem. In addition, Judaica museums proliferate, and major auction houses regularly feature Judaica objects.

The interest in Jewish art history probably owes its current impetus to three factors.

1. First was the amazing discovery in 1928 of the sixth-century C.E. Beth-Alpha synagogue mosaic and in 1932 of a mid-third-century C.E. synagogue with a complex cycle of paintings from a provincial Roman military outpost at Dura-Europos, Syria. Not only were these unusual finds totally unanticipated by scholarly reconstructions of rabbinic Judaism of the period but they actually challenged old theories that Judaism had never tolerated any visual art and that its laws strictly forbade such endeavors.

2. The creation of the State of Israel in 1948 also helped stimulate an interest in Jewish art history. Like any other nation, Israel desired to claim a national art in order to boast of a noble and ancient artistic heritage. Archaeological digs were encouraged and spectacular finds of figural syna-

193

gogal mosaic floors revealed that the Dura and Beth-Alpha synagogues were not isolated, deviant examples but part of a tradition with solid roots. Museums were built to house these finds, and art history and archaeology departments were established in order to teach and research Jewish art and archaeology.

3. And last were the pioneering efforts of Erwin R. Goodenough, whose *Jewish Symbols in the Greco-Roman Period* first drew attention to the fact that there existed a vast body of Jewish art that had been sadly neglected. Goodenough's great achievement was in calling to the attention of scholars a world of Jewish images and thus restoring to Jewish scholarship, which had been exclusively text oriented, a vital visual dimension.

Equally important for Jewish art history is the great interest and growth in the collecting of Judaica objects during the last forty years. The focus has been on Judaica objects stemming from the last five hundred years or so of Jewish residence in Islamic and Christian countries. The ensuing researches and displays of these objects by avid Jewish collectors in private synagogal and public Judaica museums deserves an in-depth sociocultural and economic study. No doubt some of the reasons for the interest in, and the collecting of, Judaica objects lie in the emotional effort of twentieth-century, largely secular, Jews to find in these ancient objects pious reminders, or sacred anchors, of a holy Judaism rapidly disappearing from their lives. To more traditional Jews, there is an implicit hope that in owning these objects they can perhaps capture a holy spark of once thriving religious communities and their leaders, all so ruthlessly destroyed in the Holocaust by the Nazi hordes. The urge in our materialistic society to possess what some consider gilt-edged investments plays a role in the ever-soaring prices of these objects at Judaica auctions. No doubt the aim in this picture-oriented culture to dramatize our Jewish heritage visually and to use displays of these Judaica objects as an educational bridge to both Jews and Christians should also not be overlooked as a factor leading to the fascination with and the burgeoning of Jewish art.

The serious study of Jewish art began only in the last decade of the nineteenth century and was largely in the hands of professionally trained art historians—Jewish and non-Jewish[1]—with little background in Judaism. These early scholarly studies were for the most part confined to the description, attribution, and stylistic analysis of objects and not only excluded all value judgments but treated Jewish art in a vacuum, divorced from the larger Jewish and non-Jewish context of which it was an integral part. These researches followed the model developed by the influential Swiss art historian Heinrich Wölfflin.[2] To Wölfflin's stylistic theories, or concerns with only formal artistic problems, early scholars of Jewish art added the analysis of content of a work of art. They felt that a study of the ideas

194

expressed in a work of Jewish art would help establish a clearer understanding of its style. Following theories on iconography and iconology formulated by such brilliant art historians as Erwin Panofsky,[3] these scholars at times saw in the specific content of a work of Jewish art the source of its distinctive style.

Although Jewish art history in the last forty years has been in the hands of scholars who frequently have a sound Judaica background in addition to good training as art historians, Jewish art history methodologically made no measurable progress beyond the formal, stylistic analysis of Wölfflin or beyond the identification of the content or the ideas inherent in a work of Jewish art, as theorized by Panofsky.

General art history, however, has moved far beyond the stage of explaining only purely esthetic phenomena of a work of art or formalistic investigations into style, subject matter, and the history of ownership of a work of art. Many contemporary art historians consider the above as necessary starting points but tend to place art within the historical, sociopolitical, cultural, and economic context of a particular era.[4] These scholars are in touch with and embrace disciplines such as psychoanalysis,[5] anthropology, linguistics, and economics.[6] They tend to emphasize the relationship of art to the sociopolitical, cultural, and economic climate of a specific time period rather than focusing exclusively on formal problems of shape, color, and composition. Jewish art history, unlike its related discipline Jewish history,[7] is still largely moored in the Wölfflin and Panofsky schools of thought and has not yet fully absorbed the newer approaches of contemporary art history.

The limited approach of Jewish art history, its primary concern with problems of style and iconography, is revealed in many studies of Jewish art of the last forty years.[8] To the above must be added the lack of agreement among scholars as to what constitutes Jewish art—how to define its parameters and perimeters.[9] Unlike the art of various countries and societies, which flourished within well-defined territorial boundaries, Jewish art, like Jewish history, is different. It simply cannot be defined in purely ethnic or national terms, nor can it be treated separately, divorced from the larger context of which it is an integral part. Jewish art, like Jewish history, has not, except in the Biblical period, been confined to one geographic area;[10] it is at the same time the history and art of ancient Western Asian cultures, the Greco-Roman worlds, the Muslim and Christian civilizations. To separate Jewish art from its larger context is to do violence not only to the art of the Jews but to the art of the larger configuration of which Jewish art forms a small but intricate part. Thus, for instance, the art of the early synagogue grows out of, and is nurtured by, Greco-Roman art, just as the art of medieval Hebrew manuscripts is inseparably linked to medieval

Christian and Muslim manuscript illumination. The styles, the decorations, the paleography, and at times even the subject matter are rooted in, and are adapted from, the dominant contemporary non-Jewish society.

The researcher of Jewish art must discern in that art the complex involvement of the Jewish minority with the art, thought, and practices of its non-Jewish host society. In addition, the scholar must probe how and why non-Jewish models and forms were adapted, what unique Jewish iconographic features were introduced, all in order to make Jewish art relevant to, and expressive of, the unique Jewish experience in whatever society or community Jews lived.

Until the nineteenth century the art of the Jews was an intrinsic part of distinct, organized, and legally-constituted Jewish communities that functioned within the larger non-Jewish society. Jewish art under these conditions expressed and reflected how each Jewish medieval community brought into being a recognizably distinct, collective way of thought, feeling, ritual, and symbolism. Thus, Jewish art until the nineteenth century primarily functioned within a religio-communal context, and the designation "Jewish art" is appropriate until about the year 1800. From that period on, the label Jewish art becomes meaningless and should be dropped. With the legal emancipation of Jews in the nineteenth century, the artist of Jewish birth was freed from the jurisdiction of a legally constituted Jewish community and could now sever the connection that bound him to that community: he no longer expressed the collective beliefs and symbols of any Jewish community. Functioning as a citizen of a specific country, he created art that expressed his private, personal feelings, beliefs, religious practices, and affiliations. Even the occasional use of Jewish symbols and subject matter bespoke his own personality and may have had little direct relation to a religio-communal background. These factors must be carefully weighed in any future assessment of the modern art[11] created by artists of Jewish birth in the diaspora and Israel.

Another major area of confusion in Jewish art history centers around the so-called Biblical Second Commandment. Until recent times Jewish art was largely ignored by Jewish and non-Jewish scholars on the grounds that Jews had no talent for the visual arts. Following essentially Hegelian racial ideas, these scholars went so far as to conclude that Jews had an inherent congenital incapacity for the visual arts—their talents were thought to lie in the domain of the audial and not the visual. Even so notable a Jewish historian as Heinrich Graetz affirmed that "paganism sees its god, Judaism hears him." Although this stance has been softened, it is still not unusual to read that the strict Biblical prohibition was formulated because the God of the Hebrews was an implacable enemy of images. Writers still claim that in most periods of Jewish history the Second Commandment hampered Jewish artistic expression, while in other periods Jews simply ignored this prohibition. What was operative among Jews, according to many scholars, was either an attraction or a revulsion toward art.

Recent studies have shown that one cannot speak of *one* Second Commandment—an unchanging concept that never transcended its original Biblical context. Thus in the course of Jewish history multiple versions of the Second Commandment appeared. The Jewish attitude toward art reflects not so much inherent forces of revulsion or attraction, of observance or disobedience of a static, Biblical divine command, but is conditioned by a dynamic interaction with the dominant official attitude toward art expressed in the non-Jewish Greco-Roman, Parthian-Sasanian, Christian or Muslim societies where Jews resided. Thus each Jewish involvement with new societies demanded a reevaluation and reinterpretation of the original Biblical prohibition.[12]

I shall now survey the major studies of Jewish art history that have appeared in the last forty years. My survey is divided by periods, from ancient to modern times, and focuses on the current state of scholarship and future research needs.[13]

Biblical Period

No major cycles of Jewish ("Israelite") paintings, distinctly Jewish sculptures, or architecture that date from the Biblical period have been excavated in the Land of Israel. Many artifacts clearly reveal their Canaanite, Egyptian, Phoenician, Mycenaean, and Assyrian origins. The major artistic monument from that period would be, of course, the Temple of Solomon. Little agreement exists among scholars on whether the Biblical narratives describe an ideal temple, Solomon's actual temple, or a later building. Nor is there a scholarly consensus on how the descriptions of the Temple in 1 Kings are related to those in Ezekiel and Chronicles. Unfortunately, but inevitably, most attempts at reconstruction are hypothetical and are based on meager archaeological evidence and the brief and unclear description of Solomon's Temple in 1 Kings 6–7.[14]

Roman-Byzantine Period

The first major period of Jewish art history dates from the late second to the seventh century C.E. It was during this time span that the Jews living under Roman and Byzantine jurisdiction created some amazing works of art that in recent times have been the focus of a considerable body of research. Foremost is the sensational discovery in 1932 of the synagogue at Dura-

Europos in Syria, precisely dated 244/45 c.e.[15] This amazing find has raised many scholarly questions, including the following six.

1. Are the origins of Christian art Jewish? Scholars who support the hypothesis that the elaborate cycle of paintings at the Dura synagogue was one of the sources for later Biblical scenes in both Christian and Jewish art base their theories on a putative existence of earlier illustrated Jewish manuscripts stemming from such large Jewish centers as Alexandria. The existence of illustrated Jewish Septuagint manuscripts in antiquity is an *argumentum ex silentio* that has little substantive evidence to support it. Illustrated narrative Christian manuscript cycles based on the Bible or illustrated narrative manuscript cycles based on Greco-Roman mythology date only from around the fifth century c.e.; Jewish illustrated manuscripts have survived only from the ninth century c.e. In the Roman world, fresco painting, and not illustrated manuscripts, was the preferred mode of artistic expression. Furthermore, rhetoric was considered the highest form of communication in the Greco-Roman society, whereas written texts were used only as necessary and practical vehicles. They were an inferior mode of communication, and both reading and writing were often assigned to slaves.[16] Since the manuscripts had no sacred value, Romans would hardly have gone to the expense of commissioning costly illuminated texts. All of these factors argue against the existence of illustrated manuscripts in pagan antiquity.

2. Do iconographic parallels exist between the scenes depicted in the Dura synagogue and in later Christian and Jewish art? Apparently not. The iconographic parallels cited by scholars are of such a superficial and general nature that no direct connection can be established.[17] Both the costumes worn and the poses of the figures in later Biblical scenes that are used for comparison are quite different from the Dura paintings, ruling out a concrete and indisputable association.

3. Does the appearance of Jewish legends—extra-Biblical stories—in later Christian, Muslim, and Jewish art automatically assure the existence of illustrated, but lost, ancient Jewish manuscripts? Jewish legends were adapted by Christians and Muslims and are found extensively in their writings, so the appearance of a Jewish legend in Christian and Muslim art does not warrant positing a direct Jewish inspiration that would at the same time support the existence of lost ancient illustrated Jewish manuscript cycles.[18]

4. What are the stylistic sources of the Dura synagogue paintings? Scholars are divided on whether to attribute the Dura style to provincial Roman or Parthian art. Recent research has shown that the hieratic, frontal, rigid, impersonal, two-dimensional figures, with large, staring eyes, so common in the Dura paintings, represent an artistic mode of presentation

that began to develop in first-century C.E. Syria.[19] A detailed study of the stylistic and iconographic sources of the Dura synagogue paintings is a much needed scholarly desideratum.

5. Is the Dura synagogue with its complex cycle of paintings a local, isolated example or does it represent a widespread practice, especially in such affluent centers as Palmyra, Edessa, and Nisibis? Until new discoveries of similar synagogues come to light, this question is best held in abeyance.

6. What religious ceremonial-theological function did the synagogue painting program serve? Most scholars agree that it had religious propagandistic aims, but cannot agree on the type of Judaism that flourished there or on the meaning of its cycle of paintings. Current scholarship has suggested Palestinian liturgical inspiration not only for the Dura synagogue paintings but for the somewhat later Palestinian figural mosaic floors found in ancient synagogues.[20]

The Dura synagogue paintings are also described in three of the thirteen volumes of Erwin R. Goodenough's opus.[21] Goodenough was convinced that the hellenization of Christianity was made possible by an older hellenized Judaism. But in Goodenough's generation virtually all scholars agreed that at least from the first century C.E. on there prevailed a universal, rigid, "normative rabbinic Judaism" that eschewed Hellenism and mysticism, and was highly antagonistic to any kind of artistic image. Archaeological finds of synagogues and catacombs revealed a Jewish predilection for an art that was Roman-Byzantine in character and in style. Goodenough therefore concluded that rabbinic literature is an unreliable guide for the decipherment of ancient Jewish art. In his conceptual approach to the material at hand he relied heavily on the metaphysical theories of the philosopher Friedrich Hegel and the pyschologist Carl Jung. He spoke of the "interpretation" of symbols (the articulate, objective explanation or meaning of symbols that change in every new culture) and the "value" of symbols (the emotional, subjective response to a "live" symbol, which remained essentially the same in differing societies). Thus according to Goodenough, the Jewish masses, divorced from rabbinic jurisdiction and influence, worshiped in synagogues decorated with "live" pagan symbols and subscribed to a popular, mystical Hellenistic Judaism whose chief literary remains are discernible in the Hellenistic writings of the first century C.E. Alexandrian Jewish philosopher Philo. Although Goodenough failed to prove his thesis, he forced a reevaluation of Jewish history and the role that art played in Judaism during that period.

The many excavated synagogues in the diaspora and Palestine have elicited much research. These scholarly writings have generally aban-

doned the earlier clear-cut three-stage typological synagogal development—
from early Galilaean to the transitional and the later Byzantine type—and
are now opting for local or regional variants in synagogue architecture. Although the second- to third-century date for the Galilaean synagogues is, in
the light of new excavations, no longer accepted, there is no common
agreement on the dating of Palestinian synagogues.[22]

The origins of the synagogue as a religious institution and as a distinctly recognizable architectural building have not been resolved either.
The origins of the synagogue as a religious institution go back to sixth-
century Babylonia, according to many textbooks, but this notion is gradually giving way to a much later dating. Scholars now agree that by the first
century C.E. the synagogue was a flourishing institution.[23] The frequently
found designation *proseuchē* in ancient writings and inscriptions has been
interpreted by scholars as "synagogue," although there is no clear evidence
presented for this conjecture. This subject demands critical scrutiny.[24] Similarly, no building can indisputably be identified as a synagogue prior to the
third century C.E. Structures excavated in Israel and dating from the first
century C.E. have been labeled "synagogues," even though the evidence
presented is largely circumstantial and no incontrovertible proof that these
structures functioned as synagogues has been advanced.[25] What is vitally
needed, first, is a detailed scholarly study of each major synagogue.[26] Furthermore, an in-depth analysis is needed of the Greco-Roman sources both
for the various synagogal architectural plans employed and for the religious
institutions that influenced the emergence of the synagogue. Such topics as
furnishings, orientation,[27] and the liturgical-theological function of the
early synagogue as revealed both in architecture and in literature demand
detailed study. A scholarly corpus of synagogue mosaics, dating from the
fourth to the seventh century, awaits research.[28] In addition, the meaning of
ceremonial appurtenances and the zodiac depicted on these mosaics deserves critical scholarly investigation.[29] That such objects as the shofar,
lulav, etrog, and menorah are symbolic of the Jerusalem Temple ritual, as
commonly claimed, is far from proven fact. These symbols may simply
express the liturgy and theology of contemporary Palestinian Judaism—a
hypothesis that merits investigation.[30]

The Jewish catacombs, especially those from Beth She'arim and Rome,
dating roughly from the third and fourth century, demand a major study.
Such a scholarly undertaking should examine the stylistic and ideological
relationship of Jewish catacombs and their art with Roman and Christian
catacomb art. The function and meaning of the decorated gold glasses and
the sculpted sarcophagi of the catacombs also merit scholarly consideration.[31] Perhaps such an investigation will explain why contemporary

200

Christian catacomb paintings employ Biblical scenes and Jewish catacombs refrain from using them, although Biblical narratives are found in synagogal decoration.

Islamic Period

From the Sasanian period no Jewish artistic artifacts or religious buildings have come down to us. From the Islamic period, however, illuminated Hebrew manuscripts, ceremonial objects, and synagogue buildings have been preserved. Illuminated Hebrew manuscripts are the only objets d'art from Islamic cultures to have been studied thus far. Although only a few Jewish ceremonial objects and synagogue structures may have survived from medieval Islam, the subject, nonetheless, deserves a systematic critical study.[32]

The famous Moshe ben-Asher codex, the oldest illuminated Hebrew manuscript, dated 894/95 c.e., from Tiberias, Palestine, has been studied, as have later fifteenth-century illuminated Hebrew manuscripts from Yemen.[33] These researches, however, need reexamination in the light of the exciting Umayyad manuscript discoveries in the great mosque of San'a, Yemen.[34] In addition, the role the Karaites may have played in stimulating the illustration of Bible manscripts merits detailed study. Placing what has been termed *masorah figurata*—the practice of having minute Hebrew letters form the shape of artistic subjects (which may or may not be related to the accompanying texts)—in Hebrew Bibles has been hailed as a distinct and unique Jewish art form.[35] Again, whether Karaites in eighth-century Iraq under the Abbasid dynasty introduced this practice and whether it is truly a unique Jewish art form or an adaptation of artistic conventions already at home in the Byzantine and Umayyad societies requires further exploration.

Christian Middle Ages

The Jewish involvement with Christian civilization in Europe between the thirteenth and the fifteenth centuries has been better studied than any other period of Jewish art history. Several fine studies on medieval European synagogues offer good stylistic analyses of synagogue architecture and give valuable historic background information.[36]

A vital dimension still missing in synagogue architecture research, however, is the study of how these buildings functioned in context, specifically, how non-Jewish architectural forms were adapted to special Jewish communal liturgical demands, and how in turn the liturgy of the synagogue—its practices, ceremonies, and prayers in each specific Jewish society—underwent changes by its interaction with and response to the liturgy, theology, religious practices, and the art-architecture of the non-Jewish world.[37]

Especially the field of Jewish illuminated Hebrew manuscripts has been an area of concentration productive of so many studies that it is next to impossible to keep up with them, or even to list them. Here luxurious facsimile editions have been produced that allow many viewers to personally experience the splendor of these priceless medieval masterpieces, which are generally hidden on the shelves of rare book rooms in libraries and are accessible only to a few scholars.[38] Although the technical reproduction of some of these manuscripts has reached a high level of craftsmanship, the accompanying scholarly texts exploring the style and iconography of the miniatures in these medieval manuscripts fail, with few exceptions, to match the thoroughness and high standards of scholarship we are accustomed to finding in comparable Christian manuscript facsimiles. The same can be said for the *catalogues raisonnés* of public collections of illuminated Hebrew manscripts that have thus far appeared. These catalogues do not show the meticulous, stylistic, iconographic and bibliographic analyses we see in catalogues of Christian illuminated manuscripts.[39]

Medieval Hebrew illuminated manuscripts in Europe span a period of about three hundred years, from the thirteenth to the fifteenth centuries. They were produced primarily in Spain-Portugal, Franco-Germany, and Italy. Each of these areas produced and favored different kinds of Hebrew manuscripts, artistic styles, iconography, and paleography.[40] Thus we find, for instance, that in Germany large synagogal illuminated *mahzorim* were favored, whereas in Spain the private illuminated Haggadah appears to have had great appeal. In Italy, illuminated medical and legal treatises are singled out. Most of the studies devoted to illuminated Hebrew manuscripts concentrate almost exclusively on problems of style and iconography.[41] What still has to be addressed are such vital questions as why the large, illuminated, synagogal *mahzor* first appears in Franco-Germany and what its relation is to such Christian church manuscripts as the Breviary—it is even called in one medieval Hebrew manuscript from Melun, France, *Breviarium Judaicum*. Similarly, research should address how the emergence of liturgical Christian books, such as the Book of Hours, affected the rise of such private liturgical books as the Haggadah. How each Jewish community responded differently to the liturgy, theology, ceremonies, and practices of its host country and how distinct Jewish ceremonies, liturgical prayers, and practices arise and how they are refracted in Hebrew illuminated manuscripts has not been adequately explored.[42]

Thus we find, for instance, that the practice of placing illuminated pages of the vessels of Solomon's Temple as frontispieces in Spanish Hebrew Bibles, called *mikdashyah,* not only expresses Spanish Jewry's sophisticated yearning for a messianic future but stems from similar yearnings among Christians and follows earlier Islamic practices as seen in Umayyad Qurʿān manuscripts. This kind of messianic image is unique to Spanish Jewry and grows out of a Jewish involvement in Spain with its Islamic-Christian environment.[43]

In like fashion, for example, the many images of *kiddush ha-shem* (Sanctification of the [Divine] Name) seen in medieval illuminated Hebrew manuscripts in the guise of the *ʿAqedat-Yitzḥaq* (Abraham's Sacrifice of Isaac: Genesis 22) stem primarily from medieval Germany. The concept of martyrdom, *kiddush ha-shem,* is foreign to medieval Spanish Jewry, but is completely at home in Germanic lands and grows out of memorializations of Jewish martyrs, which in turn are deeply rooted in and develop out of Christian martyrologies on behalf of saints martyred for the sanctification of Christ.[44]

Similarly, the opening of the door to greet Elijah, the messianic guest at the Passover seder—a ceremony that first arises in fifteenth-century Germany—is depicted in German Haggadah manuscripts of that period. These images were prompted by the unbearable miseries German Jews were subjected to in the declining economic system of medieval Germany, miseries that demanded a much-needed escape—the fervent hope for the actual coming of the Messiah on *Pesaḥ,* the night of redemption, and the return to Jerusalem. These images again are responses to and are rooted in similar Christian practices, where wooden figures of the awaited Christ, the Messiah astride his messianic ass *(Palmesel),* were wheeled at Easter time to the gates of a mock Jerusalem.[45]

Thus the images in Hebrew illuminated manuscripts, such as the messianic temple, the sacrifice of Isaac, and the Messiah at the seder, must be seen in a broader perspective than simply solving problems of style and iconography. These images belong to specific Jewish communities; they function in and grow out of the complex sociocultural, political, and economic involvement and interaction of Jews with their non-Jewish neighbors.

The Seventeenth and Eighteenth Centuries

The last significant period of Jewish art history is during the seventeenth and eighteenth centuries. Illuminated Hebrew manuscripts owing to the printing of Hebrew books now play a minor role,[46] but we find the emergence of such novel Judaica items as the illustrated *ketubbah,* the illustrated roll of Esther, and figural sculptures on tombstones. During these two hundred years, from around 1600 to 1800, some of the finest extant Jewish ceremonial objects were made.

The study of Jewish ceremonial art is probably the most chaotic and problematic of all areas of Jewish art history. Although a relatively small number of genuine objects are extant, thousands have been forged, are authenticated by self-styled and unscrupulous experts, and wind up in private and public collections. Furthermore, serious studies in the field are primarily limited to European Judaica objects, and those from the lands of Islam have been sadly neglected. The function of these ceremonial objects in Jewish ritual in the home and synagogue has been the subject of several scholarly works that have extensive bibliographies.[47] Similarly, although studies of the origins of such European ceremonial objects as the Torah ark curtain, the mezuzah, Hanukkah lamp, eternal light, and havdalah spice box have yielded some valuable observations, the origins of other ceremonial objects still await scholarly investigation.[48] Research of ceremonial objects in public Judaica collections such as the Israel Museum, the New York Jewish Museum, the Prague State Jewish Museum, the Jewish Museum of London, and the Cluny Museum in Paris has also produced some excellent catalogues.[49] Still vitally needed is a detailed corpus of all indisputably dated Jewish ceremonial objects. In addition, comprehensive research on the history of individual objects is a major desideratum.[50] These investigations should trace the emergence of each object, the various artistic forms produced in each country, the masters who produced them,[51] the relation of the Jewish objects to similar Christian and Islamic objects, and the Jewish practices that center around them in each country. Some exciting research efforts in Jewish art during this period are emerging from a generation of younger art history scholars who are conversant with newer art history methodologies. Thus we find that an in-depth study of the illustrated *ketubbah* from seventeenth- to eighteenth-century Italy places this art object within its sociocultural, historical, legal, economic, and art-historical context.[52] The same can be said for the exhaustive study of seventeenth- to eighteenth-century Sephardi tombstones from the Netherlands.[53] The illustrated Esther scrolls of that same period still await a similar treatment.[54]

The Nineteenth and Twentieth Centuries

In the nineteenth century, artistic masters of Jewish birth finally emerge. Thus we find such artists as Moritz Oppenheim appearing in Germany[55] and Moses Jacob Ezekiel in the United States.[56] These artists for the most part avoided painting Jewish subjects or working for the Jewish community. They vehemently denied being Jewish artists or producing Jewish art. This holds especially true for twentieth-century masters of Jewish origin, such artists as Chaim Soutine, Amedeo Modigliani, Adolph

Gottlieb, Philip Pearlstein, and Louise Nevelson, to name only a few. We find only two abortive attempts to create a national Jewish art—one in Israel in the early twentieth century spearheaded by Boris Schatz[57] and another in postrevolutionary Russia.[58]

Concluding Reflections

Jewish art history is still in its formative stages. Although considerable progress has been made in the areas of ancient synagogues and medieval illuminated Hebrew manuscripts, many subjects still await scholarly inquiry.

The most urgent problems, as I have indicated, center around the definition of Jewish art and the place of the so-called Second Commandment within different Jewish societies. I have pointed out that up to the nineteenth century the art of the Jews was an intricate part of distinct, organized, and legally constituted Jewish communities, which functioned within the larger non-Jewish society. Jewish art under these conditions expressed how each medieval Jewish society brought into being a distinctly recognizable collective way of thought and feeling, and a type of ritual and symbolism. Thus the designation "Jewish art" until around 1800 can adequately cover the subject and do full justice to the contradictory nature of Jewish art. After 1800 the artist of Jewish birth is freed from the jurisdiction of a legally constituted Jewish community. Functioning as a citizen of a specific country, his art expressed his private, personal feelings, beliefs, religious practices, and affiliations. Most artists of the nineteenth and twentieth centuries denied being Jewish artists or producing Jewish art. Thus from 1800 on the label of Jewish art is, in my opinion, best eliminated, since the artist now functions as part of specific secular universal art movements.

Similarly, I have underscored that we cannot speak of one unchanging Second Commandment that never transcended its original Biblical context. In the course of Jewish history multiple versions of the Second Commandment appeared, as each Jewish involvement with new societies demanded a reevaluation and reinterpretation of the original Biblical prohibition.

Most studies of Jewish art history largely focus on stylistic and iconographic problems, thus following late nineteenth- and early twentieth-century art-historical methodologies. These approaches excluded value judgments and viewed art in a vacuum. I have suggested that such approaches are limited and should be replaced by more meaningful and newer art-historical methodologies that reveal how Jewish art functioned in distinct sociocultural, political, and economic contexts within many societies. Several recent studies in Jewish art history using such newer methodologies are preparing the way for future research in the field. Vitally needed are in-depth and well-researched final reports on ancient synagogues, and *catalogues raisonnés* of synagogue mosaics, illuminated Hebrew manuscripts, and Jewish ceremonial objects.

Jewish art history—a relatively new discipline—can add to Jewish studies a vital dimension that has been largely overlooked.

Notes

1. The early scholars of Jewish art received their training in or came predominantly from Germany. Heinrich Frauberger, Rudolf Hallo, Guido Schoenberger, Franz Landsberger, Karl Schwarz, Richard Krautheimer, and Rachel Wischnitzer are some of the pioneer scholars who laid the foundations of Jewish art.

2. On Wölfflin's theories, cf. M. Schapiro, "Style," in M. Philipson, ed., *Aesthetics Today* (Cleveland, 1961), pp. 94–103; M. Podro, *The Critical Historians of Art* (New Haven, Conn., 1982); M. Lurz, *Heinrich Wölfflin: Biographie einer Kunsttheorie* (Worms, 1981).

3. Cf. M. Holly, *Panofsky and the Foundations of Art History* (Ithaca, N.Y., 1984).

4. Cf. G. Glueck, "Clashing Views Reshape Art History," *New York Times*, December 20, 1987; S. Guilbaut, "Art History after Revisionism: Poverty and Hopes," *Art Criticism* 2 (1985), pp. 39–50; W. E. Kleinbauer, *Modern Perspectives in Western Art History* (New York, 1971).

5. Cf. J. Spector, "The State of Psychoanalytic Research in Art History," *Art Bulletin* 70 (1988), pp. 49–76.

6. Cf. O. K. Werckmeister, "Marx on Ideology and Art," *New Literary History* 4 (1973), pp. 501–19.

7. For contemporary approaches to Jewish history, cf. M. A. Meyer, *Ideas of Jewish History* (Detroit, 1987). O. K. Werckmeister aptly said that [Jewish] art historians still "shy away from the conclusion that artworks, however specific their aesthetic fascination, are documents of history as far as their significance is concerned, subject to the same critique as any other historical evidence." Review of A. Hauser, *The Sociology of Art*, in *Art History* 7 (1984), p. 347.

8. Cf., for instance, such surveys of Jewish art history as C. Roth, ed., *Jewish Art: An Illustrated History*, rev. ed. B. Narkiss (Greenwich, Conn., 1971); and G. Sed-Rajna, *L'Art juif. Orient et Occident* (Paris, 1976). For concrete examples of an approach to Jewish art in consonance with newer art history methodologies, see below.

9. The problem of what constitutes Jewish art is clearly reflected in the annual publication *Jewish Art*. Here we find alongside studies dealing with the art of ancient and medieval Jewry articles on Christian and Muslim Old Testament images and Christian anti-Semitica in art—studies that rightly belong to the histories of art of Christianity and Islam. In addition, articles on contemporary Israeli architecture and art are featured, which are far removed from the pieties of Judaism; they do, however, form an intricate part of the developments in secular, universal contemporary architecture and art.

10. Even here, except perhaps during the united and divided monarchies and the Hasmonean kingdom, Israel has never been a separate, independent entity.

11. For a study of the development of Jewish art history, a critique of the definitions offered, and a discussion of the problems of art for contemporary artists of Jewish birth in Israel and the diaspora, cf. J. Gutmann, "Is There a Jewish Art?" in C. Moore, ed., *The Visual Dimension: Aspects of Jewish Art* (forthcoming). A shorter version of this paper, titled "Jüdische Kunst," was published in B. Rübenach., ed., *Begegnungen mit dem Judentum* (Stuttgart, 1981), pp. 167–79.

12. Cf. J. Gutmann, "The 'Second Commandment' and the Image in Judaism," in J. Gutmann, ed., *No Graven Images: Studies in Art and the Hebrew Bible* (New York, 1971), pp. xiii-xxx, 1–14. C. Konikoff, *The Second Commandment and Its Interpretation in the Art of Ancient Israel* (Geneva, 1973), offers no new insights on the subject; his approach is largely a philological discussion of the Biblical commandment. Cf. also W. Barnes Tatum, "The LXX Version of the Second Commandment (Ex. 20. 3–6 = Deut. 5. 7–10): A Polemic against Idols, Not Images," *Journal for the Study of Judaism* 17 (1986), pp. 177–95; J. Gutmann, "Deuteronomy: Religious Reformation or Iconoclastic Revolution?" in J. Gutmann, ed., *The Image and the Word: Confrontations in Judaism, Christianity and Islam* (Missoula, Mont., 1977), pp. 5–25. J. M. Baumgarten, "Art in the Synagogue: Some Talmudic Views," in J. Gutmann, ed., *The Synagogue: Studies in Origins, Archaeology and Architecture* (New York, 1975), pp. 79–89, cites the pertinent sources and literature on the subject. I. Z. Kahana, "Synagogue Art in Halakhic Literature," in M. Hakohen, ed., *Bet ha-Keneset* (Jerusalem, 1955, in Hebrew), pp. 255–308, cites many of the medieval sources on the subject. Both studies are invaluable for future evaluations of the Jewish attitude toward art during the medieval period.

13. Only one book exists listing most published research on Jewish art up to 1966. Cf. L. A. Mayer, *Bibliography of Jewish Art*, ed. O. Kurz (Jerusalem, 1967). Invaluable as this book is, there is a great need not only to update it but to critically evaluate the material presented. The journal *Jewish Art* lists publications on Jewish art from 1975 on. No effort is made to distinguish between popular and scholarly items, or to critically evaluate the materials cited.

14. A detailed study with extensive bibliographic citations can be found in T. A. Busink, *Der Tempel von Jerusalem von Salomon bis Herodes. Eine archäologisch-historische Studie unter Berücksichtigung des westsemitischen Tempelbaus*, vol. 1: *Der Tempel Salomons* (Leiden, 1970); vol. 2: *Von Ezekiel bis Middot* (Leiden, 1980). Busink's volume 1 should be read in light of the critical findings of J. Ouellette, "The Basic Structure of Solomon's Temple and Archaeological Research," in J. Gutmann, ed., *The Temple of Solomon: Archaeological Fact and Mediaeval Tradition in Christian, Islamic and Jewish Art* (Missoula, Mont., 1976), pp. 1–20, 147–49.

15. The magisterial study of C. Kraeling, *The Synagogue Excavations at Dura-Europos, Final Report VIII.1*, aug. ed. (New York, 1979), has not been superseded. For a summation of research since Kraeling and an analysis of the major problems, cf. J. Gutmann, "The Dura-Europos Synagogue Paintings: The State of Research," in L. I. Levine, ed., *The Synagogue in Late Antiquity* (Philadelphia, 1987); J. Gutmann, ed., *The Dura-Europos Synagogue: A Reevaluation 1932–1972*, rev. ed. (forthcoming).

16. Gutmann, "Dura-Europos," pp. 67–69.

17. Cf. J. Gutmann, "The Dura Synagogue Paintings and Their Influence on Later Christian and Jewish Art," *Artibus et Historiae* 17 (1988), pp. 25–29; and K. Weitzmann and H. L. Kessler, *The Frescoes of the Dura Synagogue and Christian Art* (forthcoming).

18. Cf. J. Gutmann, "The Illustrated Midrash in the Dura Paintings: A New Dimension for the Study of Judaism," *Proceedings of the American Academy for Jewish Research* 50 (1983), pp. 92–104; J. Gutmann, "The Testing of Moses: A Comparative Study in Christian, Muslim and Jewish Art," *Bulletin of the Asia Institute* 2 (1988), pp. 107–17.

19. Cf. B. Goldman, "A Dura-Europos Dipinto and Syrian Frontality," *Oriens Antiquus* 24 (1985), pp. 279–300.

20. For a summation of the proffered theories, cf. J. Gutmann, "Early Synagogue and Jewish Catacomb Art and Its Relation to Christian Art," in H. Temporini and W. Haase, eds., *Aufstieg und Niedergang der römischen Welt*, pt. 2, vol. 21.2 (Berlin, 1984), pp. 1313–42; and Gutmann, "Dura-Europos," pp. 62–63.

Joseph Gutmann

21. E. R. Goodenough, *Jewish Symbols in the Greco-Roman Period* (New York, 1953–68). Cf. R. S. Eccles, *Erwin Ramsdell Goodenough: A Personal Pilgrimage* (Chico, Calif., 1985), and the excellent review by M. Smith, "Goodenough's Jewish Symbols in Retrospect," in Gutmann, *The Synagogue*, pp. 194–209.

22. Cf. F. Hüttenmeister and G. Reeg, *Die antiken Synagogen in Israel*, (Wiesbaden, 1977) 2 vols.; M. J. C. Chiat, *Handbook of Synagogue Architecture* (Chico, Calif., 1982); L. I. Levine, ed., *Ancient Synagogues Revealed* (Jerusalem, 1981). Cf. also the bibliographies of Foerster, Tsafrir, Kraabel, and Meyers listed in Levine, ed., *The Synagogue in Late Antiquity;* E. M. Meyers and A. T. Kraabel, "Archaeology, Iconography, and Nonliterary Written Remains," in R. A. Kraft and G. W. E. Nickelsburg, eds., *Early Judaism and Its Modern Interpreters* (Atlanta, 1986), pp. 175–210; A. Kasher et al., *Synagogues in Antiquity* (Jerusalem, 1987; in Hebrew with English summaries). It should be noted that no synagogues have thus far been found in the great Babylonian centers of the Sasanian Empire, perhaps because no one has yet looked for them.

23. Cf. Gutmann, *The Synagogue*, pp. 2–40, and "Synagogue Origins: Theories and Facts," in Gutmann, ed., *Ancient Synagogues: The State of Research* (Chico, Calif., 1981), pp. 1–6.

24. Cf. Gutmann, *The Synagogue*, pp. xxv, 27–54, and *Ancient Synagogues*, pp. 5–6, n. 14. L. M. White, "The Delos Synagogue Revisited: Recent Fieldwork in the Graeco-Roman Diaspora," *Harvard Theological Review* 80 (1987), pp. 133–60, corrects some assumptions made by Bruneau and other scholars. Although I can agree with the author that a second-century B.C.E. private building at Delos may have been renovated and adapted by Jews as a place of assembly for religious purposes, there is no indisputable epigraphic, archaeological, or historical evidence on hand for calling the building in question a synagogue. We know the functions and practices of the synagogue, but we do not know either the liturgy or the function of the *proseuchē*.

25. Cf. M. J. Chiat, "First-Century Synagogue Architecture: Methodological Problems," in Gutmann, *Ancient Synagogues*, pp. 49–60.

26. Cf., for instance, M. Dothan, *Hammath-Tiberias: Early Synagogues and the Hellenistic and Roman Remains* (Jerusalem, 1983), reviewed by L. I. Levine, *Israel Exploration Journal* 34 (1984), pp. 285–88; E. Meyers et al., *Ancient Synagogue Excavations at Khirbet Shemaʿ* (Durham, 1976), and idem, *Excavations at Ancient Meiron* (Cambridge, Mass., 1981), reviewed by G. Foerster, "Excavations at Ancient Meron," *Israel Exploration Journal* 37 (1987), pp. 262–69; A. Seager et al., *The Sardis Synagogue and Its Setting* (forthcoming).

27. On orientation, cf. Gutmann, *The Synagogue*, pp. xix, xxvii, n. 27. The common conception that all synagogues faced toward Jerusalem is not borne out by the evidence.

28. Cf. E. Kitzinger, *Israeli Mosaics of the Byzantine Period* (New York, 1965); B. Goldman, *The Sacred Portal: A Primary Symbol in Ancient Judaic Art*, 2d ed. with introduction by J. Neusner (Lenham, Md., 1985), reviewed by J. Gutmann, *The Jewish Quarterly Review* 64 (1973), pp. 176–79; R. and A. Ovadiah, *Hellenistic, Roman and Early Christian Mosaic Pavements in Israel* (Rome, 1987), describe excavations of synagogue mosaics only up to the year 1975; their bibliographical citations are incomplete. A study that widens the scholarly horizons beyond stylistic description and dating is C. Dauphin, "Mosaic Pavements as an Index of Prosperity and Fashion," *Levant* 12 (1980), pp. 112–34.

29. Cf. the extensive bibliography cited in J. Gutmann, "Early Synagogue and Jewish Catacomb Art and Its Relation to Christian Art," pp. 1336–38.

30. Ibid., pp. 1337–38. Cf. also R. Hachlili, *Ancient Jewish Art and Archaeology in the Land of Israel* (Leiden, 1988).

31. Cf. the bibliography listed in Gutmann, "Early Synagogue and Jewish Catacomb Art," pp. 1335–36. On the sarcophagi, cf. A. Konikoff, *Sarcophagi from the Jewish Cata-*

combs of Ancient Rome (Stuttgart, 1986); cf. review by F. Monfrin, in *Revue des études juives* 147 (1988), 233–34, and L. V. Rutgers, "Ein in Situ erhaltenes Sarkophagfragment in der jüdischen Katakombe an der Via Appia," *Jewish Art* 14 (1988), 16–27; C. Vermeule, *Jewish Relations with the Art of Ancient Greece and Rome* (Boston, 1981).

32. Only a few scattered articles have appeared on the subject of medieval Jewish ceremonial objects from Muslim lands; cf. S. D. Goitein, "The Synagogue Building and Its Furnishings according to the Records of the Cairo Genizah," *Eretz-Israel* 7 (1964), pp. 94–95 [in Hebrew]; and D. Barash, "*Tiq* of the Sefer Torah," *Sinai* 15 (1952), pp. 228–36 [in Hebrew]. Medieval Jewish sources should be carefully searched for any descriptions of ceremonial objects and synagogues. Field research trips should be organized to study and record remains of former synagogues in Muslim countries. Cf., for instance, the descriptions and photographs of synagogues in Muslim lands published by the late Jacob Pinkerfeld. Even for the postmedieval period, we have only a few ethnographic exhibit catalogues that describe some of the synagogues and ceremonial objects in Morocco, Turkey, Yemen, and Bukhara. However, no scientific scholarly studies tracing the origins, meanings, and styles of Jewish ceremonial objects or comparative architectural studies of synagogues in Islamic lands have appeared.

33. Cf. L. K. Avrin, "The Illumination of the Moshe ben-Asher Codex of 895 C.E." (Ph.D. diss., University of Michigan, 1974), gives the pertinent bibliography of Jewish art in the Islamic world. Cf. also the study by R. Ettinghausen. "Yemenite Bible Manuscripts of the XVth Century," in Gutmann, ed., *No Graven Images*, pp. 429–65. The illustrated *ketubbot* in the Cairo Geniza also demand scholarly study; cf. J. Gutmann, "Jewish Marriage Customs in Art: Creativity and Adaptation," in D. Kraemer, ed., *The Jewish Family: Metaphor and Memory* (New York, 1988), p. 61, nn. 21–22.

34. Cf. H. C. Graf von Bothmer, "Architekturbilder im Koran: Eine Prachthandschrift der Umayyadenzeit aus dem Yemen," *Pantheon* 45 (1987), pp. 4–20.

35. Cf. the many studies on this subject by L. Avrin, listed and analyzed in J. Gutmann, "*Masorah Figurata:* The Origins and Development of a Jewish Art Form," in E. F. Tejero, ed., *Estudios masoreticos* (Madrid, 1983), pp. 49–62; and T. Metzger, "Ornamental Micrography in Medieval Hebrew Manuscripts," *Bibliotheca Orientalis* 43 (1986), pp. 377–88.

36. Cf. the extensive bibliographies listed in C. Krinsky, *Synagogues of Europe* (New York, 1985), and R. Wischnitzer, *The Architecture of the European Synagogue* (Philadelphia, 1964). To be singled out is the excellent study by O. Böcher, "Die Alte Synagoge zu Worms," in E. Roth, ed., *Wiedereinweihung der alten Synagoge zu Worms* (Frankfurt am Main, 1961), pp. 1–154—on one of the oldest synagogues of Europe. Now rebuilt, this synagogue had been destroyed by the Nazis. The following books might be added to the bibliographies cited in the above books: A. Parík, *The Synagogues of Prague* (Prague, 1986); J. F. van Agt and E. van Voolen, *Nederlandse Synagogen* (Weesp, Holland, 1984); H. Künzl, *Islamische Stilelemente im Synagogenbau des 19. und frühen 20. Jahrhunderts* (Frankfurt am Main, 1984). For postmedieval synagogue architecture, the following books are highly recommended: M. and K. Piechotka, *Wooden Synagogues* (Warsaw, 1959); H. Hammer-Schenk, *Synagogen in Deutschland. Geschichte einer Baugattung im 19. und 20. Jahrhunderts* (Hamburg, 1981) 2 vols.; and idem, "Historische Einführung," in R. Bothe and V. Bendt, eds., *Synagogen in Berlin: Zur Geschichte einer zerstörten Architektur* (Berlin, 1983), 2 vols.

37. Cf., for instance, J. Gutmann, "Christian Influences on Jewish Customs," in L. Klenicki and G. Huck, eds., *Spirituality and Prayer: Jewish and Christian Understandings* (New York, 1983), pp. 128–38.

38. Limited facsimile editions published in recent years are: E. Katz and B. Narkiss, *Machsor Lipsiae* (Leipzig, 1964); M. Spitzer et al., *The Birds' Head Haggada* (Jerusalem, 1967); B. Narkiss, *The Golden Haggadah* (London, 1970); J. Gutmann et al., *Die Darmstädter Pessach-Haggadah* (Berlin, 1971–72); B. Narkiss and A. Cohen-Mushlin, *The Kennicott Bible*

Joseph Gutmann

(London, 1984); A. Scheiber, G. Sed-Rajna, et al., *Codex Maimuni: Moses Maimonides' Code of Law. The Illuminated Pages of the Kaufmann Mishneh Torah* (Budapest, 1984); M. Beit-Arié et al., *Worms Mahzor* (London, 1985); K. Schubert et al., *Bilder-Pentateuch von Moses dal Castellazzo. Venedig, 1521* (Vienna, 1986); L. Mortara Ottolenghi et al., *The Rothschild Miscellany* (London, 1988). Facsimile editions made for a larger market: A. Scheiber, *The Kaufmann Haggadah* (Budapest, 1957); M. Schmelzer and E. Cohen. *The Rothschild Mahzor* (New York, 1983); E. Werber, *The Sarajevo Haggadah* (Beograd, 1985); G. Tamani, *Canon medicianae di Avicenna nella tradizione ebraica* (Padua, 1988); R. Loewe, *The Rylands Haggadah* (New York, 1988).

39. Cf. A. Luzzatto and L. Mortara Ottolenghi, *Hebraica Ambrosiana* (Milan, 1972); B. Narkiss et al., *Manuscripts in the British Isles. A Catalogue Raisonné. The Spanish and Portuguese Manuscripts,* vol. 1 (New York, 1982). See reviews of the latter publication by D. Sperber, in *Bibliotheca Orientalis* 41 (1984), pp. 158–62, and T. Metzger, *Cahiers de civilisation médiévale* 29 (1986), pp. 393–95.

40. Great strides have been made in the relatively new field of Hebrew paleography; cf. M. Beit-Arié. *Hebrew Codicology* (Jerusalem, 1981), and "Paleographical Identification of Hebrew Manuscripts: Methodology and Practice," *Jewish Art* 12–13 (1986–87), pp. 15–44.

41. For general introductions to the field, see B. Narkiss, *Hebrew Illuminated Manuscripts* (New York, 1969; rev. ed., Jerusalem, 1984 [in Hebrew]); J. Gutmann, *Hebrew Manuscript Painting* (New York, 1978). Cf. also M. Metzger, *La Haggada enluminée. Etudes iconographique et stylistique des manuscrits enluminés et décorés de la Haggada du XIIIe au XVIe siècle* (Leiden, 1973), reviewed by J. Gutmann, *Art Bulletin* 58 (1976), pp. 440–42; T. Metzger, *Les Manuscrits hébreux copiés et décorés à Lisbonne dans les dernières décennies du XVe siècle* (Paris, 1977); T. and M. Metzger, *Jewish Life in the Middle Ages: Illuminated Hebrew Manuscripts from the Thirteenth to the Sixteenth Centuries* (New York, 1982), reviewed by E. Horowitz in *Jewish History* 1 (1986), pp. 75–90; G. Sed-Rajna, *Le mahzor enluminé. Les voies de formation d'un programme iconographique* (Leiden, 1983); G. Sed-Rajna, *The Hebrew Bible in Medieval Illuminated Hebrew Manuscripts* (New York, 1987), reviewed by J. Gutmann in *Choice* (March 1988), p. 78, and T. and M. Metzger, in *Echos-Unir* 61 (1988), pp. 12–15.

42. Cf. Sperber and Horowitz reviews in nn. 39 and 41 above.

43. Cf. J. Gutmann, "The Messianic Temple in Spanish Medieval Hebrew Manuscripts," in Gutmann, *The Temple of Solomon,* pp. 125–44; and idem, "Return in Mercy to Zion: A Messianic Dream in Jewish Art," in L. Hoffman, ed., *The Land of Israel: Jewish Perspectives* (Notre Dame, Ind., 1986), pp. 234–38.

44. Gutmann, "The Sacrifice of Isaac in Medieval Jewish Art," *Artibus et Historiae* 16 (1987), pp. 72–80.

45. Cf. J. Gutmann, "Messiah at the Seder: A Fifteenth-Century Motif in Jewish Art," in S. Yeivin, ed., *Studies in Jewish History. Presented to Professor Raphael Mahler on His Seventy-fifth Birthday* (Merhavia, 1974), pp. 29–38; and idem, "Return in Mercy to Zion," pp. 240–42. The unusual animal-headed figures in medieval Hebrew manuscripts from Germany during the thirteenth to mid-fourteenth century merit an in-depth scholarly study to determine how such images may be related to the thought and practices of contemporary Cistercian and mendicant monastic orders; cf. Gutmann, "The Sacrifice of Isaac in Medieval Jewish Art," p. 76.

46. Cf., for instance, H. Peled-Carmeli, *Illustrated Haggadot of the Eighteenth Century* (Jerusalem, 1983).

47. Cf. I. Shachar, *The Jewish Year* (Leiden, 1975); J. Gutmann, *The Jewish Sanctuary* (Leiden, 1983); idem, *The Jewish Life Cycle* (Leiden, 1987).

48. Cf. the studies in J. Gutmann, ed., *Beauty in Holiness: Studies in Jewish Customs and Ceremonial Art* (New York, 1970). To the studies reproduced in the above-cited book, the

following should be added: B. Nosek, "Synagogical Tablets from the Collections of the State Jewish Museum (Textual Analysis)," *Judaica Bohemiae* 18 (1982), pp. 88–108; M. Narkiss, "Origins of the Spice Box," *Journal of Jewish Art* 8 (1981), pp. 28–41; J. Gutmann, "Die Mappe Schuletragen: An Unusual Judeo-German Custom," *Visible Religion* 2 (1983), pp. 167–73; idem, "An Eighteenth-Century Prague Jewish Workshop of *Kapporot*," *Visible Religion* 6 (1988), pp. 180–90.

49. Cf. I. Shachar, *The Feuchtwanger Collection of Judaica* (Jerusalem, 1981); Victor Klagsbald, *Jewish Treasurers from Paris from the Collections of the Cluny Museum and Consistoire* (Jerusalem, 1982); R. Barnett, ed., *Catalogue of the Jewish Museum London* (London, 1974); *Danzig 1939: Treasures of a Destroyed Community* (Detroit, 1980); S. S. Kayser, ed., *Jewish Ceremonial Art* (Philadelphia, 1959); N. Kleeblatt and V. Mann, *Treasures of the Jewish Museum* (New York, 1986); D. Altshuler, ed., *The Precious Legacy: Judaic Treasures from the Czechoslovak State Collections* (New York, 1981).

50. Cf. M. Narkiss, *The Hanukkah Lamp* (Jerusalem, 1939; in Hebrew). A revised edition in English translation is forthcoming.

51. Cf. such studies as J. Stone, "English Silver Rimmonim and Their Makers," *Quest* 1 (1965), pp. 23–29; and V. Mann, "The Golden Age of Jewish Ceremonial Art in Frankfurt. Metalwork in the Eighteenth Century," *Leo Baeck Institute Year Book* 31 (1986), pp. 389–403.

52. S. Sabar, "The Beginnings and Flourishing of Ketubbah Illustrations in Italy: A Study in Popular Imagery and Jewish Patronage during the 17th and 18th Centuries" (Ph.D. diss., University of California, Los Angeles, 1987). A forthcoming book on the *ketubbot* in the Hebrew Union College Skirball Museum, Los Angeles—*The Illustrated Ketubbah: Jewish Marriage Contracts at the Hebrew Union College Skirball Museum*—will include much of the material discussed in this dissertation.

53. Cf. R. Weinstein, "The Sepulchral Monuments of the Jews of Amsterdam in the Seventeenth and Eighteenth Centuries" (Ph.D. diss., New York University, 1979). A book on the above subject is forthcoming.

54. Cf. J. Gutmann, "Estherrolle," *Reallexikon zur deutschen Kunstgeschichte* 6 (1973), pp. 88–103.

55. E. Cohen, ed., *Moritz Oppenheim: The First Jewish Painter* (Jerusalem, 1983).

56. J. Gutmann and S. F. Chyet, *Moses Jacob Ezekiel: Memoirs from the Baths of Diocletian* (Detroit, 1975).

57. N. Shilo-Cohen, ed., *Bezalel 1906–1929* (Jerusalem, 1983).

58. Cf. R. Apter-Gabriel, *Tradition and Revolution: The Jewish Renaissance in Russian Avant-Garde Art 1912–1928* (Jerusalem, 1987). Cf. also K. E. Silver et al., *The Circle of Montparnasse: Jewish Artists in Paris 1905–1945* (New York, 1985)—these artists created not Jewish art but Parisian art—and A. Kampf, *Jewish Experience in the Art of the Twentieth Century* (South Hadley, Mass., 1984), reviewed by J. Gutmann, in *Choice* (Feb. 1985), p. 90.

I am greatly indebted to Shaye Cohen and Stanley F. Chyet for reading this manuscript and making many suggestions for its improvement.

211

III

RELIGION AND
SCHOLARSHIP

Modern Jewish Thought

15

PHILOSOPHY AND THEOLOGY

Neil Gillman

In keeping with the celebratory nature of this volume honoring the centennial of the Jewish Theological Seminary, it is appropriate to begin with a word on the study of Jewish thought at the seminary over the past century.

It is no secret that the adjective "theological," included in the name of this academic institution, has frequently been greeted with a measure of skepticism, even by the seminary's most loyal supporters. Throughout the greater part of this past century, the curricula of the various seminary schools, preeminently the Rabbinical School, have indeed reflected a striking imbalance in class time assigned to text courses in Bible and Talmud on the one hand, and theology and philosophy on the other.[1]

One can speculate why these latter disciplines did not play a more prominent role in the formal academic programs of this school.[2] In part, it reflected the ambiguous role they played throughout the course of Jewish intellectual history. With few notable exceptions, our ancestors did not feel that clarifying the belief content of Judaism was as important as analyzing the minutiae of human behavior in terms of Jewish legal norms. More specifically, the reluctance of the faculties of the seminary to conduct an intensive, critical inquiry into the central issues of Jewish religious thought—the existence and nature of God, revelation, theodicy, and eschatology, to name but a few—probably stemmed from the fact that few of them shared a sense of the problematics of Jewish religious identity in the way that many of us do today. They were, by and large, "at home" with Jewish religion

215

and its halakha; it needed no further defense or apologia.[3] The most notable exception to this pattern was Mordecai Kaplan, whose influence on American Jewish thinking was monumental, at least in part because he felt the urgency of these issues in a highly personal way.

Finally, specifically on the issue of revelation, these scholars were engaged in a perilous enterprise. Their academic background in the *Wissenschaft* movement impelled them to study and teach Torah as a cultural document, shaped as much by the distinctive experience of the Jew in every age as by its own internal impulses. This justified their use of all the tools of historical and critical scholarship at their disposal in order to understand Jewish texts and the Jewish experience. At the same time, they insisted on the binding character of Jewish law as the central, most authentic form of Jewish religious expression, and on a minimalist or, at most, gradualist approach to halakhic development. They were apparently able to live with these conflicting impulses. To open the issue of revelation could well have exploded the entire package. In retrospect, then, avoiding the issue was an effective way of defending against that threat.

It must also be said, particularly on this occasion, that the extended seminary community served as a major center for Jewish theological creativity over the past seven decades. Of the four undisputed giants among twentieth-century Jewish theologians—Martin Buber, Franz Rosenzweig, Mordecai Kaplan, and Abraham Heschel—the two who found their home in the United States taught at the seminary, Kaplan for over five decades, and Heschel for twenty-seven years, until his death in 1972. Many seminary students went on to make substantial contributions to American Jewish thought. I will mention only three of the older generation: the late Milton Steinberg and Max Kadushin, and, *yibbadel leḥayyim*, Robert Gordis, who also taught here for decades, as did Kadushin. Some of the most stimulating debates in the history of American Jewish thought took place at conventions of the Rabbinical Assembly with Kaplan, Heschel, and Will Herberg as participants along with Steinberg, Gordis, and others.[4] The late Jacob Agus, a longtime member of the Rabbinical Assembly (though not ordained at the seminary), was, I believe, the first to introduce the English-speaking theological community to the thought of Franz Rosenzweig in his *Modern Philosophies of Judaism,* which was published in 1941, a decade before Herberg's reformulation of Buberian/Rosenzweigian existentialism in his *Judaism and Modern Man* (1951) and Steinberg's critical evaluation of that position,[5] and fully twelve years before Rosenzweig's writings became available in English through Nahum Glatzer's anthology, *Franz Rosenzweig: His Life and Thought.* Seminary people, then, played a pivotal role in the transmission of European Jewish thought to America. That part of the record is also indisputable and must be acknowledged on this occasion.

To pick up on an earlier point, our century has produced four giants—Buber, Rosenzweig, Kaplan, and Heschel. Borrowing the language of Thomas Kuhn's *Structure of Scientific Revolutions,*[6] they introduced new paradigms into Jewish thought, original and revolutionary conceptualizations—Buber and Rosenzweig, using the idiom of existentialism; Kaplan, that of American naturalism; and Heschel, continental phenomenology. Since their time, the rest of us have been doing what Kuhn might call "normal theology," that is, resolving ambiguities in their paradigms, expanding the scope of the paradigms, and elaborating their potential impact. But essentially we have been standing on their shoulders, viewing Jewish thought through one of their sets of spectacles.

Our century has seen two marker events in Jewish history—the Holocaust and the creation of the State of Israel—which, like all events of this magnitude, invariably generate a sense of "crisis" regarding the existing paradigms.[7] Heschel's thought in its totality can be understood as a post-Holocaust paradigm, though it might also be viewed as a reworking of a Biblical or more narrowly prophetic and neo-Hasidic model. On the other hand, the model that was most severely affected by the Holocaust was Kaplan's theological naturalism. One of the victims of the Holocaust may well have been Kaplanian naturalism, though his civilizational model is alive and well and has in fact become mainstream American Jewish thinking. Finally, Richard Rubenstein's "death of God" theology testifies that for him at least, all of the classical Jewish theological paradigms had died and must be replaced. Significantly, Rubenstein's thesis has largely been ignored by Jews, partially because its Christian parallels have also faded and partially because it was simply too offensive to Jewish ears. This is not to diminish Rubenstein's contributions to Jewish theology and to our thinking about Jewish religion. We will return to these contributions below.

Of these, then, the existentialist model has fared best of all. There is a good deal of existentialism in Heschel as well, of course. Existentialism may well provide us with the most effective resources for handling the *theological* implications of the Holocaust, but, as we shall see, a good deal of extratheological work remains to be done on this issue as well.

For the rest, I shall deal with a series of issues that are implicitly or explicitly on the agenda of modern Jewish thought, though they may not have as yet been given the attention they deserve. They are of two kinds: some are metatheological or methodological issues, others are substantive theological or philosophical issues.

First, the methodological. One issue is agitating all segments of the Jewish community today. But typically perhaps, it is rarely addressed as the metatheological problem that it ultimately is. We have been hearing a great deal these past years on the divisiveness that racks the world Jewish religious community. To a large extent, the debate has centered on substantive halakhic questions (patrilineal descent, mixed marriages, conversion procedures), or on different approaches to what constitutes legitimate halakhic process, or finally on strategic/political techniques (how the various Jewish religious movements can be convinced to work together to preserve the integrity of the Jewish community).[8] But the real issue is none of these. In fact, the debate raises the broader questions of authority and authenticity in matters of Jewish theology, and on these metatheological issues very little has been written.

Our community is split on questions of Jewish personal status because some of us do not believe that the Torah is the explicit word of God. That's why we approach halakhic development in a more liberal way. The issue, then, is how to understand revelation. Opposing theologies of revelation yield opposing notions of the authority of Torah in matters of belief and practice. But then which of these opposing theologies are themselves authoritative or authentic? What criteria do we employ? And who decides?

We know that the Roman Catholic church has evolved an approach to this complex of questions. Judaism never has, probably because of the very different role that theology plays in the two traditions. But we have to confront the issue if we are to deal with Mordecai Kaplan's naturalist concept of God, or with Richard Rubenstein's ''death of God'' response to the Holocaust, or with Harold Kushner's response to human suffering in *When Bad Things Happen to Good People*. In fact, each of the four giants of twentieth-century Jewish theology—even Heschel, who is the most traditionalist of all—has been attacked for affirming quasi-heretical teachings in the name of Judaism.[9] The implicit criterion that is invoked here is fidelity to past or classic formulations of Jewish belief. But we know that by that criterion we could rule out many portions of the Bible itself, including the Book of Job and some of the prophetic books, let alone the writings of the mystics and of Maimonides. We can always excommunicate a Mordecai Kaplan, but that is no substitute for a more systematic metatheological inquiry into the question of authority in Jewish theology.

Authority issues are troublesome, but authenticity issues are even more complicated. We all appeal to the criterion of authenticity. Nobody deliberately seeks to be a heretic. But there has been no systematic study of the logic of the authenticity argument in Jewish theology, even though it is omnipresent in our literature. Both issues—authority and authenticity in Jewish theology—are fascinating because a prima facie case can be made for claiming that the most interesting and valuable of Jewish theological statements are so precisely because they broke with the received tradition, because they could be dubbed ''inauthentic.'' Job, for example, or Isaac Luria, or Maimonides fall into this category. And then there are those claims made in the name of Judaism that were rejected by the community. Pauline Christianity is an example of that phenomenon; so is Spinoza's thought. How does this process of appropriating or rejecting work itself out? What are the parameters and who decides?[10]

The twin issues of authority and authenticity in Jewish theology raise still further questions. One is the even broader or umbrella issue of the place of the entire theological enterprise in Jewish religion. To borrow from Kaplan, what is the relation of "believing" to "behaving" and "belonging" in Judaism? It is surely different from the relation in classical Christianity, but why? And how do *we* work out the balance? We know that many of the halakhists among us take the halakhic system as a given, as self-validating.[11] For much of our past, this validation rested on a series of implicit theological claims about the Torah. But if those claims change, surely the validity of the system *itself* has to be argued anew. In fact, we may even question if there is a single halakhic system in the first place. And does this not force us to reconsider the rather peripheral place that theology has occupied in resolving the broader question of Jewish identity?

Beyond this, let us return to revelation. We cannot even begin to deal with revelation as a substantive theological issue without opening up the question of the epistemological status of all Jewish theological claims. Here, in contrast to the first of our umbrella issues, the literature on the subject is abundant; but it has been developed by general philosophers and Christian philosophers of religion. Little of it has found its way into Jewish theology. A notable exception is Emil Fackenheim's sharp critique of John Wisdom's seminal paper "Gods" and of the "Theology and Falsification" debate that it inspired.[12] Fackenheim's claim is that much of this inquiry is infused by an idiosyncratic Christian bias and has little relevance to Judaism. However we feel about this critique, we must deal both with the larger epistemological issues and with Fackenheim's own proposals, which often are far from clear. Are Jewish theological claims—claims such as "God has chosen us from among the nations"—falsifiable? Verifiable? How? Do they constitute legitimate knowledge claims? Why? If not, then what status do they have? And is there a distinctive function to Jewish theological language? To Jewish religious language? All of these issues have been raging in the outside world for decades, but Jewish thinkers have barely touched them.

In my own theological development, this complex of questions led me back to Paul Tillich and to the notion that Torah has to be understood as the canonization of the classic, complex Jewish myth, where "myth," of course, means neither a legendary tale nor a deliberate fiction, but rather the structure of meaning through which our ancestors organized their experience of the world, of nature and history.[13] But a religious myth is much more than a theological or more broadly intellectual device. And Judaism is much more than theology—as it is much more than halakha. It is, in fact, a "religion," and a religion does much more than create *intellectual* order out of the blooming confusion of the "out there." Clifford Geertz has taught us that the function of religion is also to create what might be called an "existential cosmos," an intuitive sense of "at homeness" in the world in the face of the incipient chaos all about us. That above all is the task of religion and its myths.[14]

The study of religions as complex phenomena emerging from and having an impact on human beings and their communities—of religion as viewed from the human, together with or even as opposed to the divine, perspective—is a relatively young discipline in the scholarly world at large. Again, much of the spade work has been done by scholars in the social sciences and by students of Christianity and primitive religions. Gershom Scholem was probably the first major figure to apply the methods of this inquiry to the study of Jewish religion, specifically in his case to Jewish mysticism. But there is now a sizable group of scholars in almost every field of Jewish studies who are engaged in this kind of research. We can single out the names of two scholars whose work is distinguished both by the range of issues addressed and the refinement of the methodology employed. Jacob Neusner has pursued a decades-long and multivolumed study of the shape of Talmudic religion, asking questions of the Talmudic text that have rarely been asked before. Neusner has also encouraged his students to apply his methodology to an expanding range of issues in Jewish religion. Second, Richard Rubenstein has used the perspective of psychoanalytic theory to understand the dynamics of Jewish religious living and thinking. Not the least of their contributions has been to place these questions at the heart of the agenda of Jewish scholarship.

One of the more exciting results of this inquiry has been a renewed interest in the forms and functions of ritual in Jewish religion. If we believe that God dictated the Torah in words and letters, then the rituals of Judaism are observed because God said so.[15] The inquiry ends there. If we posit an active, substantive human contribution to revelation, however, we must also look at the human functions that ritual serves, at the process of ritualization or of the formation of rituals in life in general and in religion in particular, of the way in which ritual and liturgy combine to create an elaborate, theatrical pageant as in Jewish rites of passage or at the Passover seder, at the distinctive quality of religious rituals, and at the way in which rituals both influence and borrow from the myths to which they are related.

The literature on this topic is abundant and growing rapidly. The groundbreaking work of scholars such as Emil Durkheim, Bruno Malinowsky, Victor Turner, and Mircea Eliade has begun to be combed with an eye to discovering the distinctive character of Jewish ritual. Mary Douglas's "The Abominations of Leviticus" is a pioneering effort to apply this methodology to the dietary laws. Richard Rubenstein, as we have noted, has studied the material from a psychoanalytic perspective. Jacob Neusner has focused, inter alia, on the functions of ritual purity and impurity in Talmudic religion. A recent anthology, *Judaism Viewed from Within and from Without,* applies an anthropological perspective to a wide range of Jewish ritual practices. Lawrence Hoffman's *Beyond the Text* studies the phenomenon of ritual and the function of the liturgy in Judaism.[16] These questions are now being addressed by the Jewish scholarly world. They are even beginning to appear in the curricula of our rabbinical schools.

Parenthetically, this is a particularly appropriate time to study the process of ritualization because we are squarely in the midst of that process in at least four areas of Jewish life. We are experimenting with rituals celebrating the birth of a female child, for marking the establishment of the State of Israel on *Yom Ha'atsma'ut,* and for commemorating the Holocaust on *Yom Hasho'ah.* Further, many Jewish women are beginning to explore the rituals of *kippa, talit,* and *tefillin* in every possible combination and permutation. Here is a priceless opportunity to study how the process takes place.

When we look at Judaism from this expanded perspective, all of the classical theological issues become reframed. Take the perennial issue of theodicy, for example. We have seen that Geertz identifies the main function of religion as the attempt to formulate "conceptions of a general order of existence," to bring cosmos out of chaos, for "the thing that we seem least able to tolerate is a threat to our powers of conception, a suggestion that our ability to create, grasp, and use symbols may fail us, for were this to happen, we would be . . . helpless."[17] We cannot deal with chaos. But the experience that most starkly captures the eruption of chaos into our lives is persistent, unjustified suffering or, more broadly, the experience of evil.

That recognition puts the problem of theodicy in an entirely new light. First, it is no longer *a* theological problem. It becomes *the* theological problem—the theological problem par excellence, for it cuts to the heart of what religion is all about. Second, of course, it is no longer simply a theological or *intellectual* problem, but more broadly a *religious* problem. What is threatened is not simply our intellectual ordering of the world but much more—our most primitive sense of "at homeness" in the world. What the Holocaust conveys is the simple reality that the barbarians are at the gate, that in fact they have overrun the walls, that the structures through which we have organized our lives are destroyed, and that our instinctive, existential sense of rootedness in the world has collapsed. What we must formulate, then, are not only theological responses to suffering but religious ones as well. Suddenly the need for a liturgical and ritual observance of *Yom Hasho'ah* becomes infinitely more pressing. But we have only begun to develop Holocaust-specific liturgies and rituals. David Roskies's *Night Words: A Midrash on the Holocaust*,[18] which includes the ritual of writing numbers on the arm, is to my mind the most interesting and effective proposal thus far, though it is hardly universally accepted.

If we begin to look at Judaism as a complex religious system, it may also be possible for us to begin to explore what constitutes a "religious" Jew. The compartmentalization of Jewish studies; our tendency to study Jewish law, Jewish liturgy, Jewish literature, Jewish philosophy as discrete units; the general tendency, on the highest levels of our educational work, to emphasize text studies at the expense of a more conceptual or synthetic approach to issues in the Jewish experience—all these have made it difficult to look at the broader question of specifically Jewish models of religious authenticity. Is it the observant Jew? The believing Jew? The studying Jew? All of these together, if that is at all possible?

Why is this more than an academic issue? One example will suffice. What model of Jew should a Jewish day school try to produce? That question has to be addressed before a curriculum is created, before a faculty is hired, before the culture of the school is articulated. But most Jewish educators are, at best, struggling with alternative models of Jewish religious authenticity at different moments of the school day. We know how to teach texts, the data of Jewish history, ritual, and language skills. We could teach Jewish theology if we had teachers who had worked out a coherent personal theology and knew what they wanted to teach. What we rarely teach is how to become a "religious" Jew, how to live a Jewish religious life. One of the reasons we don't teach it is that we don't know what a religious Jew looks like, or that we have widely varying perspectives on that question.[19]

It need not be added that if this is a problem for the principal and faculty of a Jewish day school, it is an even more pressing problem for the faculties of our rabbinical schools. By and large our rabbinical schools are really Western-style graduate schools for higher Jewish studies. They do little *religious* education, however well they may do Jewish (skills, texts, and data) education and professional, rabbinic education. These are all very different educational enterprises.

One of the most noteworthy developments in the study of Jewish thought over the past three decades has been the engagement of a group of competent, trained traditionalist thinkers in Jewish theological debate. I recall, in the mid-fifties, trying to find a well-written, somewhat sophisticated, coherent statement of traditionalist Judaism written in a contemporary idiom, and being handed Samson Raphael Hirsch's *Nineteen*

Letters of Ben Uzziel. This hardly met the needs of an American educated, undergraduate philosophy major. But at that time there was little else available. Today there is much more.

In retrospect, Hirsch emerges as a figure of striking importance. He was certainly not a sophisticated theologian or philosopher. Yet he is responsible for formulating the classic Orthodox response to the tides of Reform and "Positive Historical" (soon-to-become "Conservative") Judaism, by insisting that Torah is the revealed word of God, hence absolutely authoritative. If there is to be an accommodation between Judaism and modernity, it must come from the general culture, not from Torah. Of course Hirsch did make his own accommodations to German culture; he called them *derekh 'erets,* or what we might call "civility." That entire response pervades the style of "modern" or "centrist" Orthodoxy to this day.[20]

The other thinker who has emerged as seminal for this reading of Judaism is Joseph B. Soloveitchik. In contrast to Hirsch, Soloveitchik is very much a trained philosopher, quite apart from his renown as a Talmudist and *poseq.* For many years, his reputation was based more on word of mouth than on his published work. But two of his extended studies, "The Lonely Man of Faith" and *Halakhic Man,* which synthesize Soloveitchik's reading of Biblical and Talmudic thought and a Barthian/Kierkegaardian approach to philosophical issues in religion, have been widely studied for a theological underpinning for a traditionalist approach to halakha.[21]

Beyond this, David Hartman and Michael Wyschogrod, two notable representatives of the younger generation of Orthodox thinkers, have written on a wide range of theological and philosophical issues from a traditionalist perspective.[22] The recognition by the traditionalist community that this position needs a theological defense, that it *can* be coherently defended, that the Kaplans and Rosenzweigs and their younger disciples need not have the field to themselves, is a welcome development. It can only impel all of us to sharpen our own thinking.

We must also celebrate the return of Jewish mysticism into the field of modern Jewish thought. For this we must, of course, be grateful to the late Gershom Scholem, who created the field as a modern scholarly discipline. More recently, Moshe Idel's *Kabbalah: New Perspectives* offers a fresh assessment of the original kabbalistic texts and traditions that departs from Scholem's.[23]

Scholem's impact has been felt not only in the scholarly field but also in the renewal of a mystical strain in contemporary Jewish thinking. Martin Buber and Abraham Heschel played a role in this development as well. But since the fifties, the new romanticism in culture at large has had its own impact on Judaism, blunting the drier, more critical stance of the *Wissenschaft* school, which dominated from the early nineteenth century through the first decades of the twentieth. One notable result of this new emphasis is a renewed interest in the nature of spirituality, specifically in the attempt to distinguish authentically Jewish models of spirituality.[24]

Moving away from theology, there is no disputing the need for a much more systematic inquiry into the assumptions of Jewish political philosophy than we have conducted thus far. A recently published study by Daniel Elazar and Stuart Cohen is a pioneering effort in this direction. The authors claim that there has been a strong and consistent Jewish political tradition from the Bible to this very day, with the Torah as constitution, and the ʿeda or assembly of the community, the constituent body. Within the ʿeda, the authors claim, power and authority were diffused among the three ketarim, or "crowns," cited in Mishna Avot 4:13: the crown of Torah, symbol of intellectual or pedagogic authority; the crown of kehuna or priestly, clerical authority; and the crown of malkhut or civil authority. The evolving tensions and interrelationships between these three sources of authority provide Elazar and Cohen with the structure for their study of the history of Jewish political philosophy.[25]

This inquiry is much more than an academic exercise. Its implications for the political situation in the State of Israel and in the diaspora communities are clear and immediate. For the better part of the past two centuries, we have defined ourselves in terms of a set of options that were developed close to two centuries ago at the dawn of the Jewish Emancipation. But these options have become less and less relevant. Neither the early nineteenth-century western European responses to Emancipation nor the later classical Zionist reactions to that response fully capture our situation as Jews who have chosen to live in America in the second half of the twentieth century with a State of Israel in existence. Yet much of the dialogue between Israelis and American Jews is still conducted as if those were the only two options. The result is a gulf of misunderstanding; we no longer share the same universe of discourse.

Beyond this, we have come to recognize that Ahad Haʿam may well have lost his battle with Herzl, but he clearly won the war. There is simply no questioning the impact of the State of Israel on Jewish culture broadly speaking. But the simple establishment of a Jewish state has hardly served as the immediate and automatically effective boon to Jewish self-identity that it was promised to be. If anything, it has led to a gradual polarization between two forms of identity, a Jewish and an Israeli, and we have seen that polarization gradually accentuated in recent years as the State of Israel has been forced to deal with the full implications of sovereignty and geopolitical power.

At the same time, we American Jews have become increasingly ambivalent about our own self-definition vis-à-vis America and vis-à-vis the

State of Israel. We have been exceedingly fortunate that for many years our political clout and the broad interpretation that America has given to the constitutional wall separating church and state have enabled us to handle that tension moderately well. But the Israeli sovereignty issues noted above have served to heighten our unease. Many of us are now struggling to define more clearly just what our responsibilities are both to the State of Israel and to our Jewish brethren who inhabit that state, and how both of these mesh with our loyalties to America. We need a systematic inquiry into that knotty complex of issues.

In fact, that systematic inquiry has been well launched by Arnold Eisen's masterful *Galut: Modern Jewish Reflection on Homelessness and Homecoming.*[26] Eisen not only asks all the right questions: how is it that Israeli and American Jews have so vastly different perceptions of each other? How did a religious vocabulary play such a central role in achieving a secular homecoming? What can it mean for Jews to come home to Israel and yet fail to achieve the kind of redemption promised by the religious tradition? And what can the experience of exile mean in a contemporary, "benevolent" America? He also provides a fine-tuned analysis of the range of responses to these questions, beginning with Herzl and Ahad Haʿam, their disciples Jacob Klatzkin, Yehezkel Kaufmann, Martin Buber, and A. D. Gordon, through Franz Rosenzweig, Rav Kook, Gershom Scholem, Abraham Heschel, and Mordecai Kaplan, and up to contemporary attempts to redefine the options by thinkers such as Amos Oz, Eliezer Schweid, A. B. Yehoshua, and Emil Fackenheim.

Where are we today? Eisen discerns three major strands in the contemporary attempt to define Jewish homecoming: the religious Zionist view of the state as "the beginning of the flowering of our redemption," the attempt to reformulate Herzlian or Ahad Haʿamist secular alternatives, and a middle path that sees the state as both a departure from and yet also a continuation of a (selectively articulated) religious tradition.

One concludes Eisen's study with a striking appreciation of the ambiguities that characterize what he calls the Israeli-diaspora "conversation over exile and homecoming." His analysis of the Israeli attack on the legitimacy of diaspora Judaism and the strategies that have been employed to defend against that attack, as well as his own attempt to bridge that division, constitute an indispensable point of departure for that ongoing conversation.

Finally, on an issue that straddles theology and political philosophy and that permeates Eisen's analyses, a word on Jewish eschatology. Gershom Scholem has drawn our attention to the tension between two classic Jewish eschatological voices, a gradualist or evolutionary voice and an apocalyptic or revolutionary voice. These two voices differ in their depiction of the eschatological scenario, in the respective roles assigned to God and to Israel in bringing it to pass, and in the temper or affect with which the messianic dream is articulated and pursued.[27]

We are clearly in an age of rampant, apocalyptic eschatological activity, in Islam in the Middle East, in American fundamentalist and evangelical Christianity, and among certain communities of Jews in Israel and elsewhere. Never have the dangers inherent in this eschatological voice been more starkly revealed. The nexus that links fundamentalist theology, eschatology, radical political activity, militarism, and, in the extreme, violence and terrorism is there for all to see.

The tragedy is that the apocalypticists have had the field to themselves. But the reaction to apocalyptic messianism need not necessarily lead to the abandonment of eschatology as a whole. There are ample resources in our tradition for seeing a messianic dimension in the everyday, in the common activities we do as Jews and for humanity. We must not be intimidated into losing that. But we must also work out the implications of that alternative, gradualist voice for our social and political philosophy as Jews. We too must be able to say that we do what we do in order to bring the Messiah. What better source of ultimate meaning can we give to our lives?

Notes

1. I recall, for example, that in the years 1954–60, when I studied in the seminary's Rabbinical School, Abraham Heschel's course in medieval Jewish philosophy met for one class hour over two semesters. Mordecai Kaplan's philosophies of Judaism class met for two class hours over two years. Heschel also taught an elective seminar every year that was preeminently where he shaped the education of a number of Conservative rabbis and future academicians. For many of us, it was an exceptionally powerful formative experience. In contrast, every rabbinical student studied Talmud for at least four class hours a week, and codes, midrash, and Bible for at least two class hours a week—every semester of residence. It should be noted that more recent (that is, post-1975) seminary Rabbinical School curricula have made a serious and successful attempt to redress that imbalance.

2. See my contribution to the symposium "Entering the Second Century: From Scholarship to the Rabbinate," *Proceedings of the Rabbinical Assembly* (1986), pp. 41–46, and my "Mordecai Kaplan and the Ideology of Conservative Judaism," *Proceedings of the Rabbinical Assembly* (1984), pp. 57–68.

3. My "The Jewish Philosopher in Search of a Role," *Judaism* 34/4 (Fall 1985), pp. 474–84, is an attempt to substantiate this claim in regard to the enterprise of Jewish philosophy as a whole.

4. See, inter alia, the symposia on "Authority in Jewish Law," "Theological Problems of the Hour," "Prayer and the Modern Jew," "Needed: A New Zionism to Revive the Moribund Jewish People," *"Yisrael: Am, Eretz, Medinah,"* and "Recent Theological Trends: A Survey and Analysis," in *Proceedings of the Rabbinical Assembly,* 1942, 1949, 1953, 1954, 1958, and 1959, respectively.

5. Steinberg's evaluation of existentialist theology and of Rosenzweig's thought can be found in his "The Theological Issues of the Hour" and "New Currents in Religious

Thought," both in Arthur A. Cohen, ed., *Anatomy of a Faith* (New York, 1960), pp. 155–213, and 214–300. The first of these was prepared for delivery at the 1949 convention of the Rabbinical Assembly as the major position paper in the symposium referred to in n. 4 above as "Theological Problems of the Hour." The discussants were Will Herberg and Eugene Kohn. For a different perspective on Steinberg's estimation of religious existentialism, see Herberg's "Foreword" to his *Judaism and Modern Man* (New York, 1951).

6. Thomas Kuhn, *The Structure of Scientific Revolutions*, 2d ed. (Chicago, 1970). My criteria for identifying these thinkers as "paradigmatic" is threefold. First, they have all written extensively and on a wide range of issues. Second, their published work exhibits a singular integrity or unity. Third, this integrity issues from an overall theological conceptualization that is original and revolutionary.

7. The terms "normal science" and "crisis" as applied to scientific theories are technical terms for Kuhn. See his chaps. 2, 3, 6, and 7.

8. A notable and widely influential example of the last of these is Irving Greenberg's "Will There Be One Jewish People in the Year 2000?" *Perspectives* (National Jewish Resource Center, June 1985).

9. See Eliezer Berkovits, "Dr. A. J. Heschel's Theology of Pathos" in his *Major Themes in Modern Philosophies of Judaism* (New York, 1974). This volume includes Berkovits's even more stinging critiques of the thought of Buber, Rosenzweig, and Kaplan. It is noteworthy, however, that the author does not attempt to articulate and defend the criteriology that underlies his critique, apart from a brief statement in the foreword to the effect that reformulations of Jewish theology and philosophy must "be accomplished by means of an intellectual strength that draws its creative inspiration as well as its contents from the classical sources of Judaism—Bible, Talmud and Midrash."

10. My "Authority and Authenticity in Jewish Philosophy," *Judaism* 35/2 (Spring 1986), pp. 223–32, is one attempt to answer these questions.

11. Joel Roth, *The Halakhic Process: A Systemic Analysis* (New York, 1986), is a thoroughgoing defense of that position.

12. Wisdom's paper is widely anthologized. It can be found, together with the ensuing debate, in Ronald E. Santoni, ed., *Religious Language and the Problem of Religious Knowledge* (Bloomington, Ind., 1968), pp. 295–332. Fackenheim's critique is in his *Encounters between Judaism and Modern Philosophy* (New York, 1973), chap. 1. See also Louis Jacobs, *Faith* (New York, 1968), chap. 2.

13. Tillich's *Dynamics of Faith* (New York, 1957) remains the classic statement on theological language as symbolic and mythical. Ian G. Barbour, *Myths, Models and Paradigms* (New York, 1974), is an extraordinarily lucid and helpful inquiry into the implications of this approach. See also the collection of papers in Alan Dundes, ed., *Sacred Narrative: Readings in the Theory of Myth* (Berkeley, 1984), and Will Herberg, "Some Variant Meanings of the Word 'Myth,' " in Bernhard W. Anderson, ed., *Faith Enacted as History: Essays in Biblical Theology by Will Herberg* (Philadelphia, 1976), pp. 139–48.

14. See Geertz, "Religion as a Cultural System," in his *Interpretation of Cultures* (New York, 1973), pp. 87–125, which is the seminal statement of that definition of the function of religion.

15. An exceptionally unambiguous statement of that position and its implications is in Norman Lamm's contribution to *The Condition of Jewish Belief: A Symposium Compiled by the Editors of Commentary Magazine* (New York, 1956), pp. 124–26.

16. Mary Douglas, *Natural Symbols* (New York, 1970) and *Purity and Danger* (London, 1966) are, as noted, indispensable. "The Abominations of Leviticus" is chap. 3 of *Purity and Danger*. See also: Richard Rubenstein, *After Auschwitz: Radical Theology and Contemporary Judaism* (Indianapolis, 1966) and *The Religious Imagination: A Study in Psychoanalysis and*

Jewish Theology (Boston, 1968); Jacob Neusner, *The Idea of Purity in Ancient Judaism* (Leiden, 1973); Harvey E. Goldberg, ed., *Judaism Viewed from Within and from Without* (Albany, 1987); Lawrence A. Hoffman, *Beyond the Text: A Holistic Approach to Liturgy* (Bloomington, Ind., 1987). On the Passover seder, see Baruch M. Bokser, *The Origins of the Seder: The Passover Rite and Early Rabbinic Judaism* (Berkeley, 1984); and Ruth Gruber Friedman, *The Passover Seder: Afikomon in Exile* (Philadelphia, 1981).

17. Geertz, "Religion as a Cultural System," p. 99.

18. David Roskies, *Night Words: A Midrash on the Holocaust* (Washington, 1971).

19. A notable recent contribution to that inquiry is Michael Rosenak, *Commandments and Concerns: Jewish Religious Education in Secular Society* (Philadelphia, 1987).

20. The classic statement of that defense is in Hirsch's "Religion Allied to Progress," *Judaism Eternal: Selected Essays from the Writings of Rabbi Samson Raphael Hirsch,* trans. and annotated by I. Grunfeld (London, 1956), vol. 2, pp. 224–44. More recent "modern" or "centrist Orthodox" reformulations of that position can be found in the contributions of Marvin Fox, Immanuel Jacobovits, Norman Lamm, M. D. Tendler, and Walter Wurzburger to *The Condition of Jewish Belief.*

21. The first of these was published in *Tradition* 7/2 (Summer 1965), pp. 5–67. The second originally appeared in Hebrew in *Talpiot* 1/3–4 (1944), pp. 651–735. The English translation in Lawrence Kaplan was published by the Jewish Publication Society of America in 1983.

22. See in particular Hartman's *A Living Covenant* (New York, 1985), and Wyshogrod's *The Body of Faith: Judaism as Corporeal Election* (New York, 1983).

23. Moshe Idel, *Kabbalah: New Perspectives* (New Haven, 1988).

24. See, for example, Arthur Green, ed., *Jewish Spirituality* (New York, 1986–87), 2 vols.

25. Daniel J. Elazar and Stuart A. Cohen, *The Jewish Polity: Jewish Political Organization from Biblical Times to the Present* (Bloomington, Ind., 1987).

26. Arnold Eisen, *Galut: Modern Jewish Reflections on Homelessness and Homecoming* (Bloomington, Ind., 1986).

27. See Scholem's "The Messianic Idea in Judaism," in his *The Messianic Idea in Judaism and Other Essays on Jewish Spirituality* (New York, 1971).

16

RESPONSE

Steven T. Katz

Gillman has provided us with an interesting agenda of issues and problems that confront the student of "modern Jewish thought" as we near the end of the twentieth century. In so doing, he has indicated his own specific reading of the subject matter. By contrast, however, he has offered no specific solutions to the contentious issues he has identified. As the respondent to his essay, I will follow his lead. I will suggest, highly schematically, my own estimation of the matters Gillman has called to our attention while offering a somewhat different reading of the relevant sources and personalities.

I

To begin, I am an "outsider" at the Jewish Theological Seminary and therefore unable to speak with authority on the history of Jewish thought as it has unfolded at this institution. My impression, however, is that despite the presence of both Mordecai Kaplan and Abraham Joshua Heschel on the faculty, Jewish thought has never been accorded a high priority by the institution. Kaplan's relations with the institution were *very* stormy, and Heschel is known to have repeatedly asked his few friends here, "Why do they hate me?" I do not have any doubt that at JTS "Jewish thought" has always been something of an intellectual *dhimmis,* tolerated in law, unloved, even abused, in reality. And this is no cause for celebration.

Gillman's "heroes" list of Buber, Rosenzweig, Kaplan, and Heschel is a reasonable one, though Hermann Cohen's absence is to be noted. Gillman's estimation of the respective and enduring significance of each of the four thinkers is, however, subject to reconsideration. Though he is correct that "essentially we have been standing on their shoulders, viewing Jewish thought through one of their sets of spectacles," this empirical fact is not in itself a philosophical recommendation. Kaplan's naturalism is certainly dead, as Gillman notes, though it did not require the *Sho'ah* and the State of Israel to kill it. It was intellectually naive from the outset, and only very unsophisticated minds would have ever found it suggestive. The fact that it "played" to the students at JTS and not the faculty is not a recommendation of the intellectual acuity of the student body. Heschel's thought is not, I would argue, properly understood when seen as being "in its totality . . . a post-Holocaust paradigm!" Rather, very much the reverse. Though he wrote his major works after 1945, the existential and phenomenological patterns of his thought were already firmly in place before 1940. The evidence of this is the near total absence in his corpus of any serious wrestling with either the meaning of the *Sho'ah* or the State of Israel, as well as the predominance in his thinking of the methodological maneuvers of Buber and Husserl. His beautiful, late book on Israel only confirms this judgment. That is to say, this effort represents little more than a starting point for a discussion of Zionism and the State of Israel despite the overwhelming significance of these phenomena for Jewish thought, and this because the architectonic structures of his thought were all in place before 1940.

As to the existentialism of Buber and Rosenzweig, I disagree fundamentally with the judgment that "[existentialism] is the most satisfactory way of handling the theological implications of the Holocaust"—or anything else for that matter. I do not know, despite intensive work in the area for more than a decade, any "satisfactory" existentialist response to the Holocaust. The two thinkers who one might generally see as belonging to this camp, Yitzchak Greenberg and Emil Fackenheim,[1] have not produced any substantive philosophical response that can withstand serious interrogation. And the best Buber himself could do was simply speak of the "Eclipse of God," as if this phrase explained anything rather than itself crying out for explanation. More generally still, Buber's dialogical subjectivism and theological anarchy, confused metaphysical formulations, and indefensible, self-contradictory ethical recommendations do not encourage seeking the basis for a defensible modern Jewish position in his oeuvre.[2] And with Rosenzweig, his 1919–29 efforts are endorsed only at the high price of a radical ahistoricism that can hardly accommodate itself in any sensitive and constructive way to either the obscene realities of the Nazi era or events in the Land of Israel after 1948.[3]

It behooves me to remark also on my reservations about Gillman's comment "that theology has gone as far as it can go with the Holocaust." This contention, which is repeated later in the essay, seems altogether incorrect. I argue, in the strongest possible terms, the alternate thesis that our thinking about the Holocaust has just begun. Given the magnitude of the event we seek to understand and respond to, it is not at all surprising that this should be the case; nor again is it surprising that the efforts to date have been so limited and unconvincing. All the fundamental questions remain to be asked, all the vast labor of conceptual reconstruction, for example, in regard to issues such as those arising out of a Jewish philosophy of history that would seek to accommodate the *Sho'ah*, have hardly even been formulated. The same, I might add, applies to our *philosophical* thinking about the meaning of the State of Israel, an event so radical that we seem to be unable to say anything even moderately interesting philosophically about it.

II

Now to Gillman's second cluster of concerns: what he labels metatheological and methodological issues, in particular the thorny matters of authority and authenticity. In singling out these two items Gillman has shown his perspicacity, for they are indeed, along with the substantive matter of revelation, which he also very wisely returns to several times in his remarks, the key issues. For myself, however, the subject of authority is "more troublesome," to use his expression, than authenticity, for once one establishes *authority*, then authenticity follows, in large measure if not completely, upon this prior decision. Having correctly diagnosed the problem, however, Gillman leaves us to our own devices. Yet, it is here, where there is urgent need, that more is required. Two remarks: (1) we need to reconsider the viability of nonpropositional reconstructions of revelation; (2) as a methodological concern, given that we are discussing these matters in the context of the Conservative movement, some fundamental attention needs to be given to the *status* of halakha. That is to say, relative to questions of authority and authenticity, what status does halakha, and the halakhic *process*, have in this discussion? The Conservative movement identifies itself as a halakhic movement, but is it? I'm not so sure. My doubts arise from this fact: if the notion of halakha involves in some primal logical and theological sense subordination and authority, then the correct test cases arise at just that point where halakhic norms and demands collide with competing, contrary, contemporary, "sociological" values. If, that is to say, one is a halakhic movement, one chooses to follow the halakha even when it is uncomfortable and unfashionable, unless one can find a creative halakhic solution to the specific dilemma at hand. Yet the opposite seems actually to be the case in the Conservative movement. Riding on the Sabbath, even to synagogue, was a total, nonhalakhic capitulation to suburbia. Women *hazzanim* is another case in point. It is, in other words, easy to call oneself halakhic when little sacrifice is demanded. The issue of authority raises its head here, just here, with a special ferocity.

In reflecting on this insufficiently analyzed conundrum of the Conservative position let me add that the difficulty may well stem from an uncertain self-image. We have all been taught that a group largely defines itself by who it is not, by that "other" from which it wishes to distance itself. But precisely in this context the unavoidable dilemma arises: on the one hand the Conservative movement is adamant that it not be the Reform movement and, on the other hand, that it not be Orthodox. But this double negation, this two-sided dialectic of distancing, creates a middle position that is hard to maintain, at least conceptually, whatever sociological and utilitarian advantages its maintenance offers.

I concur with Gillman's implicit call for a study of the vexing rubric *authenticity*. His examples of this phenomenon, however, suggest that the answer to what makes something Jewishly authentic lies in the concept of *tora missinai*. R. Isaac Luria and Maimonides are not inauthentic and were generally not considered as such in the annals of Jewish history (despite the Maimonidean controversy centering around the *Guide*), because, however radical their reconstructions and however novel their decoding of the canonical sources, both predicated their positions on the *authority* of *tora missinai*. Conversely, Paul excluded himself from the common norm of authenticity by his contention that the regulative authority was Jesus, not Torah, whereas Spinoza altogether denied the reality of Sinaitic revelation. Necessarily allied to this nomistic center is also the corollary commitment to *mitsvot*. For all their intellectual transmutations of the traditional rationale, neither Luria nor Maimonides, in contrast with Paul and Spinoza, denied the continuing authority of the regimen of *mitsvot,* whether understood as cosmological levers *à la* kabbala or in keeping with Aristotelian theories of intellect *à la* the rationalists. In this sense "orthopraxis" becomes the necessary justificatory measure, at least in part, of conceptual adequacy and authenticity. These brief remarks certainly only begin a conversation on these *topoi,* but they point, I would contend, in necessary directions for further investigation.

Gillman's plea for epistemological sophistication in Jewish theology is correct, as is his relatively extended reflection on the current impact of social-scientific theories and approaches on the study of religion generally, and the need to think through their implications for Judaism in particular.

Given their influence today, and Gillman's articulate plea for their employment in a Jewish theological context, I issue a warning: social science, although a necessary complement to theology, is not an adequate substitute for metaphysical and theological inquiry. For if Judaism is, in some sense, about transcendental realities, then sociology and anthropology will have only limited value as tools for deciphering its meaning. This is said as a hermeneutical—that is, a logical—observation, not a faith statement. Consider, for example, the extremely influential psychological theories of religious formation. The logical fact is that, for example, God's existence or nonexistence is not touched in any way by our psychological needs, projections, or the like. Either God exists or not, and no amount of our wishing or wanting will "create" Him, just as no amount of psychological denial or "liberation" from theological illusions will, if He exists, negate His existence.

Second, although I support the contention that these influential social science theories should be introduced into rabbinical school curricula, we should have no illusions about their role as a general panacea to the more general malaise in these institutions. Nor again should we underestimate the *negative* consequences of too radically translating *tefilla* and *mitsvot* into anthropological categories. What abiding value will, for example, the seder have if it is completely immanentized, humanized, sociologized, psychologized, and anthropologized—and all the "mystery" and transcendence is squeezed out of it?

Third, the impassioned plea for new Holocaust liturgies, a consequence of reflecting on Clifford Geertz's ruminations on religion and chaos, must be supplemented by the recognition that if the metaphysical accounting of the phenomenon of Nazism is deficient, then the long-term power of *Yom ha-Sho'ah* liturgies will be marginal. If there is no God, liturgies, no matter how profoundly we understand their "function," will have little point. Another way of putting this is to recognize that whereas theology requires religion, defined *à la* Gillman's usage, religion correspondingly requires theology, if only implicitly and by way of shared ontological assumptions.

III

Let me close by briefly responding to the "discrete, substantive ideological issues" with which Gillman concludes his essay.

I, too, applaud the growth of an "orthodox" component to the contemporary theological and philosophical discussion. The "results" produced, so far, by Orthodox thinkers are limited, but their thinking out of the rabbinic sources, especially their familiarity with the halakha, is potentially a major contribution.

233

Steven T. Katz

As to our "celebrating even more triumphantly the return of Jewish mysticism into the field of modern Jewish thought," I am a good deal more cautious. Cautious, but not altogether skeptical. My caution arises, first, from the fact that reading Gershom Scholem, genius of geniuses that he was, is not the same as studying kabbala and applying its hermeneutic to our situation. Second, Buber's influence here, his so-called neo-Hasidism, has been, in my view, almost wholly unauthentic and in many elemental ways pernicious. Third, can we have kabbala without *halakha lemoshe missinai* (deriving from Moses' teaching at Sinai)? Without propositional revelation? Without the gnostic and Neoplatonic ontology we all reject? Without a certain magical conception of the *mitsvot*? In other words, what appears to be kabbala today is only very marginally, if at all, kabbala, and its influence, in the form of the ersatz syncretism that passes for kabbala, has been dubious. Fourth, to return to Scholem's repercussive contribution: he taught us to see Jewish history pluralistically and non-normatively. (This is the real reason for the immense impact of his work.) But was he, on second thought, altogether, or even substantially, correct about this, his special reading, of Jewish history and the history of Jewish spirituality and religiosity?

We need to explore, especially because of events in *Erets Yisra'el*, the conditions for a "Jewish" political philosophy. I am not sanguine, however, that Daniel Elazar's thesis regarding covenantal rules as the basis for practical politics is historically accurate, or, still more generally, that a single model, putatively generated out of the sources of Judaism, can be formulated.

Again on the Zionist agenda: I too am more comfortable in many, though not all, ways with Ahad Ha'Am's cultural Zionism, but as a historical fact it is surely incorrect to say that "Ahad Ha'Am may well have lost the battle with Herzl but he clearly won the war." Given the fact that simple refuge has been the main, and overriding, function of the State of Israel, Zionism's child, in our century, down to the refuge given the Falashas, I do not see how Ahad Ha'Am can be said to have "won" anything. Certainly Herzl's naivete about the state ending anti-Semitism and creating *normalcy* has been shown all too transparently facile, but the rate of worldwide intermarriage and assimilation hardly vindicates Ahad Ha'Am's view, whereas it has the monumental disadvantage of being antistatist and hence antirefuge as a matter of twentieth-century reality. This is not to say, as the list of recent Israeli-related political catastrophes and the polarization cited by Gillman indicate, that sovereignty is not without its cost, but extreme caution should be exercised in this area. We do not want to delegitimize the sovereign State of Israel because its leaders are, today, craven and stupid, or because we, as American Jews, are made to feel uncomfortable by some of its decisions and actions. Nor again should the polarization in Jewish life be exaggerated. First, is it more polarized than it was, say, fifty or seventy-five years ago, when there was no state? Second, would there be no polarization if the state ceased to exist? Are, for example, patrilineal descent, women rabbis, and *hazzanim* the fault of the State of Israel? The political implications of such contentious issues are far more complex than they otherwise might be because of the actuality of Israeli life, but the issues were not created by the Israeli political reality. And to turn the issue completely on its head, is there not, in some fundamental sense, more consensus and unanimity in Jewish life today rotating around a broad pro-Israel agenda than there has been for perhaps a century or more?

Finally, on this issue, the unease Gillman rightly reminds us of regarding "dual loyalty" may well contradict his assertion that "the classic Zionist rhetoric is clearly inadequate" today. Certainly it is not altogether adequate, and this for many reasons, but the residual truth it contains should not be dismissed. Then again, if the choice is between the end of ambivalence and sacrificing the State of Israel, can there be any reasonable choice for the end of ambivalence? Indeed, in the premessianic conditions of historic existence, ambivalence and unease—the two attributes Gillman is worried about—are the normative conditions of the Jewish people, whether inside or outside the Land of Israel, whether Zionists or not. This fact, in itself, is the foundation for all Jewish thought today, as yesterday.

Notes

1. I have analyzed Emil Fackenheim's views in detail in my *Post Holocaust Dialogues—Critical Studies in Modern Jewish Thought* (New York, 1983), pp. 205–48. I discuss Yitzchak Greenberg's position at some length in a forthcoming collection of essays.

2. I critically decipher Buber's representation of Hasidism in my *Post Holocaust Dialogues*, pp. 52–94, and his more general epistemological position on pp. 1–54.

3. A fuller, more positive appreciation of what Rosenzweig's ahistoricism still can teach us is to be found in my essay "On Historicism and Eternity: Reflections on the 100th Birthday of Franz Rosenzweig," in Wolfdietrich Schmid-Kowarzik, ed., *Der Philosoph Franz Rosenzweig (1886–1929). International Kongress—Kassel 1986* (Munich, 1989), vol. 2, pp. 745–69.

Jewish Studies and the Transmission of Judaism

17

SCHOLARSHIP AND CURRICULUM: WHAT JEWISH SCHOLARSHIP MEANS FOR JEWISH EDUCATION

Joseph Lukinsky

This essay examines the potential role of Judaica scholarship for Jewish education. How might scholarship influence curriculum development and teaching?

There are different ways in which the scholar participates in curriculum development.[1] Scholars teach their own courses, but we cannot assume that their teaching communicates their scholarship! Teachers use scholars' research, reported in books and articles, as readings in courses. The purpose may be unclear. What are the criteria for choosing readings? What is their optimum use? What are students supposed to learn from them? There are a great many uninvestigated assumptions about such matters.

Scholars have been included in curriculum development outside the university. The Curriculum Reform movement of the 1960s and 1970s (the "New Math" and the like) placed the scholar at the center of the process of developing curriculum for elementary and secondary schools.[2] This approach had its Jewish versions too; witness the Melton Research Center's well-known Bible curriculum for the supplementary elementary school.[3]

Other models viewed the scholar, the subject-matter expert, as a resource for curriculum development on a par with other resources such as knowledge about the learner, the milieu, and the teacher.[4] School-based or teacher-originated curricula sometimes turned to the scholar as a respondent to curricular programs that grew out of felt needs at the later stages of a project as a check for authenticity. On occasion scholars were asked to state goals or objectives for curricula in their respective fields. Many curricular projects, in reaction to perceived failures in curriculum reform, ignored scholars altogether.

The limits on scholars' time for, and interest in, curriculum development outside (or even inside) the university have led me to suggest that scholars' written work serve as a "stand-in" for their personal involvement.[5] I mean more than reading the scholarship intensively. This work would be seen as an access vehicle to the worlds that it presents to us. Unpacking a scholar's work[6] would reveal the roots of the argument, the primary sources supporting it, the alternative sources and theories rejected, and the other scholars with whom the writer is in dialogue, whether they are mentioned directly or not; the goal would be the philosophical frame of reference of the writer and, ultimately, of a field of study. The process as it works itself out might lead us to relate to the sources differently than did the original work which was unpacked; nevertheless, it gets the curriculum specialists and teachers, who may not be scholars in the field but who appreciate scholarship, more quickly into the material than could be accomplished from scratch or from reading for conclusions only.

In short, the scholarly component is one source for curriculum making. There are different ways of using it. What can we learn for this endeavor from the essays included in this volume? Of the numerous possibilities I am limited to providing a few examples. For practical and heuristic purposes I shall consider the essay by Shaye Cohen on "Ancient Judaism" representative of the others, and the three themes he considers characteristic of his field applicable in a general way to them too. Following Cohen's lead, I will then suggest educational implications of his "separators and unifiers" theme as exemplified in the research of Jacob Neusner on the Mishna and the gemara.

Cohen's three themes may also serve as ideological boundaries for the field of Jewish studies. The first, "polemics and apologetics," addresses the need of scholarship to be as free as possible of tendentiousness and bias. The third theme, "Jewish antiquity versus ancient Judaism," carries the same point further by removing Jewish studies from its parochial context and placing it in a larger humanistic framework, the study of antiquity. Parochial scholarship is as passé as polemics or apologetics. This argument further situates true Jewish scholarship in the center of a contemporary consensus that is broad, nontendentious, and sophisticated.

The ideological point of the second theme, "separators and unifiers," seems to be that modern Jewish pluralism has historical foundations and that, though the recovery of these foundations may seem to contradict the "normative" understanding of tradition, it is a legitimate undertaking even by Jewish scholars who are committed in their personal lives to that tradition. I think that this point is the mother lode of educational implications, and I will address it further.

The most valid and useful approaches, as I read Cohen, are in the separators' camp. The separators see each text or historical artifact in its own light, apart from connections to other entities. At the current state of methodology, there is much pay dirt in the separators' retrieval of meaning that has been lost, neglected, ignored, misunderstood, or suppressed in different historical periods. This does not preclude the possibility of deeper connections between systems, and indeed, Cohen cautions against extreme separatism, the view that separate items do not form part of larger systems. The facile assumption that everything now known can be explained by everything else is, however, to be denied. In the case of rabbinic literature, for example, the view that interprets "every rabbinic passage . . . in the light of every other . . . all the texts form[ing] one seamless Torah"[7] is surely to be rejected. The separators have, in essence, recovered lost Judaisms, rendering the terms "orthodox," "normative," and "sectarian" obsolete, at least historically. What came to be "normative" did so for reasons that can be investigated, but there were options that, in their own time, were legitimate.[8] Zeroing in on separate systems might make possible more sophisticated connections.

The "separators and unifiers" section is the largest in Cohen's essay; he obviously attaches great importance to it and endorses the stance of the separators, with the caution mentioned above. Within this section he relates at greatest length to Jacob Neusner's work, which he sees as deserving extended treatment because of its impact and importance.

If there is some value besides the scholarly per se in the recovery (or construction) of historical meanings that cross the grain of previously accepted or "normative" knowledge, what would be some implications for the Jewish studies curriculum at all levels and in different settings? Within the limits of this essay, by relating to a narrow range of issues in Neusner's work, I will try to shed some light on the broader topic.[9]

On Jacob Neusner's Mishna and Gemara Consciousness[10]

Neusner's form criticism of the Mishna and Talmud (that is, gemara) has explicated two modes of consciousness that have specific and general educational significance. Building his case slowly, pericope to pericope, chapter to chapter, tractate to tractate, seder to seder, and finally reaching the work as a whole, he struggles to draw out the world-view of the Mishna as an entity in its own right. He seeks the Mishna *as such,* apart from the way it is interpreted and appropriated by the gemara, and apart from comparison to analogous sources in the Tosefta and midrashim.

The way the gemara grasps the Mishna is another datum, which he teases out in the same painstaking way. Although the interpretation of the data may be open to differences, as pointed out by Cohen, the educator must relate seriously to this careful effort. The discovery and presentation of two separate forms of consciousness reject the notion of a homogenized "rabbinic" Judaism that is the same throughout.

In Neusner's view, the Mishna is rich and varied in its vast array of contents, but abstract and simple in the way these contents are presented. Scholars could spend a thousand lifetimes on the contents alone, which is in fact what they have done and is part of the problem. Neusner has done something more intriguing in construing the *meaning* of the work as a whole not in its contents, nor in any summary of them, but in the *form* in which the contents are organized.

This formal structure is the vehicle of meaning—the message—and is manifested in the grammar, in the relatively few syntactical structures through which the contents are expressed. Whether this message was deliberately contrived or more intuitively worked out, it is a response to the primary issue of the historical period during which the Mishna was edited. The theme is expressed not as an abstract propositional argument but as the deep structure underlying the prosaic treatment of specific contents, ordinary and sublime, many of which no longer had practical bearing on the real life of the time. This underlying thrust generated a web of meaning.

The grammatical forms, imposing a unity on the diverse contents, teach that the world is ordered by God and that humans, through intellect, can come to understand this order and, more astonishingly, *create* it through their own intention by imposing it on a misleadingly chaotic world. Human will is thereby raised to high status. It becomes operative in the person who learns and knows Mishna, and who thereby becomes a vehicle for the process of creating order and meaning. In Neusner's paradigm, to *know* Mishna is to be imbued with its content, yes, but, more important, with its *process* as a creative force. It is the formation of an active Mishnaic consciousness!

The "generative problematic" that created this meaning responded to the *Sitz im Leben* of the period after the destruction of the Second Temple in 70 C.E. The abstract syntactical form, imposed on content dealing with agriculture, holidays, family life, damages, sacrifices, and purities, as if it referred to eternal issues transcending all places and times, created a document, which confronted the absence of the Temple and replaced it as a source of meaning.

The abstract formulation, moreover, expressed in the final redaction, with no attempt to replicate Biblical Hebrew style or to use the actual words of the original statements (whatever *they* were), with little reference to Biblical prooftexts or explicit reasoning, is a statement of the conviction that the Mishna is, in its own presentation, the expression of revelation. It *is* the oral half of the "dual Torah" given to Moses at Sinai. To learn Mishna, therefore, concisely and simply formulated so as to assist memorization, is to participate *directly* in a revelation that is taking place now and that is a paradigm for the continuing revelation that takes place when a "Mishnaic Jew" relates to matters of ongoing life in any time and any place. To "make Mishna" is to bring Mishnaic consciousness to bear on anything.

To enter the Mishna then, for Neusner, is to enter an idealized "nomos," transportable to every place and time, that replaced the lost Temple. To "live" there is to experience a model for living in the world that we experience daily. It is the revelation of the true, divine order of existence. Neusner has recovered for us a kind of Mishna consciousness. I do not evaluate it as "true" or "false." I assume that whether or not Neusner has indeed identified the historical context, he presents a challenging and existentially relevant world-view that makes sense of the text as a total system. It is a hypothesis to be explored educationally. This I will do after a briefer construction of his view of the gemara.

The gemara,[11] in Neusner's view, does not understand the Mishna as the Mishna understood itself. It treats the Mishna in small bits as takeoff points for its own inquiries. The search for the Mishna's sources in Scripture, for the reasons behind its apodictic statements, and for its relationship to the Tosefta and *beraitot,* makes the Mishna secondary to Scripture, or at least to the Pentateuch; this, then, is a departure from the Mishna's view of itself as a source of revelation equal to the Written Torah.

More specifically, the gemara seeks reasons for the basic statements of the Mishna. In its analysis of the Mishna, the gemara attacks, interacts, seeks, demands sources, asks why, makes distinctions, compares with other sources, seeks the underlying rule-of-law, makes unexpected connections, raises questions of logic, and constructs hypothetically the "facts" that undergird one text in order to resolve a conflict with another.

If Mishna consciousness is the basic structure of the Jewish mind, the way that mind constructs the world, then "gemara consciousness" is something else. Mishna consciousness is veritably to be reduced to the unconscious, internalized through the memorization of the contents and their powerfully controlling forms. Gemara consciousness, then, is thinking about Mishna consciousness, a kind of "thinking about thinking," secondary about primary, in which the mind turns back on itself to examine itself in depth. Mishna is socialization, intuition, heritage, and revelation. Gemara is questioning, exploration, reason, and autonomy. Mishna is thinking God's thoughts after him. Gemara is reflexive consideration of that very act.

The way of the separators, then, is an attempt to understand smaller units as integrated systems of meaning. These may be interpreted as responses to particular historical circumstances. The systemic response changes when the generative issue changes, and the earlier view may be subsumed in the later. This does not mean that it disappears. Its presence may continue to be felt, though not recognized as such. Recovering it through the critical methodology of the separators reestablishes the lost dialectic and enriches our understanding of the later system.

It is not completely clear to me whether Neusner sees the Mishna's consciousness of itself (as he interprets it) as absorbed intuitively by the gemara, even as the latter understood it explicitly as something else. If this indeed happened, then Mishna consciousness continued to operate below the surface. Judaism, as it developed from this mix, does seem to reflect both modes, but the recovery of the contrast in explicit form gives us a hypothetical construct, now generative and powerful. Paradoxically, the gemara medium also becomes liturgical and revelatory, that is, Oral Torah. In its own way the gemara is different from but also similar to the Mishna, in that its dialectical exploration of it both expands the latter's meaning and also boldly seizes the right to establish new meaning.

Application to Curriculum: A Beginning

My summary of Neusner's two kinds of consciousness is an educational construct. I shall derive some general principles from taking Neusner seriously. To move toward an actual curriculum would require further steps culminating with teaching the material in real classrooms. [12]

First, a few general comments about those aspects of learning analogous to the imbibing of a native language and culture. Both are "there" before we are; we are given them and participate in them before we understand them; and we spend our entire lives trying to understand them and to turn them to the service of our autonomous thought and inquiry. At first they control *us;* if we succeed, we make them instruments, perhaps never fully tamed, for constructing meaning.

Being socialized means being stocked with words, concepts, intuitive grammatical structures, stories, values, literary allusions, and cultural referents of all kinds. Advanced thinking, say, at the university level, represents transcending but not leaving that material received as a gift of culture. We cannot think without something to think about. The level of independent thought is based on a foundation of primary socialization.

Students do not come to advanced learning today with well-stocked minds and hearts, and the emergence of independent thinking is hindered by the lack of exemplars and adumbrations presented by rich cultures. Independent thought could emerge from a strong base of folklore, art, mythology, literature, and law, which in the main today is just not there. The wisdom of the past is encapsulated in heritage, in the narrative tradition, in law and culture, not in concepts and abstractions without roots. If socialization does not initiate people into culture, then something is missing, and some substitute needs to be found.

If, in order to think at all, we need language, values, stories, logic and grammar, the basic resources of thought, then, to think Jewishly we need the Mishna *mode,* that is, the *primary* elements of thought and action deriving from socialization. And we need the gemara mode, the autonomous activity of thinking and deliberating that transforms that which we already know into a force for creating that which we do not know yet.

How might these two modes of thought be acquired? Neusner's description of them suggests a broad way of looking at our most basic Jewish sources, in a manner that we can transfer from the narrow domain of Talmud to other domains of Jewish learning, and to education in general. If the Mishna uses a highly structured syntax as the medium for presenting its vast contents and its deep-structured message, then it follows that there is a similarity between the learning of Mishna and the way one learns a native language or culture. It is to be so thoroughly internalized and made one's own that it becomes the very "stuff" out of which the Jew perceives and constructs the universe. The well-stocked Jewish mind is to be filled with Mishna, the ordering mentality that construes everyday life as a harmonious and reasonable "place" where our responsible intentions can have a meaningful impact. To know Mishna is to absorb it at the unconscious or preconscious level, so that, like language, it functions almost effortlessly as the medium of primary Jewish conceptualization and motivation to action.

The mystery of Mishna consciousness, implicit in specifics and taught indirectly through the proper mastery of them, recalls Richard S. Peter's distinction between the "literature" and the "language" of a field.[13] It is possible to learn the "literature" (the specific substantive material) in a way that obscures and denies the "language" (the underlying meaning, the syntax of investigation and inquiry), but it is *im*possible to learn the language without the literature.

This resonates with the Jewish way of learning and constructing meaning. Jewish tradition is a narrative and legal tradition. We are asked to remember stories, to interact with and confront real people and real tasks in community. These are compelling, colorful, serious, and lively characteristics of Jewish traditional materials (on the whole) that are lost when we reduce the tradition to propositions. To do the latter is banal. There is no other way to gain the language than to enter and participate in the literature in depth. "Religion" exists only as a dimension of "world." There are two educational tasks: to learn the explicit material *and*, at the same time, to learn its underlying consciousness, its "syntax," to internalize it so that it becomes a resource and then a tool in the student's service.[14]

In a modern, open society our thinking is affected by other cultural paradigms and processes, which we may gladly embrace as a benefit of our participation in a lively pluralistic environment. We would not give them up. At the same time, as Jews, we can only stand in awe of the framers of the Mishna, who, in Neusner's view, created a medium for the transmission of basic Jewish consciousness that could withstand the intellectual and emotional pressures of powerful opposing forces. The work of sorting out the influences that bombard us daily can only be enhanced by the accessibility of a powerful integrated counterbalance, an alternative consciousness that can serve as a center for our Jewish identity.

If the Mishna mode represents socialization, the gemara mode represents autonomy.[15] If the Mishna represents the primary prism through which one fully imbued with it "sees" the world, to learn gemara is to question the instrument itself, to examine the prism, to become self-aware concerning one's own thought processes. Again, the gemara mode, like the Mishna, derives from its form, the *way* it undertakes its inquiries.

Mishna and Gemara as Curricular and Pedagogical Styles

A specific practical inference at one level of the work of Neusner the separator (to use Cohen's designation) is that the Mishna should be taught with great seriousness as a work of importance in itself. It should be taught extensively and intensively. A Mishna curriculum would aim for wide coverage but with emphasis on inner criteria. Although interesting content would be essential, it would also be necessary to promote, through the content, a sophisticated complex of pattern structures that enable a long-term generation of intuitive connections. The goal would be internalization of the systemic world-view of the Mishna, *separate from* the interpretation of the Mishna through the eyes of the gemara.

Even after the study of gemara is started, the study of Mishna in its own terms would continue in depth. This is quite different from the common approach at all levels today, in which Mishna is only a prelude to gemara, always interpreted in light of the gemara, and rarely seriously studied again once the gemara is begun.

A research issue would be whether gemara should be started at all until Mishna is mastered to a certain level. The level would be characterized by extensive and intensive knowledge; skills of learning, memorizing, and retaining; internalization of basic patterns, and what I would call associational skills, the ability to relate patterns in various combinations. What I have in mind here is best said by Neusner about

> rabbis who memorized Mishnah [who] are capable of amazingly abstract perceptions, for their ears and minds perceive regularities of grammatical arrangements running through a whole range of diverse words. What is memorized is a recurrent notion expressed in diverse examples but framed in a repeated rhetorical pattern. The diverse cases are united by a principle that is contained within all of them. But that principle is seldom made explicit. Rather it is embedded in the deep structure of thought and language and has to be discovered there by the mind of the person who memorizes and discovers the several cases.[16]

In the Mishna itself, according to Neusner, the "principle is seldom made explicit." But in *teaching* today an open research question would be whether and if so, *when* to make it explicit. To do so prematurely might be to inhibit the intuitive natural development of the understanding of deep structure. On the other hand, since the whole effort would be a conscious educational reenactment or simulation of what once was a cultural process, there is likely to be a point at which the articulation of the principle could represent a helpful focusing.

I further suggest that there is a great deal to be said for *memorization*.[17] I am well aware of the regressive possibilities inherent in this suggestion. It would have to be memorization of a certain kind, controlled by a set of criteria. Using Neusner himself as a guide (and a return to his scholarly writings in depth would be necessary at this point), I propose not memorization of contents per se, but a carefully planned memorization emphasizing the kinds of patterns that Neusner has identified with his form-critical methodology. A developmental scheme would have to be created to build up slowly the deep structure patterns that, for example, embody the power of human intent to affect the real world.[18] It goes without saying that I am not talking here about the sometimes mindless memorization that has often been advocated in the traditional school. This latter does perhaps have its long-term, indirect value for some students, but not necessarily.

Once the study of gemara is undertaken, teaching the Mishna from the point of view of the gemara's conception of it would not be ruled out. But this would be intentionally construed and perceived as something different. The main point would be to keep the two modes separate. The implicit world-view of the Mishna would not be taught apart from the contents that are its building blocks, but at the same time the scholar's analysis (here Neusner's) supplies the control that directs the choices and methods of teaching those very contents.

The implications of "gemara consciousness" are also suggestive, but here I will focus on one important distinction. There is a difference between learning to understand what the gemara is doing (with, and to, the Mishna) and learning to do something similar ourselves. It is easy to confuse the two, especially since the first is such a formidable, lifelong task. When does learning the reasoning of the gemara, the actual workings of a page of text, shape the *gemara kopf*, which enables the student to think "Talmudically" in a novel situation?[19]

In most cases that I am aware of, the Talmud curriculum spends the most time on the understanding of the text as it is, necessarily so, it would seem, in view of its difficulty. What would it take to move from this to the alternatives not presented or rejected, to the questions that could have been asked, to other possible responses? To recapture the lost possibilities is to understand better the alternative that *was* chosen, to see it, in effect *as* an alternative. The curricular research question is: how to teach the existing deliberations and, at the same time, teach the process in a way that gradually enhances our own powers of deliberation.

To extend this point beyond the field of Talmud: in all fields, what was originally an expression of autonomy, spontaneity, and choice becomes easily a matter of "tradition," something to be learned because it is "there." "Oral Torah" becomes "Written Torah." The struggle of one age to think *about* and *with* the materials of its heritage becomes the heritage of another age. This is true of modern scholarship, too. Modern scholarship can be learned as a body of new "truths," apart from the way it is produced and the paradigmatic frames of reference that make it possible. Thus a field becomes static and dogmatic.

Some Concluding Thoughts

The "separators and unifiers" theme suggested by Cohen highlights the retrieval by critical modern scholars of forms of consciousness, ways of thinking, and frameworks for the construction of meaning different from those that have constituted the "normative" tradition. Although Cohen is talking about the field of ancient Judaism, I have suggested that the issue is broadly applicable to other fields; I have amplified this in one respect by looking more closely at Neusner's retrieval of the systemic consciousness of the Mishna and its contrast with the consciousness developed later by the gemara. I have explored some educational implications of my construction of these two modes of consciousness.

The two modes are best kept separate conceptually if we are to imagine and create valid ways for them to interact in practice. This applies to Talmudic studies and, by extrapolation, to other fields, too. All learning starts with something to be learned. We are socialized to certain contexts even before we know we are learning. In Jewish education the mode of socialization to basics can be *simulated* in the curriculum. I suggest that it *should* take place as an intentional effort of the Jewish curriculum insofar as it no longer takes place naturally in a community's integrated formal and informal educational system. This would require an intensive search in every field of Jewish study for the essential substantive themes and methodological skills that are worth communicating to the next generation. What should Jews know, and what should they be able (and *want*) to do? The gemara mode of one age easily becomes the Mishna mode of another, and keeping the two separate *and* together is an ongoing educational task that is never solved once and for all.

Notes

1. Joseph Lukinsky, "Structure in Educational Theory," *Educational Philosophy and Theory* 2 (Nov. 1970), pp. 15–31; and 3 (Apr. 1971), pp. 29–36. See also Ralph Tyler, *Basic Principles of Curriculum and Instruction* (Chicago, 1949); *From the Scholar to the Classroom*, ed. Seymour Fox and Geraldine Rosenfeld (New York, 1977). I also addressed this issue in my presentation to the conference of the Association for Jewish Studies, Boston, 1985. See also my article "Jewish Education and Jewish Scholarship: Maybe the Lies We Tell Are Really True?" in *The Seminary at 100*, ed. N. Cardin and D. Silverman (New York, 1987), pp. 205–22.

2. Lukinsky, "Structure in Educational Theory."

3. The early curricular units and training programs for teachers were based on Nahum Sarna's *Understanding Genesis* (New York, 1966) and Moshe Greenberg's *Understanding Exodus* (New York, 1969). Both of these scholars were active participants in the writing of the units and the teacher training.

4. See Tyler, *Basic Principles*, and Joseph Schwab, "Translating Scholarship into Curriculum," in *From the Scholar to the Classroom*, pp. 1–30.

5. This was the main point of my presentation at the Association for Jewish Studies, Boston, 1985.

6. Joseph Schwab, "Education and the Reading Process," in his *Science, Curriculum, and Liberal Education: Selected Essays*, ed. Ian Westbury and Neil J. Wilkof (Chicago, 1978).

7. Shaye J. D. Cohen, "The Modern Study of Ancient Judaism," Chapter 5 above.

8. Cohen is of course not suggesting that what was historically legitimate or understandable is an option for today. That would be beyond his mandate as a historian. Understanding something in its historic context might enable it to *speak* to us in some valid way.

9. See Lukinsky, "Jewish Education and Jewish Scholarship."

10. My discussion of Neusner in this essay is based on selective reading and includes the following works: *Form-Analysis and Exegesis: A Fresh Approach to the Interpretation of Mishnah: With Special Reference to Mishnah-tractate Makhshirin* (henceforth referred to as *Makhshirin*); "The Talmud," in *The World of Judaism*, ed. Elie Kedourie (Minneapolis, 1980); *Invitation to the Talmud* (New York, 1973); *Scriptures of the Oral Torah* (New York, 1987). This last work has an extensive relevant bibliography. I have also read many other books and articles by Neusner over the years. Especially relevant here are his two books for children: *Learn Mishnah* (New York, 1978) and *Learn Talmud* (New York, 1979).

11. In my article "Law in Education: A Reminiscence and Footnote to Robert Cover's *Nomos and Narrative*," *Yale Law Journal* 96/8 (July 1987), pp. 1836–59, I explore the implications for education of David Halivni's interpretation of *Gemara* as reflected in his *Midrash, Mishna and Gemara* (Cambridge, Mass., 1986). Halivni's view of the relationship between the gemara and apodictic Mishna is different from Neusner's, as is his interpretation of the meaning of both. A comparison of the educational implications of the two approaches and the distinction between them will be undertaken in another paper.

12. Neusner's *Learn Mishnah* and *Learn Talmud* are unique in that very few scholars have written authentic works for children that reflect their front-line scholarship at the children's level. I think that these works do this, in a straight, didactic expository form. The question of pedagogy—that is, how the material is actually to be taught by teachers in the classroom—is not taken up. The Teachers Guide published later, not authored by Neusner, seems to me to miss Neusner's point, the very ideas that make the works interesting as reflections of a scholar's thinking.

13. R. S. Peters, "Reason and Habit: The Paradox of Moral Education," in Israel Scheffler, ed., *Philosophy and Education*, 2d ed. (Boston, 1966). This issue is developed excellently in Michael Rosenak's *Commandments and Concerns: Jewish Religious Education in Secular Society* (Philadelphia, 1987). Rosenak's book is relevant to the overall argument of this essay. Peters's use of the term "language" is analogous to "deep structure" in Neusner. In Peters's usage one learns the "literature" of a field in a way that ultimately leads to the mastery of its "language." My analogy between learning Mishna and learning a primary language includes both of Peters's terms.

14. See Lukinsky, "Structure in Educational Theory," and Schwab, "Education and the Reading Process."

15. One qualification: *within* the Mishna paradigm as Neusner interprets it, "making Mishna" also becomes ultimately, for some people, an autonomous activity. Cf. Thomas Kuhn's *The Structure of Scientific Revolutions*, 2d ed. (Chicago, 1970).

16. Neusner, "The Talmud," p. 110.

17. See *Learn Mishnah*, where Neusner suggests the importance of memorization.

18. A thorough study, for example, of Neusner's *Makhshirin* would serve as the basis of the scholarly contribution to such a curriculum. Neusner's methodology of inquiry would have relevance to the development of teaching methodology. I am of course not ruling out the use here of other scholars' writings as they become relevant.

19. See Lukinsky, "Law in Education."

18

RESPONSE

Moshe Sokolow

Interpretation has been given many felicitous descriptions. Simon Rawidowicz wrote that interpretation "bridges the gap between past and
present";[1] Gershom Scholem called it "true growth and unfolding from
within";[2] and Ralph Tyler has spoken of "the illuminating resource of Jewish scholarship of classical texts"[3] as the basis for determining Judaism's
life experiences. Interpretation, as Marvin Fox has observed, is a process
"we are always dependent on and involved in."[4] The question facing
scholar and educator alike is: what type of interpretation should we be using and encouraging our students to use?

In the introduction to his essay on the implications of Jewish scholarship for Jewish education, Lukinsky suggests that written scholarship replace scholars' personal involvement in the curriculum process. Using
Joseph J. Schwab's concept of "the unpacking process," he describes the
advantages that would accrue to education from the careful reading and
analysis of these works of scholarship and lists the following educational
derivatives: "the roots of the argument, the primary sources supporting it,
the alternative sources and theories rejected, [and] other scholars with
whom the writer is in dialogue whether mentioned directly or not."

It is my intention here to provide an illustration of the potential educational advantages of Judaic scholarship by way of a discussion of three
alternative methods of Biblical interpretation: the "traditional," the
"historical-philological," and the "participative." By demonstrating the

relative advantages and disadvantages of each, and by indicating the specific pedagogic advantages of the method called "participative," I hope to convince scholars and teachers of Bible and of other Judaic disciplines of the enormous educational potential that inheres in their combined efforts, and of the futility that will continue to characterize their every partisan effort.

The Traditional Method

The approach to interpretation exemplified by medieval Biblical exegesis consists of resolving the inherent polyvalence of a text[5] by identifying the interpretation most consistent with its tradition. Sa'adia Gaon (882–942) cautioned would-be exegetes: "It is ever incumbent upon the rationalist to grasp the Torah according to the meaning most widespread and prevalent among the speakers of its language—for the purpose of every book is to deliver its message clearly to its reader—except for those places where sensory perception or rational inquiry contradict that prevalent meaning, or in the case that it contradicts another verse of unambiguous intent, or one of the prophetically inspired traditions."[6] In our own era, Paul Ricoeur has written in a similar vein that "every reading of a text always takes place within a community, a tradition, or a living current of thought."[7]

Rashi (1040–1105), similarly cognizant of the need to resolve the equivocal nature of Scripture, also uses tradition as the yardstick of interpretation. In commenting on the seemingly oxymoronic statement of Rabbi Yehuda: "Whosoever translates only according to the literal sense of a verse is a charlatan, but whoever adds to it reviles and blasphemes,"[8] Rashi gives his approbation to the ostensible additions of Targum Onkelos by observing that "they were revealed at Sinai."[9] In resorting to the Talmudic adage "It was forgotten and reestablished,"[10] Rashi was appealing for the recognition of the unity within tradition of the text and its interpretation. Gershom Scholem has described this doctrine as "Revelation comprises within it everything that will ever be legitimately offered to interpret its meaning,"[11] and Rawidowicz observes that "equality of origin and time for the *Perush* [commentary] with the text means absolute equality of value . . . [which] is bound to lend the *Perush* an autonomy, a self-sufficiency sui generis."[12]

The advantage of the traditional method is that "it is possible for anyone of normal intelligence who operates within the structures of understanding of the faith community, and his or her own life experience, to grasp at least the basic meaning of the text."[13] It has its disadvantages, however, both methodological and educational. E. A. Speiser put his finger on the methodological shortcomings: "In course of time the content became enveloped in layer after layer of superimposed interpretation; interpretations bequeathed by scribes and rabbis, ancient versions, the vocalizers of the standard (Masoretic) text, and—not the least formidable of all—the first standard version in the given Western tongue. Each of these accretions has served as a safeguard in some ways, but as a barrier in others, a barrier to the recovery of the original context."[14]

Yehudah Elitzur, himself a religious scholar, considers excessive emphasis on classical and medieval exegesis an educational drawback: "A contemporary exegete is required, of course, to examine things in the light of contemporary knowledge. . . . If he does so, then he is following in the footsteps of the ancients even if he disagrees with them in a thousand details. However, one who only copies the ancients, shutting his eyes to newly discovered facts and knowledge, is abandoning the ways of the ancients and is rebelling against them."[15]

The Historical-Philological Method

Historical-philological ("critical") interpretation, as epitomized by the preceding quotation from Speiser, posits the existence, for each text, of a single original intent that can be retrieved via the proper use of archaeology and linguistics. If one reconstructs an original Biblical text (Moshe Greenberg calls it "penetrating beyond the text to its first form . . . to describe the process of its evolution"),[16] identifies its author(s), and circumscribes its linguistic, literary, and cultural contexts, then one has determined the text's original intent and *that* is its interpretation. Anything else, according to this method, is not exegesis but eisegesis (Speiser's "superimposed interpretation").

The ancients and medievals, it is admitted, did the best that could be expected of anyone lacking the tools of historical-philological investigation. In the absence of comparative Semitics, for instance, they imagined that they could exchange rabbinic Hebrew with its Biblical predecessor, and bereft of a tangible basis for cross-cultural contrast, they employed the literary fiction of midrash. "Later Hebrew," chides Speiser, "is by no means identical with early Biblical usage. Yet successive interpreters would tend to make the secondary usage retroactive. And because the Bible had become sacred Scripture, such anachronistic interpretations acquired a normative bearing of their own."[17] We moderns, however, are uniquely situated to perform the labor of critical interpretation denied our predecessors.

Tradition, in response, argues: (a) even were we to presume that the author of any work of literature had but one single intention, the text—by itself—does not suffice for its retrieval, as stipulated by I. A. Richards: "We have to remember . . . that what the writer meant is not to be simply equated with what he wrote";[18] (b) the nature of revelation compels us, regarding Biblical literature, to contend with intentions other than those of the author. As expressed by Rabbi Abraham Isaiah Karelitz (the "Ḥazon ʾIsh"): "The prophet often received the intent alone, and often the words as well. However, his understanding of both the words and the intent was often only of the kind available to any scholar of the Torah, and was not uniquely prophetic. Thus it is conceivable that in the transmitted words were additional intentions unrecognized even by the prophet himself."[19] The doctrine of the "sensus plenior," developed by Father R. E. Brown, also speaks of "that additional deeper meaning intended by God but not clearly intended by the human author,"[20] and Marvin Fox, along similar lines, has called historical inquiry of this sort "a kind of secularist fundamentalism."[21]

The "historical-philological" method, too, has both a methodological and an educational disadvantage. The former is its disavowal of the inherent polyphony of a revealed text. As William Braude has observed in the context of midrash, "Traditional interpreters deny the [critical] mathematical-mechanical outlook because they believe in revelation and hence in the polyphony of a text."[22] Braude calls the result of the critical method "unilinear peshat," and attributes it to three false premises: "False premise no. 1: We moderns really know Hebrew—in any event we know it better than Ḥazal [the Sages]. False premise no. 2: We have the means to recover the intent of the writer of Scripture. False premise no. 3: A great text such as Scripture, which even those who do not believe in revelation will admit that it indeed is, has one meaning and one meaning only."[23]

The educational drawback, articulated by Brevard Childs, is the excessive emphasis on the text's remote historical and linguistic origins. "An almost insurmountable gap has arisen between the historical sense of the text, now fully anchored in the historical past, and the search for its present relevance for the modern age."[24] "I am now convinced," he wrote more recently, "that the relation between the historical-critical study of the Bible, and its theological use as a religious literature within a community of faith and practice, needs to be completely rethought."[25]

The Participative Method

Childs's sentiment is echoed by Edward Greenstein, himself a historical-philologist, who writes: "The Bible has been cherished by religionists as an inspired source of truth, and by students of the past as a primary historical source. Both positions are valid, but there is something more to the Bible than this. . . . Far be it from me to say not to analyze the Bible. But in the long run, more is required of the religious person and the religious scholar."[26] What he recommends is "training in experiencing of

251

the text, so that the reader will become sensitive enough, on his or her own, to directly encounter it."[27] The "remoteness" of either historical antiquity or of traditional exegesis can be overcome only by the active and direct involvement of the reader in the interpretive process.

"Participative interpretation" is the bridge between those competing methods and the catalyst for their potential amalgamation. It is also particularly well suited for the needs and purposes of education, although it would place new and different emphases and demands on scholarship. Synonymous with the "unpacking process" with which we began, it is described by Schwab as follows: "If a reader could have access to the alternatives from which an author chose his key words, the structure of his key sentences, and his organization, he would have at hand a remarkable aid to interpretation. . . . By bringing to bear on symbols and meanings the process of comparison . . . the reader could participate in a part of the act of authorship."[28] Samuel Heilman, in his recent study of Talmud *lernen* (study) groups, makes the same observation: "The excitement in such study is to uncover for oneself the old truths . . . to feel as if one is oneself the pioneer. The traditioning 'lerner' is by no means simply mimicking or mouthing the words of the past . . . he is dramatically possessed by the text and its world; yet to him its words and reasoning seem to be his own."[29]

Conclusion

Although the preceding discussion has been drawn from the world of Biblical scholarship, the historian, philosopher, or sociologist should have no trouble reading "political options," "economic policies," and "ideological constructs" in place of "key words, sentences, and organization." I am asking my colleagues in both scholarship and education to gear their research, publication, and pedagogic agenda to assist the pursuit of that kind of interpretation that is not merely "a source of pleasure"[30] but "ultimately the determining of an ideal of life, the establishing of a preference among possible ends. It is the ordering of types of action in an ascending and descending scale of better or worse, an ordering which shapes the kind of life we choose to live. . . . Interpretation thus becomes the gateway to life and in this wide sense is synonymous with education."[31]

I conclude with a *devar torah* on "participative interpretation" courtesy of Reb Menachem Mendel of Kotzk:

If you truly wish your children to be occupied with Torah, occupy yourself with it in their presence. They will follow your example. Otherwise they will not occupy themselves with Torah but will simply instruct their children to do so.

It is written: "Beware lest you forget what you have seen . . . be sure to inform your children and grandchildren about it" (Deut. 4:9). If you forget the Torah so will they, and they will think it sufficient just to relate it to their children. Their children, too, will forget it and they will just relate it to their children.

Eventually everyone will be relating the Torah, but no one will actually understand it.

Notes

The thesis regarding education and Biblical interpretation presented herein appears in greater detail in an essay titled "The Bible and Religious Education," scheduled to appear in *Studies in Jewish Education* (The Hebrew University), vol. 4.

1. Simon Rawidowicz, "On Interpretation," in *Proceedings of the American Academy for Jewish Research* 26 (1957), p. 116.

2. Gerschom Scholem, "Tradition and Commentary as Religious Categories in Judaism," *Judaism* 15/1 (1966), p. 23.

3. Ralph Tyler, in personal conversation with the author.

4. Marvin Fox, "Judaism, Secularism, and Textual Interpretation," *Modern Jewish Ethics* (Columbus, Ohio, 1975), p. 5.

5. BT Sanhedrin 34a: "miqra' 'ehad yotse lekama te 'amim."

6. Moshe Zucker, *Perushei Rav Sa'adia Gaon liBereishit* (Jerusalem, 1984), pp. 17–18 (my translation from the Arabic).

7. Paul Ricoeur, "Existence and Hermeneutics," in his *Conflict of Interpretations* (Evanston, Ill., 1974), p. 13.

8. BT Qiddushin 49a: "hametargem pasuq ketsurato—harei ze baddai, vehamosif 'alav—harei ze meharef umegaddef."

9. "Besinai ne'emeru."

10. "Shekhahum, vehazeru veyisedum."

11. Scholem, "Tradition and Commentary," p. 18.

12. Rawidowicz, "On Interpretation," p. 92.

13. Sandra Schneiders, "Faith, Hermeneutics, and the Literal Sense of Scripture," *Theological Studies* 39 (1978), p. 732.

14. E. A. Speiser, *Genesis* (New York, 1964), p. lxiv.

15. Yehudah Elitzur, *'Emunah, Dat, uMada'* (Jerusalem, 1966), pp. 132–33.

16. Moshe Greenberg, "Biblical Scholarship and Israeli Reality," *Hammiqra' va'anahnu* (Tel Aviv, 1979; in Hebrew), p. 71.

17. Speiser, *Genesis*.

18. I. A. Richards, *Interpretation in Teaching* (London, n.d.), p. 29.

19. Yitzhaq Klein, *Nevi'ei 'Emet* (Bnei Braq, 1969), p. 158.

20. R. E. Brown, *The Sensus Plenior of Sacred Scripture* (Baltimore, 1955), p. 92.

21. Fox, "Judaism, Secularism, and Textual Interpretation."

22. Wiliam Braude, "Midrash as Deep Peshat," *Studies in Judaica, Karaitica, and Islamica in Honor of Leon Nemoy* (Ramat Gan, 1982), pp. 32ff.

23. Ibid.

24. Brevard Childs, "The Sensus Literalis of Scripture," *Festschrift Walther Zimmerli* (Göttingen, 1977), pp. 91–92.

25. Brevard Childs, *Introduction to the Old Testament as Scripture* (Philadelphia, 1982), p. 15.

26. Edward L. Greenstein, "Against Interpreting the Bible," *Ikka D'Amrei* [a student journal of JTSA] 4 (1982), p. 31.

27. Ibid, p. 30.

28. Joseph J. Schwab, "Enquiry and the Reading Process," *Science, Curriculum, and Liberal Education* (Chicago, 1978), p. 154.

29. Samuel Heilman, *The People of the Book* (Chicago, 1984), p. 65.

30. Greenstein, "Against Interpreting the Bible," p. 36.

31. Leon Roth, "Some Reflections on the Interpretation of Scripture," *The Montefiore Lectures* (London, 1956), pp. 20–21.

Concluding Reflections

19

JUDAISM AND THE HUMANITIES:
LIBERATION FROM HISTORY

Jaroslav Pelikan

The Jewish Theological Seminary of America was created during the most historically conscious of all centuries, the nineteenth, and in the heyday of humanistic historical scholarship: 1886 C.E., the year of the seminary's founding, was also the year of the death of the nestor of European historical scholars, Leopold von Ranke,[1] and the year in which Adolf von Harnack, the historian of Christianity who was to be hailed as "the bearer of German *Bildung*,"[2] published the first edition of the first volume of his *Lehrbuch der Dogmengeschichte,* the most important and most influential history of Christian doctrine ever written. Ranke and Harnack, and all those who have followed in their train, believed firmly that the best way, indeed perhaps the only way, to come to terms with a religious or humanistic tradition is to comprehend it historically, by examining its origins, development, and outcome. Thus in his famous public lectures on *Das Wesen des Christentums,* delivered to an audience of about six hundred students in the winter semester of 1899/1900 at the University of Berlin, Harnack insisted at the very outset that his answer to the question "What is Christianity?" would be put "strictly in a historical sense [*lediglich im historischen Sinn*]."[3]

Among those who have "followed in the train" of Ranke, Harnack, and the nineteenth century have been many of the most distinguished intellectual and administrative leaders of this institution, as Chancellor Ismar Schorsch pointed out earlier in this centennial observance:

I have reflected for some time [Schorsch observed on December 2, 1986] on the rather astounding fact that the Conservative Movement prefers to select historians as its chancellors. That is not the only academic field in Judaica, and yet four out of the six chancellors of this institution have been historians. . . . The selection of the historian tells us something about the character of the religion that is studied and practiced in this institution. And the fact is that Conservatism, in its European origins, was called Historical Judaism. The very word historian or history was incorporated into the character of the religious position.[4]

And it has dominated the scholarship not only of the chancellors of the Jewish Theological Seminary of America but of many of its distinguished professors and alumni, across a broad spectrum of methodology, ideology, and theology.

As a historian whose principal work bears the title *The Christian Tradition*, then, I propose to reflect on the role that humanistic historiography can play, and the role that it cannot play, in the understanding of a religious tradition. Being by instinct and training a historian rather than a philosopher or even a theologian, I have not been as sensitive to questions of method as many of my colleagues and students have. "Method is mother wit," I would personally be inclined to say, with Harnack.[5] Nevertheless, as I was writing the first volume of *The Christian Tradition*, I had the privilege, under Roman Catholic auspices, to make explicit—first in the St. Thomas More Lectures published in 1969 under the title *Development of Christian Doctrine* with the subtitle *Some Historical Prolegomena*,[6] and then two years later in a monograph called *Historical Theology*, whose subtitle read *Continuity and Change in Christian Doctrine*—at least some of the methodological and historiographical presuppositions with which I was approaching my task in writing the big book.[7] That also relieved me of the obligation to open *The Christian Tradition* itself with a lengthy dissertation on methodology.

It is delightful evidence of the ecumenical times in which we live, and that the Jewish Theological Seminary has done so much to foster, that upon completing the final volume, I have now been invited to articulate, this time under Jewish auspices, how those methodological presuppositions look to me now. "We ask you," Gerson Cohen wrote to me in his letter of invitation of 3 March 1986, "because your original theoretical work in religious cultures, religious symbols and the interpretive 'reading' of cultures has stimulated the thinking and research of some of our faculty." He continued: "A paper on a topic of your choice that advances theoretical considerations that would be of interest to scholars of any religious culture will complement our deliberations on Judaica and the history of Judaism."

In an existential sense, then, the subtitle of this essay, "Liberation from History," could simply be taken to describe the bittersweet feeling, described by Edward Gibbon, of "joy at the recovery of my freedom" and yet of sadness at taking "an everlasting leave of an old and agreeable companion,"[8] which has, I am sure, come upon every author of a multivolume book of history when, after several years or even several decades— I began planning *The Christian Tradition* as a graduate student at the University of Chicago in 1944/45—liberation from that history has finally come and the book is done. "Writing a long and substantial book," Winston Churchill once said, speaking about his own *History of the English-Speaking Peoples,* "is like having a friend and companion at your side, to whom you can always turn for comfort and amusement, and whose society becomes more attractive as a new and widening field of interest is lighted in the mind."[9] In this essay, however, I am using "liberation from history" to mean, by a play on the preposition *from* that carries over also into other languages, liberation *out of* the tyranny of the past, but also liberation *by* the past from the tyranny of the present. Both of these are, or at any rate can be, the gifts of historical study.[10]

I

The principal role that history has played in European and American humanistic scholarship, particularly during the century being observed here, has been the first of these, to liberate a community and its individual members from the tyranny of a dead past. "Tradition," I said in the introduction to *The Emergence of the Catholic Tradition,* the first volume of *The Christian Tradition,* "is the living faith of the dead; traditionalism is the dead faith of the living."[11] It is, of course, all too easy to caricature such traditionalism, whether Jewish or Christian—although one must add that it has often provided its own most vivid caricatures of itself. Yet beyond the caricatures, timeless tradition can be a religiously powerful and an intellectually appealing idea. We have it on the authority of Plato's *Timaeus,* whose similarities and contrasts with the Book of Genesis on the relation of creation and time have been a constant source of fascination and perplexity for Jewish and Christian commentators,[12] that time is "an everlasting likeness [of eternity] moving according to number."[13] Truth within time, therefore, can also be such an *eikon,* participating, to the extent that its "numerical" and sequential nature permits, in the eternal truth of the Ideas, the same Ideas which were, according to Philo of Alexandria and then according to Clement of Alexandria,[14] what was created "in the beginning." Now if this is valid when speaking about all truth, it must acquire special validity when applied to the truth of divine revelation as given to

257

the seers and prophets *in illo tempore* (whatever that may have been) and as faithfully transmitted by the elect community: "as it was in the beginning, is now, and ever shall be, world without end. Amen."

For as it is the quality of the Almighty to be able to say, by the mouth of the prophet Malachi, "I change not," and then to assure the children of Jacob that therefore they, too, will not be consumed, so it is with the truth revealed to the children of Jacob.[15] Jewish disciples of Martin Buber and Christian disciples of Søren Kierkegaard may find such "ontologism" suspect as the intrusion of an alien metaphysics into the existential language of Biblical revelation; but commenting on what John Courtney Murray once called "the towering text" in the theophany to Moses from the burning bush,[16] "I am that I am,"[17] Saint Augustine declared:

> Other things that are called essences or substances admit of accidents, whereby a change, whether great or small, is produced in them. But there can be no accident of this kind in respect to God; and therefore He who is God is the only unchangeable substance or essence, to whom certainly BE-ING [*esse*] itself, whence comes the name of essence, most especially and most truly belongs. For that which is changed does not retain its own being; and that which can be changed, although it be not actually changed, is able not to be that which it had been; and hence that which not only is not changed, but also cannot at all be changed, alone falls most truly, without difficulty or hesitation, under the category of BEING.[18]

Elsewhere he argued that "God is Truth,"[19] and that therefore the truth of God participated in his eternal and unchangeable nature. If there was change, then, it was because, as the prophet Malachi says in the very next verse after the one just quoted, "Even from the days of your fathers ye are gone away from mine ordinances, and have not kept them"[20]—words of complaint and judgment that have, alas, an ecumenical and universal applicability. The change that is characteristic of human history, and therefore also of the human handling of divine truth, is evidence of how the children of God have repeatedly "gone away from mine ordinances"; but it is not evidence that the divine truth itself, as revealed, is subject to historical vicissitude.

It is significant, both historically and theologically, that the most frequent use of what we may without fear of anachronism call "the historical method" in the study of religious traditions has been directed at identifying the way one's opponents have "gone away from mine ordinances."[21] The polemical use of historical scholarship for this purpose found application both in the conflicts between Christian sects and in the beginning of the scientific and scholarly study of the history of religions, as both of these activities were carried on by the intellectual heirs of Renaissance humanism. It had long been the general assumption, voiced in the opening paragraph of the first church history, the *Ecclesiastical History* of Eusebius at the first half of the fourth century, that continuity was the characteristic of the truth, whereas *neoteropoiia*, innovation and change, was the characteristic of error.[22] As historical scholars have frequent occasion to learn and to lament, one consequence of this assumption with far-reaching implications for the later historian is that we have ended up being better informed about the history of Christian heresy, which was thought to be constantly changing, than about the history of Christian orthodoxy, which was not thought to have had a history in the same sense because it had always been the same, *semper eadem*, and which therefore has not been documented in the same detail.

Similarly, as Augustine had already demonstrated in his *City of God,* it was possible to wield the history of religion and the history of religious philosophy as a formidable weapon in attacking the received systems both of Judaism and of classical antiquity.[23] Augustine carried out his historical polemic almost completely on the basis of what was available in Latin; for his knowledge of Greek was spotty, and, despite his occasional references to the Semitic dialects known as "Punic" as a key to the understanding of Hebrew or Aramaic terms in the Bible,[24] he did not know Hebrew. Indeed, ignorance of Hebrew was all but universal during the first millennium and a half of the history of the Christian exegesis of the Hebrew Bible, and ignorance of Greek was likewise general in the Latin West for most of that period. But when the insistence of the Renaissance humanists on the study of the original languages had provided theologians of the Reformation period with the equipment to do so, they made use of it to apply historical-critical methodology to the polemic against post-Biblical Judaism.

Nor was it accidental that the earliest Christian extensions of that historical-critical methodology from post-Biblical history to the Bible itself dealt with the "Old Testament" rather than with the "New Testament." For when, in Emil Kraeling's words, deism "got involved more and more in polemic against existing Christianity and, favoring a natural theology, assailed the theology based on revelation," it should not be surprising that "the Old Testament provided a convenient object for such attack."[25] Despite the Christian appropriation of the Hebrew Bible—epitomized in the familiar formula addressed at the middle of the second century C.E. by Justin Martyr to Trypho (whether or not "Trypho" was in fact Rabbi Tarphon),[26] that references to Jesus as Messiah "are contained in your Scriptures, or rather *not yours, but ours*"[27]—the historical criticism of the Old Testament turned out somehow to be a less sensitive area than the historical criticism of the New Testament, within which, in turn, it was safer to employ historical criticism for the study of the Pauline and deutero-Pauline epistles than for that of the Gospels. And when, to borrow the title of Frank Manuel's incisive study, the eighteenth century confronted the gods,[28] it did so increasingly by resort to the classical methodology of euhemerism, the historical explanation of mythological themes and images. Even for the critics of orthodoxy, then, history and change were what happened to error, not what happened to truth.

Once it had become the "universal solvent,"[29] however, the historical-critical method could not be confined to "error" (meaning the traditions and the sacred writings of others) without also being applied to "truth" (meaning one's own traditions and sacred writings). Cherished elements of "authentic" tradition became vulnerable to the very same historical scrutiny that had brought down the "fictive" traditions. Perhaps the most striking case study of this process was the interpretation of miracles by the rationalistic historical criticism of the eighteenth century; for in the triad of "miracle, mystery, and authority," as defined by Dostoevsky's Grand Inquisitor,[30] miracle held the key to the other two.[31] If it was methodologically sound to attack the purported miracles of paganism or of post-Biblical Judaism, why not also those in the Roman Catholic and Eastern Orthodox *Lives of the Saints* or in the Protestant *Acts of the Martyrs?* And if this included the miracles attributed to medieval saints, the process could not stop short of, for example, the *Life of Antony* by Athanasius of Alexandria—especially if that same Athanasius was also at the same time the target of attack for his doctrine of the Trinity. But then there was no way of stopping short of the privileged sanctuary of the Bible itself. Edward Gibbon explains in his *Autobiography* that the continuity between Biblical and post-Biblical miracles led him, as a young man, from Anglicanism to Roman Catholicism, but then, by a reversal of the very same logic, from Roman Catholicism to rationalism.[32] Thus, in the familiar words of Goethe's *The Sorcerer's Apprentice,*

Ach, da kommt der Meister
Herr, die Not ist grosz!
Die ich rief, die Geister,
Werd' ich nun nicht los.[33]

Once summoned, whether for polemics or for fun, the spirits refused to go back to where they had come from: historical-critical methodology was here to stay.

II

The philosophical theology of the Jewish Haskalah, no less than that of the Christian *Aufklärung,* demonstrated where "liberation from history" in that sense could end: the historicism of a night where all cats were gray, where all doctrines could be equally true because they were in fact equally false. Such relativism has often been associated with the development of toleration and religious liberty. Nevertheless, as among others Étienne Gilson pointed out, the twentieth-century outcome of the Christian *Aufklärung* also provides frightening evidence that a tolerance based on the absence of belief can be extremely fragile; for when belief, of whatever kind, is revived, tolerance can give way once more to persecution. What we need rather, Gilson insisted, is a definition of tolerance that is rooted in what we do believe rather than in our loss of belief.[34] History has been the great iconoclast, unmasking all the idols of human history as, in Winston Churchill's favorite quotation from Lord Byron,

Those Pagod things of sabre sway
With fronts of brass and feet of clay.[35]

Like all iconoclasts since the day Moses came down from the mountain, the idol smashers of the historical-critical method were confident that thereby they were only preparing the way for the true God to reign:

Heartily know,
When half-gods go,
The gods arrive,[36]

Ralph Waldo Emerson assured his readers in the final lines of one of his best-known poems. Nevertheless, the polytheism of that assurance—reminiscent of Goethe's familiar aphorism, "When we do natural science, we are pantheists; when we write poetry, we are polytheists; and when we reflect on morality, we are monotheists"[37]—does raise the question of whether the historical-critical method, once unleashed, does in fact lead to a reaffirmation of Mosaic monotheism, or whether its relativism ultimately relativizes that as well, and perhaps prepares the way for the recrudescence of polytheism.

Even short of that most momentous of all questions, the question of monotheism, the history of the historical method of studying tradition, as practiced during this past century, raises as well the question of what happens when "history" is applied to "history." Once a "liberation *from* history'' seen as the destruction (or at any rate the reduction) of the tyranny of the past has been achieved, is historical relativism the only alternative, or can there be a ''liberation *from* history'' that liberates also from relativism itself? ''We must overcome history by means of history [Wir müssen die Geschichte mit Geschichte überwinden]'' was a motto that both Adolf Harnack and Ernst Troeltsch made their own under the impact of historical relativism.[38] Yet even their most ardent defenders are obliged to admit that they were more eloquent in articulating the question than in formulating the answer. The corrective of historicism on the definition of tradition as timeless truth is an achievement of the historical methodology behind which it is impossible ever to go again: there cannot be a *status quo ante bellum*. But it is no less sure that it is both possible and necessary to go beyond historicism, not behind it but beyond it, to a ''liberation from history'' in which history will also function as what Lord Acton once called ''our deliverer not only from the undue influence of other times, but from the undue influence of our own, from the tyranny of environment and the pressure of the air we breathe.''[39]

The key issue for such a ''liberation from history'' is the reality of continuity. During the nineteenth and twentieth centuries, the historical skeptics of all the traditions seem to have proceeded on an unquestioned assumption that discontinuity was a historically verifiable fact, but that continuity could only be an article of faith, beyond any except a subjective verification. In part this may have been because they looked in the wrong setting for the locus of continuity, in theological doctrine or institutional structure rather than in ritual observance, in dogma and polity rather than in liturgy—or, to invoke an early Christian distinction,[40] in the *lex credendi* rather than primarily in the *lex orandi*. It is not mere assonance of the English language, but a fundamental corollary of historical study, that *community* is the locus of *continuity*. Each year in the Jewish community, there is one night that is different from all the nights of the year, because it was on that one night that the ''we'' of the community, past and present, were brought up out of captivity: by making that event one's own in participation and reenactment, one affirms one's share in the community, and therefore and thereby one affirms the continuity of the community itself. That affirmation of continuity is not only an article of faith, though it had better be that as well; it is the testimony of the historical record. Similarly, every day for almost two thousand years the members of the Christian community have taken bread and wine in their hands to celebrate the Eucharist.[41]

Now, unless the continuities of Passover and the Eucharist are dismissed as trivial and ''merely ritual observance,'' it would seem that the nature of the community comes to decisive expression in them. When historical scholarship does move beyond a liberation from history that performs the necessary and illuminating task of putting the Passover and the Eucharist into the context of the history of sacred meals throughout the history of anthropology, it can move to a liberation from history that comes to terms with the special role that each of these particular sacred meals has played in the community in which it has been celebrated for these millennia. And that, too, is at least in part an assignment that can be carried out by historical scholarship, indeed, one that cannot be carried out in our time without historical scholarship. For historical scholarship is in a position to investigate the cluster of meanings that have attached themselves to this "night that is different from all the nights of the year" and to this "night in which [Jesus] was betrayed," and to see how these communities and their interpreters have, over and over again and in a variety of ways, drawn upon the memory and the celebration of those nights to affirm who and what they are.

Speaking as a historian of the Christian tradition, I am obliged to say that I am struck by the remarkable historiographical coincidence that the same Adolf Harnack who could identify it as "another instance of the exceptional nature of Christianity" that "for quite a time it possessed no ritual at all" and who therefore felt justified in ignoring ritual as a key to the explanation of the history of Christian doctrine[42] was also the historian who, nearly fifty years later, could, in his last important scholarly work, formulate the following astonishing thesis: "To have rejected the Old Testament in the second century was a mistake that the main body of the Church was correct in avoiding; to retain it in the sixteenth century was a historical fate that the Reformation was not yet in a position to escape; but to go on conserving it within Protestantism as a canonical authority after the nineteenth century is the consequence of a paralysis of religion and Church."[43] For if, as various of my reviewers have suggested, whether favorably or critically, one characteristic distinguishing my history of Christian doctrine from Harnack's has been the role that the history of worship plays throughout my account of how Christian dogma has developed, it is noteworthy that another such characteristic, as they have also suggested, should be my attention in each successive volume of *The Christian Tradition* to the history of the continuing relation between Christian and Jewish teaching even and especially after the New Testament era. I am profoundly convinced that these two characteristics of my own work are closely connected, just as I cannot avoid the sense that the absence of both themes from Harnack's *Dogmengeschichte* is more than what I have called it, a mere "historiographical coincidence."

Beneath this fundamental methodological insight into the function of historical scholarship in identifying the nature of the community not only through how it is organized but through how it has maintained the continuity of faith and observance is an even more fundamental principle, ultimately identifiable as a philosophical principle: that continuity and change are not mutually exclusive, as theories of timeless truth and historical relativism both suppose despite the opposite conclusions they draw from this common conviction, but that authentic continuity is to be sought in change that is authentic (setting aside, at least for now, the delicate normative question of what is "authentic"). The name that such authentic continuity-*cum*-change acquired during what I have been calling here "the most historically conscious of all centuries," the nineteenth century, was "development." Substituting, thanks in part to the pervasive influence of Romanticism,[44] the metaphors of organic growth for those of architecture and engineering, various nineteenth-century historical thinkers sought to take up the undeniable phenomenon of change into their understanding of historical identity. And as, in a familiar nineteenth-century oxymoron, "the Child is father of the Man,"[45] not by a radical break or with discontinuity, but by the most profound continuity of all and yet with change no less profound, so it is with a community and above all with a religious tradition, for which "development" is the key to the preservation of identity. The resistance to such an understanding of tradition and identity came during the nineteenth century from those who saw, and correctly, that "development" and "timeless truth," when pressed to their ultimate consequences, were mutually incompatible. Still speaking for such resistance in the twentieth century, Jacques Maritain insisted that the idea of development "is not a metaphysical instrument and it does not concern itself with the analytical explanation of being." Rather, he continued, "it is an historic instrument and concerns the historical explanation of becoming."[46]

Fundamentally, it is that very distinction between "being" as metaphysical and "becoming" as merely historical that I am questioning here. For in the history of Israel and in the history of the church, there has been no "being" except as it has been perceived not only within "becoming," but *through* "becoming." Even the very word from the burning bush that serves as the prooftext for the "metaphysics of Exodus"[47] in Jewish and Christian ontologism may be translated to speak of an eternal becoming: "I shall be who I shall be." And liberation from history does not mean an escape out of history, but a recognition, within history, of those events in which is revealed the meaning and the promise of life and the mystery of this divine being-as-becoming. Historical scholarship as such cannot teach us that meaning and promise, nor can it induct us into that mystery. But it can enable us to see at work through the centuries the community that confesses this meaning, awaits this promise, and adores this mystery. In the words of an almost exact contemporary of Leopold von Ranke, the "apostle of development" John Henry Newman, such a community, in acquiring

264

new forms, "changes with them in order to remain the same. In a higher world it is otherwise, but here below to live is to change, and to be [mature] is to have changed often."[48] History can liberate us from history if it faces us with the reality of that continuity. The saints, sages, and scholars who have adorned The Jewish Theological Seminary of America for the past hundred years have, at one and the same time, documented and embodied such continuity, and therefore they continue to confer on succeeding generations—including, please God, the present generation, as well as others yet unborn—the blessing of such liberation.

Notes

1. On Ranke's significance for the development of the historical understanding of religious tradition, see my forthcoming essay, "Ranke as Historian of the Reformation," in James M. Powell, ed., *Ranke Centennial Essays.*

2. The title came from Paul von Hindenburg, president of the Weimar Republic, on the occasion of Harnack's seventy-fifth birthday in 1926; see Agnes von Zahn-Harnack, *Adolf von Harnack,* 2d ed. (Berlin, 1951), p. 409.

3. Adolf Harnack, *Das Wesen des Christentums,* 4th ed. (Leipzig, 1901), p. 4.

4. Ismar Schorsch, "Affirming the Religious Middle: The Path of Conservative Judaism," address delivered December 2, 1986, at the Jewish Theological Seminary (preliminary draft).

5. Quoted in von Zahn-Harnack, *Harnack,* p. 48.

6. Jaroslav Pelikan, *Development of Christian Doctrine: Some Historical Prolegomena* (New Haven, Conn., 1969).

7. Jaroslav Pelikan, *Historical Theology: Continuity and Change in Christian Doctrine* (New York, 1971).

8. Edward Gibbon, *Autobiography,* ed. Dero A. Saunders (New York, 1961), p. 195.

9. Winston S. Churchill, *The Second World War* (New York, 1961), 6 vols., vol. 1, p. 181.

10. As a consequence, I shall, rather more than is my wont, be referring to various of my own writings that document the development of these themes in my own scholarship.

11. Jaroslav Pelikan, *The Christian Tradition: A History of the Development of Doctrine* (Chicago, 1971–), 5 vols., vol. 1, p. 9.

12. Harry Austryn Wolfson, *Philo: Foundations of Religious Philosophy in Judaism, Christianity and Islam* (Cambridge, Mass., 1982), 2 vols., vol. 1, pp. 214–17.

13. Plato *Timaeus* 37E. See the important explanatory note in Francis Macdonald Cornford, *Plato's Cosmology* (New York, 1957), p. 98.

14. Harry Austryn Wolfson, *The Philosophy of the Church Fathers,* vol. 1: *Faith, Trinity, Incarnation* (Cambridge, Mass., 1956), pp. 268–70.

15. Mal. 3:6.

16. John Courtney Murray, *The Problem of God: Yesterday and Today* (New Haven, Conn., 1964), p. 5, quoting Exod. 3:14.

17. Exod. 3:14. For a brief account of the place of this text in the early fathers of the Christian church, see my *Christian Tradition,* vol. 1, p. 54.

18. Augustine *On the Trinity,* bk. V, chap. 2, par. 3; in *A Select Library of the Nicene and Post-Nicene Fathers of the Christian Church* (Grand Rapids, Mich., 1956), 1st ser., vol. 3, p. 88.

19. Augustine *On the Profit of Believing [De utilitate credendi]*, par. 33; in *A Select Library*, vol. 3, p. 363.

20. Mal. 3:7.

21. Pelikan, *Historical Theology*, pp. 33–67: "The Evolution of the Historical."

22. Eusebius *Ecclesiastical History*, bk. I, par. 1.

23. See Jaroslav Pelikan, *The Mystery of Continuity: Time and History, Memory and Eternity in the Thought of Saint Augustine* (Charlottesville, Va., 1986), pp. 34–51.

24. Jaroslav Pelikan, ed., *The Preaching of Augustine* (Philadelphia, 1973), p. 102, n. 5; p. 82, n. 40; p. 139, n. 23.

25. Emil G. Kraeling, *The Old Testament since the Reformation* (New York, 1955), p. 47.

26. For a bibliography, see Johannes Quasten, *Patrology* (Westminster, Md., 1951–), vol. 1, pp. 202–4.

27. Justin Martyr, *Dialogue with Trypho*, chap. 29, par. 2. See my discussion of these words of Justin and related ideas in *The Christian Tradition*, vol. 1, pp. 12–27.

28. Frank E. Manuel, *The Eighteenth Century Confronts the Gods* (New York, 1959).

29. See the quotations collected from Lecky and Hutton, s.v. "Solvent," *Oxford English Dictionary*, vol. 10, p. 408.

30. Fyodor Dostoevsky, *The Brothers Karamazov*, pt. II, bk. V ("Pro et Contra"), chap. 5 ("The Grand Inquisitor").

31. *The Christian Tradition*, vol. 5, pp. 61–74 ("The Objectivity of Transcendent Revelation") deals with "Miracle, Mystery, and Authority" in the eighteenth century.

32. Gibbon, *Autobiography*, p. 82–86; and the famous discussion in chap. 15 of his *Decline and Fall of the Roman Empire*, ed. J. B. Bury (London, 1896–1900), vol. 2, pp. 29–32.

33. Johann Wolfgang von Goethe, *Werke*, Festausgabe, ed. Robert Petsch (Leipzig, 1926), vol. 1, p. 122, lines 89–92.

34. Etienne Gilson, "Dogmatism and Tolerance," *International Journal* 8 (1925), pp. 7–16.

35. Winston S. Churchill, *Blood, Sweat and Tears* (New York, 1941), p. 71 (October 16, 1938), and again p. 455 (9 Feb. 1941).

36. Ralph Waldo Emerson, "Give All to Love," *The Complete Essays and Other Writings of Ralph Waldo Emerson*, ed. Brooks Atkinson (New York, 1940), p. 775.

37. "Wir sind naturforschend Pantheisten, dichtend Polytheisten, sittlich Monotheisten": *Maximen und Reflexionen*, 807, *Werke*, Festausgabe, vol. 14, p. 353 (from a letter of January 6, 1813).

38. See Wilhelm Pauck, *Harnack and Troeltsch: Two Historical Theologians* (New York, 1968), on these two scholars and the relation between them.

39. Lord Acton, *Lectures on Modern History*, introduction by Hugh Trevor-Roper (New York, 1961), p. 44.

40. See Pelikan, *The Christian Tradition*, vol. 1, p. 339.

41. Jaroslav Pelikan, *The Vindication of Tradition*, The Jefferson Lecture for 1983 (New Haven, Conn., 1984), p. 48.

42. Adolf Harnack, *Lehrbuch der Dogmengeschichte*, 3rd ed. (Leipzig, 1894–97), vol. 1, pp. 764–66.

43. Adolf Harnack, *Marcion: Das Evangelium vom fremden Gott*, 2d ed. (Leipzig, 1924), p. 217.

44. It will be evident that I have been influenced here by the work of my colleague, the historian of literary criticism René Wellek, *Concepts of Criticism* (New Haven, Conn., 1963), pp. 128–221.

45. William Wordsworth, "My heart leaps up when I behold," *The Poems*, ed. John O. Hayden, 2 vols. (New Haven, Conn., 1981), vol. 1, p. 522.

46. Jacques Maritain, *Existence and the Existent,* trans. L. Galantiere and G. B. Phelan (New York, 1948), p. 45.

47. Pelikan, *The Christian Tradition,* vol. 1, p. 54.

48. John Henry Newman, *An Essay on the Development of Christian Doctrine,* ed. Gustave Weigel (Garden City, N.Y., 1960), p. 63. I have substituted the word "mature" for the original word "perfect," which in present-day usage suggests, almost unavoidably, moral sinlessness—quite the opposite of Newman's intention.

INDEX

269

Index

Art history (*cont.*)
twentieth centuries, 204–5; of Roman/
Byzantine period, 193–94, 197–201;
of seventeenth/eighteenth centuries,
203–5. *See also* Manuscripts, illumi-
nated; Synagogues
Aschkenasy, Nehama, 176
Ashi, R., 94
Ashtor, E., 133
Asis, Y. T., 141
Assimilation, 151, 160–62
Assis, Moses, 82, 84, 85
Astour, M., 24
Augustine, Saint, 258, 259
Avery-Peck, Alan J., 86

Baer, Yizhak, 118, 134
Balaban, Meir, 145
Band, Arnold, 191
Bar-Asher, Moses, 85–86
Baron, Salo, 118, 139, 141, 146
Barton, John, 35
Bavli Talmud, 81, 83, 85, 87, 88, 95, 96,
98, 101
Beer, Moshe, 96
Benedict, Benjamin Z., 82
Ben-Porat, Ziva, 187
Ben-Zvi Institute, 148
Berdichewsky, M. J., 173, 175
Berger, D., 138
Berkovits, Eliezer, 227 n. 9
Berkowitz, I. D., 190
Beth-Alpha synagogue mosaics, 193, 194
Bettelheim, Bruno, 159
Beyond the Text (Hoffman), 221
Bialik, Chaim, 167, 171, 175, 188
Bible curriculum, 236
Biblical interpretation, 248–49; historical-
philological method, 250–51; partici-
pative method, 251–52; traditional
method, 249–50
Biblical studies: and archaeological evi-
dence, 28–30, 41 n. 57, 52, 197; and
author's meaning, 49; crisis of faith
in, 23–24, 36–37, 38 n. 2; feminist,
37; and historical reliability, 25–28,
50–52; within Jewish framework, 37–
38; literary approach to, 120; medieval,
48–49; methodological pluralism in, 52–
53; oral *vs* literary tradition in, 24–25,

28; philological analysis in, 30–31;
source-critical analysis in, 26, 27–28,
31–32, 48, 52; synchronic analysis in,
32–36, 48, 49–50
Blidstein, G., 137
Bloch, Marc, 121, 139
Bloom, Harold, 35, 175
Blumenkrantz, B., 138
Böcher, O., 209 n. 36
Bonfil, Reuven, 123, 138
Bonfils, Joseph, 48–49
Braude, William, 251
Braudel, Fernand, 121, 139
Brenner, Yosef Hayyim, 173, 174–75, 187, 188
Bright, J., 25, 29–30
Brown, C. M., 89
Brown, R. E., 251
Buber, Martin, 216, 217, 223, 225, 230, 234

Cahan, Abraham, 177
Carroll, R., 43
Cassuto, Umberto, 25
Catacomb art, 200–201
Ceremonial art, 203–4
Charlesworth, James H., 61
Chazan, R., 138
Chedorlaomer texts, 24
Childs, Brevard S., 43 n. 91, 51, 251
Christian Tradition, The (Pelikan), 256,
257, 263
Churchill, Winston, 256, 261
City of God (Augustine), 259
Clement of Alexandria, 257
Cohen, A., 133
Cohen, Gerson D., 118, 256
Cohen, Hermann, 230
Cohen, J., 138
Cohen, Mark R., 121, 133
Cohen, Naomi, 161
Cohen, Shaye, J. D., 69 n. 9, 237, 238, 245
Cohen, Stuart, 224
Collective memory, 124
Community studies, 145, 150
Concordance to the Talmud Yerushalmi, 86
Conservative movement, 223, 231–32
Crenshaw, James L., 33
Crescas, 138
Cross, Frank M., 25, 30, 50
Crossan, John Dominic, 36
Curriculum Reform movement, 236

270

Index

Index

Sa'adia, Gaon, 249
Sadan, Dov, 166, 167–68, 172, 188–89
Safrai, Shmuel, 81
Samuel, Book of, 27
Sanders, E. P., 57, 60–61, 64
Sardis synagogue, 65
Sarna, Jonathan, 161
Saul, 25–26
Schäfer, Peter, 71–72 nn. 28, 34, n.6, 79, 81
Schatz, Boris, 205
Schiper, Ignacy, 145
Scholem, Gershom, 19, 117, 135–36, 147–48, 186, 220, 223, 225, 234, 248, 249
Schorsch, Ismar, 44 n. 101, 149, 151, 160, 161, 255–56
Schürer, Emil, 69 n. 8, 70 n. 12, 86
Schwab, Joseph J., 248, 251
Schwartz, Shuly R., 153–54 n. 7
Schweid, Eliezer, 225
Second Commandment, 196–97, 205
Seltzer, Robert M., 19
Sephardic Mystique, 114–15, 116, 120, 122, 132–34
Septuagint, 33, 198
Sermonetta, G., 138
Shaked, Gershon, 43–44 n. 92, 173, 174
Shanks, Hershel, 30
Shatzky, Jacob, 145
Shavit, Uzi, 173
Shmeruk, Khone, 170, 171, 172, 187
Shpigl oyf a shteyn, A, 170
Sholem Aleichem, 166–67, 170, 172, 173, 190
Short Story Writers and Novelists (Niger), 169
Sifra, 63
Singer, I. B., 170, 172
Smith, Morton, 60, 70–71 n. 20, 208 n. 21
Social and Religious History of the Jews, A (Baron), 139, 146
Sokoloff, Michael, 81, 82, 86
Solomon, 26, 29, 197
Soloveitchik, Haym, 117, 141
Soloveitchik, Joseph B., 223
Song of Deborah, 25
Soutine, Chaim, 204
Soviet-Yiddish literature, 170
Spanish Jews, 116, 203
Spartoli texts, 24

Speiser, E. A., 23–24, 50, 51–52, 249, 250
Sperber, Daniel, 86
Spinoza, 232
Stark, Irwin, 176–77
Steinberg, Milton, 216
Steinberg, Yaakov, 173
Stendahl, K., 57
Sternberg, Meir, 36
Stillman, N., 133
Stillman, Yedida, 124
Stow, K., 138, 141
Strack, Hermann, 17
Strauss, L., 137
Strauss, Ludwig, 188
Strayer, Joseph R., 129
Structure of Scientific Revolutions (Ruhn), 217
Sum and Substance (Glatstein), 169
Sussmann, Jacob, 82, 84
Synagogues: architecture of, 66, 201–2; inscriptions in, 65–66; in Muslim lands, 209 n. 32; origins of, 200; paintings and mosaics in, 193–94, 197–99, 200–201
Synchronic analysis, Biblical, 32–36, 48

Tabory, Joseph, 84
Talmage, F., 138
Talmud, 63, 65, 77, 245
Talmudic studies: advances in, 80–81; collation of readings, 82–83; critical editions, 83–85; forms of, 93–94; higher criticism, 87–89; implications of, 95–101; linguistic features in, 85–86; source criticism, 89–93; text criticism, 81–82
Tanakh, 61, 68. See also Biblical interpretation; Biblical studies; Torah
Ta-Shema, Israel, 82, 85
Tcherikower, Elias, 145
Tel Aviv School, 171, 187, 188
Temple of Solomon, 197
Theodicy, problem of, 221
Theology, Jewish: authority and authenticity in, 217–19, 222, 231–32; and eschatology, 225–26, 233; existentialist model of, 217, 230; giant thinkers of, 216–17, 230; and Holocaust, 217, 221–22, 230–31, 233; from human

276

The manuscript was edited by Lois Krieger. The book was designed by Joanne Elkin Kinney. The typeface for the text is Times Roman. The display face is Times Roman italic. The book is printed on 50-lb Glatfelter paper and is bound in Holliston Roxite A-grade cloth. The paperback cover material is 10 pt C1S.

Manufactured in the United States of America.